INDIA-CHINA BOUNDARY ISSUES

Quest for Settlement

INDIA-CHINA BOUNDARY ISSUES

Quest for Settlement

Ranjit Singh Kalha

INDIAN COUNCIL OF WORLD AFFAIRS

PENTAGON PRESS

India-China Boundary Issues: Quest For Settlement
by Ranjit Singh Kalha

ISBN 978-81-8274-785-2

First Published in 2014

Published by
PENTAGON PRESS
206, Peacock Lane, Shahpur Jat,
New Delhi-110049
Phones: 011-64706243, 26491568
Telefax: 011-26490600
email: rajan@pentagonpress.in
website: www.pentagonpress.in

Branch:
Prime Arcade
Office #11
1154 Saifee Street
Opp. M.G.Road, Camp
Pune-411001
Email: pentagonpresspune@gmail.com

Printed at Aegean Offset Printers, Greater Noida, U.P.

This book is

Dedicated to my wife

Babli

For her unstinted support

and

to our grand-children

Fateh, Prahlaad and Alisiya

Contents

ANNEXURES

Preface

It was by chance or perhaps providence so willed it that I was nominated to study the Chinese language on joining the Indian Foreign Service. Thereafter while living and working in China, I began my long association with Chinese affairs that lasted well over a decade. It was here also that I formed my first impressions of the Chinese as a people; their nature, aptitude, their thinking, their way of life and the strength and weaknesses of their character. I studied their form of governance, the Chinese Communist Party [CCP] and understood the factors that went into decision making.

The Chinese in general, apart from Foreign Office officials, found it exceedingly hard to place me as a person. In my stay in Beijing, two incidents remain firmly etched in my memory that confirmed my observation. On my posting to China in 1972 the only route open for foreigners to travel to Beijing was by train from Hong Kong to the Chinese border and after crossing the border at Lowu on foot, on to Canton [Guangzhou] by a Chinese train. On the Chinese side of the border all passengers were served breakfast while customs and immigration formalities were completed. At breakfast, I requested for eggs, toast, bacon and tea. Everything I ordered, except the bacon, arrived. No one would tell me why the bacon was not served. Finally, my official Chinese guide whispered to me that I was not being served bacon since I was a Muslim! I showed them my passport and to put them at ease, I explained that I was a Sikh and Sikhs were certainly are not Muslims. No one would believe me. Obviously the person in authority had decided that I was a Muslim and that decision would stand! And no matter how much I remonstrated, there was no bacon for me!

On another occasion in Beijing while I was repairing a minor fault in my car, a curious crowd of locals quickly gathered to watch. They did not know that I understood Chinese. The conversation amongst them was hilarious! One old man opined that I was an Arab. He pointed to my turban and with an air of authority said that only Arabs wore such a head dress. Most nodded in agreement. Another said I might be an Afghan or maybe even Turkish as I was tall, over six feet and sported a beard. Another, who finally got it right, said maybe I was an Indian. Almost everyone loudly disagreed, for they opined that Indians were not that tall but rather short statured . As I had finished repairing my car, I thought

I would enlighten them. There was consternation all around when I spoke in Chinese and told them that I was an Indian. They all rapidly disappeared, for those days, at the height of the Cultural Revolution in Mao's China, it was highly inappropriate to be seen with a foreigner and that too an Indian! My conclusion was that most people in China knew very little about the outside world other than what the leadership told them. Therefore they believed whatever was disclosed by their leaders. It was apparent that China was a very isolated country, with most of its people bereft of any contact with the outside world.

In writing this book, I deliberately chose to begin from 1947 onwards, for it was only after independence that it can be truly said that negotiations with China were conducted keeping in mind the vital and strategic interests of India only. Earlier Britain always kept her own interests paramount and Indian policy was invariably subject to overriding imperial interests. Secondly, the pre-independence period is rather well documented and covered by many distinguished scholars and authors and therefore to do it again would only be repetitive. Nevertheless, one cannot be unmindful of history and oblivious of relationships of the past.

There is no doubt that the subject of the India-China boundary question has been under intense scrutiny ever since the first clashes took place between India and China on the high Himalayas. Many scholars have written detailed and fairly comprehensive accounts of the subject. Invariably, most have relied on the extensive archival material that is available in the United Kingdom, both at the India Office Library as also with the records of the Public Records Office in London. Private correspondence and despatches of important British dignitaries have also been tapped into for information and historical record. Few, if any, have had access to Chinese records, although only recently some records have been de-classified. Biographies of important Chinese personalities are now also available. Even in present day China most writings, official or otherwise, are invariably officially vetted before publication. This is perfectly understandable given the nature, the structure and secrecy that surrounds governance in China. Some scholars were able to access records that are available with the National Archives of India, the Nehru Memorial Library, but these mostly though not all, relate to the pre-independence period. Some recent publications contain impressive factual data, but are short on analysis of the policy issues.

Therefore most studies have necessarily been a bit one sided, depending upon the political predilections of the scholar and the time period when it was written. Some scholars have introduced facts to suit their own predetermined views or simply ignored others. Although it would not be fair to find fault with the advantage of hindsight, yet most historical data has been scrutinized without keeping in mind the period that it was written in. It is easy to be critical with the knowledge of the present. Often there are no formal conclusions, no written documents, but actions of the principal actors and the circumstances that prevailed that are well understood. Sometimes understandings are not committed to the written word, but remain verbal for well-known political compulsions. Independent India was dealt with a certain hand and realism demands that it is only with the cards that we hold that we can play. There is no point in lamenting over a situation that did not exist in reality nor to re-construct events with the advantage of hindsight.

The earliest recorded instance that negotiators were used to settle a boundary dispute was in 1222 AD, when a Commission consisting of six English and Scots representatives were appointed, to mark the limits of the two kingdoms. A chilling fact was that the Commission collapsed as soon as it set to work. And the negotiators, both English and Scots, were retired with ignominy and barely escaped imprisonment! The work of boundary negotiators is thus never easy!

I am neither a historian nor a scholar, but a diplomat who has tried to put all the facts on the table and the factors that influenced policy as faithfully and as commonly understood at that point in time. I have strongly desisted from using the advantage of hindsight to 'interpret' policies or events. It would not be fair. I have also tried hard not to be subjective or to be swayed by emotion and have refrained from being judgemental; particularly of personalities. I have also documented the influence of major world powers on the course of negotiations. The reader may not agree with most or all of my conclusions. There may also be some errors of fact and sometimes of faulty reading of the historical context and political process. While I take immense pleasure and credit for the work, I am equally solely responsible for any errors of fact and any obvious shortcomings. I am deeply conscious of my limitations.

During the many rounds of border negotiations, my Chinese interlocutors to emphasize a point would often remark, perhaps with contrived solemnity, 'it is only from facts that we can determine the truth.' Although such general statements of principle can never be points of contention, yet the question remains which set of facts are we talking about? As Nehru was to remark in the context of Sino-Indian boundary negotiations 'we have basic differences over facts.'

As to which side is right on this issue or which side has a better case; I leave it to the discerning and more discriminating judgment of the reader. Having defended India's case over the years, my own personal predilections are fairly obvious.

In making this study possible I wish to convey my grateful thanks to the Director-General of the Indian Council of World Affairs (ICWA) for his unstinting support and encouragement in the completion of this work. I also wish to thank the Director-General of the Institute of Defence Studies and Analyses (IDSA) and his staff for their help in developing the maps of the Sino-Indian border areas.

[RSK]

List of Maps

CHAPTER 1

Boundaries, Borders, Frontiers and the Imperial Inheritance

Frontiers are indeed the razor's edge on which hang suspended the modern issues of war and peace, the life and death of nations.
—Lord Curzon, Romanes Lecture, 1907

The contemporary global state system is based on the premise that nation states are territorial entities with fixed boundaries that are internationally accepted, legally concluded and physically demarcated on the ground to ensure peace, security and stability. The purpose of a boundary is to mark, in unmistakeable terms, the limits of territory upto which a state exercises sovereign power. A state without a boundary is highly improbable and within a defined territory only one fully sovereign state can exist. A state is, therefore, defined territorially and state sovereignty resides within the totality of national territory.[1] Thus, the main objective of any negotiations between nation states is to attain secure boundaries so that peace, stability and finality are obtained and that sufficient goodwill continues to exist between peoples to prevent unauthorized expansion and trespass. The mechanics of boundary making are complex and intricate and cover a wide range of issues. These include strategic state interests that are legal, political and economic while at the same time ensuring ethnic homogeneity and geographical continuity. The emotional factor, too, plays a part.

Therefore, before any negotiations commence, it is essential that negotiators from both state parties develop a common set of understandings on the exact meaning of the terminology to be used. This is not an inexact science, for over the years, a certain method has developed that is universally accepted and well recognized. However, it is entirely possible that in the national languages of various countries, the same set of words are used to describe different concepts. For example, while in the English language the words 'frontiers' and 'boundary' have different concepts, the French commonly use only a single word 'frontiere' to describe both a boundary and a frontier. Similarly, the Germans have only one word 'grenze.'

The Chinese word 'bienjie' [边界] is the commonly used word for a 'boundary', and the Chinese word for 'frontier' is 'bianjiang' [边疆]. The Chinese also have a different word for 'border'—'biankuang' [边境]. The Chinese word 'jiang'—that is sometimes translated as 'frontier'—is possibly closer in meaning to the word 'dominion.' Quite clearly, therefore, words differ from country to country and in different regions. Consequently, the adoption of common terminology or common understanding of the terminology to be used is absolutely essential to avoid any obvious differences, misconceptions or misunderstandings. In the absence of such understandings, negotiations would only be at cross purposes.

A boundary line, by its very definition, has to be very accurately depicted, with precise coordinates and marked by well-known geographical features. For it to be an effective instrument, it must not only be properly delineated on a map, but be visibly and effectively demarcated on the ground. Basically, boundary lines are of three different descriptions. These are 'natural' boundaries that follow well-known geographical features; 'mathematical' or 'astronomical' boundaries that follow latitudes and meridians and join two precise points or 'historical' boundaries that have evolved with the passage of time by usage, custom or even by conquest. The problem that arises in the case of 'historical' boundaries is how far back into antiquity should negotiators delve, for boundaries per se are never static and invariably evolve over time. It is but natural that any state party would only wish to go as far back into antiquity as it best suits its current negotiating position. As the history of previous negotiating efforts would indicate, it is rather difficult to arrive at a mutually satisfactory cut-off date, for this by itself often becomes an issue in dispute.

In the case of 'natural' boundaries that follow well-marked geographical features, the most common features normally followed are rivers, lakes, mountains or mountain ranges, often distinguished by well recognized peaks that are easy to identify. In the case of rivers, the generally accepted international practice is to follow the median line or the 'thalweg principle', unless so stipulated to the contrary by an agreement or a treaty [thalweg, a German term, refers to the middle of the main navigable or principal channel of a river]. The main problem with river boundaries is that rivers often change course, leaving the two contending states with a dispute. It is also the accepted international practice where a mountain range marks the boundary, that the watershed or water-parting is the normal guiding principle. In the past, China has generally accepted this principle of the watershed as the Treaty of Nerchinsk [27 August, 1689], the Convention of 1890 between Britain and China relating to Tibet and Sikkim, and the Convention between China and France relating to Vietnam [Tonkin] of 26 June, 1889, would indicate. In present times, China has followed the same principle of the watershed in the treaties signed and ratified between China and Nepal [1961] and China and Burma (now Myanmar) [4 January, 1961].

A boundary line is also, invariably, not only a political line separating two states but, more often than not, is also a line separating two civilizations, two distinct geographical systems and sometimes even two religious groupings. Two states divided by a boundary line may or may not be antagonistic to each other and this is largely a political question. A boundary line is also an emotional and a psychological divide. The Radcliff Line that separated India and Pakistan was a boundary line that partitioned British India into two countries on the basis of religion. It did not follow any well-known or marked geographical features on the ground. It separated two peoples, both in the West and in the East of British India that spoke the same language, were ethnically and culturally similar, but with different religious affiliations. In areas where people of different religious denominations have lived together for centuries, it becomes an exceedingly harrowing exercise to draw a boundary line, as significant minorities are often stranded on the wrong side of the line. The horrendous loss of life and property when the partition of India took place in 1947 testifies to this.

On the other hand, a frontier is but a vague and indefinite term.[2] A frontier generally has two conceptual meanings. The first concept means a political frontier that divides two states, and *it need not be under the control of either state* [emphasis added]. Since this frontier zone has both depth and width, it is possible to be imprecise as to where the line of separation between two sovereignties actually lies. Sometimes, fortifications were built to indicate an inner frontier upto which point a state exercised full control, leaving the intermediate as a kind of 'free zone.' The second concept of a frontier is with reference to 'settlements' *within a single country such* as those that existed when continental United States was being settled on its westward march. Thus, this latter concept represents the distinction between *occupied and controlled* land, as opposed to *unoccupied or open* land outside political control [emphasis added]. It also suggests that this political 'frontier' can be advanced as the settlement process unfolds and thus, by its very nature, is not considered to be a permanent one.

Frontiers face inwards as well as outwards depending on the power of the state.[3] Logically, therefore, frontiers are never static. They change over time with the ebb and flow of state power and, thus, reflect to a large extent, the political and military balance between countries. Each frontier is unique and, therefore, generalizations are of doubtful validity. Frontiers lie close to the heart of any foreign policy for they involve both the security of the sovereign state and are invariably the primary cause of anxiety of nearly every foreign office. It is said that four out of every five political treaties/conventions deal with frontiers alone.[4]

Many countries have favoured utilizing the concept of 'frontier zones' rather than specific boundary lines. In adopting such a concept, it absolves them of the need to negotiate and police specific boundary lines that may entail a heavy financial expenditure as well as a military burden. A frontier zone, unlike a boundary line, can cover extensive territory giving, it both depth and width that need not be defended, since it would imply open territory that neither state wishes to occupy. However, like a boundary line, a frontier zone, too, separates two sovereignties. Many a time, this concept is resorted to simply because some states have neither possessed the administrative aptitude nor the capacity to police such a boundary and have, therefore, preferred to forgo a definitive line in favour of a vaguer concept.

The terms 'border' and 'borderland' are generally considered to be synonymous. They usually refer to zones of indeterminate width that form the outer most parts of a state that are bounded on one side by a national boundary. It is not uncommon to find that the terms 'boundary', 'frontier' and 'border' are often used interchangeably and with loose facility. However, all are endowed with specific meanings and are not interchangeable. In any boundary negotiations, these definitions must be clearly understood, mutually agreed and adhered to by the two state parties.

Boundary making, in a way, also reflects the power balance of the day between the two state parties. More often than not, boundaries are claimed on grounds of both political and economic ambition or on expediency, and are invariably the cause of many disputes and conflicts. A militarily and economically stronger nation is unlikely to be 'reasonable' when negotiating a boundary alignment, and invariably has its way. That is why a weaker nation tends to play for time, in the hope that a more propitious situation would evolve at a later date. That was precisely the reason why the Chinese authorities in the 19th and early 20th centuries prevaricated on the boundary question when faced with a much more robust and demanding Imperial Britain. A weaker nation tends to sign rather than prevaricate only when it feels that it may get an even worse deal in the future. Sometimes, states succumb due to intense pressure, military or economic from the stronger nation or a group of nations. Often, such states then look for early opportunities to renege on their commitments. Therefore, the decision to enter into negotiations or the decision to conclude a settlement are political decisions based on a state party's overall national interests, and has very little to do with the technical aspects of boundary making.

Once there is a general political agreement between the two state parties on the broad contours of a boundary settlement, there are then three distinct phases that follow. The first phase is 'allocation', the second 'delimitation' and the third and final phase is 'demarcation.' Allocation means the initial political agreement to decide on a particular boundary alignment either verbally or by written understanding/agreement between the two state parties. It is this boundary alignment, so agreed upon, that is then clearly *drawn on a map but not marked on the ground that* is referred to as *delimited* [emphasis added]. In the final phase, when these lines drawn on a map are subsequently clearly *marked out on the ground* by the use of extensive ground markers or pillars, it is then referred to as *demarcated* [emphasis added]. Sir Henry McMahon, too, followed the same precepts at the Simla Conference when negotiating the Indo-Tibetan boundary in 1914. Sir Henry McMahon, writing years later, clarified the distinction between delimitation and demarcation as follows:

> Delimitation that I have taken is to comprise the determination of a boundary line by a treaty or otherwise, and its definition in written, verbal terms; demarcation to comprise the actual laying down of a boundary line on the ground and its definition by boundary pillars or other physical means.[5]

The concept of boundary demarcation is also of recent origin, and it was more prevalent in Europe than it ever was in Asia.[6] There was no such concept in Asia, and it is only fairly recently that the concept of fixed boundaries, up to which a state administers its territory, has begun to correspond with the realities of the situation in Asia.[7] Even in Europe, in most treaties concluded in the 17th century between two states, there is hardly any distinct provision for demarcation. It was only from the middle of the 18th century onwards that treaty texts in Europe contained references to 'commissioners.' It was the function of these 'commissioners' to be entrusted with the task of boundary demarcation on the ground. Included in the European concept of sovereignty was the belief that nation states must have 'bounded' communities and, therefore, it became necessary in order to define the extent of each state by negotiating boundaries. Thus, Lord Curzon in his Romanes lecture in 1907, could rightly claim that 'in Asiatic countries, it would be true to say that demarcation has never taken place except under European pressure and by the intervention of European agents.' Therefore, it would be a truism to say that to have well-defined and demarcated borders of a nation state is essentially a Western concept.

In the past, the Chinese became conscious of defining their borders only when they faced territorial aggrandizement at the hands of Western imperial powers. The occasion first arose when Russian military forces arrived at the gates of the Chinese empire and forced the Chinese to define their borders in line with Western concepts and sign the Treaty of Nerchinsk in 1689. Till then, the concept of defined borders had little resonance in Imperial China.

Inner Asian frontiers have always posed the greatest security challenges to the Chinese state. The construction of the 'Great Wall' of China was an attempt to gain security and keep out the so-called 'barbarians.' In a sense, this can be termed as the first Chinese attempt to demarcate its boundary. In the past, the Chinese also attempted to construct a string of 'vassal' states around its borders so as to secure the Chinese heartland from invasion. There was an inner frontier that protected the core of the Chinese state and an outer frontier within which lay the vassal states. Often, the Chinese authorities were willing to grant special rights to non-Han entities situated on the periphery of their empire to administer, to tax trade or even to discipline their own people living in Chinese territories. The Sino-Kokand Accord of 1835 is an example, and under it, the Kokand authorities even had the authority to exercise 'consular' jurisdiction over foreign traders.

Thus, as far as the outer frontier was concerned, it only indicated the limits of influence exercised by the Chinese empire and did not in all cases imply Chinese occupation or sovereignty. In line with Confucian tradition, none of these frontiers was very precisely defined. Confucian tradition held that in an ideal world there should be no boundaries between states. In line with this tradition, China did not see itself as a nation state or even as an empire, but as the centre of civilization. Thus, the Chinese state representing the 'civilized world' had moral authority over the 'barbarians' and conquest was permissible to assert its moral authority. In this context, the Chinese state rejected the concept of conducting international relations on the basis of sovereign equality. Therefore, so long as this tributary relationship remained firm, the Chinese were not very particular about the limits or definitions of their outer boundaries. In a sense, this also helped them to meet the political reality of China's shifting frontiers. At its core, the Chinese state is a homogenous one, with nearly 94 per cent of its people being Han Chinese. Therefore, it is comparatively easy to demarcate or distinguish Han Chinese areas from non-Han or minority areas. To stretch a point, the incorporation of non-Han areas into the Chinese state is also in a way China's imperial over-reach!

Like other Asian states, the demarcation of territorial boundaries for the Tibetans was a novel experience, too. In the Tibetan system the belief was that boundaries were locally determined and sanctioned, and that boundaries did not indicate that they were co-terminus with sovereignty. There were over-lapping zones between two different political entities and, as such, there was no need for external ratification of such a situation. For the Tibetans, what mattered was not where or if lines were drawn on a map, but what constituted a system of over-lapping allegiances or the sentiments of people concerned. Often, with the passage of time, these allegiances shifted and so did political control.[8] For the Tibetans, being pastoral in nature, what mattered more was the verge of grasslands, the fringe of the pine forest and their ability to access these areas, no matter of what sovereignty. Thus, boundary lines had little meaning.

One of the major problems faced by newly emerging nation states in the post-colonial period was the fact that most boundaries were drawn by the great powers of the day, keeping in mind their own strategic, political, economic and commercial interests. As Lord Salisbury remarked in 1890, 'we have been engaged in drawing lines on maps...we have been giving away mountains and rivers and lakes to each other, only hindered by the *small impediment that* we never knew where the mountains and rivers and lakes were!' Often, homogeneous communities were split and separated and their sentiments or aspirations were never considered when lines were drawn. Compromises worked out in one region were often traded for advantages in another region. Often, complicated negotiations took place thousands of miles away in the chancelleries of Europe. The 1907 Anglo-Russian Convention is one such prime example. Thus, when the time came to depart, a colonial power would inevitably bequeath numerous problems to the successor state. Therefore, should boundaries negotiated by colonial powers for their own benefit be vigorously defended by the newly independent successor state, or should completely new boundaries be negotiated *ab initio*? Should the new boundaries be based solely on ethnicity, language, culture or economic factors or on a combination of all? References to past irredentism could also not be safely set aside. Newly independent states found that neither course could be adopted with equanimity or without massive political pitfalls. How to handle this delicate situation became a moot point for most political elites in the newly emerged independent states. In the post-colonial era, this became a most important issue.

On deep reflection therefore, most newly emerged states decided that a much safer course would be to *allow the boundaries negotiated by colonial powers to stand as they were* [emphasis added]. To re-open any boundary alignment would, invariably, be far more troublesome. And to come to a settlement on a new boundary alignment would be even more incrementally difficult. Few of the newly emerged states were confident that they possessed the necessary skills to handle such delicate issues. Therefore, the principle of *uti possidetis* that is enshrined in international jurisprudence, was invariably followed. This principle states that whenever a state becomes independent, it automatically inherits colonial boundaries and that any effort to occupy or violate state territory after it became independent would be considered ineffective and of no legal consequence. This principle was recognized by the International Court of Justice [ICJ] as legally valid in the Burkina-Faso v Mali [1986] case. It is for these very reasons mentioned above that on 21 July, 1961, the Organization of African Unity [OAU] at Cairo declared that 'all member states pledge themselves *to respect the borders existing* on their achievement of national independence' [emphasis added].

Often, great powers like to project their power beyond a settled boundary line. This is done by developing, in the initial phase, the concept of 'spheres of interest.' These then further develop into 'spheres of influence' and yet again to 'protectorates' or 'neutral zones' or even 'buffer states.' Buffer states are essentially creatures of international politics and are designed to prevent the possibility of hostilities between two major antagonistic powers. A buffer state has been defined as a device likened to 'buffers;' because a buffer is a mechanical contrivance for breaking or graduating the force of impact between two heavy bodies, in the same way a political buffer checked the violence of political collision, though such buffers rarely prevented them altogether.[9] Powerful states that fostered 'neutral zones', 'spheres of influence' or 'buffer states' never precisely defined their actual responsibilities they would assume when forming such entities, save to deny the competing state any political or economic advantage in any such area. On the other hand, the imperial powers were keen that colonial boundary disputes between them remained local, were not transferred to Europe and that they did not assume international dimensions. They were afraid that colonial disputes would become the cause for exacerbation and tension between imperial

Governments in Europe.[10] The British, too, were keen that such colonial boundary disputes that existed between the major powers remained local and were not transferred to affect their relations in Europe, and thus assume a profile larger than that was necessary.

The British, while ruling in India, were adept at opting for, and following, these concepts. The British always kept the strategic or political boundary of their Indian possessions well ahead of the limits of their actual administrative occupation. It is for this reason that some 19th century maps of British India reflected only the limits of British administrative control, but *such lines thus shown were municipal and not international* [emphasis added]. The territory beyond such lines *was not considered to be a part of another adjacent state* [emphasis added]. Sometimes, the same colour wash was used to indicate that this was a British possession, but more often than not the outer boundary lines of such possessions were left vague. Maybe the British had at that point in time deliberately decided not to clearly mark the external limits of their possessions, in the event that such lines maybe needed to be suitably altered later in line with evolving British imperial interests. Politically, such a policy was rather astute, for it gave the British the necessary strategic leeway to alter boundaries at will at a later date to suit their convenience. They did not see any particular reason to clearly demarcate boundaries unless a credible security threat loomed on the horizon. The Durand Line separating Afghanistan from British India is one such example, and was hastily arrived at when a credible threat from Russian expansion in Central Asia appeared imminent. The British always preferred to deal with disputes as they arose. Being the pre-eminent imperial power, both militarily and economically, they were confident that in any eventuality, they would eventually have their way.

The Himalayas represent the perfect barrier, the perfect buffer between South Asia and continental Central and East Asia. So long as the high Himalayas remained impenetrable, there was never a clash of civilizations or empires or political ambitions. One of the main objectives of early British explorations of the high Himalayas in the 19th century was to ascertain whether a route might exist where by wheeled transport and artillery could easily penetrate the high mountains.[11] Once this fear was laid to rest by extensive explorations and scrutiny, the North-East Frontier of India could be considered dead and the British would remain content and quiescent.[12] Till the time the Chinese arrived to occupy the high Tibetan plateau in 1950, there was complete peace and a remarkable absence of disputes or incidents, largely because the Tibetan authorities at Lhasa were peaceably inclined and never exhibited any ambitions South of the Himalayan range.

Nevertheless, the British, ever conscious of the security of their Indian possessions, took no chances and took under their 'protection' the Himalayan States of Nepal, Bhutan and Sikkim. Whilst granting a large measure of internal autonomy, the British always ensured that the foreign relations of these states was kept firmly in their hands and that no other foreign power was ever allowed to obtain a foothold. And to ensure that British interests were always well protected, a Resident Commissioner was invariably stationed in these states. In the case of Tibet, the British, while paying lip service to the concept of Chinese suzerainty, ensured by treaty that no other 'foreign' influence entered Tibet. In addition, the British were acutely aware that a weak China offered no challenge to British interests or to British administered India. Britain was more interested in India's North-West frontier, primarily to ward off what they perceived was the main threat: Russian expansionary moves towards their empire in India. The British strategic assessment was that this was the primary threat to the security of India. That is why the Eastern frontier was neglected and was often referred to as the 'forgotten frontier.' Therefore, it was convenient for Britain to maintain the fiction of Chinese 'suzerainty' over Tibet to thwart what it then perceived were Russian designs on its empire in India. Britain never seriously visualized that one day it would not be the Russians, but a newly rejuvenated China, that would challenge Indian interests in the Himalayas.

The British were never inclined to incorporate Tibet into their Indian Empire. The British were very reluctant to accept the heavy financial burden that such a policy would have entailed. At the same time, they also never encouraged any move towards Tibetan 'independence,' content that with a vague Chinese suzerainty in place they would nevertheless continue to dominate the Tibetan state. Nor were the British prepared to jeopardize their lucrative trade and commercial relations with China. Having successfully met the main British strategic objective to keep Russian influence out of Tibet by means of the 1907 Anglo-Russian Convention; the British were quite content to let things be as they were. On attaining independence, India not only inherited the treaty and other obligations of the British with respect to the Himalayan states, but also those with Tibet. That essentially was the position it obtained on India's Northern frontiers on the eve of Indian independence in 1947.

Thus, the British on their departure, not only left the question of India's Northern frontier as fairly unsettled, but also quite un-policed. On the eve of Britain's departure from India, there were no police check-posts or any other administrative unit within 150 kilometres of India's Northern frontiers. In fact, along the entire Northern border, there were only five police check points altogether. Of these, three were in NEFA, two in Himachal Pradesh and none in the Western sector.

The then Governor General of India, Lord Lytton wrote in 1879: 'the concept of a frontier is a synonym for the word quarrel.'[13] His prediction literally came to be true when both the newly independent states of China and India squared off across the Himalayas, determined to occupy every last kilometre of territory that they perceived to be theirs.

CHAPTER 2

The International Scene: Post-Second World War— Was Tibet an Independent State?

Two events in the post-Second World War period have had a profound effect on the situation in Asia, particularly, as it pertained to India-China relations. The first was the emergence of the People's Republic of China. On 1 October, 1949, the Chinese leader Mao Zedung stood on the ramparts of the Tiananmen [gate of heavenly peace] and, in a highly emotive speech, ominously declared that 'the Chinese people have stood up!' Mao's speech was to reverberate throughout Asia. Nehru understood the import of this historic event. Writing to the Chief Ministers on 18 May, 1954, Nehru called it the 'greatest event in history since the Second World War.'[1] Mao's speech signalled the birth of a new China and the beginning of a new aggressive policy to reunite *all former Chinese* territories under one strong central leadership. Tibet would be no exception. Its days as an 'autonomous' or 'quasi independent' state were, thus, clearly numbered. Inevitably, newly independent India, too, would be deeply affected by these ominous developments just beyond its Northern borders. With the Chinese determined to occupy Tibet, India for the first time in recent history, faced a strong, vigorous and a reunited China all along its Northern frontier. The magnificent barrier of the Himalayas that separated the Indian sub-continent from Central and East Asia, would now be in contention. The buffer that Tibet had provided for centuries would inevitably disappear. India faced a new reality on its Northern frontier as it had never faced before.

The second cataclysmic event was the independence and partition of India. The partition of British India led to the creation of the two successor states of India and Pakistan. It effectively turned the South Asian power calculus inwards and against itself, thus making it easy for any potential aggressor. The withdrawal of Imperial Britain from India meant that the locus of power in Asia shifted from the South to the North of the Himalayas. Even Nehru admitted that the Chinese revolution bringing to power the Communists had upset the balance of power and that 'the centre of gravity had shifted...thereby directly effecting India.'[2] Independent India could also no longer rely on the reach and power of Imperial Britain, and was left alone to navigate the perilous new political power dynamic that came into being. In addition, India had to contend with the almost visceral antagonism of Pakistan. Thus, India faced potential hostility both from the North as well as from the West.

It is said that the power of Imperial Britain rested mainly on the strength of the British Navy, the undoubted prowess of the Indian Army and the not very inconsiderable political and administrative acumen of the British civil servants in India. Whereas the British, apart from their own economic and military strength, could rely on the strength of a united Indian Army, the new Indian Government was left with only 3/5th of the old Indian Army. And to make matters even more complicated, the newly independent states of India and Pakistan were soon at loggerheads with an armed conflict raging over Kashmir. With the bulk of the forces available to the newly independent Government of India deployed against Pakistan, some for internal consolidation and security, there was little left to face the looming threat from the North and North-East. The new political and military realities of South Asia, as a result of the withdrawal of Imperial British power, were not lost on the sharp political mind of the new rulers of China.

In modern times, all Chinese Governments, of whatever hue, have steadfastly held on to the belief that Tibet has always been a part of China. This has not always been so. China first occupied Lhasa in 1720, but did not displace the local Government of the Dalai Lama. For the next 200 years, Chinese authority was intermittent and at times non-existent. In 1792, a Chinese Army on the invitation of the Tibetans, helped them expel a Nepalese invasion. The 1876 Anglo-Chinese Convention was the first international document in which Tibet figured. The Manchu general, Chao Erfang, occupied Lhasa in 1908-1910, the first Chinese Army to occupy Lhasa against the wishes of the Tibetans. However, at the fall of the Manchu Empire, the Chinese garrison at Lhasa was forced to surrender and, in 1912, all Chinese soldiers were finally repatriated to China, mostly via India.

From this point onwards, the Tibetans exercised a de facto independence. Tibet's existence as an independent state was further reinforced when China agreed to participate at the Simla Conference in 1914 along with Britain and Tibet *on an equal footing with each exercising full plenipotentiary powers* [emphasis added]. The Tibetans further claimed that, like Nepal, all their obligations to China ceased with the demise of the Manchu dynasty for their obligations, such as they existed, were to the person of the Emperor and not to the Chinese state. The relationship was one of a layman and a priest, and if the priest receives help it does not mean that the priest becomes subordinate to the layman. The Tibetans often claim that there is no treaty or document that shows that Tibet was ever subordinate to China.[3] As the Dalai Lama was to remark, 'no knowledgeable person would for a moment think that the Tibetans were Chinese'! Crucially, therefore, in Tibet, just prior to the Chinese invasion in 1950, no one spoke Chinese, no taxes were ever collected by the Chinese, few Han Chinese lived in Tibet and there were no Chinese soldiers present. There was also no direct communication between Lhasa and China. Most communications had to pass through India! Even PM Zhou admitted to Nehru that 'Tibet was different from China and could not be considered as a province of China, but insisted that Tibet had always been an autonomous region of the Chinese state.'[4]

With the overthrow of the Imperial Chinese state, Sun Yat Sen 'the father of the revolution', called for the establishment of a strong Chinese state that would expel the Japanese from Manchuria, the Russians from Mongolia *and the British from Tibet* [emphasis added]. The Republican President, Yuan Shihkai, went even further and issued an edict on 21 April, 1912, declaring Tibet to be '*a province*' of China, on an equal footing with all other Chinese provinces. Even at times when the Central Government in China was weak and Tibet outside its control, China never surrendered the belief that Tibet was a part of China. Whether China was the 'suzerain' power or otherwise, it has tenaciously maintained that Tibet has always been a part of the larger Chinese family. Throughout this period China resisted all efforts by outside powers to recognize Tibet as anything other than 'autonomous.' At best, China was only willing to concede that Tibet was an 'autonomous *province*' of China [emphasis added], but nothing more.

The KMT Government of Chiang Kaishek [Jiang Jieshi] was as adamant as any other regime in China that Tibet was a part of China; in fact, it maintained that Tibet was a Chinese province. The British Embassy in Washington, in an Aide Memoir, informed the US State Department that in a meeting between Foreign Secretary, Sir Antony Eden, and the KMT Chinese Foreign Minister, TV Soong, on Tibet on 15 March, 1943, the latter insisted that: '*Eden would doubtless be aware of the fact that the Government of China had always regarded Tibet as a part of the Republic.*'[5] Chiang Kaishek in his book entitled 'China's Destiny', also makes the assertion that 'China should make plans for the restoration of our national sovereignty over Tibet.'

Therefore, it came as no surprise that the expansion of the Chinese state to incorporate Tibet has always had great prestige value in China itself. In addition, the Chinese were aware of the immense influence that successive Dalai Lamas have exercised over the Mongols and other peoples inhabiting Inner Asia, and this in turn, has added to Tibet's political value. For the Chinese, the ownership of the Tibetan landmass, which is about 25 per cent the size of Western Europe, was crucial and a strategic necessity for without Tibet, the essential unity of the 'new' China could never be realized. The Chinese considered Tibet as a bulwark against external powers that might wish to use Tibet to mount incursions from South of the Himalayas to destabilize the Chinese state. The population of non-Han minorities in China is only about 100 million, but crucially, they occupy almost half the land area! In other words, although the Han Chinese constituted nearly 94 per cent of China's total population, yet they occupy only less than half the land! It was not surprising, therefore, that China claimed and has always insisted that Tibet was a part of China.

Realizing that on the conclusion of the Second World War, Britain would soon leave India and hand over power to the new Government of independent India, the KMT Chinese Government decided to test the waters. It protested against the activities of Indian officials South of the McMahon Line, even before the British had formally handed over power. They were coolly told that this area was within the boundaries of India. Not to be deterred, the KMT authorities tried another tack, this time with the new Government of India. In 1948, the KMT Chinese suggested that the 1908 Tibetan Trade Regulations were now due for revision. This suggestion was to test whether India still adhered to the 1914 Simla Convention, since Article 7(b) of the said Convention had cancelled the 1908 Regulations and replaced it by new regulations negotiated between British and Tibetan representatives. The KMT Chinese Government was informed by India that it recognized only the validity of the 1914 Simla Convention with Tibet, and that this Convention superseded the 1893 and 1908 Regulations.

The Chinese Communists were not too far behind either. As far back as 1922, when the Chinese Communist Party [CCP] held its second National Congress, the manifesto of the CCP listed amongst its principal aims, 'the achievement of a genuine republic by the liberation of Mongolia, *Tibet and* Sinkiang.'[6] Mao Zedung, on the other hand, in July 1936, spoke of a Chinese 'federation' of which Outer Mongolia, Tibet and Sinkiang would be autonomous constituent parts.[7] Later in 1949, Mao changed his views when he noted that 'although Tibet's population is small, its international position is extremely important and *we must occupy it*' [emphasis added].[8]

Nevertheless, on attaining power the new Government of Communist China gave the concept of a 'Chinese Federation' a wide berth and reverted to the concept of a strong Central Government. There appear to be two fundamental reasons for this. The new Government was determined to eliminate all foreign influence and any vestige of China's earlier humiliations at the hands of foreigners. A key part for the restoration of national dignity involved *restoring full sovereignty over all areas that were previously considered 'Chinese'* [emphasis added]. Restoring Tibet to the larger Chinese family, thus, had deep nationalistic as well as great symbolic value. Secondly, the Chinese leadership was conscious of the fact that Tibet, a religious theocracy, was inclined towards independence and was deeply influenced by Britain and India. For China, the possibility that countries hostile to it would continue to play a role in Tibet from where they could threaten the Chinese provinces of Sinkiang [Xinjiang], Qinghai and Yunnan was clearly an unacceptable risk. The Chinese wished to maintain stability on their South-Western borders, considering that they faced 'military encirclement' and an economic embargo imposed by the US, following the victory of the Communists in China and the outbreak of hostilities in Korea.

Reflecting Mao's thinking, it came as no great surprise when the new Chinese Government emphatically declared that it would brook no interference in Tibet. It rudely emphasized to India that:

> Tibet is an integral part of Chinese territory. The problem of Tibet is entirely the domestic problem of China. The Chinese People's Liberation Army must enter Tibet, liberate the Tibetan people and defend the frontiers of China.[9]

For the hapless Tibetans, this was a harrowing experience. Tibet is the highest country in the world, with an average height ranging from 10-15,000 feet. Most of Tibet is an arid, desolate waste in the heart of Asia's steepest mountains. For the most part it is a bleak and barren plateau; an inhospitable tract of frozen wasteland[10] and its people a very hardy race. Before Buddhism arrived from India in the 11th century, the Tibetans were animist by religion, savage by nature and revelled in military exploits. Buddhism changed all that for it preaches against the killing of any living being. The Tibetans, being avid followers of the Buddha became gentle by nature. Its soldiers faded away and Tibet never threatened any one thereafter. As the Tashi Lama remarked 'we know nothing but read and pray.'[11]

The Tibetans call their country 'Po' and China as 'rgya-nag.' Nestling among the high Himalayas, with miles and miles of high tundra bereft of any sizeable habitation, the Tibetans never felt the need to establish contacts with foreigners, for they felt that Tibet was a special land protected by the Buddha. Its leaders saw Tibet's greatness in its religious institutions and held the belief that nothing should be done to 'contaminate' them.[12] Even as late as 1950, when the Chinese armies were approaching Tibet the feeling was that Tibet was a land of the 'Gods' and, therefore, it need not worry! The purpose of its Government was to be a patron of its religion and the needs and interests of its religion would have the utmost primacy.

The Tibetan ruling class never felt the need to establish diplomatic relations with other countries, nor did they feel the need for an army. Tibet is surrounded by two major countries; India and China. Although Tibet's ethnic boundaries have invariably never been congruous to its political boundaries, nevertheless in the past it served as a very useful buffer between India and China. Tibet's very remoteness and isolation was its strength. Sometimes, diplomatic notes sent even by the British were returned unopened! There were practically no roads, newspapers, factories, radios, airfields or cars in Tibet. It was perhaps the only country where there were no wheels! In the land of the Buddha, all such manifestations of a modern state had been banned. As the Dalai Lama was reported to have remarked, 'we did not know that we had to obtain approval for our independence from outsiders.' Nor did they feel the need to involve themselves in the politics of others. Tibet was a unique, gentle civilization that meant no harm to anyone. All that the Tibetans desired was to be left alone. Nevertheless, the fault for being unable to establish Tibet's international personality lay on the Tibetan elite. They made practically no effort to join the League of Nations, but only some sporadic attempts were made to join international organizations such as the Universal Postal Union. Nevertheless, Tibet did have its own army, its own currency and by 1923 it even had its own flag. The Tibetan Government was also issuing its own passports.

Although successive Chinese regimes have steadfastly maintained that Tibet has always been a part of China, other major powers have not altogether been so sanguine. In the past, as the Russian and British empires expanded into the heart of Asia, it was clear that at some point there would be a clash of interests. The advance of Russia in Asia: Tashkent in 1865, Samarkand in 1868, Bokhara in 1869, Khiva in 1873, Khokand in 1876, Turkmenistan in 1881, Penjdeh in 1885 and the Pamirs in 1895 unnerved the British administration in India. Every rumour about a possible Russian interest in Tibet was half believed and nervously watched. Such was the paranoia that in 1902, reports of a secret Russian-Tibet 'understanding', though hardly true, were given wide credence!

The Russians were acutely conscious of British sensitivity as their dominions expanded in Central Asia towards India. Sometimes, they intrigued in Tibet simply to ruffle British feathers in the hope of gaining an advantage elsewhere. The Russians were also aware that the British could inflict serious damage to their prospects in the Persian-Afghanistan region, particularly after their decisive defeat by Japan in the short but sharp Russo-Japanese War. Britain, humbled to an extent after the Boer War [1899-1902], found itself bereft of reliable friends in Europe. Under a new administration, Britain now began to seriously look for allies in Europe to counter the growing might of the German Empire. Russia, along with France, seemed to be the natural choice. As cordiality between Britain and Russia progressed in Europe, it was but inevitable that both countries would edge towards a settlement of their competitive concerns in Central Asia. The Anglo-Russian Convention of 1907 was the culmination of repeated attempts by both countries to come to terms over their respective interests in Asia. Not unnaturally, Tibet could not be left outside such an 'arrangement' and certainly could not be left in a vacuum.

It was under the Anglo-Russian Convention of 1907 that the concept of '*suzerainty*' was introduced for the first time in an international document with regard to Tibet [PRC State Council]. The Chinese felt that the two European powers, Britain and Russia, conspired together to modify Chinese *sovereignty* over Tibet into one of *suzerainty over Tibet* to the detriment of the Chinese position. In the 1907 Convention, both Britain and Russia, in reality, created the concept of Chinese *suzerainty* over Tibet in an attempt to paper over their mutual hostility and suspicions; but for the British it was both a security as well as a commercial imperative. Although a little earlier, on 27 April, 1906, under the Peking Adhesion Agreement signed between Britain and China no term was used to define the status of Tibet, yet Britain had agreed, as a concession to China, that it could not be classified as a 'foreign power' when it came to the Lhasa Convention of 1904. Nor did the Lhasa Convention of 1904 declare Tibet as an independent state. Thus, while the great powers of the day jostled for position, no one ever consulted the Tibetans on their status!

There has been considerable debate about the term '*suzerainty*.' It is basically a Western concept that had been used in the European context in defining relations between states. In international legal terms and context, L Oppenheim defines suzerainty as follows:

> Suzerainty is by no means sovereignty. It is a kind of international guardianship, since the vassal state is either absolutely or mainly represented internationally by the suzerain state.... The fact that the relation between the suzerain and the vassal always depends upon the special case, excludes the possibility of laying down a general rule as to the international position of the vassal state.[13]

Even in the US, legal experts do not consider the two terms 'suzerainty' and 'sovereignty' to be synonymous, although it was considered difficult to draw a precise line of demarcation between them. In general terms, 'suzerainty' implied less Chinese authority and more Tibetan autonomy than did 'sovereignty.' The US was never keen to enter into this debate and, therefore, reverted to the use of a more acceptable term by referring to Chinese 'de jure' authority over Tibet.[14]

In Asia, too, 'suzerainty' as it applied to both Tibet and China was rather anomalous. In the Central Asian context, in particular, this was treated as a new definition and a totally new concept. Few Asian states earlier had ever defined their mutual relationships in such terms. For the Tibetans, the correct concept was 'the Cho-Yon' [Priest-Patron] relationship that existed between the Dalai Lama and the Manchu Emperors. As the then Dalai Lama was to remind the British King-Emperor in London in a letter that 'be pleased to remember that Tibet is related to China as a priest to his disciple' [IOR 1913]. It was a person-to-person relationship and not state-to-state. Such were the relationships that had existed before the British arrived on the scene.

For the Chinese, this concept of suzerainty was something novel, too. In the Chinese scheme of things, there was the Emperor 'the son of heaven' who had unlimited authority over the 'middle kingdom' that encompassed the whole of the 'civilized world', i.e., the Chinese state. The others were simply barbarians or outsiders. There was, therefore, no question of any equality. Middle Kingdom China never recognized any state that could be considered 'equal', for they were either clients, vassals or tributary states. All states were considered inferior who as vassals of the Empire, paid tribute to the 'son of heaven.' The then British Ambassador to China, Sir Ernest Satow, in an interesting conversation in 1904 asked Prince Ch'ing how the concept of 'suzerainty' was understood in China. The Prince remarked that in China there was no proper word to describe it, '*but the word suzerain implied the shangguo or upper nation*' [emphasis added].[15]

In other words, the Chinese position was very clear. By whatever term it was defined, the Chinese view was that Tibet was subordinate to it and was a part of China. In fact Harriman, the then US Ambassador to Soviet Russia, reported an interesting conversation to President Truman from Moscow. When the KMT leader, TV Soong, met Stalin he told him that no Government in China could last if it ceded Outer Mongolia *and Tibet.* Soong emphasized that 'assertion' of Chinese *suzerainty* was embedded deep in the Chinese 'psyche'!

Thus, to treat Tibet and China in terms of Chinese suzerainty/Tibetan autonomy was a clever British strategic move to define the relationship between Tibet and China, without offending the Chinese or other Western powers. For the British, the concept of 'suzerainty' offered a practical way out of a political impasse. Britain was not prepared to accept the responsibility of taking over and governing a huge territory such as Tibet. Britain was never interested in recognizing an 'independent' Tibet or even declaring Tibet as a British protectorate. British policy on the Tibetan issue was reflected in a memorandum dated 11 July, 1912, sent by the India Office, and which clearly stated that:

> [a] HMG, while they have formally recognized the suzerain rights of China in Tibet, have never recognized and are not prepared to recognize, Chinese sovereignty over that country.
>
> [b] HMG does not admit the right of China to intervene actively in the internal administration of Tibet.[16]

The British knew that to fortify and garrison the North-East frontier of India on the same lines as the North-West frontier would be financially ruinous. As Sir Charles Bell remarked, 'it was recognized on our side from the first that this would have developed too heavy a burden upon us, the responsibility of protecting the distant and difficult expanses of Tibet.'[17] Additionally, it would have meant that Britain would have had to police an additional frontier of about 3,200 kilometres, enclosing an area of almost 800,000 square kilometres. No one in the British establishment, not even the most ardent imperialist, was ready for such a venture. At the same time, Tibet could not be left in a vacuum for other powers to exploit, for it was strategically located just North of Britain's Indian Empire. British policy was to politically sterilize and sanitize Tibet. Taking up arms for the cause of an independent Tibet was never considered a British option.

On the other hand, the British strategists knew that China of the 19th century was a weak, ineffective, struggling country beset with internal dissension and in no position to challenge British inroads into, or ambitions over, Tibet. Although under the Anglo-Russian Convention of 1907, both Russia and Britain had come to an agreement over Tibet, Britain continued to remain highly suspicious of Imperial Russia. By promoting the concept of China as the suzerain power in Tibet, Britain hoped to achieve both its aims without bearing any additional financial costs. This way, Russia would be kept out of Tibet and as China was too weak to assert anything but nominal influence, Britain could play the role it desired of being the dominant power in Tibet. British policy towards Tibet at that time was designed to ensure that Tibet constituted a buffer against perceived Russian ambitions in Central Asia. No thought was given to the fact that Britain might need Tibet as a buffer [huan zhong guo] between its Indian Empire and Chinese ambitions. Therefore, throughout this early period, it was Britain that was the principal proponent of establishing Chinese 'suzerainty' over Tibet. As Curzon was to put it, 'we regard the so-called *suzerainty* of China over Tibet as a constitutional fiction—a political affectation which has only been maintained because of its *convenience* [emphasis added] to both parties.'[18] Britain found the formula of effective or de-facto Tibetan independence coupled, with a rhetorical commitment to Chinese suzerainty, to be both politically and economically very convenient.

Whatever may have been the views of the Government of British India regarding Tibet, they were never allowed to exercise them independently. There were four principal offices that determined British policy; these were the India Office and the Foreign Office located in London, the Viceroy in India and the British Envoy to China. Often, relations and conduct of policy between these four offices was not well co-ordinated. Whether Tibet should remain under Chinese suzerainty or whether it should be allowed or encouraged to declare itself independent of China was always a question that would be decided in London. Although Indian interests were often put across very forcefully to Whitehall, nevertheless, overall British imperial interests invariably always prevailed. As the then Secretary of State for India was to so succinctly remind the Viceroy, Lord Curzon:

> Indian frontier policy could no longer be regarded from an exclusively Indian point of view, that the course to be pursued in such cases must be laid down by His Majesty's Government alone. It is essential that this should be borne in mind by those who find themselves entrusted with the conduct of affairs in which the external affairs of India are involved, and that they should not allow themselves... to forget the necessity of conforming to the instructions which they have received from His Majesty's Government, who have more immediately before them the interests of the British Empire as a whole.[19]

As for deciding where India's frontiers should lie, the British officials serving in India were duly reminded that '*Indian Frontiers cannot be decided without reference to imperial exigencies elsewhere*' [emphasis added].[20]

In the British concept, Chinese *suzerainty* over Tibet did not mean total Chinese control over Tibet. It also did not mean that Tibet was a province of China, nor did it mean that Tibet, apart from exercising complete internal autonomy, could *not conduct relations with other countries independent of China* [emphasis added]. To allow full Chinese control or even influence over Tibetan policy would mean in fact giving a veto to China. This was something that the British were not prepared to concede. The linkage between full Tibetan autonomy and allowing

China to claim *suzerainty* over Tibet was firmly established in the British mind. The two concepts were always stressed together.

Thus, when world-wide British imperial interests so demanded, Britain came to terms with Russia with the signing of the 1907 Anglo-Russian Convention. Under this Convention, Britain conceded to Russia a virtual veto over Tibet when both agreed that there would be no negotiations with Tibet except through the intermediary of the Chinese Government, and further agreed that neither country would send a Resident Representative to Tibet. British anxiety over the events in Tibet remained, particularly on the conclusion on 11 April, 1913, of the Tibet-Mongolian Treaty that was signed at Ugra. The British suspected a Russian hand and were not convinced that the Russian drive for expansion in Central Asia had abated.

It was in order to counter perceived Russian ambitions for further expansion in Asia that Britain, in order to safeguard the security of its Indian Empire, attempted to establish a more forthright position in Tibet and to delimit Tibet's frontiers with India. However, the question of China's legal position as regards Tibet remained unresolved. At this point in time, the British were convinced that the only first rate power that could threaten its Indian Empire was Russia,[21] although British apprehensions over Chinese ambitions remained. These were the main reasons why Britain attempted to come to terms with China and Tibet at the Simla Conference in 1914.

In terms of British diplomacy, the Simla Convention was a spectacular success. They had prevailed over China to agree to the participation of Britain, China and Tibet *on an equal footing, with each exercising full plenipotentiary powers* [emphasis added]. They secured a boundary agreement between India and Tibet [The McMahon Line], eliminated any Chinese influence near the North-East Regions of India and yet prevailed upon the Tibetans to save Chinese 'face' by acknowledging Chinese 'suzerainty' over Tibet. The Simla Convention, although initialled by the Chinese plenipotentiary, Ivan Chen, was subsequently not ratified by the Chinese Government for altogether different reasons that had nothing to do with the Indo-Tibetan boundary. The Chinese Government's sole objection to ratifying the Simla Convention was the proposed boundary between Tibet and China! It is a moot point, but had the First World War not commenced so soon after the conclusion of the Simla Convention, British diplomacy would have ultimately prevailed upon the Chinese Government to ratify the Convention. In any case, differences between the Tibetans and the Chinese over their boundary alignment were not of such magnitude that it would have prevented British diplomacy from prevailing. After the conclusion of the First World War, it was a different ball game altogether, for Britain was by now fatally weakened by the horrendous losses it suffered in manpower and economic strength. The baton, as the main superpower in the Western world, had passed from Britain to the United States, and the US was not interested in further weakening the Chinese state. The Chinese were not unaware of these far reaching developments and accordingly adjusted their policies.

Nevertheless, British policy in the inter-war period was firmly established. While nominally acknowledging Chinese suzerainty, they felt free to conduct relations with Tibet as they perceived in their best interests. It was a simple, pragmatic but an opportunistic policy. In this way the British hoped not to offend other Western powers suspicious of British aims in Tibet. The British did, however, make some efforts to get China to ratify the Simla Convention. On 21 August, 1921, Curzon, now Foreign Secretary and a former Viceroy of India, 'threatened' the Chinese Minister thus:

> In view of the commitments of HMG to the Tibetan Government arising out of the tri-partite negotiations of 1914, and in view of the fact that the Chinese Government accepted, with the exception of the boundary clause, the draft Convention of 1914, providing for Tibetan autonomy under Chinese suzerainty, and formally reaffirmed their attitude in this respect in their offer of 1919, HMG do not feel justified, failing a resumption of negotiations in the immediate future, in withholding any longer their recognition of the status of Tibet as an autonomous State under the suzerainty of China, and intend on dealing on this basis with Tibet in future.[22]

It was pure British bluff, for they were in no position to force the issue. The Chinese prevaricated, made the excuse of pretending to be busy with the forthcoming Washington Conference [1922] and let the British proposal lie. Conscious of the fact that its bargaining position was weak, as its strength did not match its responsibilities, Britain did not force the issue. For Britain, its own interests were above and by far more important than those of India, and in a sense this immobilized her efforts. This can also be seen in the consistent British refusal to supply arms to Tibet in adequate quantities, even though they were obligated to do so under promises made to the Tibetans during the Simla negotiations. In any case, after the First World War, the British realized that in the near future they would have to grant India self-Government and to that extent, British enthusiasm to push China for clarity over Tibet's status considerably lessened. The zeal exhibited earlier by British officials noticeably declined and, as the movement for Indian independence gathered steam and since no imminent security threat appeared over the horizon, issues pertaining to Tibet were safely put on the back burner.

Nevertheless, some dedicated British officials still persisted with trying to make the McMahon Line acceptable. Alerted by a trivial incident in 1935, when the Lhasa Government questioned the right of a British botanist, F. Kingdon Ward, to travel through Tawang to Tibet without the Lhasa Government's permission, Olaf Caroe [Deputy Secretary, Foreign Department] immediately recognized the significance of the issue. To his consternation he found that both the Assam Government and the Political Officer in Sikkim were ignorant of the position of the frontier, and accordingly complained to the India Office at London.[23]

Caroe queried the Chief Secretary to the Assam Government, Dawson, on what steps the Assam Government had taken to extend political control up to the 'Line' which had been accepted by the Tibetan Government as the delimited frontier between India and Tibet. Subsequently, the Government of India clarified unequivocally that 'HMG have now agreed that the 1914 Convention with Tibet and connected agreements should be published and that the boundary as then laid down should be shown on maps published by the Survey of India.'[24] But the British Government still insisted, as late as in 1937, that it was not open to 'HMG to repudiate Chinese suzerainty over Tibet or to support the Tibetan Government in any attempt to do so.'[25]

The Chinese were, of course, not in any position to challenge British decisions. In 1943, even at the height of the Second World War, when the Americans queried the British on their position on Tibet, the British, in line with their stated policy, were very explicit. An Aide Memoire from the British Embassy in Washington to the State Department quoting the Viceroy of India, Lord Linlithgow, clarified British policy as under:

> Ever since the abortive 1913 Convention, the attitude of Government of India has been that they wished to secure agreement between China and Tibet and were willing to advise the Tibetan Government to admit formal Chinese suzerainty, although such an admission would in no sense constitute Tibet a province of China. The Government of India has always held that Tibet is a separate country in full enjoyment of local autonomy, entitled to exchange diplomatic representatives with other powers. The relationship between China and Tibet is not a matter which can be unilaterally decided by China, but one on which Tibet is entitled to negotiate, and on which she can, if necessary, count on the diplomatic support of the British Government along the lines shown above.[26]

In similar terms, the British Foreign Secretary, Sir Anthony Eden, on 5 August, 1943, also informed the Chinese Foreign Minister in a memorandum that:

> HMG are prepared to recognize Chinese suzerainty over Tibet, but only on the understanding that Tibet is regarded as autonomous. Neither the British Government nor the Government of India have any territorial ambitions in Tibet, but are interested in the maintenance of peaceful conditions in an area that is co-terminus to the North-East frontiers of India.[27]

Despite its obvious interests in the security of its dominions in India, the other principal British objective was to ensure that its trade and commercial interests in China were not harmed. To facilitate such a policy, the British were apt to disclaim any interest in the territorial disintegration of China. As the British envoy to China, Sir John Jordan reminded his own Government that 'Britain's gigantic trade throughout China was hostage against any strong anti-Chinese policy' that the British Government might consider.[28] The British were fully aware of the need to balance their strategic interests in the Tibet region, with expected commercial gain in China and, therefore, they were not inclined to needle Chinese sentiments unnecessarily. Britain's efforts were also largely devoted to ensuring the territorial integrity of China, for if Britain engineered to slice Tibet away from China, what would prevent other great powers from similarly slicing away other Chinese territory? Thus, it was the considered opinion in Britain that the dismemberment of China would be disastrous for British trade. In 1898, the House of Commons passed a resolution declaring that 'it is of vital importance for British commerce and influence that the independence of Chinese territory be maintained.'[29] That being so, how could Britain 'detach' Tibet from China and bring it completely into the British Indian political orbit or even encourage its independence?

Britain first made commercial contact with China through the East India Company. In 1692, it was allowed to set up a trading post in Taiwan. The East India Company soon engaged in regular and direct trade with the Chinese mainland and was permitted to make visits to Canton, Amoy and Chusan. However, the foreign traders were under severe restrictions, and in a bid to by-pass such restrictions, Britain sent Lord Macartney in 1792 as a royal envoy to the Imperial Court in Peking. In 1793, Lord Macartney was finally granted an interview with the Emperor and his request for lifting restrictions on foreign trade were summarily rejected. A second mission under Lord Amherst was similarly unsuccessful. Nevertheless, trade between the two countries flourished.

Thus, by the late 19th century, Britain controlled nearly 80 per cent of China's foreign trade of which nearly 50 per cent was carried in British ships. However, by early 20th century, Britain was running huge trade deficits with the Atlantic world and this fiscal deficit could only be met by the surpluses that Britain generated in her trade with China and India. The British were huge consumers of tea that was largely imported from China, and the British exchequer gained enormously by levying a duty on Chinese tea imported into Britain. From importing just 2 pounds of tea from China in 1660, this trade grew exponentially so that by 1780, Britain was importing 15 million pounds of tea, which by 1830, increased to 30 million pounds!

At the same time, as hard as it tried, Britain just could not sell sufficient amount of goods to China to pay for its huge imports of tea. The Chinese insisted that the balance must be settled in silver dollars alone. To cover this obvious deficiency, the British hit upon the idea of selling opium grown in India to the Chinese to balance her imports of tea from China. Opium was grown in India and the British had gained the Bengal opium monopoly as a result of Clive's decisive victory at Plassey in 1757. The British by 1773, had assumed the monopoly in the sale of opium and by 1797, the complete monopoly of its manufacture. Such a monopoly yielded nearly one seventh of the total revenue of British India and it became an essential and permanent element of the Indian fiscal system.[30]

As could be expected, the British were not averse to using military means to force the Chinese to import opium [The Opium War]. During this period, the economies of China, India and Britain were linked together in a trade triangle that, till the 1860s, was one of the most important components of the world economy and continued to play a significant role in world trade. The flow of trade amongst the three countries involved the export of British manufactures to India, the export of opium from India to China and the purchase by Britain of Chinese tea, silk and bullion.[31] Thus, trade between Britain, China and India was neatly balanced. It was not until the late 19th century that Indian tea from Assam began to arrive in Britain in sufficient quantities to substitute for the China tea trade. The British were clearly dazzled by the prospects of a limitless China market and did not wish to take any political initiative that might undermine this lucrative trade.

It was British credit that was mainly used to finance the construction of railways and other infrastructure projects in China. Britain advanced loans to China and supported Yuan Shihkai against Sun Yatsen's nationalists after the fall of the Qing dynasty, mainly to enable them to continue the revenue advantages that had accrued to them under various treaties signed earlier. In 1920, a banking alliance between Britain, USA, France and Japan was negotiated and secured, mainly to supervise and oversee political loans to China. These agreements were clearly one-sided. Most British traders and financiers operated from enclaves established near the major ports of China, notably Shanghai, Hong Kong, and Canton. This enabled them to control most of the trade and access to potential markets in interior China. Extra-territoriality enabled British subjects to work outside the Chinese fiscal, administrative and judicial system. Even the 1922 Washington Conference, organized at the initiative of the US that provided for the return of sovereign rights to China, was hedged in with various conditions initiated by Britain.

Just prior to the end of the Second World War, there seems to have been a subtle shift in British opinion. Perhaps aware that they would have to leave India soon, the British were not keen any more to continue their involvement with Tibet. They now began to plan for a suitable time and an opportunity to disentangle themselves from Tibetan affairs. Understandably, Britain felt that the lead role should now be played by the new Indian Government. In a remarkably prescient note, this is what the Foreign Office in London said:

> China is bound to absorb Tibet after the war if not before and we can do nothing to prevent it. In the event of India gaining its independence, we shall be unable to help Tibet further and, therefore, it is poor service to the Tibetans to encourage them against the Chinese now...it is our desire to maintain the Tibetan buffer for as long as we are responsible for India's foreign relations...the development of modern warfare has rendered out of date the policy of buffer state...Chinese suzerainty over Tibet is very deep rooted in history and even if the Tibetans refuse to acknowledge it now, they might quite possibly do so....[32]

Therefore, it came as no surprise that when Britain finally departed from India, it largely abandoned its interests in Tibet. The US Embassy in London on 26 August, 1947, in a telegram to the State Department in Washington confirmed such a change in attitude and policy and the lack of interest in Tibet on the part of Britain. The US Embassy in London informed Washington as follows:

> The UK no longer has an abiding interest in the future of Tibet since British control was withdrawn from India.[33]

From this point on, Britain's commercial and political interests in China became the pivot on which British policy was formulated. Thus, not unsurprisingly, in 1948, Britain refused to give visas on Tibetan passports to a Tibetan delegation travelling to Britain. Two years later, the British Ambassador to the UN advised the British Government that 'what we want to do is to create a situation which does not oblige us in practice to do anything about the Communist invasion of Tibet.'[34] Later, speaking first at the UN, the British Ambassador obfuscated the issue of Tibetan independence by informing his colleagues that after half a century of 'intimate' relations, HMG felt that the status of Tibet 'was unclear' and suggested that the Tibetan appeal be postponed! Later in 1961, the British sold Vickers-Armstrong powered four engine transport planes to China, which could fly directly from China to Tibet, thus enabling China to consolidate her rule in Tibet! Even today, Britain is the largest European investor in China. And finally, on 25 October, 2008, Britain completely abandoned its century old policy at the altar of its commercial interests. The new British policy was:

> Our ability to get our points across has sometimes been clouded by the position the UK took at the start of the 20th century on the status of Tibet, a position based on the geo-politics of the time. Our recognition of China's 'special position' in Tibet developed from the outdated concept of suzerainty. Some have used this to cast doubt on the aims we are pursuing and to claim that we are denying Chinese sovereignty over a large part of its own territory. We have made clear to the Chinese Government, and publicly, that we do not support Tibetan independence. Like every other EU member state and the United States, we regard Tibet as part of the People's Republic of China.[35]

Thus, with this statement, all British ambiguity over the status of Tibet ended, once again, at the altar of her commercial interests.

But what was the policy on the status of Tibet that Soviet Russia was following? Had the policy followed by Imperial Russia changed after Lenin took over in Moscow? Imperial Russia had, in an agreement with Britain in 1907, recognized Chinese *suzerainty* over Tibet. Imperial Russia never objected to the 1914 Simla Convention or to the bilateral agreement between Britain and Tibet settling the Indo-Tibet boundary along the McMahon Line.

On the conclusion of the Second World War, Mao timed his visit to Moscow in 1949 [Dec-49/Jan 50] to enable him to participate in Stalin's 70th birthday celebrations. Mao gave Stalin a signed photograph of himself with the inscription, 'to *our leader* Comrade Stalin from Mao Zedung' [emphasis added]. Elated at such flattery, the Soviet leader was quite emphatic that Tibet was a part of China. An exchange of views on Tibet, in a meeting on 22 January, 1950, in Moscow between Mao and Stalin, aptly illustrates the Soviet Russian view:

> Mao Zedong: I would like to note that the air regiment that you sent to China was very helpful. They transported 10,000 people. Let me thank you, Comrade Stalin, for the help and ask you to allow it to stay a little longer, so it could help transport provisions to [CCP CC member and Commander of the PLA's Second Field Army] Liu Bocheng's troops, currently preparing for an attack on Tibet.
>
> Stalin: It's good that you are preparing to attack. The Tibetans need to be subdued. As for the air regiment, we shall talk this over with the military personnel and give you an answer.[36]

Stalin also advised flooding Tibet and other border areas with Han Chinese. Two years later, on 3 September, 1952, when PM Zhou Enlai sought Soviet help in subduing the Tibetans, Stalin once again emphasized that:

> Tibet is a part of China. There must be Chinese troops deployed in Tibet.[37]

Thus, when the Tibetan appeal came before the UN in November 1950, the Soviet delegate, in line with stated Soviet policy, categorically maintained that 'Tibet was an inalienable part of China and its affairs were the exclusive concern of the Chinese Government.' Not only did Soviet Russia fully support the Chinese, but went a step further when *Pravda*, on 30 May, 1951, accused Britain of 'unlawfully' taking away both Bhutan and Sikkim from Tibet in 1890! In other words, *Pravda* undoubtedly reflecting the Kremlin's views, did not even recognize independent India's relations with Sikkim and Bhutan.[38] Moscow welcomed the Seventeen-Point Agreement of 23 May, 1951, between Tibet and China, and *Pravda,* of 29 May, 1951, gave wide coverage to the statements of Mao and Zhu De. Later, Moscow also helped in the construction of an airfield in Lhasa and Soviet pilots flew test flights to Lhasa.[39]

The other major power that had influence over events in Tibet and China was the United States. From early 20th century, the US has consistently held the view that it was in their interest to 'preserve the territorial and administrative integrity' of China. The US accordingly informed major European powers of this policy.[40] A little later, Secretary Hay reiterated the same policy, once again to US Ambassadors abroad in a circular telegram on 13 January, 1905. He clarified that:

> The US has repeatedly made its position well known of its broad policy of maintaining the integrity of China.

So pleased were Chinese officials with the US position that on 5 July, 1905, the then Emperor of China expressed his gratitude to the US President thus:

> China's great obligation [to the US] for proclaiming to the whole world that China's territorial integrity must be maintained.

The American Minister [Commissioner] in Peking, WW Rockhill, in 1908 even went to the extent of making statements that 'the Lama [the Dalai Lama] was a vassal prince' and that he must 'bow to his sovereign's command' and that 'close and friendly relations with China are absolutely necessary for Tibet.'[41] The broad parameters of this view continued to be US policy throughout this period. In line with this thinking and policy, the US has consistently held the view that Tibet was under Chinese '*suzerainty.*' In 1943, the US State Department reaffirmed its views to the British Embassy in Washington. It stated that:

> With regard to the position of Tibet in Asia, the British Government has been so good as to give an account of its historical attitude. For its part, the Government of the United States has borne in mind the fact that the Chinese Government has long claimed suzerainty over Tibet and that the Chinese Constitution lists Tibet among areas constituting the territory of the Republic of China. This Government has at no time raised a question regarding either of these claims. The Government of the United States does not believe that a useful purpose would be served by opening at this time a detailed discussion of the status of Tibet.[42]

The United States was also not prepared to cause any offence to the Chinese authorities by even remotely suggesting that Tibet was not a part of, or even independent of, China. President Roosevelt was 'advised' by his Secretary of State, Hull, to be careful when addressing a letter to the Dalai Lama, so as not to hurt Chinese susceptibilities. Addressing a memo to the President, Secretary Hull emphasized that:

> The letter [should be] addressed to the Dalai Lama in his capacity of religious leader of Tibet, rather than in his capacity of secular leader of Tibet, thus avoiding giving any possible offense to the Chinese Government which includes Tibet in the territory of the Republic of China.[43]

Letters from US authorities were always addressed to the Tibetan Foreign Affairs '*Bureau*' and never to the Tibetan '*Foreign Office*'! US Assistant Secretary of State, Berle further confirmed the US point of view in a note to the Director of the Office of Strategic Services [Donovan] when he clearly stated that:

> Tibet as you know is regarded by the Chinese as a dependency of China and the Government of the United States has never taken any action in contravention or disregard of that Chinese view.[44]

Similarly, the British too were regularly reminded of the US position.[45] From the US point of view, it was essential that the territorial unity of China be maintained. For the US, at that point in time, China was an important and a necessary strategic counter-weight to Japanese expansionism in Asia. As such the US warned the Japanese that '*the US could not regard with indifference the assumption of political, military or economic domination over China by a foreign power [Japanese]'* [emphasis added].[46] It remained an axiom of US policy that it was not prepared to see the emergence of a single formidable power that could dominate the East Asian strategic landscape. Nevertheless, the US remained committed to a 'strong, peaceful, united and a democratic China.' Although the US had little inclination to interfere in the internal affairs of China since it felt that 'the management of internal affairs is the responsibility of the peoples of sovereign nations', yet it strongly urged the KMT Chinese Government to 'overlook no opportunity to adjust their [KMT and Communist] internal differences promptly by peaceful negotiations.' The US was even prepared to give political support to this position by informing the Chinese that they [the US] were prepared to seek British and Soviet Government support. Even as late as 1945, the US indicated that it was willing to work with 'any other leadership' in China, provided it contributed to achieving peace and stability in East Asia. On the other hand, the US was willing to provide both financial and military support to see that a 'unified' Chinese Government emerged. It was for this reason that it was willing to 'broker' a meeting between the Communists and the KMT Government.[47]

The US conscious of its vital interests in Asia in which China played a predominant part, was not prepared to push the line of Tibetan *suzerainty* beyond a point, and certainly not towards independence. Tibet was never a core issue of interest of US foreign policy. At best, the US was willing to exploit the situation for tactical purposes and utilize the developments to further its strategic interests. Three events bear out the truth of this policy: the Chinese invasion of Tibet in 1950, the 1959 rebellion in Tibet and the normalization of relations with China in 1972.

After the defeat of the KMT forces in China, the Communists moved rapidly to consolidate their hold over the country. It was a foregone conclusion that Tibet would be next. In line with policy, PM Zhou informed Soviet Ambassador Roschin as early on 14 November, 1949 that 'right after liberating Sichuan and Xingiang, we will attack Tibet.'[48] The US was deeply worried over the shape of events taking place in China. The collapse of the KMT regime and the rise of the Communists had a far reaching effect on US policy. If there was a time to change its attitude towards China in general and Tibet in particular, it was now. While the US attitude towards the new Communist Government stiffened, yet it was not prepared to re-consider its position towards Tibet, *even if Chinese troops moved to occupy Tibet* [emphasis added]. A Top Secret report of the National Security Council of 25 August, 1950, recommended that in the event of an attack by Chinese troops against Tibet, *the US should take political action, but was not expected to take military action* [emphasis added].[49]

The US was deeply worried that any attempt to detach Tibet from mainland China could have cascading consequences elsewhere. The Soviet Union had not as yet fully withdrawn its troops from Manchuria, and the US was worried that the Soviets too might be tempted to detach Manchuria from China, just as the Japanese had done earlier. [It may be recalled that the Soviets had successfully detached Outer Mongolia from China and formed the Mongolian People's Republic under its tutelage and had managed to obtain the acquiesce of this action from both the KMT and the Communist Governments of China.] Therefore, while the US strongly opposed the new Communist regime in China and even refused to recognize its existence, nevertheless supporting the maintenance of the territorial integrity of China remained upper most in the minds of US policy strategists. The US, thus, operated at two levels: strategically it would do nothing to violate the territorial integrity of China, while tactically it would lose few opportunities to embarrass the new Communist Government. A Memorandum from the Department of State [Far East Department] dated 12 April, 1949, *for internal circulation* spells out US policy succinctly. It says:

> We have already given renewed assurances to China [KMT] of our recognition of China's de jure sovereignty or suzerainty over Tibet...*The Department informed the Chinese Embassy [KMT] that this Government has no intention of acting in a manner to call into question China's de jure sovereignty over Tibet...a decision to recognize Tibet involves our consideration not merely of our policy over Tibet but also of our policy towards China. A basic principle of our policy towards China has been respect for China's territorial integrity.... As a practical matter, Tibet's importance both ideologically and strategically, is very limited....unless minerals are found in Tibet, the Army [US] does not regard Tibet as of strategic significance.*[50] [emphasis added]

And to confirm this assessment, the then US Ambassador to India, Henderson, informed the State Department on 12 April, 1949, that:

> Present American economic interests in Tibet are of little importance. There is no information available regarding mineral resources in Tibet. Even if found...they would be almost impossible to exploit...given the conservative, superstition-ridden Tibetan people.[51]

Nevertheless, the advantage of embarrassing the new Communist Government of China was too good to be missed. The intervention of Chinese troops in Korea also played on the American mind. The intention of the US was not to help Tibet, but only as a Cold War tactic to challenge the Chinese.[52] The cause of Tibet *per se* was of secondary importance. The US was fighting Communism and not China and was mainly concerned in preventing the spread of Communism rather than providing serious or committed aid to Tibet. As such, in practical terms, the US took every step to avoid any military confrontation with China over Tibet.

On the other hand, the US tried to inveigle the Dalai Lama to leave Tibet and seek asylum abroad. It hoped to use the presence of the Dalai Lama outside Tibet to launch a political campaign to embarrass the Chinese authorities. But here again, the US entered a caveat. It would only help the Dalai Lama if he denounced the Seventeen-Point Agreement entered into by him with Mao's China.

And the US, in line with its stated policy, would not commit to anything more than underlining *suzerainty* for Tibet. As the US Ambassador to India, Henderson, clarified:

> In case Tibetan Government should announce refusal accept Agreement [17 Point Agreement] we believe US should be prepared to issue a sharp statement denouncing Peiping machinations to force Tibetans under duress to abandon their long established rights to autonomy. Such announcement should, of course, be couched in such terms as not give undue offense to non-Communist China by questioning Chinese sovereignty over Tibet.[53]

And further, the US Secretary of State directed the US Ambassador in Delhi that:

> Implicit in this understanding, however, is US support for the Dalai Lama's return to Tibet at earliest moment as head of autonomous non-commie country.[54]

The choice had been made. The US was not willing to hurt Chinese sensitivities and, thus, would not support Tibetan independence, even in the face of Communist 'aggression' against Tibet. An autonomous Tibet, as a part of China, was the best that the US was willing to offer or support.

The US authorities even began to look for places where the Dalai Lama could be suitably settled once he decided to seek asylum outside Tibet. Both Sri Lanka and Thailand, as predominately Buddhist countries, were considered as possibilities. The US also indicated that it would finance only a part of the costs of such a venture. That the Dalai Lama decided not to accept the US offer was based on his understanding that without India's support, such a venture was unlikely to succeed and that the terms offered by Mao were decidedly better. When the revolt erupted in Tibet 1959 and the Dalai Lama escaped from Lhasa and sought asylum in India, the US was one of the few countries that supported the Tibetan cause, but only as a humanitarian gesture. The US encouraged the Tibetans in their appeal to the UN *to concentrate on humanitarian aspects and not on the political* [emphasis added]. The US did not want to take issue on whether Tibet was an independent country or under Chinese *suzerainty*, as it did not want to antagonize the Chinese further. Politically astute, the US was aware of the beginnings of a major dispute between the two Communist giants and erstwhile allies, Soviet Russia and China, and did not in any way wish to bring them closer together on any issue of importance. Thus, the US Secretary of State, Herter, cabled the US Ambassador in Delhi to inform the Dalai Lama that the US view was:

> Consultations with other UN members on the subject have confirmed our view, made known to you earlier, that wider support can be obtained for a hearing of Tibet's case if suppression of human rights aspects of it are stressed rather than matters relating to sovereignty. [55]

At this point in time, US relations with Communist China were also quite tense, particularly over the dispute over the off-shore islands [Quemoy and Matsu] held by the Taiwan based KMT Government. The US also did not want to lose this opportunity to embarrass the Chinese. While it held on firmly to its core belief of not going too far to talk of Tibetan independence, the US was not averse to supporting Tibetan self-determination. The US Secretary of State Herter's letter to the Dalai Lama dated 20 February, 1960, is the farthest that the US has ever gone for Herter mentions Tibet *as an autonomous country [Note: word used for Tibet is a country] under the suzerainty of China.* [emphasis added]

The letter from Secretary of State Herter to the Dalai Lama [20 February, 1960] reads as follows:

> As you know, while it has been the historical position of the United States to consider Tibet as an autonomous country under the suzerainty of China, the American people have also traditionally stood for the principle of self-determination. It is the belief of the United States Government that this principle should apply to the people of Tibet and that they should have the determining voice in their own political destiny.[56] [Relevant Para]

Implicit in this letter is the concept of self-determination, but this was never US policy and, soon after this letter was written, the US reverted to its familiar line of respecting the territorial integrity of China. It was also during this period that the US was doing its utmost to de-stabilize the Chinese regime in Tibet by undertaking covert CIA sponsored operations inside Tibet. Even here, the objective was not to create an independent Tibet but only an *autonomous* Tibet in pursuance of US policy objectives, as stated initially in the document NSC 5913/1. As relations between China and Soviet Russia worsened, particularly after the clashes between them in 1969 on the Ussuri River, the US sensed an opening for normalizing its relations with China. What had been obvious was now stated quite openly. The State Department on 14 April, 1970, informed the US Ambassador in Delhi that:

> Both the Dalai Lama and the Government of India presumably have been aware for some years that relations with Communist China have inevitably been an element in our approach to the Tibetan question...we believe that the US Government must give this weight.[57]

This trend of thinking in US policy that was now so apparent culminated in 1972 in the visit of President Nixon to China. The outcome of this visit was that the US put the Tibetan question in deep freeze. US policy now reverted to its familiar line. Abandoned were CIA covert operations inside Tibet, official contacts with the Dalai Lama seemed to taper off and the US now recognized the People's Republic of China as the legitimate Government in place of the KMT Government. The US did not want the issue of Tibet to become an irritant in their relations with China. By 1975, President Ford was able to assure a skeptical Deng Xiaoping that 'we oppose and do not support any [US] Governmental action as far as Tibet is concerned.' Therefore, when asked about the status of Tibet, this is what a State Department spokesman clarified on 8 October, 1987:

> We have never recognized Tibet as a sovereign state independent of China. We first made the statement that we considered Tibet to be a part of China in 1978; however, our earlier formulations were not inconsistent with the statement, and we have never challenged China's claim. No third country recognizes Tibet as a state independent of China.

As can be seen, the US completely glossed over its earlier references to Tibetan autonomy, self-determination, etc. It was a classic case of power politics.

Thus, as can be seen and as so eloquently put by the US State Department, 'no third country' was prepared to recognize that Tibet was an independent state. The major powers that could have played a decisive role in promoting Tibetan independence—Britain, India, the US and even Soviet Russia—were all interested in maintaining good relations with China. Almost all were prepared to sacrifice whatever little interests that they had in Tibet for the sake of developing friendly relations with China. Clearly, the US support for the Tibetans was not out of some moral principle or sympathy, but because of its world-wide antipathy to Communism. Once that dissipated, so did US concern for the Tibetan cause.

Nehru met the Dalai Lama in 1959 at Mussourie soon after the latter's flight from Tibet. He explained to him the intricate workings and compulsions of great powers and their politics. Nehru informed the Dalai Lama as follows:

> In America, there is no real sympathy for Tibet. Chiang Kai-Shek has no sympathy....They all want to exploit Tibet.

Much as Nehru has been maligned by his political opponents for 'losing' Tibet, was he then right in 1950? It appears to be so. Nehru was far-sighted enough and spot-on in his assessment of the situation when he penned a note on 18 November, 1950. He wrote:

> It must be remembered that neither the UK nor the USA, nor indeed any other power, is particularly interested in Tibet or the future of that country. What they are interested in is embarrassing China.

In 1958, he followed up his assessment of 1950 with a statement in Parliament that '*at no time did any country, any foreign country, consider it* [*Tibet*] *independent*' [emphasis added].[58]

Years later, the Dalai Lama, too, understood the import of international politics and the games that great powers play and resented the fact that the US only wished to use Tibet as 'a pawn' in its fight against Communism. He recognised that the US help for Tibet was primarily aimed at serving American interests rather than for Tibetans. Hence, his conclusion in his book 'Freedom in Exile' that:

> Apparently the Americans felt that it was worthwhile to provide limited assistance to the Tibetan freedom fighters, not because they cared about Tibetan independence, but as a part of their world wide efforts to destabilize all Communist Governments.

Although, strictly speaking, recognition is not a criterion for statehood, not a single major power desired or supported an independent Tibet. No one wanted to antagonize China, even less so the rising power of modern China. Tibet had achieved de facto independence in the inter-war years, but unfortunately failed to convert it to de jure independence. The fault, if any, lies largely with the myopic policies followed by the Tibetan Government in the inter-war years and the self-serving interests of the Tibetan elite that refused to contemplate any changes in policy that would have facilitated Tibet's move to full independence recognized by most countries in the world.

CHAPTER 3

Independent India's Dilemma: What should we do with Tibet?

The earliest mention of the word 'Tibet' is in the Arab Istakari's works [About 590 AD] where it is written as 'Tobbat'
—*Rockhill's Ethnology of Tibet,* p. 669

'Our desire has always been and is to retain the friendship of the Chinese people and to cooperate with them as far as possible. That will be our guiding principle.'—Nehru
—Letters to the Chief Ministers, *ibid,* vol. 11, p. 269.

On 1 January, 1950, barely twenty-four hours after India announced its recognition of the People's Republic of China, the new Chinese Government announced that the 'liberation' of Tibet would be one of the basic goals of the People's Liberation Army [PLA]. Further, on 24 January, 1950, the Chinese Communist Party Central Committee [CCP CC], acting on instructions sent by Mao from Moscow in the early hours of 2 January, 1950, issued a directive to the People's Liberation Army [PLA] 18th Army to move into Tibet. Mao was on an official visit to Moscow from 16 December, 1949 to 17 February, 1950. Mao's order to move into Tibet did not go down well with the soldiers of the 18th Army and many desertions took place. Many thought that they would never return from that far and forbidden land [Tibet]. It took extraordinary efforts by senior PLA commanders to restore order.[1]

Accordingly, on 7 October, 1950, after due preparations and calculating a suitable time, 40,000 troops from the 52nd and 53rd Divisions of the PLA crossed the Sino-Tibet border at three points and overwhelmed the small Tibetan border detachment. Also on 7 October, 1950, China announced its military support for the beleaguered North Koreans. Thus, 7 October, 1950, became a very important day for the Chinese PLA. On 19 October, 1950, the PLA occupied the border fortress town of Chamdo [Chengdu], about 480 kilometres due East of Lhasa and the Governor of Chamdo, Ngabo Ngawang Jigme surrendered to the Chinese. Of the approximately 8,000 Tibetan defenders, about 5,738 were mercilessly slaughtered. The Chinese lost only about 180 soldiers.[2] The Tibetans, poorly armed and badly led, were easily crushed by battle hardened PLA troops. Those that surrendered or injured were treated with exemplary kindness, fed and released to return to their homes. Mao had given special instructions on this as he visualized that this would create a very favourable impression of the new China, for he was determined to foster, in addition, a new 'clean' image for the PLA. Mao's assessment was spot on. Mao's policy was to 'liberate' Tibet by peaceful means and use force only as a supplement to his larger design. The new China was determined to extend its authority to every part of Asia where she had ever exercised authority in the past, no matter, however, shadowy such claims might have been.

For India, the dilemma was acute. What should India do now that Chinese troops would soon arrive at her very door-step? On 27 October, 1949, Krishna Menon, the Indian High Commissioner in London, on instructions from Nehru, approached the British Government for advice. A month later, after considerable thought, the British Government responded with an 8-Point Memorandum of which points (ii) and (v) are most important. These were (point ii) that 'India should do what it can...*short of military assistance.*' And that (point v) '*recognizing Tibetan independence must be ruled out*' [emphasis added].[3] Similarly, the British also 'advised' the US by emphasizing the following points: that [a] Britain was 'always' prepared to recognize Chinese *sovereignty* [Note: use of word 'sovereignty' and not 'suzerainty'] over Tibet, but on the understanding that Tibet is autonomous and [b] that *Tibet's inaccessibility makes it impracticable to do anything to stiffen military resistance to China.* Tibet has long been judged as incapable of anything more than nominal resistance [emphasis added].[4] The British advice seemed to be contrary to what the US Ambassador to India, Henderson's demarché to the State Department on January 1949 advocated, that the US should be prepared to recognize Tibet as an 'independent' state following the KMT rout in China.[5]

Thus, while the British Government advice was unambiguous, most strategic thinkers in India had been brought up to believe that Tibet was an essential buffer for the security of India. They felt that the occupation of Tibet by Chinese troops presented a new and an ominous challenge. Tibet, on its own, had never posed any security threat on India's Northern frontiers. In the past, it was a Chinese tradition to work through the Tibetans and claim for themselves whatever the Tibetans could influence. The new Chinese Government sought to do just that, but were not prepared to accept that Tibet had a 'unique personality' beyond being a region of China. It is possible that Mao felt that recovering 'lost' Chinese territories might be that much easier where resistance was likely to be that much feebler. That the Chinese chose Tibet first over Taiwan or Mongolia illustrates the point. To 'liberate' Taiwan or Mongolia, the Chinese would have to contend with either of the two super powers: the US and Soviet Russia respectively. Tibet was that much 'easier' since Nehru's views Nehru is regarding Tibet were probably already known to Mao, as illustrated by the fact that on 23 August, 1950, Mao informed the South-West Bureau, responsible for conducting operations against Tibet, 'that India has made an announcement acknowledging that Tibet was a part of China'! Further, Ambassador Panikkar openly maintained that the 'special political interests' in Tibet that India inherited from the British *could not be maintained and that Nehru in general, concurred with this view* [emphasis added].[6]

Nevertheless, the news of Chinese military action against Tibet aroused considerable anxiety in India. And yet protests from India to the Chinese authorities were, to say the least, rather curious. Although the protest note [21 October, 1950] from India pleaded for a *peaceful settlement* [emphasis added], there was no reference to the rights of the Tibetans, it did not question China's right to incorporate Tibet, nor that this [invasion] represented as an affront to the position of India. All that the protest note did was to plead that an 'incautious move at the present time, *even in a matter which is within its own sphere*' [emphasis added], would prejudice China's chances of occupying the Chinese seat in the UN. Further, the note advised that China should have followed the more 'enduring' method of a peaceful approach than that of undertaking military action. This was followed by another note on 28 October, 1950, which was much stiffer in tone and 'regreted' Chinese military action and felt that the '*invasion of Tibet by Chinese troops* cannot but be regarded as deplorable and not in the interest of China or of peace' [emphasis added].

Earlier, on 26 August, 1950, Ambassador Panikkar, in a note to the Chinese Government, defined India's policy towards Tibet as 'autonomy within the framework of Chinese *sovereignty*' [emphasis added]. The note was so poorly worded that it conceded Chinese 'sovereignty' over Tibet rather than the usual word 'suzerainty.' After much prevarication, some allege deliberately, Panikkar subsequently, in a note on 1 November, 1950—a good two months later—tried to rectify the 'oversight.'[7] The British view was that whether Panikkar's error was unfortunate or a deliberate attempt to appease China, the result would be that India was now committed to recognizing China sovereignty over Tibet and would find it extremely hard to retract, if she ever wished to do so.

While Nehru chastised Panikkar for making representations to the Chinese Government that were 'weak and apologetic', he took no administrative action against Panikkar for what amounted to a gross misrepresentation of policy. This lack of action lends credence to the theory that Panikkar's actions were in line with Nehru's thinking. What someone should have enlightened both Nehru and Panikkar was the fact that even the Chinese delegate to the Simla Conference in 1914, Ivan Chen, never asked for anything more than a recognition of Chinese 'suzerainty' over Tibet [See Annexure 1].

What would the Chinese have thought of these shenanigans? They deliberately attributed the 'correction' made by the Government of India to 'outside' influence, knowing full well that such an assertion would further incense Nehru and, as a result, he would incline even more towards the Chinese positions just to show his 'independence of thought'! Nevertheless, in a note on 30 October, 1950, the Chinese dismissed India's protest with contempt, curtly telling India to 'mind its own business' as Tibet was a 'domestic problem' and that no foreign interference would be tolerated. This admonition was repeated in the Chinese note of 16 November, 1950.

Slowly but surely, the stage was now set for the complete occupation and subjugation of Tibet. As no further serious military resistance was expected, Chinese troops could easily have pushed on and captured the Tibetan capital, Lhasa, without any significant opposition. And yet, soon after capturing Chamdo, Mao instructed the Chinese PLA to pause and not to push further. Two reasons are usually ascribed for this hesitation. Firstly, the war in Korea initiated by the North Koreans on 25 June, 1950, had started to go badly wrong for the North Koreans. After pushing UN [US] troops into a small perimeter near Pusan, the North Koreans were completely taken by surprise when US seaborne landings took place at Inchon. By 29 September, 1950, US troops had re-taken Seoul and had received the green light from President Truman to cross the 38th Parallel and enter North Korea. The Chinese leadership was very perturbed and concerned that US troops would now come face to face with them just across the Yalu River that separated North Korea from China. To pre-empt the Americans from reaching the Chinese border, the Chinese leadership took a major decision. They decided to confront the Americans and, on 7 October, 1950, Chinese troops in large numbers crossed the Yalu River to defend North Korea, simultaneously with their attack on Chamdo [Tibet]. The Chinese estimated that they were in for a bitter fight with the Americans where the ultimate result could not be foreseen. Strategically, it might have been unwise to fight on two fronts, for most of their resources would be needed for the fight in Korea against the formidable might of the US. But prudently, at the same time, the Chinese wished to secure their rear and not allow any foreign interference via Tibet.

Secondly, the Chinese were still not completely certain of India's reaction. Although they had made a fairly shrewd assessment that Nehru was not inclined to intervene militarily in Tibet, yet they wanted to be completely sure of his intentions. This hesitation also arose because of the 'advice' that they were supposedly receiving from Moscow. The British believed that China had decided to intervene in Tibet at such a delicate time and in such a hurry as they had received reports from Moscow that Nehru was preparing to intervene in Tibet. The Soviet press, too, harped on the same theme by alleging that the Western powers were 'hatching a scheme' to 'detach Tibet from China and establish it as a colony.' For example, *the New Times*[8] published a report that:

> New roads and aerodromes were being constructed in great haste in parts of India adjacent to Tibet. Large quantities of American arms and war material were shipped via Calcutta to Darjeeling railway terminus on the Tibetan boundary, from where they were taken to Lhasa by road. Two years ago, a chain of radio transmitters were set up along Tibet's Eastern border.

Doubtless, the Chinese would have paid due care to such reports appearing in the Soviet press, for at that time Moscow was their close ally and provided main access to the outside world. An internal Foreign Office memo by a senior British Foreign Office official, Sir Esler Dening, also reflects this belief:

> As regards Tibet, it is possible that the Chinese move was animated by a fear that if they did not move, India would. Russia would encourage such a belief.[9]

The same senior British Foreign Office official, Sir Esler Dening, told Stanton, the US Ambassador to Thailand, a few days later at Bangkok that the Chinese decision to intervene in Tibet at such a delicate time was motivated by the fact:

> that the Soviets had been very successful in persuading Chinese Communist leaders that India, at the instigation of Great Britain, had designs on Tibet, and that in consequence the Chinese Communists rationalized the present invasion of Tibet as a move to forestall the Indians.[10]

The fact that the British believed that the Chinese decision to intervene in Tibet was heavily influenced by the Russians is also corroborated to some extent by Nehru, when he cabled Pannikar on 25 October, 1950, that he believed 'Chinese policy might be independent of the Soviets *but is clearly influenced by one-sided and distorted by news coming from Moscow*' [emphasis added].[11] Echoing the same thought Nehru wrote to Chief Ministers on 1 November, 1950, that 'it seems clear that owing to development of the war situation in the Far East and accounts of repeated bombing of Manchurian towns, *the Chinese Government believed that they were threatened by war by their enemies*' [emphasis added].

Further, in an interview with the Reuters correspondent in Srinagar on 29 October, 1950, Nehru elaborated on the same point and attributed China's action to Soviet influence. Nehru recalled Soviet press reports that had alleged Anglo-American intrigues to bring Tibet into an anti-Communist orbit. Earlier, Panikkar had informed Nehru that all foreign news published in *Xinhua* was originally from *TASS*. Nehru believed that Soviet advice was that the Anglo-Americans were conspiring to occupy the region.[12] This is what Nehru said:

> The current Chinese policy can perhaps partly be attributed to the fact that although Peking's policy may not be dictated by Moscow, much of the information upon which this policy is based came through Soviet sources.[13]

The Chinese, heavily involved as they were in the fighting in Korea, needed to be absolutely certain that India would not intervene in Tibet, either on its own or in conjunction with Western powers. Every possibility, no matter how trivial, was assessed with great seriousness. Even Ambassador Pannikar refers to this aspect when he cabled Nehru that Premier Zhou, in a meeting with him on 22 August, 1950, seemed 'greatly concerned about reports that Nepalese military units had gone to the assistance of Tibet *and expected India to prevent them from entering on such an adventure*' [emphasis added]. It would be recalled that Radio Moscow had repeatedly characterized Nepal as an 'Anglo-American satellite.' This report was later personally debunked by Nehru.

On 7 November, 1950, the Tibetans decided to approach the UN for redress. The Chinese suspected that the Tibetan appeal to the UN that was so well drafted, was perhaps instigated and drafted by the Indian representative at Lhasa, Hugh Richardson.[14] In actual fact, as disclosed by India to the British Government, the Tibetan appeal was drafted not by Richardson but by another Indian official, Sumal Sinha.[15] The Chinese wisdom and canny political foresight of halting the advance of their troops after the capture of Chamdo now paid handsome political dividends. Not only did the UN baulk at any action, guided primarily by Britain and India, but not a single country except for little San Salvador came forward to help the battered and hapless Tibetans. Sir Benegal Rau, the Indian Permanent Representative [PR] to the UN, informed Nehru that not a single member of the UN Security Council was interested in raising the Tibetan question.[16] Apparently Rau was under the impression that by not criticizing China in the UN regarding Tibet, he personally might play a helpful role in mediating between China and the Western powers!

Nevertheless, in line with Nehru's thinking on the policy to be followed with regard to the Tibetan complaint, instructions from Delhi to the Indian PR at the UN were as follows:

[a] India did not like the El Salvador resolution and the PR was not to support it.

[b] The timing of the Tibetan appeal needed careful consideration. *Korea was obviously of first importance...nothing should be done which was likely to embitter relations with China at a critical state....*therefore no action be taken on the Tibetan appeal [emphasis added].[17]

From the instructions received from New Delhi to the Indian PR at the UN, it was clear that a policy decision had been taken to 'sacrifice' Tibet in exchange for Sino-Indian friendship, and for playing a role on the Korean peninsula as also on the world stage. Not surprisingly, therefore, the Indian PR to the UN, Sir Benegal Rau, 'advised' Western powers that if a debate took place, India would perforce have to criticize the Chinese action. He queried 'how then could it [India] play a mediatory role in Korea'? The British who had earlier advised Nehru on the policy to be followed towards Tibet and were already privy to Nehru's thinking on Tibet understood the significant import of Sir Benegal Rau's query. When the US State Department raised the question of whether the issue of Tibet should be pursued any further in the UN, they were advised by their Ambassador in London that the British view was that the Tibetan problem was '*subordinate to larger issues and should not be raised at the moment*' [emphasis added]. On re-consideration, the US, conscious of the thinking of the British and Indian Governments, thereafter also concurred with this assessment.[18] Further, Sir Gladwyn Jebb opined that 'what we want to do is to create a situation which does not oblige us in practice to do anything about the Communist invasion of Tibet,' and that 'whatever opinion one might hold about Chinese aggression, *the reality was that no one could give effective aid to Tibet*' [emphasis added].[19] The Foreign Office in London ruefully confirmed to the British High Commissioner in Delhi that 'neither we, nor we assume India or anyone else e.g. the US would be prepared to take armed action. It was best to let the matter rest.'[20] Thus, none of the three powers that could have helped the Tibetans India, Britain and the US for reasons of their own, declined to respond to Tibet's agonizing appeals.

On 24 November, 1950, the UN General Assembly postponed indefinitely the consideration of the Tibetan appeal after the Indian delegate stated that 'India *was certain*' [emphasis added] that the Tibetan question could still be settled by peaceful means,[21] and that such a settlement would safeguard the autonomy that Tibet had enjoyed for several decades while maintaining its historical links with China, and that Tibet's status was wrapped in 'legal obscurity'! Britain endorsed the Indian position.[22] It was obvious that India's decision to gain China's friendship far outweighed any obligations it had inherited from Britain regarding Tibet and, with it, Nehru hoped to enhance Asian solidarity and Sino-Indian friendship.

Two further Tibetan demarches to the UN, the last of which was sent on 11 December, 1950, were met with angst-ridden silence. Evidence that India's position had hardened even further came when Bajpai, Secretary General of the Ministry of External affairs, told the US Ambassador to India on 18 December, 1950, that India wished to 'delay action' on the two Tibetan demarches to the UN due to its 'efforts in achieving a cease fire in Korea' and that any criticism of China would 'adversely affect India's ability to exert influence on China in the direction of a cease-fire.'[23] Thus, both India and Britain, for reasons of their own, held the view that any action in the UN on the Tibetan question should be limited to fit into the general picture of policy towards China. When US Ambassador Henderson raised the question of Tibet with Bajpai, Secretary-General of the Ministry of External Affairs, the latter told him that the 'Government of India was so immersed in the problem of maintaining world peace that it was giving little thought to Tibet; in fact he did not recall that Tibet was even mentioned in the recent [January 1951] Commonwealth Conference.'[24] With such an attitude the two Tibetan demarches were doomed for failure from the very beginning. It was only in 1959, many years later, that the UN General Assembly finally took up the Tibetan issue as a result of blatant Chinese high-handedness. Tibet was thereafter to figure only three times in the UN General Assembly in 1959 [Res/1353], in 1961 [Res/

1723] and in 1965 [Res/2079], when resolutions were passed criticizing China's role. Since the People's Republic took the Chinese seat in 1972, Tibet has been studiously kept out of the UN. India only supported the 1965 resolution, perhaps out of self-interest, perhaps due to timidity!

With any possibility of a UN action successfully aborted and as soon as the situation stabilized in Korea, the Chinese PLA resumed its forward movement towards Lhasa. Chinese troops led by Wang Qimei entered Lhasa on 7 September, 1951. However, the Chinese Army Commander, General Zhang Jingwu, actually arrived in Tibet via India! The Chinese moved swiftly to consolidate their rule over Tibet.

The day the Tibetans appealed to the UN on 7 November, 1950, the Deputy Prime Minister of India Sardar Patel wrote a letter[25] [it is said that it was instigated and drafted by MEA Secretary-General, Bajpai] to Nehru in which he bitterly criticized Chinese actions in Tibet and outlined the dangers facing India. Nehru, perhaps aware of the real author of the missive, never responded to Patel directly in writing, but outlined basic Indian policy in a note to the Foreign Secretary on 18 November, 1950, that partially answered Patel's criticisms. Patel died on 15 December, 1950, and, thus, any opposition to Nehru's line of thinking ended rather abruptly. Nevertheless, it is important to understand Nehru's thinking and the basis of his policy line at this stage. Could India have helped the Tibetans by intervening militarily? Could Tibet be retained as an essential buffer between the two rising nationalistic states?

Just a few months prior to independence the Foreign Department of the interim Government of India in which Nehru held the External Affairs portfolio, laid down India's policy towards Tibet in the following terms:

> To prejudice her relations with so important a power as China by aggressive support of unqualified Tibetan independence is, therefore, a policy with few attractions....while GOI are glad to recognize and wish to see Tibetan autonomy maintained, they are not prepared to do more than encourage this and certainly not disposed to take any initiative which might bring India into conflict with China on this issue.[26]

As it became apparent that the Communists would win the civil war in China, it also became increasingly clear that a potentially new and dangerous situation would develop across India's Northern frontiers. It was the perception that as soon as the Communists re-unified the whole of mainland China, their attention would turn towards Tibet. None was so prescient to predict the situation as was Nehru. In a letter to Finance Minister, John Mathai, on 10 September, 1949, Nehru predicted that:

> Recent developments indicate that Chinese Communists are likely to invade Tibet sometime or the other. This will not be soon. But it may take place within a year.

Aware of the situation and anticipating a Chinese move to occupy Tibet, Nehru formulated three basic principles of the policy he would follow towards China and Tibet. These were [1] to ensure the safety and security of India; [2] acceptance of Chinese suzerainty/sovereignty over Tibet; and [3] advance friendship with China as an expression of Asian solidarity. It was Nehru's belief that once friendly relations were established with China, the right atmosphere could be created for the settlement of the border and other questions. Nehru as a realist and conscious of India's inferior military power, had to acquiesce in Tibet's occupation by China.[27] Nehru, in a note dated 18 November, 1950, conceded that 'neither India nor any other external power could prevent the Chinese take-over of Tibet.'[28]

Earlier, Nehru had publicly confirmed India's inferior military position when he told the Reuters correspondent in Srinagar on 29 October, 1950, that 'India has neither the resources nor the inclination to send armed assistance to Tibet' and that '150 years ago, an Indian Army invaded and subdued a part of Tibet, considered then, and ever since, a remarkable military feat in that unfriendly terrain. But the end result was that in the following winter the Indian Army froze to death!' Was Nehru thinking out aloud that this was the fate that awaited the Chinese PLA? Nevertheless, realism also dictated that it was more important to give first priority to economic development while maintaining friendly relations with China. It was imperative also to go about this urgent task quietly and at the same time strengthen the border with Tibet.

At this point, Nehru was clearly enamoured of China. Nehru felt that the establishment of the new Communist regime at Beijing was the 'culminating act of a century old process of revolution *and a manifestation of Asia's political renaissance*' [emphasis added],[29] and that it was not a question of 'approving or disapproving' but recognizing a 'major event of history, of appreciating it and dealing with it.'[30] Nehru felt that the politics of Asia would depend on relations between India and China,[31] since China had become a great power that was both united and strong. Nehru felt that the birth of new China was a victory of nationalism rather than of Communism and that nationalism played a far more profound and powerful role in shaping Chinese policies. As such, China was India's natural friend and ally in the construction of the post-colonial world order and that the emergence of Asia as a strong influence in the new international order was a fair conclusion. It was this vision of China's role that blinded Nehru to the fact that China might have a completely different set of priorities.[32] Nehru did not believe that China had the ability to 'threaten' India, for China's first priority would be to attend to its huge domestic problems. He termed such a possibility [of threating India] as 'exceedingly unlikely.'

The Chinese view of Nehru, on the other hand, as a leader of India at this stage was rather unflattering, although it had not always been so.[33] The Chinese felt that he was too enmeshed with Western countries to be classified as an independent leader in his own right. The Chinese leadership with little or no contact with the outside world, were clearly a baffled lot and questioned how 'a man like Nehru could be friendly, even grateful, to his late oppressors? It suggests nothing but a despicable lack of national self-respect.'[34] The Chinese had little understanding of how a democratic country like India functioned. The Chinese always considered Nehru as a bourgeois nationalist leader and, despite following left-leaning policies, never considered him as a socialist. Nehru is the 'running dog of imperialism' proclaimed the *Shijie Zhishi* [*World Affairs*, 19 August, 1949]. A few days later the same magazine [16 September, 1949] belittled Nehru and said:

> Nehru riding behind the imperialists whose stooge he is, actually considers himself the leader of the Asian people...as a rebel against the movement for national independence, as a blackguard...as a loyal slave of imperialism, Nehru has already been made the substitute of Chiang Kai Shek by the imperialists.

Nothing in the political lexicon of Communist China could have been a worst insult. And, a few days after Nehru's first state visit to the US in 1949, *Shijie Zhishi* [28 October, 1949] blasted Nehru in a commentary entitled, 'American Imperialism lays Hands on a New Slave.' Nehru was described as 'masquerading as a nationalist and that the most important objective of Truman's 'current summons is the desire to lay hands on a new stooge to replace Chiang Kai Shek.' Perhaps the Chinese media was reflecting what the Soviet media said. On 12 October, 1949, the Soviet *New Times* published a scathing critique of Nehru and posed the question, 'Was Nehru Chiang Kai-Shek's successor'? Quite gracelessly, Nehru's efforts to get the US to recognize the new Communist Government of China were dubbed by the Chinese as 'only a gesture to raise his own stature'!

The Chinese never realized that Nehru's visit to the US in October, 1949, was a political disaster. Nehru, at every step, was easily offended. His ego was bruised. At the first informal meeting with Truman, Nehru was annoyed as both Truman and Vice President Barkley discussed the merits of bourbon whisky in his presence for a lengthy period.[35] Nehru was determined that India would not ally itself with the Western powers, and was even prepared to forgo vitally needed economic aid. He insisted that colonialism—and not Communism—was the gravest danger to world peace and disagreed with Truman on the nature of the Soviet 'threat.'[36]

Nevertheless, Chinese suspicions of Nehru remained. The Indian Consulate General had been established in Xinjiang [Sinkiang] on 21 December, 1948. Less than a year later, on 26 September, 1949, it was unceremoniously bundled out by the Chinese, resulting in an exodus of over 700 refugees into India. However, as the *People's Daily* of 13 September, 1949, complained, China's main grievance remained that Nehru continued to 'plot' to detach Tibet from China and to create a 'cleavage' between the different nationalities of China. That Nehru let Hugh Richardson [British Representative] continue as independent India's first representative in Tibet for almost three years after India's independence, only confirmed Chinese suspicions. As Richardson himself remarked, 'the transition was almost imperceptible' and the only 'obvious change was the flag!'[37] Perhaps the ever wary Chinese thought so, too!

However, despite such unflattering references by the Chinese, it was amply clear from the earliest that Nehru was not going to intervene militarily in Tibet. He was clear in his mind that there was virtually nothing that India could do to militarily dislodge the Chinese from Tibet. Nehru made this obvious on numerous occasions, even before Chinese troops attacked Tibet. In various public speeches that he delivered, Nehru began to speak openly about Chinese *suzerainty* over Tibet as being a settled fact. Speaking at the Standing Committee on External Affairs meeting on 17 December, 1949, Nehru clarified that 'no one knows what will happen in Tibet. If the Chinese wish to enter Tibet, there is none to hold them back except, perhaps, the climate.' On 8 September, 1950, speaking to a Tibetan delegation led by Finance Minister, Shakabpa, Nehru put it very bluntly when he told the stunned Tibetans that '*we cannot give any help in the event of an invasion. Nor can any other country*' [emphasis added]. Further, speaking in Parliament on 6 December, 1950, when the question of Tibet was debated for the first time, Nehru confirmed that 'we did not challenge or deny the suzerainty of China over Tibet,' and that India had 'made it clear that we had no political or territorial ambitions' and that 'our relations with Tibet were cultural and commercial.' Reflecting Nehru's views, Panikkar told the British CDA in Beijing that 'the liberation of Tibet by the Chinese Government *would not be treated by the Indian Government as a very serious development*' [emphasis added].[38] Even if the British did not pass on this assessment to the Chinese, the latter could not have missed the clear signals emanating from New Delhi that their invasion of Tibet would be militarily unopposed!

Even on the question of recognition of the new Communist Government of China, Nehru held extensive consultations with the British Government. Nehru was, in fact moving in conjunction with the British. On 22 October, 1949, Sir Esler Dening submitted a draft note to the British Cabinet which concluded that the recognition of the new Communist Government of China 'cannot be said to be contrary to the principles and practices of international law.' On 27 October, 1949, the British Cabinet approved the note, subject to consultation with other Commonwealth countries. A formal note along with a detailed explanation of the thinking of the British Government duly arrived on Nehru's desk. The British note did not seek any quid pro quo from the Chinese in lieu of recognition. The British explained away this aberration as that 'the disadvantages of non-recognition were so great as to outweigh any possible advantages to be obtained from securing Chinese assurances of respect for its international obligations.' The British interests were quite different from those of independent India, but Nehru seems to have blurred these. Perhaps Nehru's own personal inclinations were in tune with the British view. In any case, on 18 December, 1949, Attlee conveyed to Nehru that the British intended to recognize the new Government of China on 2 January, 1950. This was later postponed to 6 January, 1950, at the request of the Australian and New Zealand Governments. On 19 December, 1949, Nehru replied to Attlee that India would follow suit, but would recognize the new Chinese Government on 30 December, 1949. There was no adverse reaction from the British Government. Five days later on 4 January, 1950, Pakistan also recognized the new Chinese Government.

Although Nehru was in agreement with the British approach, yet there were sharp differences within the Cabinet in India on the question of recognition of the new Communist regime of China. But despite such differences Nehru finally had his way. India officially recognized the People's Republic of China a few days later on 30 December, 1949, as indicated earlier by Nehru to Attlee.

The US did not accept the British contention that nothing should be asked of the new Chinese Government in return of recognition of the new regime. The US felt—and rightly so—that *at the very least* [emphasis added] the new Chinese Government should declare that it would honour China's past international obligations. The US accurately suspected that Nehru had moved with such alacrity to recognize the new Beijing Government *as a result of British advice* [which was correct]. Writing a personal note from New Delhi, the US Ambassador Loy Henderson reported to the State Department as follows:

> Sardar Patel told me last spring that Nehru would not have rushed so quickly with the recognition of Communist China if he had not been convinced by the retiring British Ambassador to China, and other Britishers who came to Delhi, that China should be recognized and that the UK expected to recognize China. Nehru, therefore, according to Patel took the position that since under British leadership the whole Western world would eventually recognize Communist China, India should move first. In fact, the British, according to Sardar Patel told Nehru that they had informal assurance from high American officials that just as soon as a suitable set of circumstances could be brought about, the Government of the United States would recognize Communist China.[39]

Earlier, in November 1949, Nehru also tried to explain to the US on reasons why India was keen to recognize the new Government in China. Nehru's view was that recognition did not mean approval of the policies of the new Chinese Government, but only a recognition of a political and historical fact and a delay might encourage 'wrong tendencies' in China. What these 'wrong tendencies' were, was left entirely unexplained![40]

In line with British thinking on the subject, Nehru asked nothing of China in return for India's recognition of the new regime. Even the US Ambassador in Delhi, Henderson, who was familiar with the thinking within Indian Government circles, was astonished and perplexed at such generosity. He cabled the US Secretary of State on 30 December, 1949, as follows:

> It appears clear from foregoing that India is not requesting Chinese Communists to respect Tibetan autonomy, or even to recognize previous treaties between China and pre-independence Indian Government dealing with Tibet, as prerequisite to establishment relations. Embassy inclined doubt GoI will press Chinese Communists strongly re recognition Tibetan autonomy.... since Pannikar, Indian Ambassador China, will probably not allow question of future of Tibet disturb cordial relationship he hopes establish between Indian Government and Chinese Communists.[41]

However, much as Nehru wished to generate goodwill by the early recognition of the new regime in China, the hard headed new leaders of China were not about to reciprocate such idealistic sentiments so easily. The Chinese were aware that Nehru had synchronized his decision to accord recognition to the new regime with the British, and this in turn perplexed them whether India's foreign policy decisions were truly independently taken or continued to be under British influence. They, therefore, insisted that while recognition was one thing, establishing diplomatic relations was quite another. The Chinese asked India to send a 'negotiating team' to discuss the establishment of diplomatic relations. On 1 Januray 1950 Mao explained the Chinese position to Soviet Ambassador Roschin as follows:

> that if they were sincere in their wishes to mend diplomatic relations with the People's Republic of China, then they must first completely break all ties with Jiang Jieshi [Chiang Kaishek] unconditionally, refuse any kind of support and assistance to this regime making it an official declaration. Under these conditions the Government of India may send representatives to Beijing for negotiations.

Nehru was irritated by this demand, but nevertheless, acquiesced in it. Not for the first time had the Chinese put Nehru in a fix and it certainly would not be the last! To press forward would mean acceptance of Chinese terms; to retract would have shown him in poor light as being unable to read Chinese intentions. Nehru prided himself on his understanding of China and thus did not wish to be shown to be wrong. Therefore, he had no choice but to persist.

An official from the former Indian Mission in Nanking, AK Sen, was asked to proceed to Beijing for 'preliminary and procedural' discussions. The Chinese recognized Sen only as the leader of the 'negotiating team' and not as CDA of a diplomatic mission. Before according Sen diplomatic recognition, the Chinese authorities asked Sen to 'explain' India's voting patterns in the UN and secondly, wished to know what India intended to do about KMT properties in India. For once, Nehru's stance and reply was emphatic. No one had any right to question which way India voted and India did not intend to explain its vote! Fortunately for Nehru, the Chinese realized the folly of their stance and quickly reversed themselves. They needed Nehru's help in Tibet as also in Korea. On 15 March, 1950, Vice-Foreign Minister Zhang Hanfu conveyed acceptance of establishment of diplomatic relations and within a week cleared the appointment of KM Panikkar as India's first Ambassador to the People's Republic.[42]

While Nehru had given every indication that India would not intervene militarily to oppose the Chinese occupation of Tibet when Chinese troops first entered Tibet in October 1950, the question of whether a military option existed or not refused to die down. It was not a decision that Nehru had arrived at without taking the advice of his military chiefs, or had taken it lightly. There were sound reasons for this decision. Nehru knew that the Chinese PLA was heavily armed with the latest American weapons captured from KMT forces and that the Indian Army was not yet prepared to confront the PLA. Having just gone through the dramatic days of partition and division, the Indian Army was heavily involved in Kashmir and with internal security duties. It had no spare troops available for action in Tibet. At a meeting, the then Army Chief, General Cariappa, emphasized that at best he could spare only a battalion and even that would have to be deployed at Yatung and at the limit no further than Gyantse. The Army Chief also cautioned that Indian troops were not sufficiently acclimatized to operate in Tibet.[43] General Cariappa's military advice was sound. On the other hand, Nehru's concept of India's security was based on the belief that no country would tolerate the idea of another acquiring the commanding position that England had occupied for so long in India. If any power was covetous enough to make such an attempt, then all others would combine together to trounce the 'invader.' Thus, the mutual rivalry that any 'invader' faced would itself be the surest guarantee against an attack on India.[44] However, Nehru obviously under estimated what modern technology, rapid development of communications, and what a determined Chinese Army [PLA] could achieve in a limited time frame.

Another factor playing on Nehru's mind was the advice that he received from the British Government that the Government of India 'should not take any steps which could be considered open defiance of Chinese Communists such as recognition of an independent *Tibet or sending brigade troops to Lhasa. They think, however, that India should not let it be known that it does not intend to oppose a Chinese Communist invasion of Tibet*' [emphasis added]. While Nehru might have discreetly followed the above advice, his Ambassador in Beijing certainly made it known widely that India had no intention of opposing the Chinese.[45]

The US Ambassador in Delhi was also cautioning the State Department that regardless of what India's foreign policy might be, it [India] should 'not expect any substantial quantities of arms from the US' in the near future. This view was probably also known to Nehru.[46] The US Embassy in London was also reporting to the State Department on similar lines. It quoted the Foreign Office in London as advising the Indians that 'Britain is prepared to support any action India may take to assist Tibet in maintaining its autonomy, but would wish *to discourage direct military intervention by India*' [emphasis added].[47] The advice from the British High Commissioner in Delhi, Sir Archibald Nye [a former general], was on similar lines. Sir Archibald Nye believed that 'no resistance on the part of Tibet could possibly be successful.'[48] No doubt this was sound military advice, as a British Foreign Office memorandum makes it clear:

> geographical obstacles would make it difficult to supply military material on a large scale to Tibet. It is the opinion of the Chiefs of Staff that Tibetans would be incapable of making effective use of any material that might be supplied [including shortage of mules to transport it]. It follows that we would be unwise to press the Indians to give increased aid to Tibetans [emphasis added].[49]

Nehru was quite receptive when he received similar advice from Lester Pearson, the Canadian Foreign Minister, with whom he had an excellent rapport. Pearson, who met Nehru on 30 January, 1950, told him that 'India should do nothing as the country [Tibet] was so remote that it was of little practical importance whether or not the Communists moved in.'[50] Nehru was himself also acutely aware of the ruggedness and the unsettled nature of the Tibet-Indian border. To intervene militarily in Tibet there was only one route available and that route lay through Yatung and Gyantse. Militarily, it would have been an extremely hazardous project, the success of which was highly problematical. Both the major Western powers, Britain and the US, would have had to support India militarily and financially in case India decided to act on exercising the military option; but both were strongly disinclined to do so and were, in fact, discouraging India from exercising this particular option. Nehru was, therefore, right in following a policy of non-intervention. India could not have gone in alone. Even the British acknowledged that:

> India has done more than we might have expected for Tibet, even to the extent of endangering her own relations with China.[51]

Whether British advice was selfless or subject to its commercial interests in the 'China market' is a moot point. The British also needed to take into account the security concerns of Hong Kong.

It was, therefore, not surprising that when the first Indian Political Officer in Sikkim, Harishwar Dayal, visited Lhasa in August 1949 and the Tibetans formally requested him for arms and ammunition, the Tibetans were advised that the primary task of the Government of India was only to train their troops. Earlier, however, in June 1949 India had agreed to supply a limited amount of arms and ammunition.[52] Nevertheless, when the Tibetans sent a delegation to India seeking aid against the Chinese invasion, they were advised by the Government of India to reach an understanding with the new Chinese Communist Government by 'peaceful' negotiations, for as the then Foreign Secretary informed the US Ambassador 'the Indian Government had definitely decided to take no action over Tibet...which might have the effect of lessening their influence with the Chinese People's Government.'[53]

That Nehru recognized that China would be a problematical neighbour was understood, but he seemed to have an excessively simplistic and naive faith in Chinese motives. Consider his belief that the Chinese occupation of Tibet presented 'no military threat' to India:

> Whatever may be the ultimate fate of Tibet in relation to China, I think there is practically no chance of any military danger to India arising from any possible change in Tibet. Geographically, this is very difficult and practically it would be a foolish adventure. If India is to be influenced or an attempt made to bring pressure on her, Tibet is not the route for it. I do not think there is any necessity at present for our Defense Ministry, or any part of it, to consider possible military repercussions on the Indo-Tibetan Frontier. The event is remote and may not arise at all.[54]

And again:

> From the military point of view [the Chinese occupation of Tibet] has no great consequence and involves no particular danger to India. Tibet is a very difficult country with an average altitude of 12,000 ft. and then there is the great Himalayan barrier. It is an exceedingly difficult matter for any considerable body of men to cross to India over the barrier.

To be fair, Nehru was not alone in making this assessment. The British High Commissioner in India, Sir Archibald Nye, also held a similar view. Writing to the Secretary of State for Commonwealth Relations, Philip Noel-Baker, Nye [a former British Army general] felt that 'India need not, therefore, fear any serious danger from China directly in the near future.'[55] Nehru also felt that the Chinese were a rational people and not given to emotion. He told the then Canadian High Commissioner, Escott Reid, that a 'military attack by China on India was not rational. Moreover, India was defended not only by the barrier of the Himalayas, but by the fact that in order to reach the border between India and Tibet, the Chinese would have to traverse the whole of Tibet, which was the most inhospitable country in the world.'[56] The Indian leadership was convinced that the rugged, inhospitable and mile upon mile of high tundra of Tibet would ensure India's safety from any Chinese military threat.

Most officials in India went along with Nehru's stated views for they felt that a person of such stature could not be challenged. And after Home Minister Patel's demise in 1950, there was no one in the Cabinet who could match Nehru's standing in the country. Any view to the contrary that the Chinese occupation of Tibet would have repercussions all along the Southern slopes of the Himalayas was simply brushed aside.[57] No official had the temerity to raise it thereafter. Nehru in a note to the Foreign Secretary on 26 December, 1957, termed such views as 'static and even out of date of the forces that are at work in the world.' When US Assistant Secretary of State, McGhee, broached the subject of inherent Chinese aggressiveness and reminded Nehru of the danger China presented to India's security on the border, Nehru cut him short by saying that China's hands would be 'full for a decade.' McGhee was disappointed and wryly noted 'I doubt that we would ever forge a firm relationship with India while Nehru was PM.'[58]

Nehru was perhaps correct in his assessment at that point in time that the Chinese occupation of Tibet presented no military threat to India. But the critical mistake seems to have been made when this assessment was elevated to the level of a mantra, in that it became a truism for all time to come. As time rolled on, the Chinese not only quickly consolidated their hold over Tibet, but energetically pushed forward the programme of building major communication networks in Tibet. In a short period of time, they were able to deploy far greater resources on the border than India ever could, and thus nullified Nehru's thesis that the Chinese occupation of Tibet presented no military threat to India. The fault in India lay in the fact that Nehru's assessment was not re-assessed, modified or revised with the passage of time as the threat became ever more apparent. No one in authority in India had the courage to challenge Nehru's thesis. It was a complete systems failure. At this point in time the Indian Ambassador to China Panikkar was reporting that there was no doubt that the Tibetan issue notwithstanding, there was a certain keenness on the part of the Chinese to build a healthy relationship with India.[59]

The Seventeen-Point Agreement between the Chinese and the Tibetans signed on 23 May, 1951, ended any hopes of genuine Tibetan autonomy. It also signaled the end of Tibet's pre invasion de facto independence. There were many in Tibet, particularly within monastic circles, that supported the Agreement. For the ruling elite in Tibet the Agreement protected their privileges, their religious freedom and made very little difference to them if Tibet was considered as apart of China or not, so long as this internal autonomy was guaranteed.[60] It was the first written agreement between Tibet and China since 821 AD, in which the Tibetans recognized Chinese sovereignty. The concept of 'suzerainty' was finally shelved in the Sino-Tibetan context.[61] The British assessment was that:

> this clearly prepares the way for the complete absorption of Tibet by China and its eventual transformation into a Chinese Communist province. There is no doubt that these terms have been forced on the Tibetans by intimidation.[62]

It is significant that it was only with Tibet that China entered into an official Agreement to formalize the process of 're-incorporation', thus tacitly recognizing that Tibet was significantly different from the rest of China. If Tibet had always been a part of China, as claimed by Chinese authorities, then where was the need to enter into a formal Agreement? Incidentally, Article 2 of the Sino-Tibetan Agreement states that 'the Tibetan people shall *return* to the big family of the motherland.' An indirect admission, if any, by the Chinese that the Tibetans had been free from the control of the central authority and were independent as they were only now 'returning'!

In the Seventeen-Point Agreement, the Chinese also gave a hint of what was in store for India. The first point states that the Tibetans shall unite to 'drive out the imperialist aggressive forces from Tibet.' As the British had long since left India, who were they referring to? It could only be newly independent India that they had in mind. The second point is even more revealing. 'The local Government of Tibet shall *actively assist* the PLA to enter *and consolidate national defence*' [emphasis added]. Defence against whom? There is little doubt that the Chinese had India in mind! India had been forewarned, only the Government in India failed to notice or to correctly decipher the signals!

On the other hand, this Agreement came as a great sense of relief for Indian policy makers. Indian policy makers felt that the issue of Tibet could now be safely put aside. Nehru had been irritated by the Tibetans when, in a thoroughly inexplicable move, the Tibetans sent a note on 16 October, 1947, to the newly independent Government of India 'demanding' the recognition of Tibetan claims to large parts of India that included Darjeeling, Sikkim and Bhutan. This distaste probably lingered in Nehru's mind for in a note to the Secretary General [MEA] on 25 October, 1953, Nehru categorically asserted that 'we cannot support feudal elements in Tibet.' But the humanist in Nehru was also evident when he surmised that the Tibetans had accepted the Agreement 'without joy and under the compulsion of circumstances.'[63] The general view those days, however, amongst official circles in South Block was that this was 'good riddance.' Another popular refrain those days was that 'the Chinese must under no circumstances be upset.' There was only marginal sympathy for the hapless Tibetans and in influential quarters in Delhi there was a general welcome for the 'modernization' process ushered in by the Chinese.

Nevertheless, there were more pressing matters to attend. Sir Girija Shankar Bajpai, Secretary General [MEA], informed the US Ambassador that the 'Government of India is at present *so immersed in problems of maintaining world peace that it was giving little thought to Tibet*.'[64] Although this was stated to the US Ambassador in early 1951, it continued to form the core of thinking in the Foreign Office in India. Earlier, Bajpai had opined that militarily, Tibet was in a 'hopeless position that there was little likelihood of any foreign power being able to lend it assistance which could enable it to halt Chinese Communist invasion.'[65] In any case, Indian policy makers at this stage were not too concerned about a possible Chinese military threat to India and had reconciled themselves to a Chinese military occupation of Tibet. On the other hand, some perceptive observers felt that this 'needless, nervous and desperate hurry to normalize relations cost us the larger perspective of action.'[66] This view was largely ignored.

The official policy of India regarding a Chinese military threat to India continued to be as stated by the Secretary-General of the Ministry of External Affairs, Pillai, that, 'we may be stupid or completely blind but where we do not see the menace we cannot pretend to do so, merely because we are so advised by no doubt wiser people.'[67] Perhaps the basis of this belief rested on the view that the Chinese would be very busy in pacifying Tibet, building the infrastructure necessary to 'control' Tibet and, therefore, there was no danger from Chinese 'expansionism' and as such any view to the contrary was both impractical and unrealistic. Great stress was placed on Nehru's belief that the Chinese were 'very rational' people and, hence, unlikely to create trouble under the present circumstances.

While on one hand, Nehru's naivety was on full display when he opined that a Chinese occupied Tibet presented no military threat to India, yet his realism was also on display when he started taking active steps to prepare for such an eventuality. Nehru knew that whatever happened in Tibet would have repercussions all along the Southern slopes of the Himalayas. He realized the importance of fastening the Himalayan states to the Indian orbit. The security of the North-East Frontier was essential. Therefore, Nehru moved energetically to firm up defence arrangements with the strategically important sub-Himalayan states of Nepal [31 July, 1950], Sikkim [15 December, 1950] and Bhutan [8 August, 1949]. China watched these moves very carefully. Apart from a *People's Daily* article of 13 September, 1949, which criticized Nehru's policy towards Bhutan by stating that the Nehru Government had 'no legal right to announce its protectorate over Bhutan', there was little else. The Chinese were engrossed and quite focused on the takeover of Tibet. They were conscious of their immediate need to be on good terms with India while they pacified Tibet.

Nehru was deeply conscious of the importance of NEFA. This area consisted of three parts: the Western part comprising Tawang and Subansiri regions is inhabited by Monpas, Akas, Daflas and the Apa Tanis tribals. In 1919 this area came to be known as the Balipara Frontier Tract. The Central and Eastern parts consist of the Dihang and Lohit regions and are inhabited by the Abors and Mishmi tribals. In 1919, they were combined to form the Sadiya Frontier Tract. It may be noted that all the tribes living in this region are non-Tibetan in origin. To consolidate India's position, administrative units were moved right up to the McMahon Line in the Eastern sector. The Balipara Frontier Tract and the Sadiya Frontier Tract were combined to form a new administrative unit called the North-East Frontier Agency [NEFA]. It was put under the direct control of the Central Government by detaching this area from the administrative control of the Assam Government. On 20 November, 1950, Nehru declared in Parliament that the McMahon Line was our boundary, 'map or no map' and that 'we stand by that boundary and we will not allow anybody to come across that boundary.' Detailed provisions were laid down for the administration of NEFA in the Sixth Schedule of the Constitution of India that came into effect on 26 January, 1950. In 1956 the Indian Frontier Administrative Service [IFAS] was created to provide administrative support to the Agency. Realising the importance of the Eastern sector, it would be recalled that the last of the Tibetan ecclesiastical officials were evicted from Tawang only on 12 February, 1951 when Major R [Bob] Khating arrived to take over the administration. Later, Nehru was to clarify that 'it [Tawang] was on our side of the McMahon Line, but it had not been occupied by us and was practically under Tibetan control till then.'[68]

There was no Chinese protest to India over the eviction of Tibetans from Tawang. Neither did the Chinese offer any protest about Nehru's statement about the McMahon Line, nor about the inclusion of NEFA as a territory of India in the Constitution of India! The question of what type of Tibetan control of Tawang existed is in essence the heart of the matter. The Chinese themselves have repeatedly emphasized that there is a difference between ecclesiastical authority and political control. As the Chinese delegate, Ivan Chen himself informed the delegates to the Simla Conference on 7 March, 1914:

> What is termed spiritual influence should not be confused with what is termed as temporal authority. The sphere within which his [Dalai Lama's] spiritual influence is extended can under no circumstances be claimed as the extent of his temporal authority...what is paid to the Tibetans is not in the shape of revenue in the ordinary sense of the word...it is rather charity than tax.

And on 13 June, 1914, the Chinese Foreign Minister, Sun Paochi, was even more explicit:

> The Tibetans are affected to think that they have right over all the places inhabited by the Lamaists, but this was not so. The Lamas might have ecclesiastical authority, but this did not necessarily mean that these places belonged to Tibet.[69]

Therefore, the Tibetan control of Tawang was essentially ecclesiastical and not political. The Chinese authorities themselves, years later on 27 October, 1962, through the medium of *The People's Daily*, admitted that Indian 'action' to takeover Tawang was allowed to go unchallenged because 'new China had no time to attend to the Sino-Indian border.' A complete afterthought, if any! The truth of the matter was that the Chinese knew that Tawang was *South* of the McMahon Line and hence in Indian territory and, therefore, there was no protest.

Nehru had realized that the Eastern sector was the most important sector on India's Northern frontiers, and that it was militarily essential to secure it. Therefore, he set up the Himmatsinghji Committee to advise on measures to be taken to secure the entire Sino-Indian border, particularly the Eastern sector, following the Chinese occupation of Tibet. In March 1952, Nehru also authorized Indian intelligence agencies to start collecting intelligence on Tibet/China.[70] The difficulties faced in moving administrative and police personnel to the frontiers were enormous. In the Eastern sector, the McMahon Line runs along mountain ranges as high as 14,000 to 16,000 ft and to reach the area from the Brahmaputra valley is a stupendous task. Not only steep and thick jungles have to be traversed, but this area receives rainfall in buckets [200 inches average] during the monsoon season, making road building and movement a nigh impossibility. In the Western sector, the Ladakh and the region beyond is alpine desert with temperatures going down to –20°C, thus making life very miserable.

The belief that the Chinese occupation of Tibet did not represent any military threat to India had an unintended deleterious effect on the armed forces in India. On 1 November, 1950, Nehru declared in Parliament that he had instructed the Defence Ministry to reduce the size of the army as also defence expenditure. India's defence expenditure was pegged at 1 per cent of GNP. Nehru felt that India needed a 'highly mechanized and a relatively small army rather than a large ill-equipped foot force.' Accordingly, in 1951, as the Chinese were moving in to occupy Tibet, about 50,000 Indian Army personnel were in the process of being demobilized. On the eve of partition in 1947, the strength of the Indian Army stood at 500,000 personnel. It came down to 280,000 personnel at partition. In 1951, a further reduction of 50,000 personnel was contemplated! Expenditure on the armed services was also reduced from Rs.165 crore [1951-52] to Rs. 160 crore [1952-53]. A fixed cap of Rs. 35 crore was placed on capital expenditure. Even the manual of Chinese infantry tactics, available with UK and US and required by the army was denied on orders of Nehru lest it alarm the Chinese![71] Similarly, Nehru turned down a proposal to post an intelligence officer to the Consulate in Lhasa on the plea that it would attract attention and might prove embarrassing. Writing to the Foreign Secretary on 10 May, 1959, Nehru felt that 'under the present conditions it was doubtful if any real intelligence work could be done in Tibet.'

It was only later, when realization dawned that the Chinese presence in Tibet may not be benign, that the armed forces were once again built up. This was done gradually. The Army's strength was increased from 280,000 to 550,000 personnel as was the strength of the Air Force, from three squadrons to 20 squadrons.[72] Time was of the essence as the Chinese were not only rapidly consolidating their hold over Tibet, but were also increasing the deployment of their troops near the border with India. Infrastructure, particularly roads, were being built at a frenetic pace near the border with India. India's efforts, in contrast, were hampered by red tape, poor planning and an equally poor and shoddy execution. India's efforts fell far behind the Chinese in the building of roads to the frontier. The result was a poor mismatch and that is where India lost the plot.

Thus, far, India's policy appears to have been to do nothing to militarily oppose the induction of Chinese troops into Tibet. A subtle change in that policy now took place. From this position of non-intervention, the policy moved to assist the Chinese in Tibet in order to earn their goodwill and friendship. Thus, in an extremely poor judgment of the situation, India actually became instrumental in helping to feed PLA troops in Tibet and thereby actively abetted the Chinese to consolidate their occupation of Tibet. When Chinese troops occupied Tibet, the Chinese leadership realized that providing food for them would be a major problem due to the vast distance of Tibet from mainland China. Also, Tibet by itself just could not provide enough food grains for the sudden and large influx of troops. As the fundamental political strategy of 'peaceful liberation' precluded the taking of food grains by force, the Chinese were left with no option but to import food grains from India *or to limit the number of troops that China could induct into Tibet* [emphasis added]. The long-term strategy followed by China was to build a secure motor road system linking Tibet with mainland China, but till then, if there was no food, Chinese troops stationed in Tibet would have starved. This was the grim reality. The Indian Mission in Lhasa in 1951 informed the Government of India that the arrival of large number of Chinese troops had left the local economy to deal with high inflation, making scarce such commodities as butter, meat and firewood.

In April, 1952, Panikkar reported from Beijing that Zhou Enlai, in a meeting, informed him that for 'many years' Tibet would have to depend for 'daily necessities' on India. Zhou requested that transport facilities be made available for transportation of food grains to Tibet via Calcutta. The Chinese were near starvation in Tibet, for there were no grains available to feed the newly arrived Chinese troops. 'We were eating wild berries for food', wrote a PLA soldier. Such was the discipline of Chinese soldiers that they would not cut the trees near Lhasa to use the wood to heat their food, but preferred to eat it cold![73] The PLA in Tibet was a highly disciplined and motivated force. Even the Tibetans acknowledged this.

When Panikkar informed Nehru of Zhou's request, Nehru recognized the implications of Zhou's request almost immediately. Nehru cabled Panikkar on 12 April, 1952, that presumably 'these supplies were meant for the Chinese Army in Tibet...which is in great need of them.' Having recognized the implications, Nehru once again appears to have prevaricated and given in to the advice of the naïve and besotted Panikkar. On 24 May, 1952, Nehru informed Panikkar that 'we have agreed to grant transit facilities for food grains up to the end of 1952 at the rate of 500 tons/month. Later at the instigation of Panikkar once again, Nehru agreed to increase the amount to 3,500 tons/month![74] It is estimated that a thousand mules were constantly on the move for several months between Gangtok and Yatung [Tibet].[75] Later in a note dated 14 November, 1959, to Nehru, the Foreign Secretary confirmed the above estimate, but categorically stated that rice did not come from India. It was Chinese rice that India allowed China to transit through India [Calcutta] to Tibet.[76]

The Chinese recognized the political implications of these shipments. These would not only significantly lessen the Chinese dependence on Tibetan food grains, but more importantly, demonstrate to the Tibetans that if they thought that they had other options, besides co-operating with the Chinese, these were closed. The Indian leadership never realized that to limit the supplies of foodgrains to Chinese soldiers in Tibet would also mean that the Chinese would be able to deploy only a limited number of troops and thus pose less of a danger to Indian security. While it may have been part of *realpolitik* not to come to the rescue of the Tibetans militarily; it was quite another to actively assist the Chinese Army to consolidate its control over Tibet. The message this act conveyed would not have been lost on the Tibetans. In Tibetan eyes, India was not a benefactor but had become an accomplice of the Chinese in their occupation of Tibet!

Similarly, in another blatantly supine act, Panikkar informed Nehru by cable on 15 June, 1952, that Zhou Enlai presumed that '*India had no intention of claiming special rights arising from unequal treaties of the past and was prepared to...the transformation of the Indian Mission in Lhasa into a proper Consulate-General as an immediate practical step.*' This Zhou suggestion was made to Panikkar as the Chinese were keen to do away with the last vestiges of any extra-territorial rights that India had inherited from the British. Zhou need not have worried, for the Indian Ambassador, despite the fact that India was the only foreign power [besides Nepal] that maintained a diplomatic mission, was already loudly proclaiming that the Indian Mission at Lhasa was an 'office of dubious legality.'[77] All this was being advocated despite Indian irritation at the way Chinese troops were behaving on the Tibet-Sikkim border. The Chinese refused to let Indian diplomatic bags for its Mission in Lhasa pass without opening them. It took considerable diplomatic efforts to make the Chinese resile from their position and let diplomatic bags pass unopened.

Nehru could not have consulted the Cabinet for, as events show, he immediately replied by cable on 16 June, 1952, that 'as for our Mission in Lhasa being converted into a Consulate-General, we have no objection.' An official announcement was made by the Ministry of External Affairs on 16 September, 1952, that the Indian Mission at Lhasa would be 'wound up' and replaced by a 'Consulate-General' that would 'report to the Indian Ambassador at Beijing', and as such, would be accredited to China! It was another 'friendly gesture' from Nehru with the intent to emphasize that India had no political interest in Tibet.[78] Nevertheless, Nehru again cautioned Panikkar:

> We would like you to consider however how far it is desirable to have these piecemeal arrangements. *We would naturally prefer a general and comprehensive settlement which includes the Frontier* [emphasis added].

No thought was given to the grave implications of such a momentous change for it was not a simple change of nomenclature. The change to a Consulate-General indicated that from this point onwards India would accept that Tibet as a state did not exist but only as a province of China and that China exercised full sovereignty. It was a practical dimension of the fact that Tibet had ceased to be independent.[79] Forgotten were all the old formulations about suzerainty, the Tripartite Simla Convention and all other rights in Tibet that India inherited from the British. Forgotten and abandoned also was the basic fact that all along so far India had negotiated *directly* with Tibet or at least with Tibet as one of the parties. The McMahon Line was the product of one such agreement. But what was even worse, no attempt was made to link these huge and practically unilateral concessions to the Chinese to the recognition of the Indian alignment of the Tibet-India boundary, which had now in effect become the India-China boundary.

Nehru was aware of the significance of the change and he did make references to the need to link all such matters, including the need for a fresh Chinese affirmation of the frontier. Earlier, Nehru had issued instructions to Pannikar to take up all these issues *together* with the Chinese. But Pannikar ignored Nehru's instructions and only took up cultural and trade matters in his next meeting with Zhou. Panikkar's thinking was that if India raised the border issue, the Chinese would be forced either to accept the Simla Convention [i.e., the McMahon Line] or to refuse such acceptance, but offer negotiations. It was highly unlikely that China would accept the first option and he felt that the second option would not be advantageous to India. However, if the Chinese raised the issue of the border themselves, India could refuse to reopen the issue and take the stand that territory South of the McMahon Line is 'ours' and that, therefore, there was nothing to discuss.

Pannikar averred, rather incorrectly, that Zhou Enlai's silence indicated Chinese acquiescence of the alignment of the India-Tibet boundary [now India-China] as shown on Indian maps. Pannikar cabled Nehru on 17 June, 1952, that:

> Chou Enlai's [Zhou Enlai] silence on the subject of the Frontier and his not having even indirectly alluded to Sikkim or Bhutan during his conversation would mean acquiescence in, if not acceptance of, India's position. He added that India must stick to the position that the Frontier had been defined and there was nothing to be discussed.[80]

Although Nehru's instructions to Panikkar showed that his apprehensions of the Chinese and appreciation of issues was spot on, yet once again Nehru prevaricated. Despite advice to the contrary from Bajpai, the former Secretary General of the Ministry of External Affairs, who had advised Nehru on 21 November, 1951, to make the recognition of the boundary as a part of a general settlement, Nehru to his and India's great misfortune, gave in and opted for Panikkar's line of thinking.[81] Further, Nehru confirmed his acceptance of Panikkar's line of thinking in a note addressed to the Foreign Secretary on 6 September, 1952, in which he noted:

> On reconsideration, I accept Shri Panikkar's advice that we should not make specific reference about the frontier.

Perhaps two other factors influenced Nehru. Panikkar had cabled to Nehru earlier on 28 September, 1951, that Zhou told him that '*there was no territorial dispute or any controversy in this matter between India and China and the question of the stabilization of the Tibetan frontier was a matter of common interest to India,*

Nepal and China' [emphasis added].[82] This was the first time that Zhou raised the border question. And that, too after Nehru had categorically told Parliament on 20 November, 1950, that 'the frontier from Bhutan eastwards had been clearly defined by the McMahon Line, which was fixed by the Simla Convention of 1914' and that 'the frontiers from Ladakh to Nepal are defined chiefly by long usage and custom...our maps show that the McMahon Line is our boundary.... And we shall not allow anybody to come across that boundary.' Zhou could not have missed Nehru's public assertions and thus, India's position would have been well known to him. It should also be noted that Zhou's remarks contained no reference to the Tibet-Bhutan, Tibet-Sikkim or the POK-Tibet border. Zhou *gave the impression* [emphasis added] that India was competent to discuss all these sectors as well. It is a matter of common failure and a fatal one indeed to read into Chinese intentions what we wish to read. Later when relations with India soured, the Chinese changed their position and refused to discuss any of these sectors with India!

Secondly, Mao told the new Indian Ambassador Raghavan on 26 September, 1952, that 'India had nothing to fear from China and China had no fears on her South-West frontier', thus confirming Nehru's thinking that India need not expect any aggression from China and that the border was not an immediate issue. Nothing contained in these formulations suggested an explicit recognition of the border, but Nehru took it otherwise. Hence Nehru issued a directive on 30 August, 1953, that the border issue need not be raised 'for the present.'

Thus, the border issue was not raised, nor was it linked to the settlement of India's rights in Tibet which were unilaterally given up, one at a time, salami style, to China's great advantage. This was a grave error of judgment. It showed what a poor reading Panikkar had of the Chinese mind. But Nehru, too, cannot be absolved of all blame. If Nehru wanted all the issues to be considered and resolved at one go, as several instructions from him to Panikkar indicate, it then remains inexplicable and remiss on his part why he acquiesced again and again to the entreaties of Panikkar. Nehru should have been firm with Panikkar and insisted that his instructions be carried out in full.

Foreign diplomats stationed in Delhi took a more forthright view that 'Panikkar had consistently and deliberately misled Nehru about China.'[83] The Prime Minister, they felt, 'had an infatuation for Krishna Menon and an admiration for Panikkar.'[84] As for the quality of Panikkar's reporting from Beijing and his understanding of the situation there, the general feeling was that he was apt to give every benefit of doubt to the Chinese and often did not distinguish between points raised by the Chinese and those raised by himself. For a man who had authored an article in an international publication only a year before independence, claiming that both Tibet and Sinkiang constituted the outer ring for the 'real security' of India,[85] to now advocating Chinese 'sovereignty' over Tibet was an astonishing leap of faith and a complete volte face. It clearly indicated that Panikkar was only too keen to project what he thought Nehru wanted to hear. He was a quintessential time server and a consummate flatterer, who was too engrossed in promoting his personal interests and in ingratiating himself with Nehru. If that meant changing his views with the season, so be it. Nehru had recognized this fatal flaw in Panikkar' character and dubbed him as 'an unscrupulous time server' rather indiscreetly to the then US Ambassador, Chester Bowles,[86] but astonishingly continued to persist with him, which lends credence to the belief that Panikkar was only reflecting Nehru's views. Panikkar was, indeed, a very poor choice for being appointed as independent India's first Ambassador to the People's Republic.

Krishna Menon was the other person who had the closest intellectual affinity to Nehru.[87] He was the only person amongst Nehru's colleagues in the Cabinet with whom Nehru could relate. Other Cabinet colleagues neither had the knowledge nor the interest in any issue outside India. Both Nehru and Menon were comfortable with each other.[88] Nehru felt that Menon was the one colleague who interpreted his 'ethics, ideologies and policies more faithfully than any other.'[89] Nehru relished Menon's tart cleverness, his barbed wit and astringent conversation. Nehru remarked that he had 'hardly come across a keener intelligence and brain.'[90] Krishna Menon spoke the same political and social language and idiom that Nehru did, although Menon nuanced his with Marxist inflections.[91] Most diplomats stationed in Delhi thought that Menon spoke, whether truly or not, in the name of the PM.[92] Some felt that he was 'one of the Nehru family [in a way no other Minister is or has been]...indeed Nehru behaved towards Menon in a manner so paternal so as to suggest that he saw in Menon the son that he had always so much wanted to have.'[93] Later US Ambassador Galbraith wrote to President Kennedy that 'in a curious sort of way he [Menon] is the 'Hindu' Dulles—alienating people as he goes.'[94] That successive US Administrations hated his generally anti-Western stance, his sarcasm and biting tongue is a truism. Eisenhower, after meeting Menon in 1955, termed him as a 'menace and a boor.'[95] That Menon equally thought poorly of the US is also a truism. He told the British High Commissioner in India that he considered them [the Americans], 'newcomers and naïve, impulsive and inexperienced,' and that they dealt with India 'in an intolerable manner.'[96] Menon was not the only official who felt that way about the Americans. Even the generally pro-US, Sir Girija Bajpai, Secretary General of External Affairs, termed the Americans as 'arrogant.'[97] Menon had also been Nehru's literary agent in the UK for the publication of his various books.[98]

Meanwhile, in line with Nehru's policy of promoting friendship with China and yet in another curious act of misreading China's ultimate intentions, India permitted the export of thorium nitrate to China. Thorium nitrate is radio active source material used mainly for research and production of nuclear fuel. India has 25 per cent of the world's total reserves. Earlier, realizing the importance of this strategic mineral, the British Government had, just prior to independence, entered into secret conversations with the then ruler of Travancore to secure for

Britain in post independent India this strategic asset. That its plans did not succeed does not detract from the importance of this asset.

On 17 July, 1953, the US discovered that the Polish freighter, SS Mickiewicz, had loaded two tons of thorium nitrate valued at Rs. 40,500 which was exported by Indian Rare Earths Limited and bound for the Chinese port of Taku Bar.[99] The US protested vigorously as this violated the Mutual Assistance Control Act of 1951 [Battle Act] and would have hobbled US aid to India completely. When the US Ambassador Allen met Nehru on 28 July, 1953, to remonstrate, Nehru was very belligerent. He declared:

> India had never and would never submit to derogation of its national sovereignty in permitting US law to determine with whom and in what commodities India could trade.[100] Nehru insisted that India would never accept aid that came attached with 'political strings.'

While it may have been patriotic to sound belligerent, the main point was being totally missed. Did India wish to assist China to develop nuclear weapons even at the cost of forgoing all US economic aid to India? Happily, better sense prevailed and a compromise was worked out in which the US would henceforth import all the thorium nitrate that India produced at a rate mutually agreed and in return, India would henceforth not export such items to China. In assessing this episode it seems as if the political leadership in India continued to be quite oblivious to the impending threat from the North and the fact that at some stage, it would need US help.

US Secretary of State Dulles visited Delhi from 20-22 May, 1953. During his visit Nehru told Dulles that:

> India has a two thousand-mile frontier with China and a deep concern with its relation with China. India has proclaimed that the Himalayas are its frontier and that it will not tolerate a penetration to the South. China like Russia was going through an expansionist phase and that this was not wholly due to Communist rule.[101]

Because of the very nature of the regime, Nehru prophesized that China would split from Russia in the next 10-15 years [How correct he was!]

Secretary of State Dulles, however, had a totally different world view. Dulles felt that the Communists were monolithic and controlled from Moscow, and the felt need was to build military alliances to contain Communism, just as they had done in Europe. Although Dulles termed 'neutralism' as immoral and a short sighted conception, he committed to Nehru that 'the US had *no present plans* [emphasis added] that would bring it into a military relationship with Pakistan.' Dulles reported that Nehru was satisfied. Dulles knew that there were active plans to give military aid to Pakistan for that was what he had recommended in a memorandum to the White House on 16 February, 1953; a good three months prior to his visit to Delhi for talks with Nehru. Dulles was thus misleading Nehru.[102]

Dulles' commitment was 'to whatever served his current need, interest or convenience, and that he was devious to an accomplished degree.'[103] Despite the apparent circumspection, Dulles' real view of Nehru was that 'he was an utterly impractical statesman.'[104] The aversion appeared to be mutual, for during Nehru's visit to China in October, 1954, he told Mao that Dulles was 'self-righteous, moralistic and without any understanding, and that he expected that every single person should agree with his opinion.'[105]

However, when Dulles reached Pakistan, General Ayub Khan, the Pakistani Army Chief, told Dulles that the US:

> should not be afraid to openly aid those countries which have expressed a willingness, and even desire, to cooperate with the United States. He reiterated the potential, both in manpower and bases that are available in Pakistan and that his country under the present Government is extremely anxious to cooperate with the United States.[106]

Dulles was hugely impressed with, and flattered by the Pakistanis. The US Embassy in Pakistan impressed upon Dulles that Ayub was the 'strongest individual in Pakistan *and the man to talk to*' [emphasis added]. Dulles felt that 'Pakistan is the largest of Muslim nation and occupies a high position in the Muslim world. The strong spiritual faith and martial spirit of the people *make them a dependable bulwark against Communism*' [Dulles Radio Address, 1 June, 1953] [emphasis added]. How utterly infantile this assessment was, for the Pakistanis were simply looking for outside support against India. To think that the Pakistani Army could stand against the might of the Soviet Union was sheer fantasy. The Pakistanis felt that this way they could inveigle the US for military, political and economic support in their struggle against India.

The US could not resist such blandishments for long and when Ayub visited the US in September 1953; serious talks were initiated for a Mutual Defence Assistance Agreement. Dulles assured Ayub he was fully prepared to assist Pakistan militarily 'regardless of India's attitude.' There is little doubt that US thinking at that time was influenced to take this policy option by the rather assiduous pleadings of a former British official, Sir Olaf Caroe [Former British Foreign Secretary in India]. State Department officials were encouraged to consider that Pakistan was a natural candidate, as a Muslim country, to help in the defence of the Middle-East and its vast oil wealth against Soviet depredations. The Western powers needed a base in North-West Pakistan from which Soviet Russia could be militarily threatened. It was estimated that 77 per cent of Soviet cities would be vulnerable to an air attack from aircraft based in North-West Pakistan.[107] Caroe's thesis upon which this strategy was based is amplified in his book 'The Wells of Power', which was widely read and circulated to leading decision makers within Washington. The decision taken by the US to enter into a military arrangement with Pakistan thus stemmed not from considerations concerning South Asia, but from Western strategic requirements concerning the Middle-East. In the event, the US secretly installed electronic equipment at Peshawar that could track Soviet missile capabilities and was also able to mount U-2 flights from there.

Quite sagaciously, Pakistani officials deliberately leaked to James Callahan of the *New York Times* stationed in Karachi, reports of the impending 'military alliance' between the US and Pakistan.[108] The Pakistani establishment correctly surmised that this was the best way to push the US into taking a decision. Nixon, then Vice-President, also pleaded for Pakistan and claimed that 'if the President backed down now [over India's objections], the US could count on losing most of the Arab-Asian countries to the neutralist bloc.'

The US was not unmindful of the extremely adverse reaction this action would have on India, but felt sufficiently sanguine on being able to handle the fallout. The press leaks were probably designed to test the waters. Even the British Foreign Secretary, Sir Anthony Eden, in his meeting with Dulles on 7 December, 1953, at Bermuda advised Dulles against going ahead, but to no avail. Eden's thinking was 'if they could not be with us, we must not make them against us.'[109] The British view was that 'the US proposal will spoil the more immediate prospects of improved relations between India and Pakistan.' In 1949, when Pakistan offered to sign a Defence Agreement with Britain, the latter had turned down the offer for fear of offending India. And more importantly, the British stressed that the political co-operation received from India was far more important than the advantages of a defence pact with Pakistan. Although the US Ambassador to India denied as late as November 1953 [Pillai, Secretary General with US Ambassador, 16 November, 1953] any intention of a military alliance with Pakistan, Nehru was not convinced. He wrote to Krishna Menon on 14 February, 1954, that serious US-Pak talks were on. The US-Pak Agreement was eventually signed on 19 May, 1954, and in line with NSC Document No.5409, was seen by the US as strengthening the 'defence of the region' against Communism. It was not US intention to make Pakistan 'the dominant state of South Asia.'[110]

Nehru had been aware of developments taking place between the US and Pakistan. In a letter to Chief Ministers on 15 November, 1953, Nehru wrote that 'the ground was being prepared in last few months in various ways and we may see its finalization.' Nehru quoted the '*US News and World Report*' that observed that Pakistan looks like 'an answer to a prayer because it will supply a vast army to fight Communism in the Middle-East.' Nehru felt that giving military aid by the US to Pakistan in the peculiar circumstances of an Indo-Pak conflict was a 'clear breach of neutrality by the US.'[111] The US, henceforth, could not be considered to be a neutral country in so far as disputes between India and Pakistan were concerned. Nehru's feeling was that 'as a matter of fact, outside interference that is troubling *us is American and not Chinese*' [emphasis added] [note to SG 25 October, 1953]. The US decision directly challenged India's pre-eminence in the sub-continent. No ruler in India, including Nehru, could have let this challenge pass.[112] The US had brought the cold war to South Asia, and Nehru's dream of keeping South Asia outside super power rivalry lay shattered with the signing of the US-Pakistan Military Assistance Agreement. Later Nehru during his visit to China in October, 1954, was to inform Zhou of the circumstances leading to the US-Pakistan Military Assistance Agreement. Nehru said:

> When Pakistan asked for American military aid, we were in the middle of negotiations; we had even reached a preliminary agreement. After Pakistan obtained military aid, I told them, the situation had undergone a basic change; one needs a new basis for consideration. They denied that the situation had undergone any change. Thus, our talks were broken off. The reason for breaking them off was America's military aid and not any internal rationale.[113]

Inwardly, Nehru seethed with rage over US meddling in South Asia.[114] He was also personally peeved and miffed at the US attitude, for it only confirmed his earlier assessment and which he had expressed in a letter to his sister [Mrs. Pandit, 10 May, 1950] that:

> I must say the Americans are either naïve or singularly lacking in intelligence. They go through the same routine whether it a Nehru, Shah of Iran or Liaquat Ali [Pakistan PM] [emphasis added].

Nehru's ego had been hurt. Nehru considered US military assistance to Pakistan as an 'unfriendly act' and an unwarranted induction of the cold war into South Asia. For the US the importance of bringing in Pakistan for the defence of the Middle-East was more important than maintaining 'pleasant relations with Nehru.'[115] Years later, the US was to realize that this decision to arm Pakistan was a 'monumental strategic blunder.'[116] Eisenhower lamented that 'the military commitment to Pakistan was perhaps the worst kind of plan and decision we could have made. It was a terrible error.'[117]

Nehru, conscious of the changed circumstances, now began to look seriously at the Chinese option. Nehru felt that it was important for India not to face two hostile and aggressive neighbours at the same time. In view of India's military weakness, it was not in a position to protect and preserve its security if it had to simultaneously face two hostile powers on its borders.[118] Of the two powers—Pakistan and China—Pakistan was viscerally antagonistic and Nehru felt that there was little hope the Pakistanis would ever be mollified, more so now that they had entered into a military relationship with the US. Nehru had a very poor view of the Pakistani leadership. With biting sarcasm he told Zhou '*that these were the same people who sided with England and opposed independence. They only depend on religion and have no political or economic base.*'[119]

Pakistan averred that its membership of CENTO and SEATO was a quid pro quo for Western military and political support to it in its disputes with India. The US reading of the situation was that 'India was against a militant approach towards China because of a desire to get along with a powerful neighbour as long as India was militarily preoccupied with Pakistan.'[120] Nehru's thinking was that 'our one major possible enemy is Pakistan...if we begin to think of and prepare for China's aggression in the same way, we would considerably weaken on the Pakistan side.'[121] Nehru now made a strategic decision of far reaching importance. The decision was to continue to confront Pakistan militarily, but to deal with China diplomatically and to continue to seek China's friendship, for he felt that Pakistan had become 'an American colony.'[122]

Therefore, in continuation of this policy, Nehru felt that it was important to reach complete settlement with China over Tibet. Whatever hesitation Nehru might have had now disappeared. In a note to the Foreign Secretary on 18 June, 1954, Nehru explained his rationale thus:

> There is not the least chance in the world of China leaving Tibet or being driven out of Tibet, unless China is defeated in war. Of that there appears to be no chance. Therefore, adventurous tactics beyond the borders of Tibet have no meaning.

And in any case, with China in full control of Tibet, there was little that any Government in India could have done otherwise. India's options were limited, but not entirely inconsequential. Nehru was conscious that defending such a long border with China would be an expensive proposition and financially debilitating, but he was not in any way blind to the potential dangers that might develop in the future [Nehru's conversations with Ambassador Chester Bowles]. Nehru felt that friendship and stable relations with China constituted the best way to redress the strategic balance of power in South Asia.[123] Later, in 1956, Nehru explained it as such to Eisenhower that this approach helped to keep defence expenditures down since it minimized the chances of conflict. Nehru further clarified that if he did not follow this policy he might fail in his primary responsibility of raising the standard of living of his people, which would otherwise mean an internal collapse leading to the rise of Communism. In reaching a settlement with China, Nehru hoped that a two front adversarial situation could be avoided, in addition to the huge expense of policing such an extensive border. Not all agreed with Nehru's thinking as the then British High Commissioner, Sir Archibald Nye [a former general] felt that Nehru had 'yielded to *self deception* that the Chinese had no aggressive designs, despite their invasion of Tibet.'[124]

At this stage, the Chinese, too, were not unwilling for with Tibet still unsettled, they wished to limit their differences with India. They had no 'apprehension that India would harm us.'[125] In strategic terms, the Chinese, too, needed friends for they continued to face military encirclement and an economic embargo imposed by the US on their Eastern sea-board. They did not want to open another front; at least not just yet. To pacify Tibet, it was crucial to seek the co-operation of India. As India was not allied to the US and as it espoused nonalignment, the Chinese reasoned that it was possible to consider India 'as a friend.'[126] This new stance was further reiterated by Mao himself, when at the Republic Day Reception at the Indian Embassy at Beijing on 26 January, 1951, he told the Indian Ambassador that 'it is a great day; the Indian people are a fine people.' The Indian Ambassador reported to Delhi that Mao spoke warmly about Nehru and expressed the wish to see Nehru soon in China.[127] This friendship, as it stood, became an important part of Chinese strategy to confront the US in Asia.[128] In any case, the Chinese were well aware of India's military weakness.

Thus, at this stage both India and China, for strategic reasons of their own, needed to come to an accommodation. Nehru moved decisively to normalize relations with China and seek its friendship by seeking an understanding over Tibet. On 2 August, 1952, a note was sent to the Chinese Government offering to discuss all pending matters and to 'modify certain practices and even remove some of them if they are considered as affecting the dignity of China.' On 2 September, 1953, Nehru took a further initiative by writing a letter to Zhou offering to discuss with the Chinese issues that still remained unresolved. In the letter Nehru said, 'Government feels that it would be advantageous to both [India and China] to deal *with all remaining problems together. Piecemeal consideration of each problem does not lead to satisfactory solutions*' [emphasis added]. But exactly the opposite was eventually done!

In his letter, Nehru also seems to have hinted to the Chinese that he was prepared to write off India's interests in Tibet when he informed Zhou that '*we have recognized this situation and are fully prepared to adapt ourselves to it*' [emphasis added]. Zhou responded with alacrity on 15 October, 1953. He agreed to commence negotiations, but insisted that they be conducted in Beijing and suggested that they commence in December that year. To insist that negotiations take place in Beijing was the Chinese way to publicly show which way the wind was blowing, for ironically the Simla negotiations in 1914 on Tibet had taken place in India! This time there were to be no Tibetans and this time they would be held in China. Thus, even before actual negotiations commenced on 31 December, 1953, Nehru gave more than ample hints that India would surrender all its rights inherited from the British in Tibet! The hapless Tibetans did not even figure in the correspondence and Nehru seems to have written them off completely, without even informing them!

Nehru was concerned that the situation on India's borders with China was far from satisfactory. Yet in a move that can only be described as incomprehensible, Nehru issued a directive to the Indian negotiators through the Secretary-General on 3 December, 1953, once again reiterating that:

> We should not raise this question [boundary]. If the Chinese raise it we should express our surprise and point out that this is a settled issue. Our delegation cannot discuss it.

There seemed to Nehru no reason to depart from the formulated policy that the boundary alignment was a settled fact except for a few minor tracts, and that it need not be raised with China.

Nehru was exasperated over the slow progress being made in the talks with the Chinese that began in December 1953. He cabled Ambassador Raghvan in China on 16 April, 1954, that:

> A very grave situation had arisen because of the new policy enunciated by Dulles. We are much concerned with this... If the India-China agreement on Tibet is signed and announced soon it will have a salutary effect. If, however, this is postponed indefinitely it will have a contrary effect...I suggest you point all this to the Chinese Government.[129]

To say the least, these negotiating tactics with the Chinese were rather strange, incomprehensible and poorly thought through. Firstly, India's position in Tibet was written off in advance of the negotiations and officially hinted as such to the Chinese. Secondly, it is almost a given that never negotiate with the Chinese if time is of the essence. They will see through it and take maximum advantage. And never leave anything open ended, as the Chinese will take further advantage and squeeze further concessions. Unfortunately, this is precisely what happened. Anyone can be forgiven for thinking that India's attitude amounted to dumping the Tibetans at any cost.

The Chinese were well aware of the difficult situation faced by India with the US decision to arm Pakistan, ostensibly for combating Communist 'advances.' The Chinese also knew that Pakistan had no such intentions of opposing them, and that these newly acquired sophisticated US weapons, such as Patton tanks, could only be used in the plains and against India. The Pakistani PM, Suhrawardy, on a visit to China had already assured them that this was indeed so. The Chinese correctly surmised that the Indo Pak cleavage was far too wide for it to be ever bridged. Thus, the room available for bargaining that India had vis-à-vis China and Chinese control over Tibet, had indeed significantly contracted by this thoughtless act [US-Pak Mutual Defence Agreement] on the part of the US. Nehru was in danger of being out-manoeuvred and squeezed from both the West and the North.

For China, the 1954 India-China Agreement on Trade and Intercourse between India and the 'Tibet region of China' was a major achievement. It amounted to the counter-signature by India on the death warrant of Tibetan independence,[130] such as it was. It was one of the biggest concessions made by India in Asian history. For Nehru, this Agreement was an attempt to insulate at least one frontier and to avoid being squeezed simultaneously both from the North and the West. Uncertain of US intentions, Nehru wanted to avoid trouble with both China and Pakistan at the same time. By incorporating the 'five principles of peaceful coexistence' Nehru hoped to hedge China in so that it would be *committed in a formal document* to adopt 'peaceful methods' in solving the boundary issue, as and when it was raised [emphasis added]. To Nehru this was an important point, for he realized that with People's Republic of China not yet a member of the UN, it had no commitment to solve disputes 'peacefully' as per the UN Charter. Present

Chinese writings give no credit to—and even deny—that Nehru was the originator of the 'five principles of peaceful co-existence', attributing this honour exclusively to PM, Zhou.[131] And the Chinese insist that they clearly told the Indian negotiators that '*issues like the border problem which are not mature can be kept pending*' [emphasis added]. But should India have given in on almost all points even before the negotiations began? Was Nehru chasing rainbows? Not only was Tibet recognized as a 'region of China', but all of India's rights in Tibet so painstakingly acquired over the years were *unilaterally* given up in one clean sweep. To have surrendered all the special rights and privileges that India had acquired, without referring to the document [the Simla Convention] under which they were enjoying these rights in the new 1954 Agreement, was a diplomatic blunder, for with it went the chance to force the Chinese to accept the McMahon Line. Thus, inexplicably, nothing tangible was asked for from China in return. This would, no doubt, have astonished the Chinese negotiators. It was particularly unfortunate that the right to station troops at the trade marts was given up, for it was here that Indian troops could acclimatize themselves to the harsh Tibetan climate and gain experience of Tibetan conditions. But for Nehru, the presence of Indian troops in Tibet was a 'symbol of British imperialism' and he had no hesitation in withdrawing them.[132]

Under Article 1 [2] of the Agreement, India was allowed to set up a Trade Agency at Gartok [Western Tibet]. But the Chinese, sensing that an Indian presence in Western Tibet might possibly detect Chinese road building activities in Aksai Chin, never allowed it to function on one pretext or the other. The only saving grace was that six passes in the middle sector were specified as points through which traders and pilgrims could pass. Interestingly, the Chinese refused to specify them as 'border passes.' They pointedly refused to name Demchok in Ladakh as a pass through which trade could take place. Instead the 1954 Agreement has the following obscure formulation: 'the customary route leading to Tashigong along the valley of the Indus River may continue to be traversed.' The excuse put forward informally by the Chinese was that Demchok [Ladakh] was in Kashmir, and that they did not wish to be 'involved' in a India-Pakistan dispute! This, too, was swallowed by the hapless Indian negotiators.[133]

In another inexplicable act, Indian negotiators sold the entire network of postal, telegraph system, public telephone services and equipment and rest houses inherited by India in Tibet from the British for a paltry sum of Rs.3,16,828 [Joint Communiqué on handing over the Indian Communications Facilities in Tibet to China, 1 April, 1955]. The Chinese probably astonished at the naivety or misplaced generosity of the Indian negotiators, promptly paid the amount by 31 March, 1955.

The signing of the 1954 agreement with China meant the complete formalization of all developments since the invasion of Tibet by China, and the total elimination of Indian political influence in Tibet. For the first time ever

India, in a formal document, recognized Tibet as an integral part of China. In international legal terms it, signalled the fact that the only country that had special relations with Tibet had now agreed to relinquish these and did so without any reference or consultation with the Dalai Lama or even with the Tibetan Government.[134] For the Tibetans, it can be said that the curtain was finally drawn on Tibet's aspirations to be an independent state or even an autonomous one.

On 25 October, 1953, Nehru clarified to the Secretary-General of External Affairs Ministry that 'we cannot support feudal elements in Tibet.' There was never much sympathy for the hapless Tibetan Government. Krishna Menon, a Nehru confidante, emphasized later to Michael Brecher that 'whatever may be the position today, we had no sympathy with the reactionary theocratic Lama regime either. There was no question in his [Nehru's] mind of any rights in Tibet.'[135] Nehru now described the historic rights and privileges that India enjoyed in Tibet as 'tainted by British imperialism.'[136] Nehru was loathe to defend the Dalai Lama-led regime in Tibet, as that would tantamount to defending 'feudalism' and as he himself was to remark, 'we can hardly stand-up as defenders of feudalism!' This was pure and simple expediency, for if this was so then why had Nehru not given up these very rights when India attained independence in 1947? On the contrary, India had confirmed to the Tibetan Government in a note in 1947 that 'the Government of India would be glad to have an assurance that it is the intention of the Tibetan Government to continue relations *on the existing basis*' [emphasis added]. The Tibetan Government had, indeed, given such an assurance.[137] Later, the Dalai Lama was to hint that even the McMahon Line was a product of such British 'imperial' rights that were consolidated under the 1914 Simla Convention. Nehru conveniently glossed over this assertion of the Dalai Lama.

But Nehru had no regrets. He was indeed ecstatic over the signing of the 1954 Agreement. He proudly proclaimed, 'we have done nothing better in the field of foreign affairs during the last six years than signing this Agreement over Tibet. I have not the slightest doubt about it. This Agreement is good not only for our country but for the whole of Asia and the rest of the world.'[138] On 15 May, 1954, an ecstatic Nehru told the Lok Sabha 'this area of peace should be spread over the rest of Asia and indeed over the rest of the world.' Writing to G L Mehta, on 29 June, 1954, Nehru added 'we have only given up what we in fact could not hold and what in fact had in reality gone.' An Indian official [RK Nehru] explained to the British Deputy High Commissioner that the reference to 'Tibet region of China' was a 'concession to realism.'[139]

Nehru was not only convinced that he had done the right thing, but when questioned about India's rights in Tibet boldly answered that 'if we had not withdrawn voluntarily we would have been forced to do so. There is no doubt on this score.'[140] It was good to give them up 'gracefully', added Nehru. When sceptics lamented the loss of Tibet as a buffer state, Nehru was at his sarcastic best when he taunted them by asking the rhetorical question 'buffer between whom?' Nehru even wrote to the Chief Ministers that two important aspects of this Agreement were [1] that 'indirectly the question of our long frontier is settled' and [2] the principles of non-aggression and non-interference are laid down.[141] This totally untenable assessment was to haunt Nehru in his later years.

The unusual vehemence that Nehru displayed in defending the 1954 Agreement was probably based on his belief that the Chinese had acquiesced in the border alignment as shown on Indian maps. This belief was strengthened when the Chinese did not raise the border issue at any time during the discussions leading to the signing of the 1954 Agreement, and also agreed to mention the six passes in the middle sector. The six passes mentioned were: Shipki La, Mana, Niti, Kungri Bingri, Darma and Lipu Lekh. From what was a belief, this was, in an act of self delusion, turned into a fact that the Chinese Government had not only no dispute with the Indian border alignment, but in fact acknowledged the traditional customary line as shown by India! A senior Foreign Office official, writing under the pseudonym of 'Kautilya,' defended the 1954 Agreement and wrote that 'our PM has declared more than once, in Parliament and outside, that we stand by our present frontiers. China has never questioned this. Besides, the Tibet Agreement itself expressly recognizes our frontier at the six passes mentioned therein and *we have no reason to believe that any frontier dispute exists. None has come to light so far*' [emphasis added].[142] It was an exercise in extreme self-delusion.

Nevertheless, the Parliament of India approved the Agreement on 3 June, 1954. There was much adulation in the press too. The *Amrita Bazaar Patrika* of 7 June, 1954 thought that the Agreement gave 'tacit Chinese approval to the McMahon Line.' The *Indian Express* of 5 May, 1954, thought that 'alleged maps establishing Chinese claims to certain tracts this side of the McMahon Line were the products of the malicious imagination of mischievous outsiders'! *The Times of India* of 1 May, 1954, felt that the Agreement with China was an 'acknowledgement of the validity of the existing boundary line.' Many speeches were made by leading personalities, several articles were written by leading journalists on the theme that for 'thousands of years' there had been undisturbed peace and brotherhood between the two great Asian friends and neighbours. Euphoria was unbounded. Krishna Menon spoke eloquently at the 9th session of the UN General Assembly, and extolled the virtues of the 1954 Agreement as having made a 'great contribution to peace in the Asian world.' Nehru was convinced that the coming together of India and China, despite differences, was a 'major event for Asia and perhaps, even for the world.' Nehru, speaking in the Lok Sabha on 15 May, 1954, thought that by this agreement 'we would ensure peace to a very large extent in a certain area of Asia.' The Chinese, realistic as ever, made no such claims. The Agreement over Tibet did not buy the peace that Nehru thought he had negotiated. It was a case of excessive faith in moral imperatives and a poor understanding of the reality of power. More than ever, the two front threat to India's security persisted, as the boundary question remained unsettled.

Having achieved a major strategic aim of getting India to recognize its position in Tibet de-jure as well as de-facto, the stage was now set for a confrontation on the border as there was no confirmation by the Chinese in the 1954 Agreement that they agreed, or even acquiesced, with the alignment as shown on Indian maps. When Ambassador Raghavan, at the end of the negotiations, tried to put a spin and proposed a toast, 'let us drink to the settling of *all our differences* through this agreement,' Zhou, ever vigilant, significantly responded 'to settling all those points *which are ripe for settlement*' [emphasis added].[143] The writing was on the wall. Indian policy makers should have become alert, but unfortunately the significance of Zhou's remarks was totally missed!

Further evidence of China's uncompromising attitude was also soon available. The Chinese Government, despite repeated requests by the Government of India, refused to intervene to pay compensation to Indian nationals retrenched by the Shanghai Municipal Corporation. Nor were they prepared to settle the claims of Indian nationals in Xinjiang [Sinkiang] when their properties were confiscated by local authorities. The contrast in attitude is, indeed, vivid when seen that the Government of India gave up all its rights in Tibet for a paltry sum!

Despite Nehru's effusive efforts to show friendliness to China, the Chinese never openly acknowledged that Kashmir was a part of India. Even in 1954, during a meeting in Delhi when Nehru gave Zhou a detailed and precise account of Pakistan, its origin, its policies and its joining the US sponsored security pacts ostensibly against Communism, Zhou kept silent. He never spoke ill of Pakistan. An alert Nehru should have noted it, but if he did, he seems to have glossed over it. During Nehru's visit to China in October 1954, Zhou put forward a feeler to Nehru when he suggested that Nehru might consider negotiating with the Pakistani PM over Kashmir. Nehru point blank refused.[144]

Earlier on 7 October, 1954, Zhou had told a Pakistani Women's delegation visiting China that 'China maintains a cool head and *a neutral stance on the Kashmir issue*' [emphasis added].[145] This assertion by Zhou was made barely a few days prior to Nehru's visit to China. Even when the US-Pakistan Mutual Assistance Agreement was signed in 1954, the Chinese attitude towards Pakistan barely changed. Although Zhou verbally told the Indian Ambassador on 16 March, 1956, that 'the people of Kashmir had already expressed their will on the accession to India',[146] China completely denied it.[147] Later that year, on 25 December, 1956, Zhou disclosed at Karachi at a press conference that he actually had talked with Nehru about Kashmir but declined to reveal the substance of his talks. Thereafter, whenever Zhou was asked about Kashmir, he always evaded giving a direct answer. He would pretend that China had 'not studied' the issue! When confronted with a direct question [*Amrita Bazaar* correspondent] this is what Zhou said:

> We hope that the Kashmir question would be settled amicably as India and Pakistan are sister countries. The people are of the same race. There can be no dispute between them which cannot be settled.[148]

However, Zhou made an interesting observation at a press conference at Colombo on 5 February, 1957, that China 'always' held the view that the Kashmir question should not be referred to the UN as this would offer the 'imperialists' the opportunity to 'exploit the issue for their own ends.'[149] Thus, China's position remained ambivalent throughout the honeymoon period with India, a point not unnoticed by the Pakistanis. The Chinese later, when relations with India became problematical, pointedly asked Indian interlocutors to cite a single official Chinese document that stated that Kashmir was a part of India. None could be cited!

At this point, however, Nehru's faith in Zhou Enlai was complete. He thought that Zhou was a reasonable man and easy to deal with, and this had helped Nehru to confirm his predilection for a deep and abiding friendship with China. Krishna Menon reinforced this view when he cabled Nehru on 21 January, 1954, that Zhou was a 'fine and, I believe, a great and able man...he is extremely shrewd and observant, very Chinese but very modern.' The theme of 'Hindi-Chini' brotherhood was common not only within the ruling circles around Nehru, but with most people in India including some members of the press who too bought this line of thinking. A foreign Ambassador stationed in Delhi observed that Nehru had more faith in Zhou than he did in Dulles [US Secretary of State].[150] Perhaps Nehru could be forgiven for forming such an assessment, given the way that Dulles had treated his confidence. Privately, though, Nehru's doubts remained. It was this public faith in the Chinese, so eloquently and conspicuously expressed, combined with nagging private doubts about China's ulterior motives that made Nehru appear ever so naïve and faltering. And yet, Nehru was soon to learn another equally hard lesson from the shrewd and observant Zhou Enlai.

CHAPTER 4

The Beginning of the Dispute [1954–59]

'To remove every subject of discord, every occasion for quarrel, one should make with clarity and precision the limits of territories'

[Vettel, 1758]

From the time that China occupied Tibet in 1950 to the signing of the 1954 Sino-Indian Agreement on Tibet, there were no Chinese incursions [apart from crossing the Aksai Chin] across the boundary alignment as shown by India, nor were there any incidents. It was a very peaceful border. The Chinese were being very discreet and had no inclination to precipitate matters just yet. Despite the euphoria generated in India as a result of the 1954 Sino-Indian Agreement on Tibet, Nehru still remained apprehensive. He still felt uneasy. On 18 June, 1954, Nehru sent a note to Secretary General [MEA], in which his doubts about China's intentions still continued to vex him. He wrote:

> No country can ultimately rely upon the permanent good-will or bona-fides of another country, even though they may be in close friendship with each other....certainly it is conceivable that our relations with China might worsen....therefore we have always to keep in mind the possibility of change and cannot be taken unawares. Adequate precautions have to be taken.[1]

These doubts about China's ultimate intentions remained, as he was not unmindful of the fact that there was no Chinese agreement on the boundary. Aware of what Zhou had earlier informally told Panikkar on 27 September, 1951, that 'there was no territorial dispute or controversy between India and China' [Statement in Parliament, 25 November, 1961], Nehru was not totally convinced of Zhou's protestations. And if a gentle reminder was needed, the Chinese published a map in 1954 showing Sikkim, Bhutan, Nepal and NEFA as parts of China.[2] The Chinese were, yet, still not ready to disclose their hand fully as they felt that more time was still needed to pacify Tibet. Although working at a furious pace, the Chinese had not been able to fully complete the construction of the new highways linking mainland China with Tibet and needed more time to improve the infrastructure. China was also busy constructing feeder roads to the Sino-

Indian border as also the Aksai Chin road linking Xinjiang [Sinkiang] with Tibet. Reports about the construction of this road had also started to come in from Bhutia traders who often visited Tibet, particularly in the summer months.[3]

Meanwhile, the Chinese, in line with their policy of playing for time, continued to shower adulations on Nehru. They knew the weakness of their position in Tibet and judged that they still needed the goodwill of Nehru. Zhou flew directly from Geneva to Delhi and stayed as a guest of Nehru from 25-28 June, 1954. It was a seminal moment in Sino-Indian relations. Even relations between the Dalai Lama and the CCP, always a key factor in Sino-Indian relations, had taken a positive turn. It seemed as if Tibet was moving forward to carve itself a niche within the People's Republic.[4]

Zhou arrived in Delhi, on his first visit to India to flatter Nehru. 'Your Excellency has more knowledge about the world and Asia than I have', said Zhou, and being the clever man that he was, added for emphasis that 'Your Excellency has participated much more in international affairs than I have' and insisted that he had come to 'learn' from Nehru. Nehru, never immune from flattery, was suitably touched. Most of the pressing problems facing the world were discussed, *but the boundary question was not touched upon* [emphasis added], perhaps with Nehru still not convinced that China had any ulterior motives other than friendship with India.

Nevertheless, soon after Zhou left Delhi, Nehru by way of abundant caution decided to firm up India's position on the issue of the boundary alignment so as to leave no doubts. While in the Eastern sector the McMahon Line indicated India's boundary quite clearly, the position in the Western sector was not that precise. Looking at the maps produced by the Survey of India since 1889, while the Aksai Chin is shown as a part of India yet the boundary line is shown as 'undefined.' Interestingly the Survey of India maps of 1903, 1917, 1929, 1936 and 1938 do not indicate any precise boundary in the Western sector. However, the Survey of India map of 1945 showed India's present boundary alignment with the same colour wash as for other areas of India, but still showed the boundary as 'undefined.' A similar position obtained in 1950, 1951 and 1952. It is interesting to note that the colour wash is the same as was shown for the tribal areas of the North-West frontier.

Accordingly, Nehru issued instructions on 1 July 1954 that:

> All our old maps dealing with this frontier should be carefully examined and where necessary withdrawn. New maps should be printed showing our Northern and North-Eastern frontier without any reference to any line. These new maps should also state that there is no un-demarcated territory. Both flowing from our policy and as a consequence of our agreement with China, this frontier should be considered firm and a definite one, which is not open to discussion with anybody. Our frontier has been finalized, not only by implication in this agreement, but the specific passes mentioned are direct recognition of our frontier there.[5]

Thus, the first map of the Western sector showing the boundary alignment *without any qualifications* was issued in 1954, after Nehru's above instructions. Armed with what Nehru then thought was a settled boundary alignment, he arrived in China to pay a return visit from 18-30 October, 1954, as the first non-Communist head of Government to do so. Nehru, accompanied by Zhou Enlai, drove in an open car from Beijing airport to the city centre. Nearly a million people lined the streets of Beijing to welcome Nehru. All the adulation paid by the Chinese was beginning to have an effect on Nehru. In a letter to Edwina Mountbatten written on 2 November, 1954, Nehru confessed, 'I had a welcome in China such as I have in the big cities of India and that is saying something. The welcome given to me was official and popular.... One million people took part on the day of arrival in Peking. I would have been less than human if I had not been influenced by all this.'[6] Nehru, in his exhilaration, wrote that the meeting between the PMs of China and India are a 'world event.' This was the high point of Nehru's odyssey with China.

While in Beijing, Nehru met Mao twice on 19 and 23 October, 1954. The meeting disappointed Nehru, for Mao's thesis that they were not afraid of a nuclear war even if it meant the annihilation of millions of people, rankled Nehru's pacifist thoughts. Nehru also never liked the way he was led in to meet Mao. Nehru felt that it was like meeting an 'emperor' and this hurt his sensibilities. In a curious omission of diplomatic propriety, Nehru never invited Mao to visit India. Was Mao waiting for an invitation? It would seem so.[7] A little later in 1955, Mao would have noticed that Nehru had invited the Soviet leaders Khrushchev and Bulganin to India where they had received a huge, rousing welcome. This, too, would have rankled with Mao for he was convinced that after Stalin, he was the 'tallest leader' within the socialist bloc! On the other hand, if Nehru had been a little more circumspect, he would have noticed that the Chinese were playing a double game which is clear from the message Mao sent to the Communist Party of India [CPI]. Mao told the Indian comrades that:

> I am deeply convinced that by relying on the unity and the heroic struggle of the courageous CPI... India will certainly not remain long under the yoke of imperialism and their collaborators...and just like free China, a free India will one day emerge in the socialist and people's democratic family.[8]

In other words, in Mao's view India under Nehru was neither a socialist nor an independent state and that it was still under imperialists and their collaborators! [Did he mean Nehru?]

Nevertheless, still uncomfortable about the boundary, Nehru took up the issue of Chinese maps with Zhou in Beijing during his visit. Nehru told Zhou that Chinese maps still showed 'portions of India as if they were within Chinese territory.' Nehru then confidently stated, 'we are not much concerned about this matter *because our boundaries were quite clear and were not a matter for argument*' [emphasis added]. Krishna Menon also confirmed Nehru's views when he told

Michael Brecher that 'at that time the PM's view was that there should be no argument about the border; the border was there, the McMahon Line is our border.'[9] Zhou cleverly side-stepped the issue by stating that these were 'old maps' and China had not done 'any surveying to draw new maps nor had they had the time to revise them and, therefore, they were still only printing old KMT maps.' Nehru then repeated that 'there was no doubt about our boundaries and I was not worried about them. But I wondered how China would feel if a part of Tibet had been shown as part of India in our maps.'[10]

The Chinese version of this part of the conversation is at variance with Nehru's version. Chinese records show that Nehru raised the issue of maps, but only in the context of smaller countries of Asia feeling 'uncomfortable' with the growing stature of both India and China. Chinese records quote Nehru as saying:

> The maps in question were published in Peking [Beijing], but depicted territories that belonged to Burma [Myanmar] and India as Chinese. This created 'unease' amongst the Burmese [note: Nehru did not mention 'unease' in India]. Admittedly these maps are old, but why hasn't the Chinese Government clarified the matter?

Zhou replied as follows:

> This is a problem inherited from history. [You] are not mistaken; the maps published by China are all old maps because we have not reconnoitred and have not discussed it with all concerned countries...we have unstable borders not only with Burma and India, but with USSR and Mongolia...PM U Nu established talks on this problem; he said in the past, the KMT Government, the Manchu/Qing Governments all did not discuss this problem. We are willing to discuss this problem, but we ask for a little time.

According to the Chinese version, Nehru did not carry the conversation further, nor did he say anything about India's boundaries being 'clear and were not a matter for argument.'[11]

Later, Nehru himself admitted to Krishna Menon in a letter written on 6 May, 1956, that 'China never clearly accepted our frontier as it is. All that they have said is that the old maps are not reliable.' It seems that Zhou deliberately asked for time for he wished to keep the South-East Asian states 'off-balance' and ever so slightly nervous, considering that they faced not only an uncertain border, but also were unsure of the loyalty of their large overseas Chinese populations. Burma in particular, was conscious of this. Interestingly, Zhou suggested to Nehru that they issue a joint communiqué at the end of their talks. But for some inexplicable reason, Nehru demurred. Had he agreed to do so, much trouble may possibly have been avoided later, for Zhou would have had to spell out in writing China's position on the border question.

Soon after Nehru's return from China, the Chinese Embassy at Delhi on 1 November, 1954, distributed revised editions of old KMT maps showing even larger areas of India as parts of China. These were circulated with copies of the fortnightly 'People's China.'[12] Unfortunately, a spokesman of the Ministry of External Affairs completely ignored the issue.[13] Nehru, perhaps a little wiser, told a private meeting of senior Foreign Office officials that he had 'received a powerful impact of China's arrogant nationalism which had only a thin veneer of international Communism.' Nehru emphasized that '*sooner or later this nationalism would assert itself and when that happened China would pose a problem for the whole of Asia*' [emphasis added].[14] Nehru's hesitations were about Chinese nationalism and not about Chinese Communism. At this point, despite his private hesitations, Nehru seems to have been easily satisfied with Zhou's reply on the question of erroneous alignment of the boundary as shown on Chinese maps.[15] Escott Reid, the then Canadian High Commissioner, recalled that he spoke with Pillai, MEA Secretary General, who told him that the issue of the Sino-Indian boundary had not been raised with the Chinese as Nehru felt that 'the time was not ripe', although the question of wrong Chinese maps had been raised.[16]

It was Zhou, during his visit to India in December 1956 – January 1957, who took the initiative to raise with Nehru the issue of Tibet and the McMahon Line. The question of incorrect maps was never considered.[17] When Zhou raised the Tibetan issue, Nehru probably had at the back of his mind a telegram sent by the Indian Ambassador to China on 28 October, 1956,[18] warning him that Zhou had told the Burmese leader, U Nu, that the McMahon Line was 'immoral' as it was based on an 'unequal treaty.' But for the sake of an agreement the Chinese would accept it as a *de facto* border. After his meeting with Zhou, Nehru penned a minute that this time Zhou told him verbally that they [the Chinese] proposed to recognize the McMahon Line with India just as they proposed do so with Burma. Zhou also confided to Nehru that the Tibetans had asked the Chinese Government to raise the issue of the boundary with India during the 1954 negotiations, but that the Chinese Government had declined to do so. An important point to note is that Zhou surprisingly, did not raise any issue regarding the Western sector, for he [Zhou] would by now be totally aware of the Indian alignment of the boundary in this sector. Undoubtedly, the Chinese Embassy in Delhi would certainly have communicated the new maps issued by India under Nehru's directive of 1954, that indicated a firm alignment in this sector. Why Zhou did not do so is not clear, but it had the effect of confirming in Nehru's mind the correctness of his decision in 1954 to show the alignment in the Western sector by a firm line.

The Sino-Burmese Boundary Agreement ratified later on 4 January, 1961, confirms the McMahon alignment along the Burmese section of the McMahon Line. Incidentally, when the Simla Agreement was signed in 1914, Burma was a part of India. The McMahon Line runs for about 192 kilometres in Burma. Nehru, despite being forewarned, still maintained his trust in Zhou and did not, for some inexplicable reason, insist that this assurance as conveyed by Zhou, on the McMahon Line be formalized and put in a joint communiqué. Nor did Nehru give Zhou a map, officially informing him about the Indian alignment. This was on the suggestion of the then Foreign Secretary who, in a rather poor advice, expressed the thought that 'we should not be impolite to our guests.'[19]

Nevertheless, Chinese duplicity was evident when these so-called 'old' maps showing redrawn and revised boundaries in other sectors, in one case to 'restore' considerable territory to Burma and in another to 'cede' some territory to Mongolia, were being openly distributed by them.[20] This pretention, that these were only old KMT maps, was further punctured when the Indian Political Officer in Sikkim reported in 1956 that the Chinese were distributing, in their thousands, recently produced 'old' maps of the Himalayan region with Tibetan markings. These 'maps' showed China and Tibet as the palm of the hand with Ladakh, Nepal, Sikkim, Bhutan and the North-East as the five fingers; thus indicating that these territories were a part of Tibet (China). When queried, the Chinese once again dodged the issue by saying that these were not 'official maps.'[21] It was also noticed that the Chinese Embassy in London did the same [Nehru to Foreign Secretary, 8 April, 1958]! What the Chinese were actually doing on the ground could only have added to the misgivings that were beginning to gain ground in Nehru's mind.

However, to be fair to the Chinese, Zhou at no point ever said that he disagreed with the alignment shown on 'old' Chinese maps, nor did he commit himself or comment on the alignment as shown on Indian maps. He simply emphasized that they were willing to discuss the issue, but needed a little time. Years later, Nehru told the Rajya Sabha on 9 December, 1959, that India had opted *not* to take up the boundary issue with the Chinese because '*we felt we should hold by our position and that with the lapse of time and events would confirm it and by the time, perhaps, when the challenge came to it we could be in a much stronger position to face it.*' Nehru to his own regret many years later, speculated that he should have forced the issue then and there or even much earlier, but certainly before signing the 1954 Agreement. But that was being wiser after the event for with the signing of the 1954 Agreement, all the cards that India held had totally lost their value.

While India's preparations to consolidate its position on the border were ponderously slow, China, from the time of her occupation of Tibet, began to visibly strengthen her position with a single-minded purpose. In the First Five Year Plan [1953-58] China spent a staggering US$ 4.3 billion on 'transportation and communications' that constituted some 11.7 per cent of the total development expenditure, the bulk of which was spent on building roads to connect mainland China with Tibet.[22] On 25 December, 1954, regular motor traffic was opened on the 2,300 kilometre Lhasa-Chamdo highway built at an average elevation of 390 metres that crosses 14 major mountain ranges and 12 major rivers, including the Mekong and the Salween. The 2,100 kilometre Xining-Lhasa highway completed in 1955 was paved with asphalt and built at an average elevation of 400 metres.

A year later both these highways became all-weather highways. Thus, by April 1956, more than 4,300 kilometres of roads had been built within Tibet, including feeder roads right up to the Indian border. The significance of these stupendous engineering feats with a concise strategic intent was clearly missed by the Indian leadership. Chinese resoluteness in developing its highway and communications systems, as opposed to India's tardy progress was there for all to see.

It was the Chinese who first brought the boundary dispute to the fore. Less than three months after the 1954 Tibet Agreement was signed, China decided to test the waters and also to signal that she did not accept the boundary alignment as shown on Indian maps. Very carefully, so as not to arouse any suspicions in the Indian mind, a small party of Chinese soldiers crossed the Tunjun La pass in the middle sector and as there was no Indian presence there, occupied an area about three to four kilometres *South* of the pass. The Chinese renamed the Tunjun La [Pass] as Hu Ji and set up a PLA post there. The Chinese claimed, in a formal note on 17 July, 1954, that Indian troops had intruded into 'Wu-Je of the Ali area of the Tibet Region of China.'[23] The Chinese also claimed that this area was 'one day's journey from the Niti Pass.' It will be recalled that Niti Pass is one of the passes that is mentioned in the 1954 Agreement, but the Chinese note did not clarify whether the 'Ali area' is South or North of the Niti Pass or the Tunjun La [Pass], or even its exact location.

India not only denied the presence of any troops in the 'Ali' region, but stated that a party of the Border Security Force was encamped at Hoti Plain, which is South-East of Niti pass, and none had crossed the Niti pass which is mentioned in the 1954 Agreement.[24] It was later clarified that Indian border security forces were at Bara Hoti on the Hoti Plain which was actually South of the Tunjun La [Pass].[25] The Barahoti grazing ground is a vast amphitheatre at an elevation of about 14,000 feet and the fact that it is South of the pass was also proven when an Indian patrol that visited the area saw the arrival of a Chinese PLA party coming over the pass! There is a stream that originates from the pass, flows South and joins the Dhauli Ganga, leaving no one in any doubt that the pass is indeed the watershed.[26] When, in a meeting on 19 April, 1958, Indian officials asked the Chinese to give the exact longitude and latitude of the area claimed by them, the Chinese refused to do so, blandly stating that these were 'imperialistic' terms! The real reason came out two years later when the Chinese claim was amplified many times and expanded to about 2,500 square kilometres.

This local dispute at Barahoti has its origins in British times and had lingered on for many years, with correspondence between local Indian and Tibetan officials that started from about 1894 to the time of India's independence. However, the real importance lies in the fact that, for the first time, the new Chinese Government laid claim to Indian territory *South* of the Himalayas. Other incursions soon followed. In the middle sector, intrusions took place at Dam-Zan, Nilang and Shipkila Pass. Nehru was taken by surprise. But he was still unconvinced that these incursions represented any large-scale territorial claims. He later clarified on 17 November, 1959, that as regards Barahoti 'there was a minor dispute with old Tibetan Government officials...but no conflict as there were complaints by us to them and them to us. They used to send their tax collectors who used to collect grazing fee and other fees.' Nehru attributed Chinese actions due to the excessive zeal of local officials.[27] Nehru thought that by attributing Chinese incursions on the border to 'local zeal', the Chinese would be able to safely withdraw without any loss of face. Nehru wanted to show a way out for the Chinese. No one in the Indian establishment questioned why such 'zeal' had not been shown by 'local' Chinese officials before the 1954 Agreement was signed. Indian officials did not correctly assess the signals emanating from Beijing, that by crossing the boundary alignment as shown by India, China was clearly signalling that it did not accept the Indian alignment. Even at this stage, Nehru felt that such differences could be settled quietly through diplomatic negotiations and, therefore, decided that these incursions need not be made public.

Although outward calm prevailed in Tibet, Chinese high handedness with local Tibetans soon reached a point of open resistance. Tibetan resistance was also, no doubt, fuelled by soaring inflation, particularly of food-grains. By April 1953, food inflation had risen by 50 per cent over the previous month and obtaining foodgrains was beyond the reach of the common man.[28] At first, the Chinese encouraged the Dalai Lama to come out of his Palace, thinking that this would lower his god-like image. It was a major miscalculation by the Chinese, for the more the Dalai Lama came out, the more his image with the Tibetans improved. The Tibetans felt an affectionate regard for him and the more he was seen, the more he was loved. In public perception, the entire blame for the sorry conditions in Tibet was laid at the door of the Chinese and not, as the Chinese had hoped, on the Tibetan Government of the Dalai Lama.

Chinese officials were fixed, dogmatic and inflexible in their dealings with Tibetans. It was only a matter of time before trouble erupted. Resistance against the Chinese first started in Eastern Tibet where the Khampas, organized as guerrilla bands, started attacking roads and bridges and isolated Chinese convoys. According to the Dalai Lama, the main reason for the revolt was the introduction of agrarian reforms by the Chinese and their interference with the social and economic life of the people.[29] The Khampas are tough, touchy and a flamboyant people who had never been under the sway of the Chinese or the Tibetan Government in Lhasa. At best, they only owed nominal loyalty to the Lhasa authorities. When the Chinese initiated military action against them, a large number of fighters gravitated towards Lhasa, further escalating the situation. When combined with the disaffected people in Lhasa, the combination became volatile.

Few Chinese officials could travel inside Tibet unless accompanied by military escort and that too in large convoys. Apart from Lhasa, Shigatse and other towns as also the main highways, the rebels controlled most of the countryside. The

Chinese estimated the strength of the rebels somewhere between 23,000 to 85,000 fighters.[30] The reaction of the Chinese authorities to the revolt was swift as it was brutal. They not only used harsh repressive measures, but bombed the historic monasteries of Changtreng, Litang and Batang.[31] Chinese aircraft flattened many towns and villages with savage, repressive air action. There were huge casualties.

As the 2,500th anniversary of Buddha's attainment of salvation fell in November 1956, India decided to invite the Dalai Lama to participate in the celebrations. Accordingly, in 1955, an invitation to the Dalai and Panchen Lamas was issued through the Chinese Embassy. However, in February 1956, the Chinese told the Indian Ambassador that the Dalai Lama could not participate due to preoccupations 'at home.' When the Indian Consul-General in Lhasa queried the Dalai Lama, the latter expressed surprise as he had not received any invitation, nor had he been consulted! In July 1956, after much hesitation and dithering, the Chinese finally allowed the Dalai Lama to visit India to attend the 2,500th birth anniversary of Lord Buddha.

The Dalai Lama and the Panchen Lama arrived by separate planes in Delhi on 24 November, 1956. Nehru received them at the airport. The Dalai Lama received a tremendous welcome wherever he went. The Chinese were clearly rattled and very nervous. Zhou Enlai rushed to India and was in India thrice in the short space of two months [28 November, 1956 to 10 December, 1956, 30 December, 1956 to 3 January, 1957, and 24-26 January, 1957]. The Chinese wanted to know why the Dalai Lama had received an official welcome on a scale usually reserved only for a visiting Head of State. The Dalai Lama complained to Nehru about the bleak and tense situation prevailing in Tibet and said that he was contemplating seeking political asylum in India. Even Zhou, in his meeting with Nehru, expressed apprehension of such a move.[32] Nehru, though mentally cool to the Dalai Lama's entreaties, took the unusual step of informing Zhou of Dalai's complaints. Zhou promised to rectify the situation and respect Tibetan autonomy as per the Seventeen-Point Agreement of 1951. Based on this assurance, Nehru, with great difficulty, was able to persuade the Dalai Lama to return to Lhasa.[33] The Dalai Lama was not very happy and told Apa Pant, the then Political officer in Sikkim, that 'the medicine that the Doctor [Nehru] is proposing for my weakness seems to be bitter and unpalatable. I do not know whether I would really get well with that medicine.'[34] Disillusioned and bitter, the Dalai Lama very slowly made his way back to Tibet reaching Lhasa only in March 1957.

Present Chinese writings paint a very different picture of what actually happened during the Dalai Lama's visit to India. According to the Chinese, the visit of the Dalai and Panchen Lamas was for the Indian Government a 'golden chance to incite the Dalai Lama's determination to go on the path of Tibet's independence.' And that Nehru met the Dalai Lama on the 27 and 28 November, 1956, and on both occasions pointed out that if China goes beyond the scope of the Seventeen-Point Agreement, 'Tibet will face difficulties; but that India will help Tibet.' Chinese writings give full credit to PM Zhou for persuading the Dalai Lama to go back to Tibet and, thus, 'India's attempt regarding changing Tibet *as its protected state* [emphasis added] once again suffered a setback.'[35]

The Chinese, who should have been grateful to Nehru, instead never forgot this humiliation of Nehru's well meaning intervention to resolve what they considered to be a purely 'internal' matter. Zhou also took it personally, for it showed that Nehru had far more influence in Tibet than Zhou did. For a time the Chinese, in a show of conciliation, postponed any further 'reforms' in Tibet and even thinned out PLA troops. But this did not affect Chinese determination to continue to consolidate their hold over Tibet and to progressively dilute the Dalai Lama's administrative control. The Tibetan issue now evolved into something wider and less manageable.[36]

The situation in Tibet, however, was grim and deteriorating rapidly. Inflation and a general price rise, aggravated further by a large influx of Han Chinese settlers, soon led to further clashes and unrest. The Tibetan economy could not sustain such a large influx of soldiers and settlers at the same time. Inevitably, repression followed and this led to the postponement of Nehru's projected visit to Lhasa, which had been scheduled for May 1958 [Chinese Note, 15 July, 1958]. The invitation to visit Tibet had earlier been sent by the Dalai Lama soon after his visit to India in 1956, via the Chinese authorities. The Dalai Lama's invitation letter was heavily amended by the Chinese and a fresh draft was prepared, which the Dalai Lama was asked to sign. It took them nearly a year to forward the invitation to Nehru! Soon after seeking a postponement, the visit was totally abandoned. This represented another loss of face for the Chinese. Nehru, instead of visiting Tibet went to Bhutan, but had to cross Tibetan territory where he received rather cavalier treatment from Chinese officials present. Nehru confided to the Bhutanese King that there was much discontent in Tibet and, in fact, Tibet was an occupied country.[37]

The situation in Tibet was fast developing to a point where a major conflagration was in the offing. Perhaps the Chinese were aware of the dangers ahead. With Eastern Tibet in turmoil over the Khampa rebellion and the general unrest it generated, the Chinese were very concerned with their lines of communications to Tibet. By this time, the Chinese were also aware of the 'foreign hand' in propelling the Khampa rebellion. Ever since 1956 the CIA had begun to undertake covert action to stoke the fires of the Khampa rebellion. The CIA programme was based on 'US Government commitments to the Dalai Lama in 1951 and 1956.' It consisted of political action, paramilitary and intelligence operations towards 'lessening the influence and capabilities of the Chinese regime' and towards the creation of capability of resistance against the Chinese 'in line with US policy objectives as stated in National Security Council Document No.5913/1.'[38] Between September 1957 and January 1960 the CIA made 19 airdrops of 47 trained Khampas and 18 airdrops of arms inside Tibet.[39] In early

1958, the PLA captured some of the Khampas and, undoubtedly, the whole exercise would by then be known to the Chinese. This US instigated effort, poorly funded and ill-planned, lasted till 1971. It was totally abandoned when Sino-US reconciliation took place that year. The Dalai Lama felt that the CIA effort 'caused more harm to the Tibetans than the Chinese.'

It would be extremely naïve to imagine that the Chinese did not suspect an Indian hand *in collusion* with the CIA [emphasis added]. By 1956-57, the Chinese had become highly suspicious of India and felt that Nehru was indulging in 'bad faith' and 'surreptitiously' meddling in Tibet.[40] The Chinese hinted at such an involvement when they officially protested to India on 10 July, 1958, in a note by alleging that Kalimpong was being used by 'Tibetan reactionaries, Americans and by the Chiang Kaishek clique' as a base to actively incite 'a handful of reactionaries hidden in Tibet for an armed revolt there.' Much later, Zhou confirmed Chinese suspicions of Nehru's involvement when he told Neville Maxwell, in an interview published on 19 December, 1971, that 'Nehru had been intriguing with the Dalai Lama and Panchen Lama since 1956, with big power backing and encouraging them to rebellion.' It was obvious that Tibet was destined to become the central issue between India and China as the situation in Tibet worsened. But it was also obvious to any impartial observer that India had very little to do with the revolt in Tibet and the subsequent alienation between Lhasa and Beijing. To ascribe the revolt to machinations of Indian intelligence agencies is to give them far more credit than is due.

As major lines of communications from mainland China to Tibet in the East passed through this turbulent and rebellious territory, it, therefore, became essential that the Western artery linking Sinkiang with Tibet be kept safe and secure. The Chinese had used this Western route from Khotan in Sinkiang earlier to cross the Aksai Chin to enter Tibet during their invasion in 1950. Earlier in 1716, the Dzungars [a Central Asian tribe] had used the same route when attacking Western Tibet and, eventually, Lhasa. The trouble, however, was that this route passed through what was ostensibly Indian Territory. It, therefore, had the potential of becoming a major flash point and a major dispute with India. The Chinese were totally aware of this. They were prepared to take the necessary risk of alienating India for the possession of this road-link, since it was a strategic necessity for them and they were prepared to face the consequences of their action.

It was the Chinese who first brought the question of the Aksai Chin road into the public domain. The Chinese probably waited to do so till the Dalai Lama was safely back in Lhasa, and had given up all thoughts of staying back in India. Till then, Chinese had quietly and steadily built the road across the Aksai Chin. Zhou Enlai told Kissinger that they had started the construction of the road in 1951 [Kissinger's meeting with Zhou on 10 July, 1971, Beijing]. This road is now known as NH219, and covers a distance of about 160 kilometres inside Indian Territory. The first inkling that something was afoot came in 1955 from

India's Trade Agent for Western Tibet, Laxman Singh Jangpangi, who informed Delhi that the construction of such a road was underway. The report was overlooked.[41] In January 1955, the Chinese Embassy in Delhi also circulated an official magazine containing a map of China that showed the North-East border as claimed by it.[42] This, too, was suppressed. By May 1956, the Government of India had sufficient reports that the Chinese were building and regularly using the Aksai Chin road.[43] Nehru confirmed later [Lok Sabha/23 February, 1960] that by 1955, reports had reached India of Chinese activity on the Aksai China road but, 'we were not clear whether this motor way crossed our territory.' As there was no conclusive proof, no protest was lodged with the Chinese then. Zhou was later to complain quite facetiously to Kissinger in a meeting on 10 July, 1973, that Nehru 'suddenly' raised the issue of the road with him *in 1956* [emphasis added]. [In actual fact Nehru never did in 1956] Kushak Bakula, the Ladakhi Buddhist leader on a visit to Tibet in early 1957, also picked up information that a new road had been constructed linking Tibet with Xinjiang [Sinkiang]. He duly informed New Delhi. No one in Delhi paid any attention.

On 2 September, 1957, the *People's Daily* published a small map [2 ¼" × ¾"] showing a road linking Xinjiang [Sinkiang] with Tibet. On the same day the Indian Embassy in Beijing reported that:

> Chinese have announced today that a motorable road from Yeh near Yarkhand across Karakoram to Ladakh and Gartok has been built and will be open to traffic in October. Road appears to pass through Aksai plain which is Kashmir territory.[44]

It was too small a map to indicate for certain whether the road crossed the Indian Territory of Ladakh [Aksai Chin] or not. From Delhi instructions were sent on 7 September, 1957, to the Embassy in Beijing to ascertain which of the two routes the Chinese were referring to for there were two routes that could possibly be followed from Xinjiang [Sinkiang] to Western Tibet. The Embassy could not give a precise answer. The question, therefore, was what should be done? To remind the Indians, just in case they had missed the *People's Daily* article, *China Pictorial* [No. 95, pp.20-21, July, 1958] along with the Soviet Weekly 'The New Times', both having extensive circulations, published the road alignment yet again in July 1958. Nehru, for obvious reasons, down played the Soviet publication and later speaking on 22 April, 1959 in the Lok Sabha said that 'so far as the Russian maps are concerned, I think they had merely copied them from Chinese maps without probably going into the matter.'

The Chinese decision to publish the map showing the road linking Xinjiang [Sinkiang] with Tibet and cutting across Aksai Chin vividly demonstrated that India was not in control of territory claimed by it. Thus, the decision taken in 1954 by Nehru to show by a firm line India's boundary in the Western sector was not followed up with any action on the ground to secure India's borders. This was quite unlike the Eastern sector, where Indian administration was energetically established right up to the McMahon Line. Therefore, the claimed boundary line in the Western sector remained on paper only and was easily overturned by China as and when it wished to do so. The Chinese had decided that the time was now 'ripe.' And they chose the Aksai Chin in Ladakh in the Western sector to make their point. The Western sector was, for the first time, now confirmed publicly as in dispute.

Due to severe winter conditions it was not till June 1958 that India decided to send out two patrols to check the veracity of the *People's Daily* report. Of the two patrols that set out from Leh, a party from the army led by Lt. Iyengar went North and a police party led by DSP, Karam Singh, went to the Southern extremity of the road. After a long and arduous journey, the Southern party reached the Southern extremity of the road and returned with the information that the road did indeed cross Indian Territory. As there was no information about the Northern party, the Chinese were formally asked in a note on 18 October, 1958, about their whereabouts. The Chinese responded on 3 November, 1958, that the Indian party was detained on 8 and 12 September, 1958, on the Xinjiang-Tibet highway and that the captured Indian personnel were being 'deported' via the Karakoram pass on 22 October, 1958. It was really fortuitous that they were found stranded near the pass. The Chinese just left them there to make their own way back!

Earlier, on 21 August, 1958, India while drawing attention to the *China Pictorial* Issue No. 95 of July 1958, protested to the Chinese for constructing the road through Indian Territory. Included in the protest note was an offer to supply a copy of the 'Political Map of India', 3rd Edition issued in 1956. *This was possibly the first time ever that India had officially offered to supply to China the map showing the alignment of the India-China boundary as depicted by India!* [emphasis added]

The Chinese, hoping to lull Nehru into inaction responded on 3 November, 1958, by stating the Chinese Government had not as yet 'undertaken a survey of China's boundary, nor consulted the countries concerned...and that a new way of drawing the boundary of China will be decided in accordance with the results of the consultations and the survey...and that it would not make any changes of the boundary on its own.' The sting was in the last sentence. The Sino-Indian boundary dispute and particularly the dispute over the Aksai Chin was now out in the open.

The Aksai Chin is a bleak, blistering alpine desert that is about 17,000-18,000 ft high. There is no human habitation there and no sign that any has ever existed in time. It is bereft of any vegetation, except for a few bushes here and there and the plateau has existed over several millenniums in complete, isolated and stark desolation. The water in the lakes is brackish and there are no fish in the waters. No birds can be seen anywhere. To paraphrase Nehru's famous quotation, 'it is a territory where not a blade of grass grows!'[45] For India, it was just an alpine desert, of no particular value, but for China it was an important passage. It was a strategic necessity.

Why did the Chinese publish the map in 1957 and thereby awaken a sleeping India is a matter of conjecture. It is clear that this news item could never have been published in the *People's Daily* without clearance at the highest level, for after all, till 1957, the Chinese had maintained complete silence. To publish and highlight the construction of the road was to deliberately make the dispute public and, thus, put Nehru on the back foot. Having claimed Aksai Chin as a part of Indian Territory, how could Nehru not have known about the road that the Chinese had built? The Chinese would later taunt Nehru precisely on this point. To be fair it does not take much to build a road in such a terrain. As Nehru pointed out in Parliament on 31 August, 1959, 'roads in such desert areas are of a peculiar type. The only thing that you have to do to build a road is to even the ground a little and remove the stones and shrubs.' It was for this reason perhaps that detection of Chinese activities went unnoticed.

Meanwhile, the Indian Ambassador in China was also reporting in 1957 that a 'certain coolness' was developing towards India. The Chinese press began to equate India and Pakistan on Kashmir and Zhou, in a speech to the NPC, minimized India's role in promoting world peace. Probably the huge, tumultuous and very warm welcome received by the Dalai Lama in 1956 in India had alarmed the ever suspicious Chinese.

At this point, the Chinese perception was that the usefulness of Nehru to their cause was over. They had obtained what they wanted when Nehru acquiesced in the Chinese occupation of Tibet, for Nehru should have known that diplomatic goods, once delivered, are never returned. The Chinese now wrote Nehru off as a 'bourgeois nationalist' and they were determined to undermine his position in the world so that India's position as an alternative model of development, too, would simultaneously diminish. Accordingly, the Chinese now began to belittle India, to diminish its stature as an alternative model of development and to undermine its status as a leader of the non-aligned nations.[46] The Chinese view of Nehru underwent yet another metamorphosis. From being a 'lackey of Western imperialism' and another 'Chiang Kaishek', to 'a friend' who was feted in Beijing by the Chinese leaders, including Mao, Nehru was now dubbed as 'arrogant.' Zhou was reportedly to claim to *The Times* of London later that 'I have never met a more arrogant man than Nehru.' The Chinese view of Nehru seemed to change colour as political expediency demanded. Clearly, Sino-Indian relations were now destined for very rough weather. Perhaps the Chinese correctly assessed Nehru's innate distaste for war, for Nehru firmly believed that a modern civilized statesman should remain above such barbarism.[47] Later, Mao contemptuously belittled India when he told Kissinger that 'India did not win independence. If it did not attach itself to Britain, it attaches itself to the Soviet Union.'[48] The inference being that the Indian leadership *did not fight* for independence, but were simply given a hand-out [emphasis added].

It is also equally clear that the Chinese had carefully surmised that they need not fear any military retaliation, for India was in no position to do so. What then were Chinese motives? What did they hope to achieve by publicly igniting a dispute with India at this juncture, or was this a part of the larger Sino-Soviet rivalry, of which India was one of the key points of contention? Was Tibet an issue or did this initiative to make this dispute public have a bearing on domestic Chinese politics?

On 25 February, 1956, Khrushchev made a secret speech at the CPSU 20th Party Congress, denouncing Stalin that reverberated throughout the socialist world. While initially silent, the Chinese took it rather badly. Khrushchev's speech was an unintended assessment of Mao's recent mistakes.[49] Relations between the two Communist giants started deteriorating, principally over what policy should be followed to usher in a socialist society at home and over policy towards imperialism. Implicit in this was the attitude towards non-aligned and neutral countries such as India. The dispute had ideological, political and economic underpinnings, as both Soviet Russia and China were at different stages of development. As Khrushchev began to preach the virtues of 'peaceful co-existence' with the West, the dispute soon became both bitter and shriller as the Chinese surmised that Khrushchev had no stomach left for a fight against US 'Imperialism.'

At the same time, leadership conflicts within China led Mao Zedong to exploit these differences to outflank his opponents at home by tarring them with the brush of being revisionists in league with foreign elements. Facing acute economic distress, Mao replaced the development model that the People's Republic of China (PRC) had inherited and hitherto followed, with a development strategy resembling earlier Soviet policies that had already been openly discredited in Soviet Russia. Mao pushed for the Great Leap Forward with disastrous results. There was rural distress and famine stalked the land, particularly in provinces such as Gansu and Sichuan, considered to be China's rice bowl. In 1960, grain production in China plummeted to 75.5 per cent of that in 1958. In many provinces, people started fleeing as they have always done in China's history.[50] Chinese statistics published later in 1990 indicated that nearly 310,000 people died in 1959 and a staggering 13$^1/_2$ million died in 1960.[51] Jung Chang, in her recent book on Mao, records a figure of 38 million dead for the period 1958-62. Journalist Yang Jisheng suggests a figure of 36 million dead for the period 1958-62, based on officially published statistics.[52] No matter whatever the figures are, there is no doubt that millions of Chinese simply starved to death. That there was a severe shortage of food is also underlined by the fact that in 1961, China produced only 160 million tons of foodgrains [Zhou to Lord Montgomery] and had to import nearly three million tons at a cost of US $200 m.[53] So severe were the conditions that in 1962, in one month alone, nearly 170,000 refugees fled to Hong Kong.[54] No period in recent Chinese history parallels the economic decline that occurred at this point in time. In 1961 alone, China's GDP declined by a whopping 27 per cent! [55]

The Indian Embassy from Beijing, too, reported the acute distress that was quite noticeable in China. Even in Beijing, the Embassy reported shortages of food, black marketing and disappearance of meat from the market and closure of restaurants. Disaffection and indifference of Chinese officials was noticed, too. The Chinese authorities explained to Indian officials in Beijing that 'shortages' were due to the unprecedented adverse international situation that China faced and the need to 'stock-up' food grains for strategic reserves. The spectre of a foreign 'threat' was used by the leadership to dampen growing internal dissidence. Astutely, the Indian Embassy opined that China as a last resort, 'might adopt diversionary tactics and assume an international violent posture to wade over internal difficulties.'[56] It was to prove to be a very prescient assessment. Shrewdly, Mao exempted the PLA from such hardships and food was always made available for the troops.

Nevertheless, Mao's prestige plummeted and fell rapidly at home. On 27 April, 1959, Mao was replaced as the President of the People's Republic by Liu Shaoqi. There were sufficient indications that serious internal dissensions within the leadership were on the rise that eventually culminated in the sacking of the Defence Minister, Peng Dehuai. Mao, determined to regain absolute power, now began to plot the overthrow of his detractors. He shrewdly linked them to Soviet 'revisionism' and to prove his point, it became necessary to radicalize policy. The radicalization of China's domestic policies over the years also made it necessary to radicalize its foreign policy and to make it even more confrontational. There was a close enmeshing of foreign and domestic policies.[57]

Khrushchev's open espousal of a policy of peaceful coexistence with the West caused immediate tension with China and, as differences over this policy grew, it tended to dominate the Sino-Soviet discourse. In November 1957, at the 40th anniversary celebrations of the Great October Revolution in Moscow, Mao took the line, 'that the East wind prevails over the West wind' and that in the newly liberated countries of Asia *unless a positive militant line was taken*, 'Communism would lose to the nationalist bourgeoisie' [emphasis added]. Mao was determined to act and found it exceedingly difficult to believe that a country that could launch the Sputnik in 1957 would opt for peaceful co-existence with the capitalist West. Flowing from this were differences over Soviet Russia's refusal to hand over designs for a nuclear bomb as promised earlier, the handling of the Taiwan Straits crisis in 1958 precipitated by China and economic disagreements—in particular trade, leading to the sudden withdrawal of Soviet specialists from China. The Chinese sensed that Soviet Russia would not back them militarily in case of a conflict with the US over Taiwan. Their fears were confirmed when Khrushchev signed a communiqué with Eisenhower on 27 September, 1959, stating that 'all outstanding international questions should be settled not by the application of force but by peaceful means through negotiations.' The British assessment was that this was 'an admonition to the Chinese.'[58]

The US had, meanwhile, hinted very broadly that should China invade Taiwan, nuclear weapons might be used. The Chinese were, thus, stopped in their tracks if they had ever contemplated 'liberating' Taiwan. The personality clashes between Khrushchev and Mao, too, were a factor. The Chinese side was far more active in pursuing the Sino-Soviet dispute and, from 1959 onwards it was Mao who pushed for the collapse of the Sino-Soviet alliance, as he became conscious of the fact that the Soviets would not risk a conflict on their behalf with the US.[59] Chinese policy towards both the US and Soviet Russia had reached a dead end, with little to show for concrete results!

Flowing from its policy of peaceful co-existence was Soviet Russia's open espousal of non-aligned India. Starting with Malenkov's praise of India's non-aligned foreign policy at the 19th Party Congress in October 1952, the Soviets consistently praised India. The Soviet approach was to boost the prestige of India and induce it to take over the leadership role of the Afro-Asian countries. As the *Pravda* of 14 December, 1955, declared, 'India as a great power should be given the first place amongst the great powers of the world.' The *Izvestia* of 4 April, 1957, went even further to state 'that without the participation of India not a single major problem of Asia and the world could be solved.'

The Chinese suspected that the Soviets were deliberately building up India to do them down. As the Soviets praised India, the Chinese disliked it for the very same reasons. Deterioration of Sino-Soviet relations ran parallel to the deterioration of Sino-Indian relations. In contrast to the wholesome praise by the Soviets, the Chinese were very sceptical of India's non-aligned and domestic policies. 'It is impossible to build socialism in India under a reactionary like Nehru', declared the *Hongqi* [Red Flag] of 21 October, 1959. A little later [22 October, 1959] the same magazine asked the question: 'What has Nehru got to show for his socialism? And again: 'India's growing reliance on imperialism has disastrously blocked the development of the Indian economy.'

The Chinese also bitterly complained that Soviet Russia had promised 'Indian reactionaries' Rs 5 billion [US $135m] from 1955 onwards *to begin their campaign* against China! [Actual figure was US $325m] On 13 September, 1959, the Soviets extended a further US $375m to India to help finance its Third Five Year Plan and in August, 1960, it supplemented this loan with a promise of an additional US $125m. This doubled the aid previously given.[60] Earlier, to add to Chinese chagrin, Khrushchev had proposed on 19 July, 1958, that a summit meeting be held attended by the Soviet Union, US, UK, France and India to 'devise ways of solving international tensions.'[61] Significantly, while India was invited, China was left out. The Chinese were miffed.

Nehru visited Washington for the second time in December 1956. Unlike his last visit in 1949, the Americans this time went flat out to flatter Nehru. He was given a 19 gun salute on arrival, an honour normally reserved only for visiting

Heads of State. President Eisenhower and Nehru talked for over 14 hours, spread over two or three occasions. Eisenhower received Nehru at the White House on Christmas day and took him personally to his farm at Gettysburg. 'All very unusual' remarked Nehru, but ever so clearly delighted [Note by Nehru on 8 January, 1957]. Unlike in 1949, Nehru, too, was in a chastened mood for he desperately needed US economic aid if India's five year plans were to succeed.[62] The British also suspected that this transformation lay in Nehru's recognition that the success or failure of India's development plans hinged, to a substantial degree, on the continued flow of US capital investment. Nehru was too shrewd a politician to let his personal distaste impinge on Indo-US relations, for he recognized that Eisenhower was in a position to 'make a great difference.'[63] After his extensive talks with Nehru in Washington in 1956, Eisenhower had come to the conclusion that India's non-aligned policy was not against US interests. Eisenhower began to criticize 'our tendency to rush out and seek allies' as not very sensible and also called into question the decision to sign the 1954 US-Pakistan Mutual Assistance Agreement, terming it as 'a terrible error.' Not surprisingly, therefore, the US revised its attitude towards India. National Security Council Document of 10 January, 1957, reflects this change and states as follows:

> While respecting India's choice of an independent foreign policy...which will on occasion bring India into opposition to US programs...India must have external (economic) assistance to attain goals of the 5-Year Plans as now envisaged.[64]

The US was now determined to help India. The US was by now aware of the developing Sino-Indian differences on the border and over Tibet, for Nehru went to Washington after he had talked to the Dalai Lama in Delhi.

The Chinese also watched with obvious envy the decision of the Western allies, prompted by the US at the end of August 1958, to pledge US$600 million in new aid to the Indian economy. In May 1960, India and the US signed a US$1.276 billion PL480 Food Agreement, under which 12 million tons of US wheat would be exported to India over a four year period, thus providing India with a much needed cushion.[65] It would be recalled that due to drought conditions, food production in India had fallen by about 10 per cent for the period 1956-58. But for timely US help under PL480, the situation might just have veered out of control. Prices of food grains had also risen 50 per cent for the same period.[66] In addition, by mid-1958, it became obvious that India continued to face a serious foreign exchange crisis. Its reserves were down from US$ 1.5 billion in March 1956 to just about US $457m by June 1958. In an obvious show of support the US Department of State announced shortly thereafter that the US 'desired to assist India in meeting her economic problems.' As a result US aid to India increased sharply, particularly from 1957 onwards, as can be seen from the table below:

(US $ million)

1953	1954	1955	1956	1957	1958	1959	1960	1961	1962
45.1	88.9	113.6	92.8	364.8	305.1	366.7	758.4	667.8	775.1

Not only did US economic aid flow to India, but so did political support. In 1959, President Eisenhower received a rapturous welcome when he visited India, which was undoubtedly partially as a result of China's belligerence on the border. Senator Kennedy called India 'the hinge of fate in Asia' and wanted 'India to win that race with China.'[67] Economic pressure, conceded Nehru, made India reluctant to appear 'as a crusader on the world stage.'[68]

As economic help and political support poured in, Nehru's policy of non-alignment and peaceful co-existence seemed to be spectacularly successful, both with the US as well as with Soviet Russia, in contrast to China's own utter failure. Rebuffed both by Khrushchev and Eisenhower, excluded from both the Western and Soviet power centres, China looked to Asia to provide a platform to raise her flag.[69] A Polish Communist Party delegation that visited China in 1959 came away with the impression that, miffed at being left out of high level negotiations between the US and the Soviets, China had decided to stir up trouble on the Sino-Indian border just as a reminder to the two super powers that there were important areas in the world that could not be settled without China's participation.[70] At this juncture, China was at logger heads with both the US and Soviet Russia and had poor relations with both.

The US assessment, too, was that economic difficulties at home and the increasingly bitter debate with Soviet Russia caused the Chinese to adopt a hard line approach to issues, such as the border dispute with India. That Soviet Russia began to see China as a potential rival has also been underscored by the revelations of the former US Ambassador to India, Chester Bowles. In a meeting in February 1957 largely devoted to Indian issues, Khrushchev did not disagree with Bowles when the latter remarked that both the US and Russia might ultimately face 'a common problem with regard to China.' This meeting took place before the Sino-Soviet break became publicly open. On 10 September, 1959, the then CIA Director, Allen Dulles, gave his assessment of the situation prevailing in China. This is what he said:

> Chinese Communist leaders were in an ugly mood because of their lessened prestige due to the failure of their economic program. However, they refused to admit failure; they maintain the 'leap forward' program is still in force and blame shortcomings on drought. The image of Mao as the 'all-wise father' has been somewhat impaired. The Chinese are showing exasperation at Soviet criticism.... In their present mood, the Chinese leaders are not disposed to retreat from any international positions they have taken [Sino-Indian border].[71]

Therefore, did the Chinese bring the dispute over the Aksai Chin into the open just to show that no matter, however, much both Soviet Russia and the US tried to bolster India, it remained a weak, disorganized country and whose prestige as also that of Nehru could be punctured ever so easily? According to Khrushchev, it was Mao himself 'who stirred up trouble with India, precisely to draw the Soviet Union into it, leaving it [Soviet Union] with no choice but to support him' [Mao].[72] If Mao could not get his way with the Soviet Union or with the United States, this was one way he could dramatically underline the power of China and show its importance. It was a felt strategic need. Mao could also stare down his domestic opponents. For this, a soft target was needed. India, indeed, provided such a target. It appears that differences with India were prompted by 'China's own actions and ambitions.'[73]

By the autumn of 1958, the situation in Tibet began to deteriorate significantly. The guerrilla movement had grown strong enough to ensure that Tibet South of the river Tsangpo [Brahmaputra] was largely out of control of the Chinese. The rebels besieged the Chinese garrison at Zedong [48 kilometres South East of Lhasa], which they had to abandon after taking severe casualties.[74] Similarly, in January 1959, the town of Dongqing was invested. Gradually the fighting spread towards Lhasa, where a large number of disaffected persons arrived to take shelter. The Chinese were only able to maintain their position by air lifting additional troops to Tibet and by the land route through the Aksai Chin road, and the newly constructed route through Qinghai. In early March 1959, Lhasa became tense with the arrival of a large number of fighters from other parts of Tibet. The situation was ripe for exploding!

Reports started reaching India of serious tension and agitation in Lhasa. Apparently, the Tibetans gave credence to, and became highly agitated, on hearing rumours that the Dalai Lama was to be kidnapped and taken to exile to mainland China. This apprehension arose due to the rather ineptly worded invitation sent by the local Chinese military commander inviting the Dalai Lama to come to Chinese military headquarters in Lhasa on 10 March, 1959, to witness a dance performance, without his usual military escort. Soon, the Norbulinka Palace of the Dalai Lama was surrounded by thousands of Tibetans who refused to let the Dalai Lama proceed. Some women demonstrators approached the Indian Consul General and requested him to accompany them to the Chinese military headquarters to witness the handing over of a memorandum. This, the Consul General could not do, and rightly refused.

For the first few days the Chinese authorities did not react; presumably they were waiting for orders from Beijing. As could be expected in such tense situations, firing broke out. The Tibetans alleged that on 17 March, 1959, at about 4 pm the Chinese fired two shells towards Dalai Lama's palace, which fell short by about eighty yards. The upshot was that the Tibetan leadership advised the Dalai Lama to leave Lhasa and head towards India to seek shelter there. He did so at about 10 pm on the night of 17 March, 1959. The same night, the Indian Consul-General in Lhasa, Chibber, informed Delhi that the Dalai Lama had left Lhasa in disguise. Braving unprecedented hazards, with a Chinese military unit in hot pursuit, the Dalai Lama finally arrived near the Indian border on 31 March, 1959, and crossed over at Lumla at about 12:30 pm on 3 April, 1959. On the Dalai Lama's written request, he was granted asylum as a humanitarian gesture. Earlier, the Indian Consul-General was informed by Delhi on 19 March, 1959, that the Dalai Lama would, if he so requested, be granted asylum in India.[75] But as the Dalai Lama had already left Lhasa, this information could not be made available to him. Within the Government, only Krishna Menon seemed to have doubts, but these were easily brushed aside by Nehru.[76]

The Chinese were clearly miffed at this action by India, although in 1954 Zhou had personally told Nehru that he had told Panikkar that if such an occasion arose, China would have no objection. Chinese sources much later, perhaps as a face saver, indicated that they were quite 'content' to let the Dalai Lama escape to India. But this was clearly an afterthought. There are reports available that suggest that along the way to India the Dalai Lama was helped by the CIA who not only air dropped food and ammunition, but were in radio contact with the Dalai Lama party through the CIA station at Dacca.[77] Beijing Radio announced the arrival of the Dalai Lama in India on 31 March, 1959. When the Foreign Secretary informed the Chinese Ambassador on 3 April of the arrival in India of the Dalai Lama, the latter must have been quite amused. The fact that the Chinese knew even before officials in Delhi did,[78] does indicate clearly that Chinese intelligence was rather good. The Dalai Lama crossed over to India with an entourage of 80 mules and 96 Tibetans, including his mother and younger sister.

Would the Chinese attitude towards India have been any different if India had refused asylum to the Dalai Lama? Would they have been more forthcoming over the boundary question? There was never any doubt in Nehru's mind at all that he was doing the right thing in offering asylum to the Dalai Lama. Nehru, a freedom fighter and a disciple of Mahatma Gandhi, knew of the natural reverence and respect that the people of India have for holiness and had Nehru not consented to give asylum to the Dalai Lama, considered holy and revered by millions of Indians, his own political future would have been in jeopardy. The Dalai Lama is not only considered the reincarnation of the previous 13 Dalai Lamas, but is considered a reincarnation of Avalokiteshvara or Chen Rezig, the Bodhisattva of compassion, and holder of the White Lotus. The Dalai Lama himself confirms this in his autobiography [From Birth to Exile].

The Chinese also knew that it is the inherent right of a country to offer asylum. They themselves had done so in the case of K I Singh, a Nepalese dissident. PM Zhou admitted as such when he told the then Home Minister Pant [21 April, 1960] that China did not object to India granting asylum to the Dalai Lama, but objected to his carrying out 'anti-China' activities. Khrushchev reminded the Chinese, that they, too, had North Koreans dissidents living in China whom they had not returned to Kim Il-sung. Morarji Desai, the then Finance Minister, reminded Zhou [22 April, 1960] that Karl Marx had himself lived in exile in Britain and there had been no restrictions placed on his political activities. There was no response from Zhou. There is no doubt that had India not granted asylum to the Dalai Lama, the Chinese would have surmised that their pressure on India was working, and that it was necessary to assert even greater pressure to gain even more concessions from India.

The escape of the Dalai Lama from Tibet advertised to the world the utter failure of Chinese policies towards Tibet. It was a blow to their prestige. The main Chinese worry was how could they pose as true advocates of Afro-Asian unity and 'liberators' when they treated the Tibetans so harshly? The Chinese decided to 'control' the situation as quickly as possible. The Chinese crackdown in Tibet started on 23 March, 1959. Thereafter, followed a wave of severe Chinese repressive measures in which thousands of Tibetans were brutally gunned down and a large number fled from Tibet. A captured PLA document states that between March 1959 and September, 1960, nearly 87,000 Tibetans were exterminated [Xiaomie/消灭] through military action.[79] The Chinese abolished any vestige of Tibetan political autonomy and utilized the Tibetan revolt to impose their complete political and military control over Tibet. Even the fig leaf of 'autonomy' was removed.

Externally the Chinese decided to 'seal' the Indo-Tibet border and on 23 April, 1959 the Military Commission of the Chinese Communist Party [CCP] Central Committee issued instructions to PLA units stationed in Tibet to 'control important roads and passages close to the unsettled Indo-Tibet border, including close to the McMahon Line, construct defence works and prevent treacherous bandits from crossing the border in both directions.' Thus, the border that had been peaceful till then became a line of confrontation and as PLA troops moved close to the border, it was a foregone conclusion that this would ultimately precipitate a clash.[80]

Chinese brutality in Tibet aroused strong anti-Chinese feelings in India. In Parliament, in the press and elsewhere there was near unanimous support for the Tibetan cause. Nehru rejected President Rajendra Prasad's suggestion that the actions of the Chinese be denounced as 'new colonialism.'[81] Similar was the reaction in South Asia as also in other parts of the world.

Even the then Pakistani Foreign Minister, Manzur Qadir, appalled at Chinese action against Tibetans said in Washington that 'expansionist tendencies were more noticeable in China than in Russia.'[82] Earlier, Ayub had arrested most Communist leaders, including pro-Chinese leaders such as Maulana Bhasani and Fiaz Ahmed Faiz. Pakistan, despite recognizing the People's Republic as the legitimate Government of China and maintaining warm diplomatic relations with her, consistently voted to postpone the question of seating the PRC in the UN till July 1961. When the question of atrocities committed in Tibet by the Chinese came up before the UN General Assembly on 21 October, 1959, Pakistan unlike India, voted for its inscription. President Ayub Khan instructed the Pakistani

Ambassador at the UN to fully back the Irish-Malaysian resolution that deplored the forcible denial by China of 'the fundamental rights and freedom to the Tibetan people.' The Pakistani representative, Prince Aly Khan, explained Pakistan's position as follows:

> The people of Pakistan have been greatly concerned over the unfortunate events in Tibet. The Tibetan people are our close neighbours. For hundreds of years, they have pursued their traditional way of life. They have a right to choose the way in which they wish to live. Equally, it is the duty of the rest of the world to respect their choice. We consider that the Tibetan question raises above all a profound question of conscience for all members of the UN [emphasis added].[83]

The Chinese reacted violently. Beijing cautioned Pakistan not to 'play imperialist propaganda tunes.'[84] Further, in a note to the Pakistani Government [21 July, 1959] China bluntly warned:

> From 7 April to 12 May, 1959 the Pakistani Foreign Minister...went sofar as to make repeated utterances on the Chinese Government's putting down of the rebellion of a handful of reactionaries on its own territory of Tibet, a purely China's domestic affair—utterances wantonly slandering China, flagrantly interfering in China's internal affairs...should the Pakistani Government continue...it must bear full responsibility.

Undeterred, Pakistan even invited a Muslim Haj delegation from Taiwan, which arrived at Karachi on 29 June, 1959, while on its way to Mecca. This seriously alarmed and irritated China. The Chinese saw in this not just religious compassion but an attempt by Pakistan to foster a 'two-China policy.' President Ayub's offer of joint defence made to India on 24 April, 1959 [*Dawn*, 25 April, 1959], was dubbed by China as 'vicious' and Pakistan was advised to 'pull up the horse before the precipice.'[85] Sino-Pakistan relations were probably at their lowest ebb.

There was considerable confusion in India about Ayub's offer of 'joint defence,' for it was surmised that this offer was only on the table if the Kashmir problem was satisfactorily resolved. High Commissioner Rajeshwar Dayal, was asked to give his assessment and, after a series of meetings with Ayub, he reported to Delhi as follows:

> President has omitted all references to a solution of the pending disputes as an essential pre-condition. He has explained this concept as merely implying that instead of two armies facing each other in mutual hostility across the cease-fire line [CFL] and the two Punjabs, they should pay heed to the real danger from the North and North-West. In my last talk with the President, reported vide HC/438/59 of 5 November, 1959, he went so far as to imply that if some of our forces from the Western border were to be diverted to meet the Chinese peril, Pakistan would not take advantage of the situation.[86]

At about the same time Ayub conveyed through the Indian High Commissioner, Rajeshwar Dayal, a proposal for a meeting with Nehru and also praised Nehru. Ayub said 'I regard him as a very great man indeed... Please assure him and give him my word as a soldier and as a honest man that I am sincerely anxious to build...best possible relations with India.' Dayal, who had served together with Ayub in pre-partition India, conveyed these sentiments to Nehru. Ayub made this offer *after* [emphasis added] Nehru had publicly acknowledged that China had built a road across the Aksai Chin and that there had also been clashes between the two countries.

That China was rattled by Ayub's offer can be seen in the fact that the People's Daily accused Pakistan of playing 'a vicious role.'[87] The Chinese were thoroughly upset with the Ayub Government and, as a *People's Daily* commentator remarked 'since the Ayub Government has come to power the Pakistani Government's attitude to China has become worse than before.'[88] Interestingly, even the Chinese intrusions and subsequent clashes were reported in the Pakistani press as acts of 'intrusion' into India. For example, on 29 August, 1959, the *Dawn* newspaper reported this item under the heading, 'Chinese troops *invade* Bharat on the Tibetan frontier' [emphasis added].

Ayub's offer might possibly have been suspect, might possibly have been linked to Kashmir, but Nehru unfortunately and without realizing the consequences for India, instead of trying to widen the yawning chasm developing between Pakistan and China, let both countries off the hook by publicly belittling Ayub's offer while speaking in the Rajya Sabha on 4 May, 1959, with the remarks, 'joint defence against whom?'[89] It was a thoughtless remark. Nehru realized his folly and later recanted, when he told a press conference in London [on 20 May, 1959] that the Ayub offer was made in a 'friendly spirit.' But it was too late. Ayub was deeply hurt. Indian foreign policy strategists missed a splendid opportunity for further widening Sino-Pak differences. Nehru tried to make amends by writing to Rajeshwar Dayal on 20 May, 1959, that he 'much appreciated his message from Ayub', but also clarified that the question of joint defence did not arise since the approach of the two countries to 'world affairs' was different. It was, indeed, a much softer and a nicer way to state the obvious.

Leaders in India should have been aware of China's consistent wooing of Pakistan. They should have analyzed and thought through carefully why Pakistan was so important for China. Pakistan was the first Muslim country to recognize China on 4 January, 1950. On the Chinese occupation of Tibet, Pakistan maintained complete silence, with PM Liaquat Ali justifying the silence by saying that the events were 'too far away.' Hardly true, for POK is contiguous to Sinkiang/Tibet! Pakistan PM Mohammed Ali met PM Zhou at Bandung. Later speaking at the Political Committee of the Bandung Conference on 23 April, 1955, Zhou told the delegates of his meeting with the then Pakistani PM and disclosed that:

> He [Pak PM] told me that although Pakistan was a party to a military treaty Pakistan was not against China. Pakistan had no fear that China would commit aggression against her. As a result, we achieved mutual understanding.

Zhou went public with Mohammed Ali's private assurances to test whether the Pak PM was sincere or whether he was simply posturing. When Mohammed Ali stood by what he had said and publicly affirmed so, Zhou was convinced in his mind that Pakistan's alliances with the West were only designed to bolster its position against India and were not anti-Chinese in nature. Zhou confirmed to the Pakistani PM that China 'understood' the reasons why she had joined SEATO and Baghdad Pacts.[90] China never publicized the fact that she had protested to Pakistan over the latter joining SEATO. Despite Pakistan joining Western sponsored alliances, China-Pak trade continued to prosper. For example, in 1953, Sino-Pak trade totalled US $ 83.8 million, almost twice as much as Sino-Indian trade, and this trade was not based on defence items!

That Zhou was free from rancour against Pakistan was carefully noted by the then Indian Foreign Secretary.[91] Zhou felt that Pakistan was a state in 'genuine' fear of a larger neighbour. Later it was reported that Pakistan received a private message from Beijing that there was 'no conceivable clash of interests between the two countries which could imperil their friendly relations, but that this position did not apply to Sino-Indian relations.'[92] Zhou in his meeting with Nehru in Beijing in October, 1954 used a very carefully chosen Chinese word 'tuanjie' when suggesting the need for the two countries [India and Pakistan] to interact with each other. Zhou was at his ambiguous best. This word 'tuanjie' is vague in its meaning. It can be translated both as 'co-operation' as well as 're-unification.' Thus, when talking to Indians, Zhou's interpreter would translate it as [re-unification], which would be 'music' to Indian ears and with the Pakistanis it would be translated as [co-operation]![93]

At the conclusion of Zhou's visit to Pakistan in a joint communiqué on 24 December, 1956, both countries reiterated that 'there is no conflict of interests between the two countries.' Beijing had well understood the importance of Pakistan in limiting the role of India to the sub-continent, as also in helping China to gain access to the Muslim countries of West Asia. Zhou shrewdly assessed that it was imperative not to allow Pakistan and India to come closer to each other, as that would be to its [Chinas] detriment. Zhou never gave up on Pakistan. His was a very mature judgment. He recognized the immense value of Pakistan to irritate India.

Therefore, it should have come as no surprise when both China and Pakistan made up this obvious hiccup within a short period of time and were soon to establish a firm understanding much to the detriment of Indian interests. Both realized that they needed each other to contain India. Pakistan thereafter, despite strong US pressure to the contrary, assumed an active role as China's stalking horse in South Asia. Pakistan became a very useful ally in advocating China's cause and a valuable instrument to be used whenever the Chinese leaders wished to 'needle' India. On the other hand, whenever the occasion arose, China ensured that Pakistan received sufficient help so that it could withstand Indian pressure.

China, despite Pakistani rhetoric to the contrary, never allowed the relationship to reach a point where Pakistani adventurism had to be underwritten by the Chinese by actually taking part in hostilities on Pakistan's behalf. The Chinese ensured that they 'used' Pakistan, but never allowed Pakistan to 'use' them instead. China's policy was always covert and subtle.[94]

Not to be left behind, PM Koirala of Nepal on 11 August, 1959, issued a statement that in 'view of the Tibetan developments, Nepal can no longer remain defenceless on its Northern borders.' It increased its defence expenditure. The Nepal Government party issued a statement saying Tibet provides an 'Asian parallel to Hungarian annihilation and that the tragedy of Tibet should be a lesson to other Asian countries.'[95] The Bhutanese were incensed as eight Bhutanese enclaves in Tibet were forcibly taken over by the Chinese. The Chinese image in Asia took a massive nosedive, especially in Asian Buddhist countries. India took little or no advantage of China's poor image and predicament, particularly in Asian Buddhist countries.

The Chinese were livid over the events in Lhasa leading to the flight of the Dalai Lama from Tibet. It showed them in very poor light particularly in the Afro-Asian comity of nations. Instead of introspecting over the folly of their own policies, they sought to lay the blame squarely at Nehru's door. In order to defend the credibility of its leadership, the Chinese political leadership decided that the charges against India—and in particular, Nehru—had to be sharp, pointed and consistent. The Chinese accused Nehru of following a policy of protecting Tibetan 'splitists.' The main Chinese grievances were as follows:

> [a] The Indian Consul-General in Lhasa met Tibetan demonstrators and helped them draft a memorandum, [b] They gave asylum to Dalai Lama, [c] They maintained official contact with the Dalai Lama at PM's level and treated him as a honoured guest, [d] Allowed the foreign press to meet the Dalai Lama, [e] Allowed the Dalai Lama to appeal to the UN, [f] Granted asylum to thousands of Tibetans, [g] Allowed anti-China activities at Kalimpong, [h] Encouraged the Indian press to publish anti-Chinese and pro-Tibetan articles, [i] Raised the Tibetan issue in the Indian Parliament, [j] De-faced Mao's portrait in Bombay and, [k] Restricted trade with Tibet and lastly allowed the Dalai Lama to call his administration as the 'Tibetan Government-in-exile.'[96]

Bereft of any outside support the Tibetan revolt, as could be expected, was shortlived. The Chinese put it down systematically and with savage ruthlessness. Director, CIA, Allen Dulles admitted that:

> The Chinese Communists had put on a very effective military showing. They were making use of veterans of the Korean War and they were also making very efficient use of aircraft. It looked as though the rebel forces in the Khamba area had been pretty well knocked to pieces. The same was probably true of the rebel forces in the Lhasa area.[97]

Nevertheless, deep suspicions of Nehru in the Chinese mind became even more confirmed. At a Politburo meeting on 17 March, 1959, Zhou Enlai claimed that the rebellion was 'connected with the Indian Government.' He speculated that both Britain and the United States had provided active support to the rebels behind the scenes and had worked with India as a frontline state. According to Zhou 'this was the reason why the commanding centre of the rebellion has been established in Kalimpong on Indian Territory.'[98] Zhou's conclusion was that 'without external encouragement and incitement, this kind of rebellion would not have erupted.'[99] The Chinese Vice-Foreign Minister, in a meeting with the Indian Ambassador, was more specific than Zhou and blamed 'US and KMT elements' for the revolt.[100] Zhou was being dramatic and only attempting to cover-up China's own failures, apparent to everyone else.

Chinese suspicions of Nehru were further fuelled when they received his letter of 23 March, 1959, just a few days after the revolt erupted at Lhasa, giving in detail India's territorial claims both in the Eastern and Western sectors. The Chinese suspected that Nehru was trying to compromise their hold over Tibet at this critical juncture by questioning China's control of the Xinjiang [Sinkiang]-Tibet road link through the Aksai Chin. It was also at about this time that India took the step of banning the exports of food grains to Tibet. This was to have far-reaching consequences, for the Chinese surmised that this was yet another attempt to undermine their control over Tibet. Chinese conclusions were further reinforced when India, in September 1959, banned the export of steel products and in October 1959, banned fuel oil, auto parts, and clothing, tea, sugar and hand tools. The Chinese sensed that India was 'in league' with Tibetan rebels and Western powers and wished to help Tibetan rebels by instituting an economic blockade of Chinese-controlled Tibet.

Further, at a meeting on 25 March, 1959, Deng Xiaoping asserted that the Indian Government and—Nehru in particular—had been deeply involved in the rebellion in Lhasa. Nonetheless, Deng argued that the time had not yet come for Beijing to voice public criticism of India. This was not because he believed that the actions of the Government of India were acceptable. On the contrary, Deng insisted that several of Nehru's speeches about the Tibetan situation, together with the fact that the headquarters of the rebellion was located in Kalimpong 'left no doubt that the Indian Government was behind the rebellion... *and, when the times comes, we certainly will settle accounts with them*' [emphasis added].[101] Deng's threat was serious and should not have been taken lightly.

Another reason why the Chinese were so incensed with the role of India was the statement of 18 April, 1959, issued by the Dalai Lama. The Chinese suspected the 'hidden hand' of India behind the statement, particularly the opening sentence, which was:

> It has always been accepted that the Tibetan people are different from the Han people of China. There has always been a strong desire for independence on the part of the Tibetan people.

The statement then went on to say that the Seventeen-Point Agreement was signed under the '*pressure of the Chinese Government.*' This assertion completely undercut the basis of Chinese rule in Tibet. The Dalai Lama further emphasized that he had left Tibet '*of his own free will and not under duress.*' Again, this completely challenged the Chinese position, which was that the Dalai Lama had '*been abducted to India by Tibetan rebels.*' But what rattled the Chinese even more was the following sentence in the Dalai Lama's statement:

> *Ever since the Dalai Lama entered India at Kanzey Mane, near Chuthangmu, he has experienced in full measure the respect and hospitality extended to him by the people of the Kameng Frontier Division of the North East Frontier Agency and the Dalai Lama would like to state how the Government of India's officers posted there had spared no efforts in making his stay and journey 'through this extremely well administered part of India' as comfortable as possible.*

The reference to NEFA being a 'well administered part of India' by the Dalai Lama and the open and implicit recognition by the Tibetans that Khinzemane [Kanzey Mane] and NEFA [Now Arunachal Pradesh] were a part of India, completely undercut the Chinese position, for Chinese claims in the Eastern sector [Arunachal Pradesh] are nothing but Tibetan claims. A key point to note is that the reference to Khinzemane would indicate that the Tibetans had accepted India's position that the McMahon Line in this sector ran along the Tangla Ridge (i.e. the highest water-shed).

India officially denied any hand in authoring the Dalai Lama's statement of 18 April, 1959. The Chinese also alleged that the Dalia Lama's statement was *not only distributed by an official of the Ministry of External Affairs but also carried on official bulletins of Indian Embassies abroad! Xinhua* of 21 April, 1959, quoted an *AFP* dispatch from Delhi to say:

> The statement was issued apparently with the approval of the Indian Government...in approving the Dalai Lama's statement wished to say indirectly certain things it would be difficult to say it directly.

Later, the Beijing *Guang Ming Ribao* pointed to the role played by a 'certain official.' The *People's Daily* of 23 April, 1959, now warned:

> There can be no greater tragedy for a statesman than miscalculation of a situation. If the Indian expansionists are seeking to pressure China, they have picked the wrong customer.

Years later, it was candidly admitted by the Indian official concerned [Jagat Mehta] that the Chinese were largely correct, as can be seen from the following admission:

> I took the draft of a statement to the Prime Minister at his house around 10.30 at night and he edited it personally. I transmitted the final version to PN Menon for submission to the Dalai Lama as a suggestion from the Government of India... I suppose I was the only person who knew of Nehru's

semantic inputs. It was also admitted that Indian Embassies carried the Dalai Lama statement.[102]

The Chinese now followed up their propaganda barrage by publishing a scathing article in the *People's Daily* of 6 May, 1959, entitled 'The Revolution in Tibet and Nehru's Philosophy.' This article, purportedly written by Mao himself, was an open indictment of India's interference in the internal affairs of China and carried a personal attack on Nehru, perhaps for the first time since the 1954 Tibet Agreement. However, a demarche delivered by the Chinese Ambassador to India to the Foreign Secretary on 16 May, 1959, although written in undiplomatic language, is most noteworthy. It was reportedly personally drafted by Mao and hence no Chinese diplomatic official would have the temerity to amend the demarche so as to put it into 'proper' diplomatic language. The demarche, after a long rambling litany of alleged Indian misdemeanours in Tibet, makes a most interesting observation. It states:

> The enemy of the Chinese people lies in the East—the US imperialists have many military bases in Taiwan, South Korea, Japan and in the Philippines—which are all directed against China. China's main attention and policy of struggle are directed to the East, to the West Pacific region, to the vicious and aggressive US imperialism and not to India.... India is not an opponent but a friend of our country. China will not be so foolish to antagonize the US in the East and again to antagonize India in the West. The putting down of the rebellion....in Tibet will not in the least endanger India. You can wait and see.... This is our state policy... Our Indian friends! What is in your mind? Will you be agreeing to our thinking regarding the view that China can only concentrate its main attention eastwards of China but not South-West-ward of China, nor is it necessary for it to do so.... Friends! It seems to us that you too cannot have two fronts.... Is it not so? If it is, here lies the meeting point of our two sides. Will you please think it over?[103]

On receiving the Chinese Ambassador's demarche, Nehru would have recalled what Mao had told him during their meeting in Beijing in October 1954 that:

> Between friends, there are times when there are differences; there are also times when there are fights—even fights till we become red in the face. But this type of fight is different in character from the sort of fight we have with Dulles. China needs very much. We are a new country. Although we are counted as a large country, our strength is still weak. Confronting us is a larger power America....therefore we need friends. PM Nehru can feel this. I think India also needs friends.[104]

The message that the Chinese Ambassador delivered on 16 May, 1959, was essentially the same that Mao had verbally told Nehru in 1954.

The response to the Chinese Ambassador's demarche of 16 May, 1959, was personally drafted by Nehru who assessed the demarche as very objectable and 'discourteous.'[105] The tragedy lies in the fact that this demarche and its contents were taken as a personal affront and the hapless Foreign Secretary directed to respond within a week on 23 May, 1959, to say that the statement was 'wholly out of keeping with diplomatic usage and courtesies due to friendly countries.'[106] And further, in response, the astonishing remark was made that 'the Government of India do not consider or treat any country as an enemy country, howsoever much it may differ from it' [Was Pakistan then a friendly country?]. The Chinese view of India's response was that while they had 'unfolded all [their] trump cards on the table and tried hard to relieve the misgivings and worries of the Indian Government', their Ambassador had been unnecessarily subjected to 'angry remarks.'[107] Further, the Indian press lampooned Chinese Ambassador, Pan Tsuli, in several sarcastic articles. The Chinese, knowing who the real author of this demarche was, would have taken it as a massive affront to Mao personally.

It was obvious that no effort was made to study the Chinese offer in detail or to assess clinically what its potential or consequences were. With Sino-Pakistan relations at their lowest ebb, with China's relations with both the superpowers at an awkward and a difficult stage, a China that faced hostility and isolation internationally due to its brutal crackdown in Tibet and with a host of internal difficulties, a real opportunity for exploring a settlement of all issues with China was missed. What was in the Chinese demarche that was so discourteous? Was a deal with China possible? Maybe or maybe not, but at least the contours of a possible settlement could have been seriously explored. Indian diplomacy was poorly served. Later, when Zhou came to India for border talks with Nehru in April 1960, he repeated the same theme by stating to Secretary-General of the External Affairs Ministry, RK Nehru [21 April, 1960] that '*Chairman Mao has said that our enemy lies in the East and will come from the sea.* We take India as a friendly country and we cannot turn our Southern border into a national front' [emphasis added].[108] As earlier, no one seemed to care or to take notice of Zhou's hint.

The rejection of the Chinese suggestion, as contained in the demarche of 16 May, 1959, made the Chinese leadership very wary of Nehru's attitude. The Chinese assessed that Nehru was, on one hand, a leading member of 'the Indian bourgeoisie' that had led the fight for independence and, on the other, could not let go his 'lust for expansion.' The Chinese surmised that it was this latter manifestation that led him [Nehru] to support and instigate the revolt in Tibet. The Chinese leadership's negative feelings for Nehru, already so evident, thereafter increased dramatically. From this point onwards, the relationship went rapidly down hill, spurred on by a regular occurrence of border incidents. The Chinese assessment was that India had moved away from the true spirit of Sino-Indian friendship.

Soviet Russia was alarmed and perplexed. How should it handle this looming dispute between a fraternal country and a friendly one? When the Tibetan revolt broke out in March 1959, the Russians sided with the Chinese. Pravda of 28 March, 1959, blamed 'imperialist provocation' and collusion between 'reactionary'

Tibetans and 'imperialist circles' abroad for the rebellion. 'Tibet is an inalienable part of China and crushing the reactionary ruling clique is solely the internal affair of the Chinese people', declared *Pravda*. Further, on 22 April, 1959, *Pravda* echoed the Chinese line by alleging that the Dalai Lama's flight from Lhasa was an 'abduction' by Tibetan reactionaries and the view that he [Dalai Lama] left 'on his own' was a 'fabrication by the Western media.' The Chinese even admitted receiving Russian intelligence help. But when the Chinese press started to berate Nehru personally, Soviet Russia went stone dead.

On 6 May, 1959, the Chinese leadership—consisting of Mao Zedong, Zhou Enlai, and Chen Yi [PRC Foreign Minister]—met with senior diplomats from the Soviet Union and ten other socialist countries to tell their side of the story. Zhou went to great lengths to explain Beijing's perception of the nature of the Tibetan rebellion and India's connection with it. He argued that Nehru's 'unspoken purpose' was to 'establish a buffer zone [in Tibet] under India's sphere of influence, with Tibet as its protectorate and to force the PLA to withdraw' [from Tibet].[109] Zhou further clarified that 'this was their [India's] main ideology; it is also the centre of the controversy between China and India.'[110] Mao, on the other hand, emphasized that Beijing's criticism of Nehru was not meant to push the Indian leader into the arms of the imperialists. This assertion was designed to undercut Soviet accusations that the Chinese, by their actions, were pushing Nehru closer to the Western powers.

As Chinese troops fanned out towards the border, clashes seemed imminent. The most serious of these was at Longju [25 August, 1959]. The clash at Longju was the first time the two sides opened fire at each other. The case of the Chinese attack on Longju is, indeed, most peculiar. Just a month prior to the incident, India had, in a note on 24 July, 1959, informed the Chinese Foreign Ministry that they wished to para-drop a doctor to Longju and requested that 'necessary immediate warning be issued to neighbouring Chinese posts of this operation.'[111] The exact co-ordinates and grid references of Longju [GRID MJ 7924, Long. 93.32E, Lat 23.37N] were also conveyed to the Chinese, who responded that it was 'not necessary to bring activities in Indian territory to their notice.'[112] Thus, Longju was clearly *South* of the McMahon Line and that Chinese troops had intruded across the line by at least two kilometres [Annexure to PM Nehru's letter to PM Zhou, dated 26 September, 1959]. Allen Dulles, Director CIA, confirmed the Indian position when he told the US National Security Council on 10 September, 1959, that 'the Chinese attack on Longju on 26 August, *resulted in a penetration three miles beyond the McMahon Line*.'[113] According to Chinese sources the clash at Longju necessitated an investigation, which Zhou immediately ordered. On 8 September, 1959, Mao convened a Politburo meeting in which it was agreed that China would seek a negotiated settlement with India and that before negotiations began, China would offer to India that both sides maintain the status quo.[114]

On 9 September, 1959, just prior to Khrushchev's visit to Beijing, the Soviets took the highly unusual step of issuing a statement published by TASS. The Chinese tried hard to stop its publication. On 6 September, 1959, the Chinese briefed the Soviet CDA, Sergei Antonov, on the clash at Longju and even went to the extent of showing Antonov an advance copy of Zhou's letter to Nehru dated 8 September, 1959, that had not yet been despatched to India.[115] But Antonov was not convinced and reported to Moscow that it was 'logical that the Chinese side had started the skirmishes.'[116] Mao was so upset that he did not hide his feelings that Khrushchev had betrayed a friend.[117] On Mao's instructions, on 13 September, 1959, the CCP took the unusual step of protesting to the CPSU [Moscow]. The Chinese felt that the *TASS* statement of 9 September had supported the Indian position and 'revealed to the whole world the divergence of views of China and the Soviet Union regarding the incident on the Sino-Indian border, and which brought joy and jubilation to the Indian bourgeoisie and to American and British imperialists.'[118] The Chinese felt that this was 'the first time a socialist country had condemned another fraternal socialist country which was confronted by such armed confrontation.' It was also the first time that Sino-Soviet differences were on full public display. Years later, the Chinese described the *TASS* statement as a 'gift' to Eisenhower by Khrushchev and an attempt by him to please American imperialism.[119] Two days later, the Soviets provided India with subsidized credits of US$ 385 million over five years. The Chinese were to claim later that their leadership met with the Soviet Ambassador at Beijing six times between 10 December, 1959, and 30 January, 1960, to persuade the Soviets to maintain 'strict neutrality' on the dispute.[120]

Khrushchev after his successful summit meetings with Eisenhower [15-27 September, 1959], rushed straight to Beijing. In a tumultuous meeting lasting nearly seven hours with Chinese leaders both sides chided each other on the events on the Sino-Indian border. It was the first face-to-face acrimonious meeting between Khrushchev and the Chinese leadership led by Mao.[121] Khrushchev began the discussions by saying that:

> *we do not understand in particular your conflict with India.... You have had good relations with India for many years. Suddenly, here is a bloody incident, as result of which [Prime Minister of India] Jawaharlal Nehru found himself in a very difficult position. We may say that Nehru is a bourgeois statesman. But we know about it. If Nehru leaves, who would be better than him? The Dalai Lama fled from Tibet, he is a bourgeois figure. This issue is also not clear for us. When the events in Hungary took place, then Nehru was against us, and we did not take offense at him, because we did not expect anything from him as a bourgeois statesman. But although he was against it, this did not prevent us from preserving good relations with him. If you let me, I will tell you what a guest should not say the events in Tibet are your fault. You ruled in Tibet, you should have had your intelligence [agencies] there and should have known about the plans and intentions of the Dalai Lama.*

Mao Zedong: *Nehru also says that the events in Tibet occurred because of our fault.*

Khrushchev: *Do you really want us to approve of your conflict with India? It would be stupid on our part. The TASS declaration [9 September, 1959] was necessary.*

Mao Zedong: *Our mistake was that we did not disarm the Dalai Lama right away. But at that time we had no contact with the popular masses of Tibet.*

Khrushchev: *You have no contact even now with the population of Tibet.*

Mao Zedong: *We have a different understanding of this issue.*

Khrushchev: *Of course, that is why we raised this issue. One could also say the following: both you and we have Koreans who fled from Kim Il Sung. But this does not give us ground to spoil relations with Kim Il Sung, and we remain good friends. We believe that the events in Tibet are the fault of the Communist Party of China, not Nehru's fault.*

Mao Zedong: *No, this is Nehru's fault. ....*

Khrushchev: *Why did you have to kill people on the border with India?*

Mao Zedong: *They attacked us first crossed the border and continued firing for twelve hours.*

Khrushchev: *Although the Hindus attacked first, nobody was killed among the Chinese.*

Zhou Enlai: *But what are we supposed to do if they attack us first? We cannot fire in the air. The Hindus even crossed the McMahon line. Besides, in the nearest future [Indian] Vice President Radhakrishnan comes to China. This is to say that we are undertaking measures to resolve the issue peacefully, by negotiations. In my letter of 9 September to Nehru we provided detailed explanations of all that had occurred between India and us.*

Khrushchev: *Comrade Zhou Enlai, you have been Minister of Foreign Affairs of the PRC for many years and know better than me how one can resolve disputed issues without [spilling] blood. In this particular case I do not touch at all the issue of the border, for if the Chinese and the Hindus do not know where the borderline goes between them, it is not for me, a Russian, to meddle. I am only against the methods that have been used.*

Zhou Enlai: *We did not know until recently about the border incident, and local authorities undertook all the measures there, without authorization from the Centre.*

Khrushchev: *That the Centre knew nothing about the incident is news to me.*

Mao Zedong: *The border conflict with India—this is only a marginal border issue, not a clash between the two Governments. Nehru himself is not aware what happened there. As we found out, their patrols crossed the McMahon line. We learned about this much later, after the incident took place. All this was known neither to Nehru nor even to our military district in Tibet. When Nehru learned that their patrols had crossed the McMahon Line, he issued the instruction for them to withdraw. We also carried out the work towards peaceful resolution of the issue. The rebuff was delivered on the decision of local military organs.... You will see for yourselves later that the McMahon Line with India will be maintained, and the border conflict with India will end.... The border issue with India will be decided through negotiations [excerpts relating to Sino-Indian relations].*[122]

Soon after Khrushchev's meeting with Chinese leaders in Beijing on 20 October, 1959, another serious clash took place at Kongka La in Ladakh. The Chinese opened fire killing five, wounding four and capturing ten Indian policemen. India protested vehemently to China. Kongka La was at least 65 kilometres inside the traditional frontier and well within Indian Territory. Later, the Chinese were to allege that the Kongka La incident took place because 'the Indian forces got Soviet protection and support, became arrogant and were further incited.'[123] The Kongka-La incident marked a new low point in Sino-Indian relations. To rub Nehru hard and in an attempt to hurt his sentiments, the Chinese handed over the dead bodies and released captured Indian personnel on 14 November, 1959. It was a birthday present from the Chinese to Nehru! The Chinese Vice-Foreign Minister, knowing full well the significance of the day, expressed 'gratification' to the Indian Ambassador in a note on 28 November, 1959.[124] It was tasteless and a needless provocation, and from this point onwards, Nehru became totally adamant.

The Soviets were being briefed regularly by India. Khrushchev in an interview to *The New Age*, characterized the clashes as 'stupid and sad' and took the occasion to address the Supreme Soviet on 31 October, 1959, where he deplored the incidents and expressed hope that they would not be repeated. While conscious of seeking Soviet friendship, Nehru knew that [Soviet] relations with China were strained and thus they could offer little help. Soviet Russia, caught between fraternal Socialist China and friendly India, could not play the role of a mediator without violating the principles of 'proletarian internationalism' and, therefore, remained deaf to any proposals for mediation. In a meeting on 12 February, 1960, Nehru tried to test the waters when he told Khrushchev 'I will be glad to supply any material [on the border dispute] which you may wish to have', but Khrushchev turned him down flat by stating that 'It will be difficult for me to take a position on the merits involving two friends' and that 'even if the two sides requested mediation, it will be very difficult for a third person to mediate.' Thereafter, Nehru did not think of asking the Soviets to use their good offices in settling the dispute.[125] The Chinese were deeply resentful of Soviet Russian neutrality on the border issue and alleged that Khrushchev, in his meeting with Nehru, reached an agreement to 'supply India with fighter planes and other equipment.'[126]

It was Chinese policy to contain the Tibetan rebellion and restore peace quickly. The Chinese anticipated that they would face no problems from the Indian Army. They would also not have been unaware of the disarray within the top echelons of the Indian defence structure. When one general raised the issue of the looming threat from China, Krishna Menon put him down in his usually acerbic and sarcastic style that there would be 'no war between India and China and [if there was] he was quite capable of fighting it himself at the diplomatic level.'[127] Whenever there was tension between India and China, particularly at the border, Krishna Menon would try to divert public attention by playing up some issue or the other with Pakistan. In this context, Pakistan, too, would 'help' by raising the Kashmir issue in the UN, which would give Krishna Menon the opportunity to fully display his histrionic talents and thus divert public attention from the imminent threat from the North.

In early August 1959, a tussle that had been brewing broke out into the open between Krishna Menon, the Defence Minister, and General Thimayya, Army Chief, that eventually led to the latter's resignation on 31 August, 1959. By the following day, the entire press corps in Delhi was awash with reports of Thimayya's resignation. The bone of contention was the unpreparedness of the Indian Army to face the upcoming threat from China as also certain senior army promotions. Thimayya had correctly surmised that to recover areas occupied by the Chinese in Ladakh would require a major military effort and from India's strategic point of view, the Aksai Chin was more 'a liability than an asset.'[128] Similarly, Thimayya felt that the 'actual McMahon Line was militarily indefensible.'[129] Although this episode was settled by a sleight of hand on the part of Nehru, yet nothing materially changed as far as the army was concerned. Menon remained at his job. Nehru would not listen to anyone who criticized Krishna Menon.

The Chinese closely observed the events in Delhi. They were aware of Nehru's public statements as also of the actual state of affairs within the Indian Army. The Thimayya episode would only have confirmed their assessment that militarily India presented no challenge. Nevertheless, they viewed Thimayya with trepidation; for they felt that he was a 'hardliner' and a 'rightist.' Strangely, a little earlier [23 January–2 March, 1958], a Chinese military delegation headed by Marshal Ye Qianying was allowed to witness exercise 'Dhanush' a combined Army/Air Force 'fire power' demonstration at Ambala, and also important military installations. No doubt they would have closely assessed the preparedness of the Indian Army. The firm belief held by Krishna Menon and Nehru that there was no military threat from China would soon be tested.

Chinese anger over the events in Tibet leading to the flight of the Dalai Lama to India had barely subsided when the Dalai Lama decided to make an appeal to the UN. The Chinese were very angry and blamed India over the turn of events. Chen Yi, the Foreign Minister, charged Nehru with having adopted, 'two faced tactics by permitting the submission of the Tibetan question to the UN and allowing the Dalai Lama to exceed by far what is permissible under international practice.' The *People's Daily* of 16 September, 1959, demanded 'India's *withdrawal from Chinese territory* [emphasis added] and an end to the anti-China campaign.' It seemed that further clashes on the border were imminent.

Nothing could have been further from the truth about the Chinese Foreign Minister's charge that India had sponsored Tibet's case in the UN. In fact, the Indian Foreign Secretary informed the US Ambassador that India would not sponsor Tibet's case for the following reasons:

[a] No one is willing to go to war over Tibet. So the only 'effective' action would be more harsh words during the debate.

[b] It will only result in more reprisals against Tibetans.

[c] Soviet Union is very quiet over Tibet and the Sino-Indian border problems, which might indicate that they do not approve of Chinese actions, particularly regarding India.

[d] If a debate is to take place, the Soviet Union would be forced to completely side with China.

[e] We have to be 'friends' with a powerful country [China] with whom we share a border of 2680 miles.[130]

Whatever might have been the thinking in official circles within the Government of India, but after the clashes at Longju and at Kongka La, where Indian blood had been shed, public opinion in India was totally aroused as never before at what was considered to be Chinese perfidy. Members of Parliament became suspicious and mistrust mounted that the Government had something even more serious to hide. Nehru was now forced to explain and to defend his foreign policy moves. He could not, as in the past, simply announce them. A foreign Ambassador noted that Nehru's monopoly in conducting Indian foreign policy was 'broken.'[131] Nehru's political opponents, whether from the left or from the right, had found an issue on which they could berate him in unison. Politically, Nehru was now pushed into a cul-de-sac. Personally, too, Nehru had become disillusioned with the Chinese. PM Zhou's letter of 23 January, 1959, confirming that a border dispute 'did exist' and the brutal crackdown of the Tibetan rebellion confirmed Nehru's worst fears. Nehru thought he had an 'understanding' with Zhou and was profoundly embarrassed when he found that it was all illusory. Nehru now fully conscious of the Chinese threat, was a changed man. He became very adamant. He openly spoke of a 'new chapter' in Sino-Indian relations and noted that 'the whole world, except China, is trying to work towards peace.' Nehru now began to publicly refer to Chinese 'arrogance.' The Chinese, on the contrary, claimed that it was India that had 'instigated' the incidents.[132]

With the people of India now demanding utmost transparency, from this point onwards, Nehru's room for manoeuvre was considerably curtailed. Even if he wished to, Nehru could not compromise on the border issue with the Chinese in the face of rising frenzied nationalism. His perceived earlier softness in dealing with the Chinese now brought him unprecedented criticism in the press, in Parliament and even within his own party. On 4 November, 1959, Nehru met with over one hundred Congress MPs who pushed him to take a tougher line. The MPs expressed disbelief when Nehru suggested that a tougher line might make an agreement with China that much more difficult. To meet the rising chorus of disbelief, in a move that would inhibit decision making for the foreseeable future and without much serious reflection, Nehru decided to publish all the correspondence with China in the form of White Papers, including the important Chinese demarche of 16 May, 1959, and India's response. The first such White Paper was placed on the table in Parliament on 7 September, 1959. This unthinking move, although an attempt to introduce transparency, compromised confidentiality which is essential when serious diplomatic moves are afoot. It seriously limited India's options and field for manoeuvre. Compromise, as a solution to the boundary dispute, therefore became even more politically untenable. Nehru now admitted that India and China had fallen out and even though some kind of relative peace may continue to exist at the frontier, yet it would be 'an armed peace and the future appears to be one of continuing tension.'[133]

If the Chinese were indeed sincere in settling the boundary issue with India then it was rather ham-handed of them to first push Nehru in to a tight corner, and then expect and hope that Nehru would negotiate with them. If instead of openly denigrating him, [*People's Daily* Article of 6 May, 1959] the Chinese had instead courted him by making some meaningful gestures, Nehru could have easily fended off his detractors and tried settle the border question. Till 1959, Nehru never seriously thought that the boundary issue would snow-ball into a major confrontation between India and China. The Chinese knew perfectly well that India was a democracy with a free press, and once the dispute came out into the open, there was little that any ruler, including Nehru, could have done. It would have been a faulty reading of the situation to suggest that Nehru could have over ridden an aroused public opinion to come to an understanding with *China based on further concessions.* [emphasis added]. If the public opinion in India was aroused against the Chinese, it was largely the fault of poor Chinese diplomacy. The alienation of Nehru, as a friend of China, must rank as one of modern China's most glaring foreign policy failures.

Thus, by the end of 1959, it was clear that events had brought the latent boundary question not only into the open, but that the differences were major and not confined to minor rectifications of a settled boundary line. Nehru's policy of friendship towards China lay in tatters. Nehru characterized China's claims and hostility towards India as nothing 'short of a tragedy,' particularly for those who [like himself] had envisaged India-China friendship '*as the basis for peace and solidarity in Asia.*' [134] India would now have to face pressure and threats both from the North [China] as well as from the West [Pakistan] *simultaneously, a position that Nehru had tried so hard to avoid* [emphasis added]. For India, it was a painful lesson, that you cannot purchase national security with friendship![135]

CHAPTER 5

First Attempts at a Settlement [1959–62] and the 1962 Conflict

'The Chinese are a very difficult people when it comes to a question of boundaries'

Sir Ernest Satow [British Ambassador to China] writing to Lord Curzon on 6 April, 1905.

When the Sino-Indian boundary question finally emerged in the public domain, it was clear that this issue did not simply require only minor border changes. Despite this fact being very obvious, Nehru speaking in the Lok Sabha as late as 4 September, 1958, still continued to maintain that:

> *So far as the broad boundary, the international frontier between India and the Chinese state including the Tibetan region is concerned, it is not a matter of dispute so far as we are concerned. It is a fixed thing. There is nothing to talk about.*[1]

The Indian position on the boundary question, therefore, was that:

> *The Sino-Indian boundary is based on custom and tradition; it follows natural features and, for the major part this customary and traditional boundary, is also confirmed by treaty and agreement and that this boundary throughout has been fixed and well known for centuries. According to international usage and practice, a customary boundary which follows well known and unchanging natural features like main watersheds, stands defined and does not require further and formal definition.*

The Chinese position on the boundary question was in contradiction to the Indian position. The Chinese maintained that:

> *The Sino-Indian boundary has never been formally delimited [the Chinese often deliberately confuse between 'delimitation' and 'demarcation'] and there does not exist between India and China any treaty or agreement delimiting their boundary. The boundary alignment as shown by China is the true traditional customary*

boundary line between the two countries. It follows, therefore, that a new boundary line must be negotiated. In the meanwhile, both sides should maintain the status quo of the line of actual control [LAC].

Apart from having very differing positions on the Sino-Indian boundary question, even the facts pertaining to the boundary are in contention. The Indian position remains that the Sino-Indian boundary is 3,488 kilometres in length [This includes the 523 kilometre POK-China section]. On the other hand, China maintains that the Sino-Indian boundary is only 1,700 kilometres in length.[7] China refuses to include the POK-China section of the boundary and maintains that the Sino-Indian boundary begins only from West of the Karakoram pass.

To illustrate the differences in greater detail—both on facts and on principle and for the sake of convenience—the Sino-Indian boundary can be divided into three sectors: Western, middle and the Eastern sector.

Western Sector

In the Western sector, the boundary line is divided into two parts, with the Kongka La [Pass] as the dividing point. The sector West of the Kongka La is the boundary between Sinkiang [Xinjiang] and Ladakh. The sector East of the Kongka La is the boundary between Tibet and Ladakh.

In the Western sector, there are three mountain ranges running parallel to each other in a generally East to West alignment. The Kuen Lun range is in the North, the Karakoram in the middle and the Himalayas in the South. Between the Kuen Lun and the Karakoram mountain range lies the territory of Aksai Chin. There was, in the past, no clearly determined boundary line that both India and China had formally accepted, although the traditional boundary alignment was rather well known to all. Neither India nor China exercised *any settled jurisdiction or regular administration* in the Aksai Chin area. Regular Indian administration stopped short of the Karakorams to the North and similarly regular Chinese administration stopped short of the Kuen Lun to the South. Thus, there existed in between an administrative vacuum. As Nehru was to clarify when speaking in the Lok Sabha on 12 September, 1959, *'This place, the Aksai Chin area, is in our maps undoubtedly, but I distinguish it completely from other areas. It is a matter of argument as to what part of it belongs to us and what part belongs to somebody else. It is not at all a dead clear matter.'*

Nevertheless, the Indian position remains that the boundary in the Western sector is 1,597 kilometres in length. The Chinese stated position is that the boundary in this sector is only 600 kilometres in length. According to India, the Chinese at present occupy 38,000 square kilometres of Indian Territory in this sector, whereas the Chinese claim jurisdiction and occupation over only 33,000 square kilometres, which they say is 'indisputable' Chinese Territory. Further, India maintains that under the Sino-Pak Agreement of 1963, Pakistan illegally ceded to China about 5,180 square kilometres of territory in Northern Kashmir. China flatly denies any such illegality and maintains that this was a perfectly legitimately concluded Agreement.

Middle Sector

In the middle sector the boundary alignment runs along the crest of the Himalayas. It is the least disputed sector and the dispute in this sector exists only in four areas. These are [a] Spiti Area; [b] West of Shipki pass; [c] Nilang-Jadang; and [d] Barahoti. All these areas are *South* of the Himalayan crest and, therefore, Chinese claims are at best tenuous, although it is their belief that they are only pressing traditional Tibetan claims. The total area in dispute is about 2,000 square kilometres and the Chinese concede that all the disputed area is under Indian control.

Nevertheless, the Indian position is that the boundary line in this sector is 545 kilometres in length, whereas the Chinese position is that it is only 450 kilometres in length.

Eastern Sector

The Eastern sector is clearly delimited by the McMahon Line that follows the Himalayan crest and the main watershed in the area. The Chinese have accepted the Himalayan crest as the boundary with regard to the Tibet-UP [now Uttarkhand], Tibet-Himachal Pradesh, Tibet-Nepal, Tibet-Sikkim and Tibet-Bhutan borders; the unanswered question, then, is why not accept it further in the case of the Arunachal-Tibet border also? And yet, the Chinese have formally, in a treaty with Myanmar, accepted the McMahon Line alignment as it runs along the China-Myanmar border! It is obvious, therefore, that no well known internationally accepted geographical principle is the issue in the dispute. The Chinese position has more to do with the political aspects of the boundary question than with any other geographical principle.

The Indian position is that the boundary, which is the McMahon Line, is 1346 kilometres in length, whereas the Chinese maintain that it is only 650 kilometres in length and along the Himalayan foothills. They refuse to accept the McMahon Line. The disputed area in this sector is about 90,000 square kilometres. The Chinese concede that the entire area is under Indian administration.

In overall terms, therefore, the Sino-Indian boundary question is a dispute not only over territory, but also over the length of the boundary. Even the facts are in dispute.

Till 2005, China did not recognize Sikkim to be a part of India and, therefore, till then, refused to discuss the Sikkim-Tibet boundary with India. This was not an insurmountable issue, for the Sikkim-Tibet boundary [220 kilometres] was recognized by China and, therefore, no dispute existed in this sector. This sector had already been negotiated with the Chinese under the Anglo-Chinese

Map 1: Chinese Alignment of Sino-Indian Border

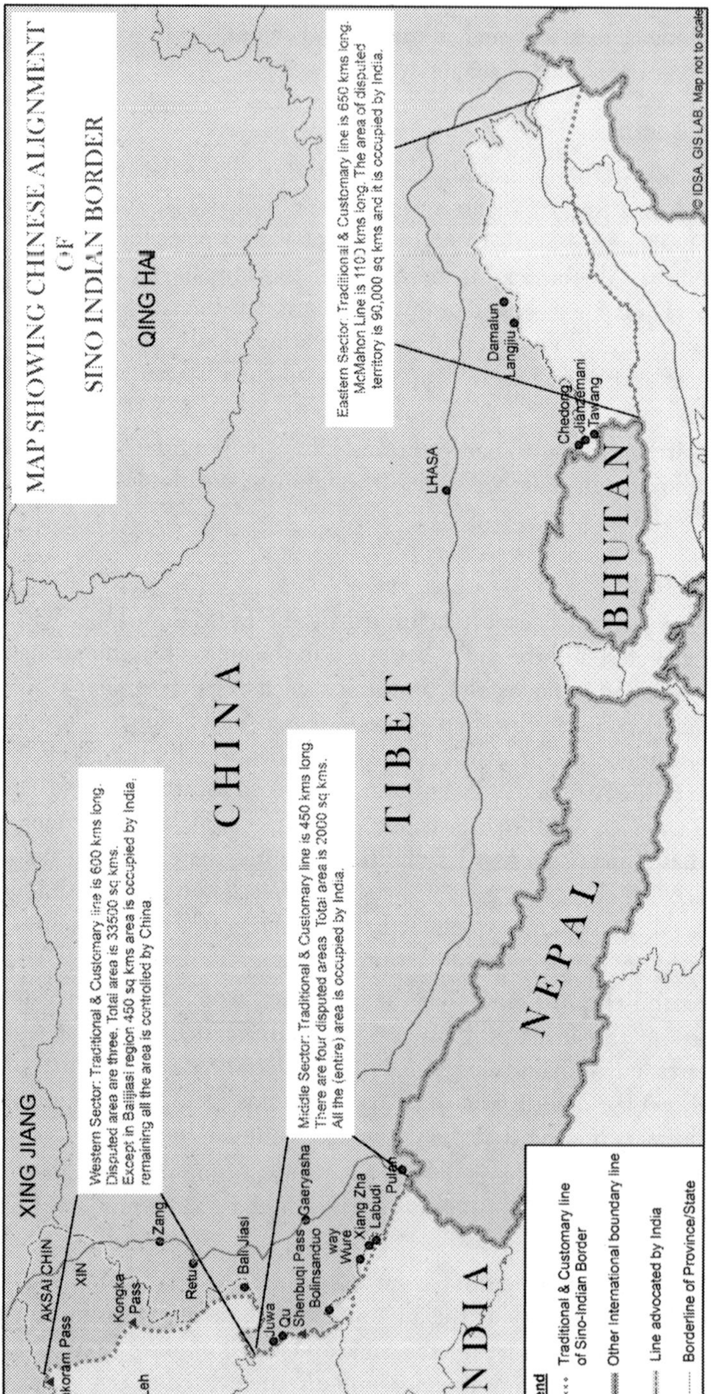

Map 2: Indian Alignment of Sino-Indian Border

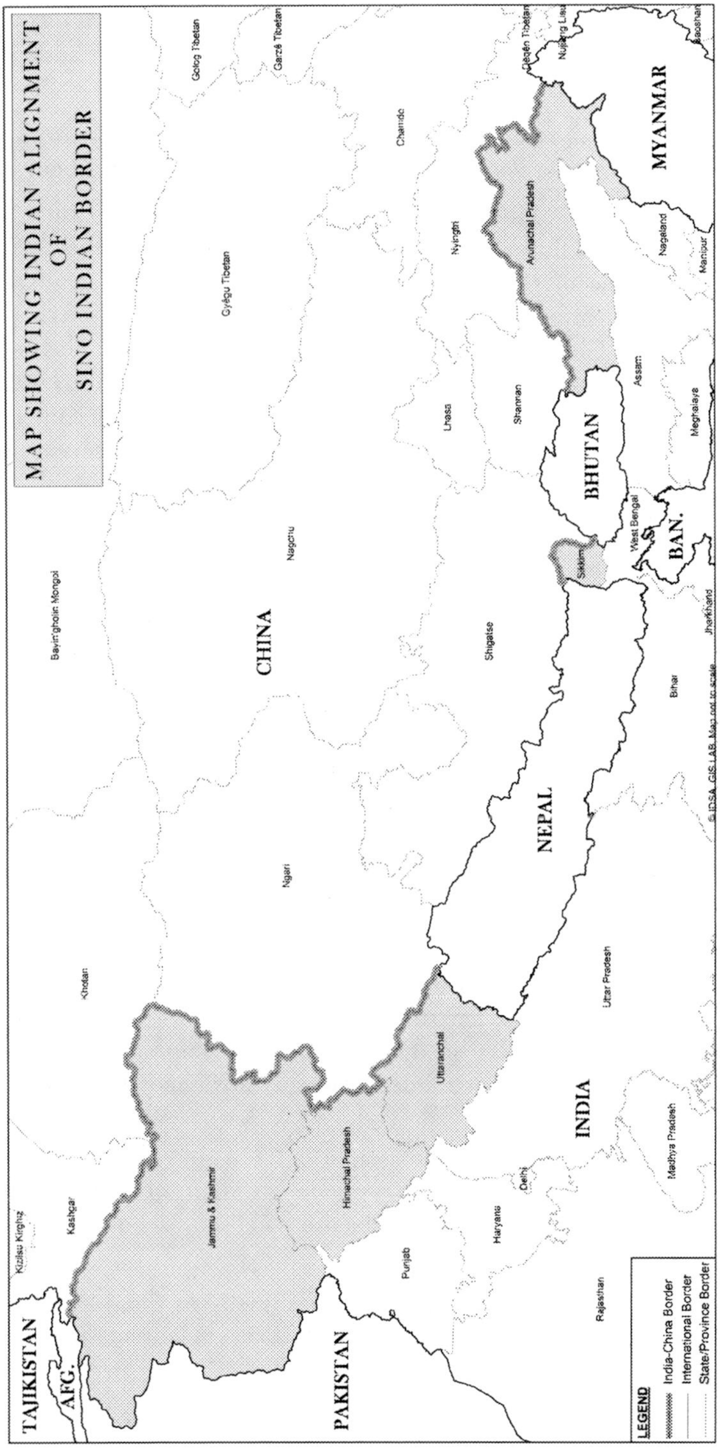

Convention of 1890 and demarcated in 1895. The Chinese Ministry of Foreign Affairs confirmed this in their note of 26 December, 1959, addressed to the Embassy of India, Beijing, stating that:

> *The boundary between China and Sikkim has long been formally delimited and there is neither any discrepancy between the maps nor any disputes in practice.*[3]

When the issue of the Sino-Indian boundary question first came into public domain, India, in line with the policy guide-lines set by Nehru, continued to maintain that the international frontier between India and China was not a matter of dispute. Therefore, the first demarche sent by India to the Chinese Government over the Aksai Chin road constructed by the Chinese reflected this confusion. Hence, the note sent by the Foreign Secretary on 18 October, 1958, was an *informal* note only [emphasis added]. The note if not farcical in content, certainly had its comical moments too, for it was rather poorly drafted. The note complained:

> It is a matter of surprise and regret that the Chinese Government should have constructed a road through indisputably Indian Territory without first obtaining the permission of the Government of India and without even informing the Government of India.

And the comical part:

> No applications for visas from Chinese personnel working on the road or even from Chinese travelers traversing the road have been received by the Government of India.

And then, the note asked for assistance:

> An Indian party of three officers,...were out on patrol near Shinglung. Since August there has been no news...since there are now Chinese personnel on Indian Territory, the Government of India would be grateful for any information that the Chinese Government might have.[4]

If this was indeed Indian Territory, as claimed; then why seek Chinese help? What would the Chinese have made of this demarché ? The Chinese reply on 3 November, 1958, said that in the 'spirit of friendship,' these Indian personnel were being *deported* [emphasis added] through the Karakoram Pass on 22 October, 1958.

And further, the Indian Ambassador in China in yet another poorly crafted note, addressed to the Vice-Minister of Foreign Affairs of China on 8 November, 1958, admitted, contrary to all that Nehru had been strenuously maintaining so far, that:

> The question whether the particular area [the Aksai Chin] is in Indian or Chinese territory is a matter of dispute which has to be dealt with separately.[5]

With this note, the Indian Ambassador admitted that there was 'a dispute' in the Ladakh area, contrary to what the Government of India maintained all along that there was no boundary dispute and, at best, only minor rectifications were necessary. Such was the looseness of language used that it is astonishing to say the least.

Probably Nehru sensed that his officials were getting nowhere and, therefore, decided to take up the issue at his level with Zhou Enlai. On 14 December, 1958, Nehru, for the first time, wrote a letter to Zhou on the boundary issue. In his letter, Nehru said that when the Sino-Indian Agreement over Tibet [1954] was concluded 'no border questions were raised at that time and we were under the impression that there were no border disputes between our respective countries.' Further, Nehru wrote that 'we thought that *the 1954 Agreement had settled all outstanding problems*' [emphasis added]. Nehru then quoted from a Minute that he had penned after his talks with Zhou in 1956:

> Premier Zhou referred to the McMahon Line and again said that he had never heard of this before, though of course, the then Chinese Government had dealt with this matter and not accepted that line. He had gone into this matter in connection with the border dispute with Burma. Although he thought this line, established by British imperialists, was not fair, nevertheless, because it was an accomplished fact and because of the friendly relations between China and the countries concerned, namely India and Burma, the Chinese Government were of the opinion that they should give recognition to this McMahon Line. [emphasis added] They had however not 'consulted' the Tibetan authorities about it yet. They proposed to do it.[6]

It is interesting to note that Nehru, in his letter by 14 December, 1958, to Zhou did not refer to the Aksai Chin road, the detention of Indian personnel or for that matter to India's protest in this regard. His letter appears to largely concentrate on the Eastern sector of the boundary.

In his response on 23 January, 1959, Zhou *did not dispute Nehru's version of their talks in 1956* [emphasis added], but was adamant that the Sino-Indian boundary had never been formally delimited and that historically no treaty or agreement on the Sino-Indian boundary had ever been concluded between the Chinese Central Government and the Indian Government. In a very carefully drafted letter, Zhou repudiated all past settlements, and his letter was the first such formal intimation that a dispute existed. Zhou admitted that the boundary question was not raised when the 1954 negotiations were held, but that was because the conditions were 'not yet ripe' for a settlement and that the Chinese Government had had no time to study the question. As for the McMahon line, Zhou said that it was a product of the British policy of aggression against the Tibet region of China. Zhou admitted *that Tibetan local authorities had signed the related documents,* but were dissatisfied with the unilaterally drawn line. Zhou then affirmed '*that the Chinese Government finds it necessary to take a realistic attitude towards the McMahon line* [emphasis added], but cannot act but with prudence and needs time to deal with it.'[7]

While Zhou might have told Nehru verbally about consulting 'Tibetan authorities' as mentioned by Nehru in his letter of 14 December, 1958, in his written response Zhou now completely omitted any such reference. To have done so would have been a grave error, for the Chinese had always maintained that the Tibetan authorities had never been independent and never had any role to play in foreign policy matters. Secondly, Zhou referred to 'Tibetan dissatisfaction with the unilaterally drawn line.' Was he, in actual fact, preparing the ground for advancing Chinese claims *South* of the McMahon Line? Thirdly, Zhou linked the question of taking a 'realistic attitude' to the McMahon Line to the behaviour of India when he referred to the fact that India was a 'friendly' country and that they 'needed time to deal with it.' Zhou's formulation raised a delicate question in the minds of the Indian leadership. What if the Chinese came to the conclusion, at any time in the future, that India's behaviour was 'not friendly'? Would they then revise their opinion of the McMahon Line? It is possible that by now Zhou was worried by the internal situation in Tibet and wanted to establish a link between India's restraint to the events unfolding in Tibet and the acceptance by China of the McMahon Line.

As regards the Western sector, Zhou was deliberately vague. He never gave precise indications as to where the Chinese alignment lay. By doing so, the Chinese were able to progressively advance their claims; maintain one position in 1956, another in 1960 and yet another in 1962. To sound reasonable, Zhou also proposed that the two sides temporarily maintain the status quo, pending a solution through consultations.

The fat was now truly in the fire. A full blown dispute of India's Northern borders now existed. With the advantage of hind sight, it is possible to say that the boundary issue should have been allowed to rest at this point following Zhou's response to Nehru's letter. Each side could have kept what it had occupied. However, if Nehru had let things rest as they were, there were other dangers lurking that were inherent in the situation. Could it be that the Chinese were simply seeking a respite to consolidate their gains and then move further forward into Indian Territory, particularly in Ladakh? Although Zhou's letter proposed that both the Chinese and the Indian sides maintain the status-quo, there was no clarification as to what constituted the status-quo. Nor did Zhou indicate whether the status-quo coincided in the Western sector with the 1956 claim line of the Chinese in Ladakh, or in the Eastern sector with the McMahon Line. With an aroused public opinion pushing him, Nehru did not have the luxury of time to ascertain Chinese intentions. Just a week before the receipt of Zhou's letter of 23 January, 1959, the Yugoslow leader Tito on a visit to India, had coutioned Nehru that the Chinese hostility towards Yugoslavia was 'primarily dictated by ideological and domestic compulsions.' Nevertheless, Nehru was taken by surprise at the harshness of the tone of Zhou's letter and its uncompromising stance.[8] As a result, Nehru's faith in Zhou was truly shaken and he did not trust Zhou anymore. Therefore, letting matters rest was not an option available to Nehru. He also sensed that the Chinese were now determined to undermine his position as a leader of the Non-Aligned Movement.

On the other hand, Nehru was also conscious of the fact that if he entered into negotiations with the Chinese, it would imply that he had decided to compromise India's case, for had he not made it known, as per his directive of 1 July, 1954, that the 'frontier should be considered firm and definite *and not open to discussions with anyone*' [emphasis added], and this position he had publicly confirmed as late as September 1958? It would also have meant that he had decided to violate his own policy directive. The question in Nehru's mind was: could the Chinese Government be trusted? As Nehru's faith in Zhou was completely shaken by this time, the answer in Nehru's mind could only have been negative. Nehru's political options were becoming narrower by the day.

Even before Nehru's first letter [14 December, 1958] to Zhou had been despatched, the US sensed, and was conscious of, the opportunity that had opened up as a result of deteriorating relations between India and China. It did not let this opportunity slip. President Eisenhower paid close attention to the developments in Sino-Indian relations. He surmised correctly that the fear of Chinese aggressive intentions would open a window of opportunity for the US to promote a 'better understanding between India and Pakistan,' a key Western objective at that time.[9] The British, too, felt the same.[10] In a letter designed to flatter Nehru, Eisenhower wrote to him on 27 November, 1958, that:

> Universally you are recognized as one of the most powerful influences for peace and conciliation in the world. I believe that because you are a world leader for peace in your individual capacity... your influence is particularly valuable in stemming the global drift towards cynicism, mutual suspicion and finally disaster.[11]

The US Ambassador in Delhi reported that Eisenhower's letter was very well received. In fact, efforts were made by [PM's Staff] to publish it in its entirety for the benefit of the members of the public and no doubt for the Chinese as well. Meanwhile, leading US public figures such as Walter Lippmann received wide coverage in the Indian press when they identified India as a 'key country.'

Nevertheless, Nehru was convinced that India had a water-tight case on the boundary. Public opinion in India was stridently anti-Chinese and, therefore, there was little room for compromise. Internally, China was in acute distress over the rebellion in Tibet and also because of enormous economic mismanagement. Internationally, both the major powers, the US and Soviet Russia, for reasons of their own, seemed to favour India. Conscious of these developments and confident that the international situation was tilting towards India, Nehru now decided to take a tougher line with the Chinese.

Nehru replied to Zhou's letter of 23 January, 1959, by sending him a detailed response on 22 March, 1959, at the height of the Tibetan rebellion. Was the timing of Nehru's response deliberate or was it a mere coincidence? Nehru was conscious of the timing for he admitted in a note on 20 March, 1959, to the Foreign Secretary, S Dutt, that:

> The idea struck me that in view of developments in Tibet, perhaps this was not the best time to send this letter. But, on re-consideration, I think it is right for us to send it as soon as possible.[12]

Doubtless, the Chinese, suspicious as ever over India's attitude towards Tibet, would have suspected an ulterior motive on the timing of Nehru's letter.

In his letter of 22 March, 1959, Nehru conceded that the Sino-Indian frontier was not demarcated on the ground 'in all the sectors', but reiterated that the 'Sino-Indian frontier follows, in the main, the geographical principle of watershed on the crest of the high Himalayan range and that most parts have the sanction of specific international agreements between the Governments of India and China.' In the Western sector, Nehru cited the 1842 Treaty that 'mentions' the India-China boundary and referred to the fact that in 1847, the Chinese Government 'admitted that this boundary was sufficiently and distinctively fixed.' In the Eastern sector, Nehru mentioned the Simla Convention and the McMahon Line. Nehru said that 'there is nothing to indicate that the Tibetan authorities were in any way dissatisfied with the agreed boundary.' Nor is there anything to indicate that the Chinese Government ever expressed any reservation on 'the India-Tibet frontier either during discussions or at the time of initialling the Convention.'[12] It will be seen that the facts support Nehru on this point, for in a telegram dated 25 April, 1914, from the Chinese Foreign Office handed over to Sir Henry McMahon by the Chinese plenipotentiary Ivan Chen, the Chinese Government specifically confirmed that:

> With the exception of Article 9 [which refers to the boundary between Inner and Outer Tibet] of the draft Convention, we are prepared to take the main principles embodied in the other Articles into our favourable consideration, which is, again, a further great concession from us.[14]

From the contents of this letter, it is obvious that there was no 'dis-satisfaction' evident, and it seems that Zhou was simply embellishing his case. Moreover, the McMahon Line has the advantage of running along the crest of the high Himalayan range and separates the Tibetan plateau in the North from the sub-mountain region in the South and is, thus, in conformity with the main geographical principle that China had accepted in other sectors of the boundary.

Further, Nehru also took up the Sikkim-Tibet boundary and reiterated that it was defined under the 1890 Anglo-Chinese Convention and jointly demarcated on the ground in 1895.

As for the middle sector, Nehru did not go into detail but said that the boundary line was 'traditional' and confirmed by old revenue records, the exercise of Indian administrative authority and by maps. Nehru emphasized to Zhou that there was 'sufficient authority based on geography, tradition as well as treaties for the boundary to be *shown as shown in our published maps*' [emphasis added]. Nehru also took the opportunity to agree with Zhou's suggestion that neither side should take 'unilateral action', but added a rider that '*if any possession has been secured recently, that position should be rectified*' [emphasis added].[15] By this Nehru meant that the entire area between the Kuen Luen and Karakoram mountains ranges—loosely referred to as the Aksai Chin—should be vacated by the Chinese. On the other hand, Zhou's reference to the status quo earlier was on the basis that the Chinese had *always* been in possession of the Aksai Chin [not correct] and, therefore, there was no question of withdrawal. Thus, while both Nehru and Zhou Enlai proposed accepting the status quo, the status quo meant two different things to both India and China. While Nehru wanted *a restoration* of the status quo, Zhou wanted *maintenance* of the status quo [emphasis added].

Zhou took his time to respond, for the Tibetan revolt was at its height. Nehru showed slight irritation at the delay when he told a press conference on 7 August, 1959, that the Chinese were 'maintaining a strange silence.' The Chinese were busy putting down the Tibetan rebellion and coping with the international consequences of the flight of the Dalai Lama from Lhasa. On 9 September, 1959, to further complicate matters the Dalai Lama, contrary to Nehru's advice, appealed to the UN.

Nevertheless, Zhou responded in detail on 8 September, 1959. While reiterating that the Sino-Indian boundary question was a 'complicated question left over by history', he emphasised that the 'over-all settlement should be sought taking into account the historical background and *existing actualities*' [emphasis added]. In other words, China would continue to keep what it had occupied. It was obvious that the Chinese, incensed over the events in Tibet, were now adopting a hardline. Gone were Zhou's earlier hesitations and tentativeness. The tone of the letter was hard, too.

Further, Zhou went into greater detail and clarified that in the Western sector, while accepting that the 1842 Treaty was indeed concluded by 'local authorities of China's Tibet and Kashmir,' emphasized that the 1842 Treaty did not contain any 'specific provisions or explanations regarding the location of this section of the boundary', nor that the Central Chinese Government had 'ratified it or sent any representatives.' Further, Zhou asserted if this treaty had indeed 'delimited the boundary,' then why did the British Government formally propose an alignment to the Chinese Government in 1899 [MacDonald proposals]? In an apparent contradiction to the above stance, Zhou claimed that there was a 'customary line derived from historical traditions,' and that Chinese maps had always drawn the boundary 'in accordance with this line,' which corresponds fairly closely to the line drawn in the map contained in Cunningham's book *Ladakh*.[16]

In the Eastern sector Zhou, in contradiction to his earlier position that China finds 'it necessary to take a realistic attitude towards the McMahon Line' [letter of 23 January, 1959], now completely repudiated it. He now maintained that:

> Contrary to what was said in your letter, the so-called McMahon Line was never discussed at the Simla Conference, but was determined by the British representative and the representative of the Tibet local authorities behind the back of the representative of the Chinese Central Government through an exchange of secret notes in Delhi on 24 March, 1914, that is, prior to the signing of the Simla Treaty. This line was later marked on the map attached to the Simla Treaty as part of the boundary between Tibet and the rest of China. The so-called McMahon Line was a product of the British policy of aggression against the Tibet Region of China and has never been recognized by any Chinese Central Government, and is, therefore, decidedly illegal. As to the Simla Treaty, it was not formally signed by the representative of the then Chinese Central Government, and this is explicitly noted in the treaty. For quite a long time after the exchange of secret notes between Britain and the Tibet local authorities, Britain dared not make public the related documents nor change the traditional way of drawing this section of the boundary on maps.[17]

Here Zhou was being economical with the truth that the '*McMahon Line was determined behind the back of the Chinese Government*' for if that was so, then why did the Chinese Foreign Office, in a Memorandum on 29 June, 1914 [soon after their refusal to sign the Simla Convention], implore the British Government to continue to act as mediators? The Chinese Memorandum requested that:

> It is earnestly hoped that His Majesty's Government will still consent to continue in its original intention to act as mediator between China and Tibet, in order that the questions between these two countries [Note: the word used is country to describe Tibet] may reach a harmonious conclusion.[18]

Further, as the Simla Conference records show, the Chinese delegate, Ivan Chen, never at any stage, objected to the bilateral India-Tibet Boundary Agreement [McMahon Line].[19] In fact, he was present at the signing on 3 July, 1914. It would be incredulous to imagine that Chen did not know what was happening.

Having taken the hard line in his letter of 8 September, 1959, Zhou softened his stance in the same letter by stating that although China 'absolutely does not recognize the so-called McMahon Line', yet '*Chinese troops had never crossed the line*' [emphasis added]. On the other hand, he accused India of occupying areas *North* of the McMahon Line at Shatze, Khinzemane and Tamaden. And, for effect, Zhou stated that 'like Bhutan, the Sikkim-Tibet boundary does not fall within the scope of our present discussion.' The implication being that India had no legal jurisdiction or *locus standi* over Sikkim.

Just a few days prior to the receipt of Zhou's letter of 8 September, Nehru had received a very warm and encouraging letter from President Eisenhower that was sent from Paris. In his letter of 2 September, 1959, Eisenhower said:

> I have been distressed to learn from your statements in Parliament that India is experiencing serious trouble with the Chinese Communist regime over border incursions and certain matters concerning Tibet. Those difficulties are of concern to India's friends... I would like you to know that I am personally following these events with concern and that I fully appreciate the problems which they have created for you.[20]

Eisenhower sent Nehru another letter on 16 September, 1959, lauding him for his efforts to settle the border issue through 'peaceful methods.' Nehru, having received two very encouraging letters within the space of two weeks from Eisenhower, was now much more confident. The *TASS* statement of 9 September, 1959, issued by Soviet Russia despite urgent requests from the Chinese not to do so, further strengthened Nehru's belief that his policies were on the right track. The *TASS* statement blamed neither side, but was plainly in favour of India. It riled the Chinese no end. Nehru sensed that he had the support of both the super powers and this considerably strengthened his belief that his policy of non-alignment was correct and that his handling of the Chinese on the boundary question was also on the right track.

At this point in time, it seemed as if the Chinese, too, were beginning to sense their isolation. The Indian Ambassador in China reported that he was once again being received by the Chinese Foreign Minister, and that the guards surrounding the Indian Mission at Lhasa had been removed. Separately, Zhou also sent a much warmer message to Nehru stating that '*current differences were only an episode in the story of age old friendship*' [emphasis added] and on 24 October, 1959, Zhou sent an invitation through Nehru to the Vice-President of India to visit China. Dr Subandrio, the Indonesian Foreign Minister, returning from a visit to Beijing said that 'he was sure that China wanted to settle the border with India peacefully as soon as possible.' Nehru, too, began to sound conciliatory. Nehru opposed the reference of Tibet to the UN and told a press conference on 7 September, 1959, that the issue of Tibet in the UN would mean that it would become a part of the 'cold war.' Speaking in the Lok Sabha on 12 September, 1959, Nehru said that 'the Aksai Chin area is in our maps undoubtedly. But it is a matter of argument as to what part belongs to us and what part of it belongs to somebody else...the matter has been challenged for a hundred years. *There has never been delimitation there*' [emphasis added]. Nehru had also earlier told the Lok Sabha on 28 August, 1959, that 'nobody had marked the Ladakh-Tibet Boundary.'[21] Here was an opportunity that had, ostensibly, now opened for both sides for a compromise, for if the delimitation in the Aksai Chin area was in doubt then it would be easy to agree with the Chinese to go in for a fresh delimitation. Sadly, it seems to have been missed.

The main culprit that induced Nehru to return to a hard line posture seems to be the Chinese Foreign Minister, Chen Yi, who, in an unprovoked vitriolic attack against Nehru at the National People's Conference called him 'two-faced.'[22] Nehru could not hide his sense of betrayal. He wrote to Zhou that he felt 'greatly surprised and distressed.' [Letter of 26 September, 1959]

Nehru replied to Zhou's letter of 8 September, 1959, on 26 September, 1959, and gave a point by point rebuttal to Zhou's assertions, as also a very detailed expose of India's position. On the question of using force, Nehru stressed that far from trying to use 'force,' as alleged by Zhou, India had kept under wraps China's creeping forward movements in the hope of settling the matter peacefully. Nehru cited the building of the Aksai Chin road, the entry of Chinese survey parties in the Lohit Frontier Division in 1957, the establishment of a camp at Spanggur in 1959, the despatch of armed personnel to Bara Hoti in 1958 and the use of force at Longju as examples of China's violations of the status-quo.

On the Ladakh-Tibet border Nehru vigorously countered Zhou's assertion that China 'did not send anyone to participate nor did it ratify the 1842 Treaty.' The 1842 Treaty was signed by a representative of the Emperor of China. It implicitly says so, as does the original Tibetan version. While it is true that it refers to 'old established frontiers' and the 1842 Treaty did not specify where the boundary lines were, yet there is a reference to 'old and well established [boundary line]' that is easily understood by all. Even Cunningham, whom Zhou had quoted with approval, toured the area in 1846 and stated in 1854 that the Eastern boundary of Ladakh was 'well defined by piles of stones which were set up after the last expulsion of the Mongols in 1687.'[23]

Even the British historian, Alaister Lamb, admits that the Cunningham-Strachey Boundary Commission constituted by the British in 1847 was 'greatly helped by the clear marking of much of the Tibet-Ladakh border *by boundary pillars set up in 1687'* [emphasis added]. [24] Further in 1893, the Chinese themselves put *up a stone marker and a board at Karakoram pass on which was written in Chinese characters 'This is under the control of the Emperor of China'* [emphasis added]. The British responded to Chinese activity by stating that 'it will be best to say that we see no occasion to remonstrate with the Chinese *on account of the erection of those boundary pillars'* [emphasis added].[25] Thus, for nearly two centuries the boundary was well recognized by both sides and clearly *demarcated* at important points; rendering Chinese claims that it has never been 'delimited' [or demarcated] quite untenable!

As for Zhou's denial that the Chinese had not ratified it [the 1842 Treaty], Nehru quoted a Chinese official, K'e-ying, the Chinese Viceroy at Canton, telling Sir John Davis, British Commissioner at Hong Kong, in 1847 that:

> The borders of these territories have been sufficiently and distinctly fixed so that it will be best to adhere to this ancient arrangement, and it will prove far more convenient to abstain from any additional measures for fixing them.'[26]

Thus, how could it be surmised that the 1842 Treaty, which specifically refers to a restoration of boundaries as '*fixed* from ancient times' and using the key word '*fixed boundaries* of Ladakh,' be said to have been used without any intent and purpose [emphasis added]? It is also interesting to note that *all other provisions of the Treaty, such as exchange of goods etc, were in operation right up till 1946, and the Chinese Government never objected or hindered these provisions from implementation* [emphasis added]. As for 1899 MacDonald proposals, Nehru felt that these referred to the Northern frontier of Ladakh with Xinjiang [Sinkiang] and not to the Eastern frontier of Ladakh with Tibet.

On the Eastern sector, Nehru was even more forthright. He stoutly defended the McMahon Line, refuting Zhou's charge that it was a product of 'British policy of aggression against China.' The Chinese representative not only fully participated as a delegate, but on an *equal footing with the Tibetan representative.* All arrangements at Simla were made with the knowledge and consent of the Chinese authorities, and the Chinese Foreign Minister wrote to the British Government on 7 August, 1913, that the Chinese plenipotentiary would proceed to India to 'open negotiations for a treaty *jointly with the Tibetan and British plenipotentiaries*' [emphasis added]. That Tibet participated on an equal footing with China is further supported by the inescapable fact that the three countries formally exchanged and recognized the credentials of each other at the start of the conference. In fact, the Chinese President, Yuan Shih-kai, issued a Presidential Order on 21 April, 1912, declaring Tibet to be an administered province of China. To emphasize the tri-partite nature of the Simla Conference, the 1912 Presidential Order *was specifically revoked on 13 June, 1913,* and the Chinese Government accepted that *all three participants were on an equal footing* [emphasis added].

As for Tibet's international personality and its competence to conclude foreign treaties, Nehru cited the 1856 Treaty between Tibet and Nepal as also the 1904 Lhasa Convention reached between Tibet and Britain, with the active assistance of the Chinese Ambassador in Tibet to prove that Tibet had the right to conclude international treaties.

Not only were the frontiers of India and Tibet discussed at the conference, but at no stage either at the conference or subsequently, did the Chinese object; for the Chinese representative at Simla, Ivan Chen was fully aware of the McMahon Line. It would be a travesty to suggest otherwise. Discussions on the India-Tibet boundary between the British Indian Government and Tibet took place from 15-31 January, 1914. At the 4th meeting of the full conference on 17 February, 1914, McMahon tabled a statement on the territorial limits of Tibet. In a map attached to the statement, the 'historic frontiers' of Tibet were shown for acceptance that later came to be known as the McMahon Line. There was no Chinese dissent. Discussions between Britain and Tibet followed, and that resulted in an agreement which is fully recorded in the exchange of letters between McMahon and Lonchen Shatra. The draft Indo-Tibet boundary was formally confirmed on 24 and

MacDONALD PROPOSAL, 14 MARCH 1899

On instructions of the British government, Sir Claude MacDonald the British envoy to China, wrote a formal letter on 14 March 1899 conveying to the Chinese Government the following: [relevant excerpts]

[a] It is now proposed by the Indian Government that for the sake of avoiding any dispute or uncertainty in the future, a clear understanding should be come to with the Chinese Government as to the frontier between the two states.

[b] From the Karakoram Pass the crests of the range run East for about half a degree [100 li], and then turn South to a little below the 35th parallel of North latitude. Rounding then what in our maps is shown as the source of the Karakash, the line of hills to be followed runs North-East to a point East of Kizil Gilka, and from there in a South-Easterly direction, follows the LakTsung Range until that meets the spur running South from the K'un-lun range, which has hitherto been shown on our maps as the Eastern boundary of Ladakh. This is a little *East of longitude 80^{0} East longitude* [emphasis added].

[c] ...you will see by examining this line that a large tract of country to the North of the Great Dividing Range, shown in Hung Chun's map as outside the Chinese boundary, will be recognized as Chinese territory. [*In other words, India would cede territory]*

****

The Chinese Government never acknowledged this proposal.

Hung Chun was a senior Chinese Government official, who as the Chinese Minister at the Court of St. Petersburg [Russia], had, in 1893 presented *an official map to the British Indian Consul at Kashgar, for onward transmission which showed both LingziThang and the Aksai Chin as outside Chinese territories and as a part of British India [emphasis added].*

25 March, 1914, and submitted at the 7th full meeting of all delegates on 22 April, 1914.

On 26 April, 1914, Ivan Chen, the Chinese plenipotentiary, officially communicated the Chinese Government stand to McMahon and stated:

> With the exception of Article 9 of the draft convention, we are prepared to take the main principles, embodied in the other articles, into favourable consideration.[27]

And just prior to the signing of the Simla Convention on 3 July, 1914, by the British and Tibetan representatives, the Chinese Government, once again, conveyed as follows:

> This Government has several times stated that it gives its support to the majority of the articles of the Convention. The part it is unable to agree is that dealing with the question of the boundary.[28]

The British Government, in a further effort to convince the Chinese Government to accept the Simla Convention, informed the Chinese Government on 25 June, 1914, that:

> As it is, the patience of HMG is exhausted and they have no alternative but to inform the Chinese Government that unless the Convention is signed before the end of this month, HMG will hold themselves free to sign separately with Tibet.

Similarly, on 8 August, 1914, the British Foreign Office told the Chinese Ambassador that:

> Chinese adherence or recognition was not necessary for the Anglo-Tibetan Convention of 3 July, 1914, and the boundary agreement of 25 March, 1914, for it to be valid.

Therefore, there was no attempt by the British Government *to sign* the Simla Convention 'behind the backs' of the Chinese delegate, for otherwise why would the British Government go to all the trouble of informing the Chinese Government? And, in a book published in 1924 and written by Sir Charles Bell, one of the principal architects of the Simla Conference, he specifically refers to the Indo-Tibetan Agreement of 1914. This is what he says in his book:

> The opportunity was also taken to negotiate the frontiers to be established between Tibet and North-East India...it proved fortunately possible to establish the frontier between India and Tibet over 850 miles of difficult and dangerous country. We have, thus, gained a frontier standing back everywhere about 100 miles from the plains of India.[29]

There was again no Chinese protest.

Earlier, on 13 June, 1914, the Chinese had made fresh proposals to the British Government on the Inner-Outer Tibet boundary. There was no mention of the

India-Tibet boundary. Similarly, five years later, on 30 May, 1919, the Chinese again made fresh proposals suggesting modifications of the Simla Convention. These, again, related to Inner Tibet and Outer Tibet and Inner Tibet and China. Significantly, there was no reference to India-Tibet boundary [McMahon Line]! Similarly, the Chinese Foreign Office issued the China Year Book 1921-22 and in it published the Chinese official version of the Anglo-Chinese negotiations over Tibet. Here again, there is no mention of the McMahon Line or that there was a dispute over it! The McMahon Line, in fact, represents the customary boundary of the area, and it formalized the natural, traditional, ethnic and administrative boundary. As for the map quoted by Zhou in his letter to Nehru in support of the Chinese claim line in the Eastern sector, i.e. the 1929 edition of the Encyclopedia Britannica, this very map also shows the whole of Aksai Chin in India! Zhou should have known that you cannot selectively quote parts that suit you.

Nehru also contested Zhou's assertion that the British Government had 'dared not published in Simla Convention' by asserting that this was done primarily in the hope that there would be an agreement about the status and boundary of Inner Tibet.' In any case, the Simla Convention was published by the British in the 1929 Edition of Aitcheson's Treaties, and the McMahon Line shown in official maps from 1937 onwards. These maps were circulated widely and were never contested by the Chinese as being incorrect.

From the time of the Simla Convention of 1914 till 23 January, 1959, the Chinese Government has never officially *in any document*, ever challenged the McMahon Line. Even official Chinese maps of the late 19th century showed the boundary in this sector as approximately to the Indian alignment. In addition, international law is quite clear on the subject:

> If a state acquires knowledge of an act which it considers internationally illegal, and in violation, and nevertheless, does not protest; this attitude implies a renunciation of such rights, provided that a protest would have been necessary to preserve a claim.[32] This view is further reinforced by the ICJ judgement in the Indonesia vs Malaysia Case.[33]

Thus, the Chinese had no case even as per international law on this subject.

Much is made by some scholars that the Simla Convention was not signed but only initialled by the Chinese delegate, thereby suggesting that it was not a legal document. The fact of the matter is that the Tibetan plenipotentiary [LonchenShatraPaljorDorje] put his full signature, as per Tibetan custom, for it is not possible to initial in the Tibetan language.[30] The two maps of 27 April, 1914, and 3 July, 1914, showing the India-Tibet boundary, bear the full signatures of the Tibetan plenipotentiary. The map of 27 April, 1914, bears the full signature of the Chinese plenipotentiary, Ivan Chen. The British plenipotentiary, McMahon, initialled the map of 27 April, 1914, but signed in full the map attached to the 3 July, 1914, Convention, as also the Trade Regulations of 3 July, 1914.

Here is a list of significant official Chinese communications where there is no mention or their objection to the India-Tibet Boundary [McMahon Line]:

[1] On 30 October, 1913, during the Simla conference the Chinese delegate presented 'counter proposals'. Point 7 of these proposals read as follows: 'the frontier between China proper and Tibet is now roughly indicated in the accompanying map'. The boundary line drawn by the Chinese ran *North* of Tawang.

[2] On 3 April, 1914, the Chinese presented a 5-point proposal. There was no reference to the border with India.

[3] On 20 April 1914, a telegram was sent by the Wai Chia Pu [Chinese Foreign Office] to the Chinese plenipotentiary at the Simla Conference, Ivan Chen, and it listed seven points on which China would never give in. There was no mention of the boundary with India in any of the seven points.

[4] On 25 April, 1914, a telegram from the Wai Chia Pu [Chinese Foreign Office] to the British authorities hinted that but for the China-Tibet boundary, the rest of the decisions of the Simla Convention were acceptable. A memo was accordingly handed over to the British Ambassador, which ignored the Tibet-India boundary.

[5] On 1 May, 1914, the Chinese President sent a Secretary to the British Ambassador, Sir John Jordan, with the message that '*only the question of the China-Tibet boundary was not acceptable*' [*the reference was to the inclusion of Chiamdo and Kokonor in Tibet*]. There was no mention of the Tibet-India boundary.

[6] On 13 June and 29 June, 1914, the Chinese authorities sent a memo to the British along with a map. The map centred only on Inner-Outer Tibet. The red line indicating the McMahon Line remained unaltered. A yellow line boundary showed the partition line as originally claimed by China. A brown line showed the compromise that China now offered.

[7] On 6 July, 1914, the Wai Chia Pu [Chinese Foreign Office] informed the British Ambassador in Peking that 'it is much to be regretted that *that boundary* [*Inner-Outer Tibet*] *and that alone has prevented an agreement*'.

[8] On 13 May 1919, China again sent proposals to the British Government that referred only to the Inner-Outer Tibet boundary. The Chinese wanted that Batang, Litang and Ta Chien Lu be made a part of Szechuan province.

[9] The 1921-22 China Year Book by HGW Woodhead, published by Tientsin Press, has on p. 617 the following statement by a Wai Chia Pu [Foreign Office] official:

China dis-satisfied with suggested division into an Inner and Outer Tibet, the boundaries of which would involve the evacuation of those districts actually in Chinese effective occupation, but is 'otherwise in accord with the general principles of the Draft Convention' [*Simla Convention 1914*], *though the initialled draft is in no way binding on her.*

[10] On 26 January, 1950, the Constitution of India came into force; with NEFA included in the 6th Schedule. It is a public document. There was no Chinese protest.

[11] On 20 November, 1950, Nehru stated in Parliament that 'map or no map, the McMahon Line was India's North-East frontier. There was no Chinese protest.

[12] On 12 February, 1951, Major Khating took over Tawang Administration from the Tibetans. Again, no Chinese protest.

[13] On 22 March 1951, Lhasa was officially informed of the intention of the Indian Government that 'regular administration' would be extended right up to the international frontier, i.e., the McMahon Line. There was no Chinese protest, even though they were by now fully ensconced in Lhasa.

The above contention falls flat, for even Zhou never denied that the Tibetans did not sign the Simla Convention. Zhou's objection was that Tibet had 'no right to conclude treaties separately.'[31] In international practice, initialling a treaty signifies assent to its contents, with the proviso that it will come into force only after the necessary constitutional procedures of the signatory states are complete. The text of the proposed agreements, so negotiated, are frozen and not subject to revision. Even official Chinese writings do not lay too much stress on this controversy [signature vs initialling], for perhaps they are aware that under the Vienna Convention on the Law of Treaties, Article 12(2a) initialling a text is considered as valid signatures of the text. [The Vienna Convention is a codification of all existing customary international law of treaties.]

Further, to address other points made by Zhou in his letter of 8 September, 1959, Nehru in his reply on 26 September, 1959, to Zhou admitted that on enquiry it was found that Tamaden was *North* of the McMahon Line and stated that India would withdraw from this area. However, Nehru insisted that Longju was South of the Line and that, as China had occupied Longju by force, it should withdraw from it. Similarly, if the status quo was to be maintained, then China must withdraw from areas it has recently occupied such as Spanggur, Mandal [Eastern Ladakh] etc. Nehru attached a detailed note on the Sino-Indian border along with his letter [26 September, 1959] to Zhou Enlai.

Zhou Enlai responded on 7 November, 1959, to Nehru's letter of 26 September, 1959, after another clash had taken place at Kongka La [Pass] on 21 October, 1959. Indian blood was once again shed. This time, Zhou did not reply on the merits of the case but made two proposals. These were [a] that both sides '*to withdraw 20 kilometres at once from the so-called McMahon Line in the East, and from the line up to which each side exercises control in the West and that the two sides undertake to refrain from sending again their armed personnel to be stationed in and patrol the zones from which they have evacuated their armed forces.*' And [b] Zhou also proposed an immediate PM's meeting.

Zhou's initiative to propose a meeting at PM's level was in line with a decision of the Chinese Politburo taken on 8 September, 1959, to resolve the Sino-Indian boundary dispute through negotiations.[34] This line was confirmed by Mao after an informal meeting of senior leaders on 3 November, 1959, that had met to consider the situation along the Sino-Indian border.[35] These decisions were probably based on the realization that China was losing political ground as both the US and Soviet Russia seemed to be firmly on India's side. World opinion, particularly within Asian-African nations, was also turning against China, alarmed at China's aggressiveness on the border against a leading non-aligned country. This was the main reason for the urgency in Zhou's letter in pressing for an immediate meeting with Nehru.

Nehru responded rather quickly. In his reply of 16 November, 1959, Nehru said that in the Eastern sector, it would be very difficult to establish a 'new line', some 20 kilometres from the McMahon Line, because of the difficulties of the terrain. Instead, Nehru proposed that since none of the border posts of the two countries were in sight of each other and if both sides desisted from sending patrols, any chance of a clash would be minimal. Secondly, '*we cannot agree to any arrangement, even as an interim measure, that would keep your forcible possessions intact.*' Nehru suggested that China withdraw from Longju and that India would not occupy it. Nehru also reiterated that at no point on this border have '*we taken any post from you*' [emphasis added]. The Indian Army leadership was also against any 'pull-back,' for the Chinese could easily reinforce their troops at the border whilst Indian troops would have to traverse several mountain ridges to do so.

For the Western border, Nehru made a counter-proposal. India would withdraw *West* of the line as shown by the Chinese side in its 1956 map, and similarly, China should withdraw *East* of the international boundary as described by India. This would eliminate all chances of a clash, as the distance between the two positions would thus be vast. Nehru indicated a willingness to meet with Zhou, but suggested that as a large mass of data was involved, some preliminary steps need to be taken to 'lay the foundation of our discussions.' 'We should' Nehru felt, concentrate on reaching 'an interim understanding' so as to ease present tensions. Nehru's reply indicated a hardening of India's stance for after the Kongka La incident, where Indian blood had been shed, Nehru was very reluctant to offer any concessions under duress. He was convinced that India and China had fallen out completely and that in the future it would be an era of 'continuing tension.'[36]

Meanwhile, President Eisenhower visited India from 9-14 December, 1959, and received a rousing welcome of such warmth that he probably had never anticipated. However, Eisenhower was aware of the reasons why this had happened. In a meeting on 10 December, 1959, Eisenhower assured Nehru that should India have serious difficulties with China, he would ensure that there was no back stabbing from Pakistan. Eisenhower emphatically told Nehru that 'I give you a guarantee that we would not allow Pakistan to do so. I have told Ayub that anyone using US arms would have us on the other side.'[37] Eisenhower confided in Nehru that although the US had supplied military weapons to Pakistan, yet the supply of ammunition was under firm control. In fact, Pakistan *had only ten days supply of ammunition* [emphasis added] and, therefore, could not act unilaterally against India even if it wished to do so. Nehru was deeply assured and felt that he could now face the imminent threat from the North with greater confidence. The Chinese perception of Eisenhower's visit to India, however, was that he 'promised Nehru that in case India fights a war with China, it can look forward to America for help, even if both countries never had any military alliance.'[38]

Zhou, fully aware of the tremendous reception that Eisenhower had received in India, would naturally have suspected that the US was fully behind India. Zhou's reply dated 17 December, 1959, to Nehru's letter [16 November, 1959], thus began on a conciliatory note. Zhou proposed that how far each side should withdraw its armed forces could be worked out 'through consultations.' As for Chinese withdrawal from Longju, Zhou made a counter demand. India should vacate Khinzemane in the Eastern sector and in the middle sector should withdraw from Shipki Pass, Parigas Sang, Tsungsha, Puling-sumdo, Chuva, Chuje, Sangcha and Lapthal all 'occupied after the signing of the 1954 Agreement.' As for Nehru's proposal for the Ladakh sector, Zhou termed it as 'unfair.' This area 'does not belong to India' and China would have to withdraw from 33,000 square kilometres with all its personnel. This area was of 'great importance to China as it has been a traffic artery linking vast regions of Sinkiang with Western Tibet.'

Zhou then made a counter-proposal. Why not apply the same principle to the Eastern sector also? In other words, India would have to withdraw from NEFA down to the Line claimed by China, and China would stay North of the McMahon Line! In his letter of 17 December, 1959, Zhou made two very significant statements. Firstly, that:

> '*the Government of the People's Republic of China has strictly abided by its statement of absolutely not allowing its armed personnel to cross this line [McMahon Line] in waiting for a friendly settlement of the boundary question*' [emphasis added].[39] In other words China would honour the McMahon alignment.

And

> *secondly that in the Western sector the 'Chinese map published in 1956, correctly shows the traditional boundary between the two countries in this sector.'*[40] In other words *for the first time* China confirmed its version of the border alignment in the Western sector. [emphasis added]

Zhou also said that the reason why he had insisted on a meeting of the two PMs was to 'reach some agreements of principles as a guidance to concrete discussions as otherwise the two sides would get bogged down in endless and fruitless debates.' He invited Nehru to China or, if that was inconvenient, then he suggested Rangoon. It was quite obvious that exchanges between the two PMs were leading nowhere as the differences between the two sides remained huge.

Nehru was very disappointed with Zhou's response. But Nehru was considerably heartened by Eisenhower's forthright support and he wrote a note on 21 December, 1959, to the Foreign Secretary that inter alia, stressed that huge differences had opened up between India and China:

> I have read this letter with regret. It does not accept the reasonable and practical proposals I made to PM Zhou in order to secure an immediate lessening of tension along the Sino-Indian border, and to create the necessary atmosphere for a peaceful settlement of the border problem. I cannot see how we can reach an agreement on principles when there is such complete disagreement about the facts.

From the period September 1959 to March 1960, India and China exchanged nearly thirty notes, eight letters and six memorandums on the boundary question, but to no avail. By now, Nehru was totally convinced, having seen and been briefed by officials on all material available both in London and New Delhi, that India's historical case on the Aksai Chin was indeed very strong. Nehru told Parliament that India's case was 'fool-proof.'[41]

Khrushchev visited India twice during February 1960. When Nehru obliquely raised the question of the boundary dispute, Khrushchev stated that the Sino-Indian Boundary dispute represented for them a 'most embarrassing question...the difficulty is that we think of you and China as friendly peace-loving countries...we would not like our relations with either of our friends to cool off.' While declining to intervene, Khrushchev said that Soviet mediation would only 'make matters worse.' He strongly urged a bilateral approach.[42]

With the Sino-Indian relationship at an impasse, Nehru decided to make one more effort to seek a solution. Nehru invited Zhou to Delhi for talks, but was careful to say that he had decided on this course of action before Khrushchev's visit to India, so as not to give the impression that he had succumbed to Soviet pressure. While inviting Zhou to India, Nehru on 18 January, 1960, publicly clarified that 'in our opinion we have nothing to negotiate; our minds are quite clear. That is one thing. But so far as we are concerned we are always ready to talk.' Nehru was careful to make a distinction. These were 'talks,' he said, and 'not negotiations.' This is important as Nehru was under tremendous pressure domestically not to give an inch to the Chinese. The Soviets were pleased with Nehru's initiative and expressed the hope that 'time is not far when both China and India will do away with their differences and restore good relations.'[43] China was also in a concilatory mood, having agreed on a tentative boundary settlement with Burma on 28 January, 1960; [ratified on 4 January, 1961] hinted that this could also take place with other 'countries.'[44] [China accepted the McMahon alignment with Burma]

Zhou visited India from 19-25 April, 1960. There were seven meetings totalling about twenty hours between the two Prime Ministers, all one to one. Zhou's main effort was to get Nehru to agree to 'six common points.' The most important of the six points were three points which were: [1] there exists a dispute with regard to the boundary [2] there exists a 'line of actual control' upto which each side exercises administrative jurisdiction and [3] a settlement should take into account the national feelings of the two peoples towards the Himalayas and the Karakoram mountains. India could not accept any of these points. Acceptance of point [1] would mean admission that there was no traditional frontier and the entire length would have to be discussed and delimited, and eventually demarcated afresh. Acceptance of point [2] would imply that India accepted that China in Ladakh had always been in possession of territory right up to their claim line, a suggestion that India had strongly denied. Acceptance of point [3] would imply that India would be amenable to a barter deal which was hinted at. India was not ready to do so at this stage. Separately, Foreign Minister Chen Yi told Swaran Singh that China would never accept the 'Simla Convention and the McMahon Line' as the basis of any border settlement. Chen Yi never clarified whether they would accept the McMahon Line *alignment.*

Interestingly, Chinese accounts of the Nehru-Zhou meetings, published subsequently, tell a different story. Was a package deal offered? Chinese writings indicate that in their first meeting, Zhou stated that although the area South of the McMahon Line was once part of Tibet, yet China would be 'practical' and not raise new demands.[45] In their fifth meeting, Zhou stated that the customary 'line of actual control' be treated as the basis of a settlement. This implied a recognition of Chinese position in the West and India's position in the East. In the sixth meeting, Zhou further clarified that in the Eastern sector we recognize the line reached by India's administrative jurisdiction and in the Western sector, India should recognize the line of China's administrative jurisdiction.[46] This was the basis of the claim made by Chinese writers that a 'package deal' had, indeed been made by Zhou during this meetings with Nehru.

As opposed to the above account given by Chinese sources, Zhou's Indian interlocutors completely differed. S Gopal, who was the Head of the Historical Division of the Ministry of External Affairs and later Nehru's biographer, was of the view that at no time did Zhou offer to swap recognition of the McMahon Line for the cession of Aksai Chin.[47] There was no concrete suggestion about this either in a letter or in the talks. There was no such offer.[48] On the other hand, Pillai [MEA Secretary General] told the British High Commissioner that 'the Chinese would be prepared for some sort of a deal on the basis of a status quo in NEFA and other areas, for an Indian concession in Ladakh.'[49] Vice President Radhakrishnan told the British High Commissioner, MacDonald, that this was a 'sensible bargain' and that if in Ladakh the Chinese accepted Indian sovereignty, 'in theory' India would 'agree to them remaining in practical occupation of territory they now occupied.'[50] Whether it was the intention of the Chinese PM to settle the issue or offer a bargain is a matter of surmise,[51] although there is a stray reference to Zhou's offer to link a settlement on the basis of the status quo as it obtained both in the Aksai Chin and NEFA areas, as contained in a circular telegram issued by the Foreign Secretary on 27 April, 1960, and addressed to all Indian Heads of Mission.[52] Thus, as matters progressed, the Chinese were never seriously tested. In any case, the entire Cabinet was united in its opposition to any 'barter deal'[53] and, therefore, Nehru held firm to India's position and ruled out any 'question of a barter.' Nehru's belief was that even if India 'gave in' and accepted Chinese claims in Ladakh, other demands would not be long in coming, for Nehru's suspicions were by now totally aroused. The Secretary General [MEA] explained Nehru's feelings to the British High Commissioner in a meeting on 25 April, 1960, as follows:

> If we gave way now on this matter, it would only encourage the Chinese to

> feel that they [India] were weak and to press even more ambitious claims later on.[54]

The joint communiqué issued on 25 April, 1960, after the talks ended, tersely stated 'that the talks did not result in resolving the differences that had arisen.' Nor did it mention the five principles of peaceful co-existence. The ultimate fact is that the talks were a failure. As there were differences of opinion on facts and documents, Nehru offered to have them studied 'here and now.' The Chinese refused saying that all their documents were in Beijing.

Would the refusal to give the Dalai Lama political asylum in India in March 1959 have helped matters? It is quite doubtful, for there is no reason to believe that the Chinese would have abandoned their suspicions of Nehru. At this point in time, they were convinced that he was in league with the Western powers. On the other hand, any denial of asylum to the Dalai Lama would have been seen as evidence that Chinese 'pressure' on India was working and proving to be fruitful. This would have encouraged them to make even more demands to gain further concessions from India.

The visit of Zhou to Delhi was a diplomatic disaster. Nehru's attitude was cold for he wanted to indicate the depth of his hurt feelings and those of the Indian people over China's actions. Politically, neither country was in a position to compromise on the boundary issue as inevitably that would be seen as a 'sellout.' That Nehru had held firm came as a sense of relief within India. As Nehru explained to the Lok Sabha on 26 April, 1960, 'our whole argument was based on Chinese forces having come into our territory. Their [Chinese] argument was that they had always been there. That was such a variance in factual state, that there was no meeting ground...this basic disagreement about historical and actual facts came up again and again.'[55] Nehru clarified the same point to Eisenhower that there was 'a strong disagreement on facts' and that the difficulty was that the Chinese 'will not say exactly where they think the border should run.'[56] Nevertheless, the two Prime Ministers did not wish to abandon the effort for a solution and both agreed that the dialogue should continue. The decision to enter into official level talks was designed to avoid an open and final break. It was agreed that the officials would '*examine, check and study all historical documents, records, accounts, maps and other relevant material on which each side relied in support of its stand, and draw up a report for submission to the two Governments.*' The officials had no authority or competence to suggest a solution or recommend anything. All they could do was to examine the facts and report.

The official level talks took place in Beijing [15 June-25 July, 1960], Delhi [19 August-5 October, 1960] and Rangoon [7 November, 1960-12 December, 1960]. India presented 650 items in support of its case whilst the Chinese could marshal only 245 items. China had no map available for the purpose of discussions on a scale greater than 1:5 million. Whilst the Indian presentation could perhaps be faulted for prolixity, the Chinese displayed utter disrespect for logic when they denied Tibetan competence to negotiate the McMahon Line, but used the same Tibetan competence to put forward their case in the middle sector! To any objective reading of the report, it is quite clear that the Chinese presentation of their border claims was scanty, which demonstrated little precise or detailed knowledge. Nevertheless, the results were on expected lines. There was no breakthrough. It was a complete stalemate. Nevertheless, Nehru speaking in the Lok Sabha on 3 April, 1961, felt that the Officials Report brought out the basic facts 'so clearly that I thought even the Chinese Government would be affected by them, not suddenly, but gradually.'

After the officials of the two sides submitted their report in February 1961 there was no further discussions on its contents. The report did not resolve the boundary question, but instead only tended to harden attitudes. Nehru's decision to present the report to Parliament on 14 February, 1961, clearly signalled that the room for a compromise had indeed narrowed considerably, if not completely vanished. If what evidence India had presented to China was indeed as comprehensive as the report testified, then where was the room for any compromise? Politically, Nehru was in no position to compromise, for it would have been political suicide to do so. With members of the public now fully aware of the strength of India's case and with Nehru openly terming it as 'almost fool proof,' the time for a compromise had clearly passed. Incidentally, China withheld the publication of the report till April 1962, perhaps embarrassed by the weight of evidence pointing in India's direction.

Any impartial observer could see that the evidence produced by India in support of its case was 'meticulously prepared, carefully documented and the evidence impressively compiled;'[57] whereas the Chinese evidence was wafer thin. The issue had now assumed a dimension where symbolism was more important than the actual solution itself. Neither side could now afford to go back on its stated position without losing face. Nonetheless, the Chinese attributed the failure of negotiations squarely on Nehru. A Chinese Foreign Ministry internal document [1961] stated that:

> Our Premier took the initiative in going to New Delhi to negotiate with Nehru and exposed the refusal of the Indian ruling group to settle the border dispute. In the diplomatic struggle between India and China the initiative is in our hands. Thus, we prevented the anti-Chinese intrigue of India.[58]

In a talk with the then Soviet Ambassador to China, Chernenko, on 17 May, 1960, Deng Xiaoping emphasized that Zhou Enlai's visit to India fully confirmed 'our previous opinion and position in relation to Nehru.' Further, Deng made two points. Firstly, that 'Nehru is the central figure in the anti-Chinese campaign in India. Nehru is not in a position where rightist and other reactionaries are putting pressure on him; he himself seeks the attainment of his goals by all means possible. Nehru has never lost control over the situation in the country, nor has the situation ever gotten out of hand. Nehru knows how to hold the country firmly in his hands.' Secondly, the trip [Zhou's visit] confirmed that Nehru 'does not want to solve the issue of the Chinese-Indian border under any circumstances, even for some sort of limited period. In this, he is operating on the basis of his interests, both internal and external. Nehru speaks out against the Communist Party of India [CPI]; for this reason, it does not profit him to resolve the border issue with China. Also, for foreign-policy reasons, it is not profitable for him to resolve the issue.' Deng Xiaoping said that if Nehru had eliminated the conflict with China, he would not have received the latest American aid, a sum of US $1.2 billion. Deng Xiaoping noted that 'at present in the Chinese press, articles are being published which are uncovering Nehru's real face.' He further said that 'many political figures in the countries of Asia—Nasser [Egypt], Kasem [Iraq], Sukarno [Indonesia], U Nu [Burma]—are taking the same positions as Nehru. Nehru stands out from them [in that] *he is the cleverest. It was not in vain that he studied in England; in India he is called a half-Englishman and the English are more experienced than the Americans in [playing] political tricks*' [emphasis added].[59]

Meanwhile, the forward movement of Chinese troops continued in Ladakh. After the failure of the Nehru-Zhou talks in April 1960, Zhou wrote to Mao on 6 May, 1960, that 'as no agreement had been reached...it was imperative to strengthen China's military presence in the Western sector.' Zhou suggested that Chinese forces should seize the opportunity and favourable weather conditions to establish additional posts inside China's claim line. Mao approved the proposal and Deng Xiaoping was entrusted with the responsibility for its implementation.[60] Acting on Mao's instructions, by the summer of 1961, the Chinese had advanced in the Western sector nearly 112 kilometres South-West of the positions they held in 1958 and began to set up several forward check posts backed by strong bases in the rear. Nehru confirmed this new Chinese forward movement and told the Lok Sabha on 28 November, 1961, that the Chinese had advanced even beyond their 1956 claim line in Ladakh to establish new bases such as at Nyagzu and Dambuguru. Nehru felt that these moves were an example of China's new 'aggressive activities,' despite their protestations to the contrary. Nehru's views of the Chinese now seemed to become even more harsh. He confided to a diplomat that the Chinese were 'very cold blooded, unemotional people.' He even complained bitterly to British Premier Harold Macmillan. The latter felt that Chinese conduct was 'a grievous blow to him [Nehru] and a source of bitter complaint.'[61]

On 26 September, 1961, the Intelligence Bureau submitted a comprehensive paper on Chinese activities in the border areas and forecast that the 'Chinese would like to come up to their claim line of 1960, wherever we are not in occupation but where even a dozen of our men are present, the Chinese have kept away.' The IB also recommended that in line with this assessment, posts be opened in unoccupied areas of Ladakh.[62] It was to counter such forward movement that Nehru, based on the advice of the Intelligence Bureau, issued orders on 2 November, 1961, that Indian patrols were to move as far forward as possible to prevent the Chinese from moving even further into Indian Territory. The expectation was not so much that territory would be recovered, but primarily to halt further Chinese expansion. It was just a screen. The policy was to build posts and show the flag in the expectation that diplomacy and negotiations would play the dominant part. There was no expectation that the decisive factor would be military force.[63] The hope was that the Chinese, sensing a build-up of Indian military strength, would come to terms and 'satisfactory' arrangements would be worked out.[64]

Nehru's directive issued on 2 November, 1961, stated as follows:

> [a] As far as Ladakh is concerned we are to patrol as far forward as possible from our present positions towards the international border. This will be done with a view to establishing our posts which should prevent the Chinese from advancing any further and also dominating from any posts which they may have established in our territory. This must be done without getting involved in a clash with the Chinese unless this becomes necessary in self-defence.
>
> [b] As regards the middle sector and other Northern areas there are not the same difficulties as in Ladakh. We should, therefore, as far as practicable, go forward and be in effective occupation of the whole frontier. Where there are any gaps, these must be covered either by patrolling or by posts.
>
> [c] In view of the numerous operational and administrative difficulties, efforts should be made to position major concentrations of forces along our borders in places conveniently situated behind the forward posts from where they could be maintained logistically and from where they can restore a border situation at short notice.[65]

While the Army Chief, General Thapar, circulated the above instructions to Army Commands, he inexplicably, left out the point about troop concentrations in the rear.

In the context of the fact that Chinese claim lines kept shifting, from the 1956 line to the line put forward at the meeting of officials in 1960 to the line the Chinese eventually reached in 1962, this policy certainly had merits. At some point, the advancing Chinese forces had to be met, as otherwise what would prevent them from reaching the Indus river valley in Ladakh? A vacuum could not have been left for the Chinese to occupy. Nehru was in no position to answer a political onslaught that would have inevitably followed in just such a contingency. Nehru realized that his political fortunes were at stake and closely linked to the evolving situation on India's Northern borders.

While Nehru was determined to meet China's creeping forward movements, there was no thought given that this might lead to large-scale conflict across the borders. The incremental addition to Indian military strength sustained over lengthy and arduous lines of communications could hardly be viewed as signalling any threat to the Chinese military position along the border.[66] On the other hand, Nehru was convinced that any conflict with China would lead to a world war, an indefinite war which could even develop into a nuclear war! He never anticipated a limited conflict. Nehru discounted the rather harsh rhetoric used by the Chinese and told the Lok Sabha on 5 December, 1961, that he did not believe that the Chinese would use force. He said, 'other factors work also.'

The fact that no military conflict was ever anticipated, or even sought as a solution to the boundary question, is substantiated by the fact that India's Defence Budget for the years from 1957-60, declined from US$ 539.11 million [1957-58] to US$ 526.95 million [1958-59] to US$ 481.81 million in 1959-60.[67] If India was looking for a military confrontation this was hardly the way to go about it. Needless to say, the Chinese were well aware of the situation, for if anything they would have closely scrutinized all published figures pertaining to the Defence Ministry and come to the inescapable conclusion that India's military challenge was anything but serious.

The belief that there would be no large scale clashes could also have been due to Soviet advice. This belief appears to have been widespread within the Government of India. No one in India, including within the Armed Forces after initial hesitations, ever thought that a military conflict was imminent. The then Foreign Secretary, MJ Desai, confided that he had received assurances/assessments from the Soviets that China would not militarily attack India.[68] Similar was the belief in the political circles in Delhi. The principal advisor to Nehru on China was Krishna Menon. The latter functioned on the firm belief that China would not seriously hurt Nehru's India or hurt a single Indian soldier.[69] On 16 November, 1956, Krishna Menon, speaking in the UN General Assembly, told delegates that 'so far as Asian people are concerned, we have no reason to think that these people [the Chinese] are *expansionist or belligerent or imperialistic in any way* [emphasis added]. It is their desire to live in peace with their neighbours.' Later Krishna Menon admitted that 'their' assessment of China was wrong when he candidly stated that 'at that time, we certainly had no idea that the Chinese were going to wage war on us.'[70] Menon reportedly felt that in the ultimate analysis, the Soviet leader Khrushchev could be persuaded to help tone down and provide a tangible deterrent to aggressive Chinese policy. Krishna Menon claimed that Chen Yi had told him in Geneva that China would never fight with India over the border issue.[71] It was, therefore, not surprising that whenever trouble with China seemed to hover over the horizon, Krishna Menon would try and divert public attention towards Pakistan, for whom he had an inveterate hatred. On Krishna Menon's resignation after the Chinese attack, his departure was most acutely felt by the Soviets. The CPSU circulated a secret communication to other Communist parties in which they lamented the fact that Chinese aggression had 'resulted in the loss of one of our most faithful friends amongst the Indian leaders and that also because he relied on our help.'[72]

Similarly, Nehru, too, seemed to be convinced that the Chinese would not make any major incursion into Indian held territory. Perhaps Krishna Menon had convinced him so. Nehru told General Thapar [then Army Chief] that 'he had reliable information' that the Chinese would not offer resistance if there was a show of force to make them vacate the check-posts.[73] The events in the Galwan Valley [May 1962] seemed to confirm Nehru's thesis, when Chinese troops advanced right up to the Indian post, surrounded it, but did not open fire and eventually withdrew. This was not the message that the Chinese wished to convey. They intended it as *a warning that they could eliminate any Indian post at any time,* but Nehru misread it and reached the opposite conclusion that China would not fight. Much later, Nehru speaking in the Lok Sabha [8 November, 1962], confirmed the above assessment when he said:

> Even the aggression on our border during the last five years, bad as it was and indicative of an expansionist tendency, hardly led to the conclusion, though it troubled us greatly, that the Chinese would indulge in a massive invasion of India.

Present Chinese writings indicate that Nehru had arrived at this conclusion that China would not react militarily due to his 'wrong assessment of the Chinese situation.' This 'wrong' assessment had as its basis the belief that 'the Chinese economy was facing a very difficult situation...due to certain policies...withdrawal of Soviet experts and the military harassment of Chiang Kai-Shek group in coastal areas of South-East China.' It was also as a result of Nehru's desire to change the status quo at the border in favour of India.[74]

What was the basis of such a conclusion reached by the Indian leadership is a matter of speculation. Was this assessment based on its own understanding of the situation, or did the Indian leaders receive positive assurances from elsewhere, particularly from the Soviet Union? It would be recalled that Khrushchev had clearly told Nehru that the Soviets would not like to 'interfere.' In his meeting with Nehru on 12 February, 1960, when Nehru tried to hand over documents, Khrushchev told Nehru that, '*even if the two sides requested mediation, it would be very difficult for a third person to mediate. You and the Chinese are right in not asking for mediation.*' On the other hand the Indian leadership could not have been unaware of what Mao told Khrushchev during their meeting in Beijing on 2 October, 1959, that 'the McMahon Line will be maintained' and later Mao himself volunteered to the Soviet CDA to China, Sergey Antonov, in a meeting on 21 October, 1959, that 'we will never, *under any circumstances,* [emphasis added] move beyond the Himalayas.'[75] It is probable that too much reliance was placed on this assurance. It is also probable that Mao knew that the Soviets would eventually pass on this information to the Indian leadership, and it is also equally probable that Mao was hoping to lull the Indian leadership into inaction. And yet, Zhou in his letter to Nehru on 17 December, 1959, had also assured that:

> The Government of the People's Republic of China has strictly abided by its statement of absolutely not allowing its armed personnel to cross this line [McMahon Line] in waiting for a friendly settlement of the boundary question.[76]

Incidentally, a highly confidential internal Chinese Foreign Ministry document accessed by the CIA, specified that in South-East Asia, 'India is our main target.' Therefore, had the Chinese leadership already taken a decision to 'teach India a lesson?' and were China's top leaders enacting a diplomatic bluff, both written and verbal, or just plain subterfuge to lull the Indian leadership into inaction?

At about this time the Chinese while still at pains to keep the diplomatic dialogue with India open, continued to take a hard line on the ground. When Harriman met Nehru on 23 March, 1961, in Delhi, Nehru told him that the Chinese were at the 'height of their aggressive intentions and that the situation was dangerous.' Nehru also said that he had tried to negotiate with Zhou on the boundary question, but had 'got nowhere.'[77] Nehru's feeling was that the Chinese had become arrogant because of their internal difficulties, and that the more these difficulties increased, so did their arrogance. The Chinese, in a note on 30 April, 1962, informed India that they had resumed 'border patrolling' in the Western sector from the Karakoram Pass to the Kongka La [Pass] and threatened that if 'India continues to invade and occupy China's territory...then China would be compelled to resume border patrols along the entire Sino-Indian boundary.' And yet in an editorial on 3 June, 1962, *The People's Daily*, while expressing regret at India's refusal to renew the 1954 Trade Agreement, affirmed that the Chinese Government and people will 'never change their stand of safe-guarding Sino-Indian amity' and that the 'radiance of the principles of peaceful co-existence can never be obscured.' It seemed as if the policy of 'san he yi shao' [三和一少] [peaceful co-existence, peaceful competition, peaceful transition and reduction of support and assistance to liberation struggle of other peoples], advocated by an influential section of the Chinese leadership led by Wang Jiaxiang, perhaps still held vogue.

Wang Jiaxiang had attended the Sun Yetsen University in Moscow and, after the founding of the People's Republic in 1949, was appointed as the first Chinese Ambassador to Moscow. It would be recalled that on 27 February, 1962, Wang as Head of the CCP International Liaison Department, had proposed that in view of China's internal difficulties, China should 'relax' its foreign policy and 'buy' time. Specifically, Wang proposed that China avoid conflicts and find a way to break the stalemate with India, noting that 'Nehru was not an enemy of the Chinese nation.'[78] Later, Mao shot down Wang Jiaxiang's suggestion, declaring that 'in our party there are some who advocate the 'three modernizations, one reduction...this is a revisionist line.'[79] Wang was criticized by Mao on 9 and 29 February, 1964, and subsequently purged and stripped of all his positions.

As there seemed to be no solution in sight for the Sino-Indian boundary, both China and Pakistan announced that they were beginning negotiations over the POK-Xinjiang sector. Clearly, this was designed to provoke India, which, as expected, protested vigorously to China. India felt that China had gone back on a commitment made earlier to India. In a note on 10 May, 1962, India protested as follows:

> The Government of India had so far believed that the Government of the People's Republic of China had accepted this basic position [Kashmir as a part of India] without any reservation. This was confirmed by Premier Chou-Enlai when he stated to the Indian Ambassador in Peking on 16 March, 1956 'that the people of Kashmir had already expressed their will' on the issue of Kashmir's accession to India. The same impression was gained at the meeting between the Secretary General of the Indian Ministry of External Affairs and the Chinese Prime Minister in July 1961.... This is reversal of the attitude of the Government of the People's Republic of China in regard to India's sovereignty over the entire State of Jammu and Kashmir is obviously a step in furtherance of the aggressive aims that China has been pursuing towards India in recent years... It is clear that the Government of China are, in this matter, acting in furtherance of their aggressive designs and are seeking to exploit the troubled situation in Kashmir and India's differences with Pakistan for their advantage.[80]

The Chinese response was to categorically state that 'the boundary negotiations between China and Pakistan do not at all involve the question of ownership of Kashmir.' And further asked the rhetorical question to the Indian side: 'to cite one single Chinese document that stated that Kashmir was a part of India?'[81] None could be produced.

On 23 June, 1962, the UN Security Council voted on the issue of Kashmir. Pakistan, despite serious US reservations, had taken the issue to the UN Security Council. The results were a foregone conclusion, thanks to a Soviet veto. Nehru expressed 'deep regret and sorrow,' and publicly complained that the US and UK are 'invariably against us.' Their actions [US and UK], said Nehru, 'had hurt and injured India' and created doubts about their 'goodwill towards India.'[82] Nehru's outburst in Parliament was badly received both in Washington and London, and the upshot was a worsening of relations between India and Britain and the United States. The British High Commissioner in Delhi felt that 'over the last year the Indians in their attitude and policy towards Britain, have done little to prepare sympathy for themselves.'[83] The US, too, was miffed and even contemplated holding back vital economic aid to India. The US experience in this entire episode was a very unhappy one. Pakistan, despite US support, remained dissatisfied; it continued its negotiations with China, despite US wishes to the contrary. In the bargain, the US received bad press in India and the Soviet position in India immeasurably improved. The Chinese would have been extremely satisfied in that a wedge had been successfully driven between India and the Western powers. Once again, the Chinese needed to thank Pakistan for its help!

What changed the Chinese mind to adopt a more belligerent attitude towards India and the border dispute? It seems that two factors played out. Firstly, Chinese patience with the situation prevailing on the Sino-Indian border was running out. Secondly, the Chinese leadership saw a chance in that a serious confrontation was developing between the two superpowers. It made both take their eyes off on the developing situation on the Sino-Indian border. In planning for their offensive against Indian positions on the frontier, the Chinese were always wary of the reactions of the two super powers. In the Chinese mind, India was seen as a 'junior partner' of the two super powers. Cautious as ever, the Chinese needed to neutralize the effects should either of the two super powers contemplate coming to India's aid. Mao understood the international situation well and assessed that 'our struggle with India is a complicated international issue, not only is it [an] Indian problem [as] American Imperialism and Soviet Union are supporting India.'[84] It was for this reason that the Chinese hesitated to take immediate military action, but on 23 June, 1962, the international situation took a dramatic turn and the heavens seemed to have smiled upon China.

Earlier, Pravda had marked the 12th anniversary of the Sino-Soviet Treaty of Friendship [14 February, 1950] by repeating Khrushchev's pledge made during the 1958 Taiwan crisis that 'an attack on the People's Republic of China—which is a great friend, ally and neighbour of our country—is an attack on the Soviet Union.' The Chinese reciprocated the gesture with a *People's Daily* editorial on 14 February, 1962, which commemorated the 12th anniversary of the Sino-Soviet Treaty of Friendship by praising the alliance and the policy of the two countries to 'assist, support and cooperate with each other.'

In the summer of 1962, the Soviets re-published maps of the Sino-Indian border showing both the Aksai Chin and NEFA as parts of China. Earlier, in 1955, the Soviet Embassy at Delhi had presented a copy of the Soviet Atlas to President Prasad that did not conform to India's position in depicting India's Northern frontier. On 1 August, 1960, India publicly revealed the Soviet position when the Parliamentary Secretary to the Prime Minister told Parliament that the Soviet maps were showing the 'India-China boundary as delineated on Chinese maps; that is, including Aksai Chin, Nilaang-Jhadang and a greater part of NEFA [Arunachal Pradesh] were shown as in China.' It was confirmed to Parliament that India had taken up the matter with the Soviet Government, which 'promised to look into it', but to which 'we have not so far received any reply.' Although reminders were sent in 1957, 1958 and 1959 and in November 1960, the Ministry of External Affairs verbally once again took up the matter with the Soviet Embassy in Delhi, yet there was no response. However, what caused even greater worry for India was the discovery that the 1959 edition of *Atlas Mira* showed Sikkim as an independent state! Earlier, it had been shown as an Indian protectorate. It was obvious that Soviet Russia had no desire to irritate the Chinese and still held firmly to the belief that there was room for reconciliation between the two countries.

From about mid-April to end May 1962, about 60,000 ethnic Kazakh Chinese Muslims fled to the Soviet Union from Ili prefecture and Tacheng in Xinjiang [Sinkiang]. The Chinese suspected not only Russian intrigues, but active connivance. This suspicion arose as the Soviets suddenly started giving large scale Soviet resident certificates to the disaffected Muslims. This set alarm bells ringing in Beijing for they feared concerted and coordinated efforts to create difficulties for them in Chinese minority areas such as Tibet and Xinjiang. In a mature display of astuteness, the Chinese never published any anti-Soviet articles in the Chinese press, but to the contrary, Zhou reportedly apologized to the Soviets for any inconvenience caused to Soviet Border Control personnel![85] Quietly, the Chinese now began to plan a counter strategy.

What came as huge relief for the Chinese were the events in Cuba. The decision of the Soviets to introduce offensive missiles into Cuba created a completely new ball game. The Soviets were extremely keen to enlist Chinese support. One issue where they thought they could mollify the Chinese was to take 'the Chinese side' on the Sino-Indian boundary issue. Meanwhile, the Chinese kept Moscow informed of most developments that were taking place between China and India. On 8 October, 1962, Chinese leaders informed the Soviet Ambassador in Beijing that, 'China knows that Indian forces are planning to launch a large scale attack in Sino-Indian frontier regions, and if India launches a attack than we will resolutely carry out self-defence.' On 13 and 14 October, 1962, Ambassador Liu Xiao met Khrushchev and the latter told him that the 'information received by the Soviet Union regarding India preparing to launch an attack on China *is same as conveyed by China*.'[86] Further, Ambassador Liu secured from Khrushchev 'guarantees' that if China was attacked and a China-India conflict ensued, *the Soviets would 'stand together with China'* [emphasis added].[87] On 20 October, 1962, Khrushchev in a letter to Nehru, rebuked him for failing to show 'due urge for reconciliation' and urged him 'to agree to Chinese proposals.'[88] This new tough line was confirmed when MJ Desai [then Secretary General, MEA] told US Ambassador Galbraith in a meeting on 23 October, 1962, that 'in the past few days, the Soviets have taken a tough line with the Indians—including advice to settle on Chinese terms.'[89] The Soviets had no option as they were deeply engaged in a serious confrontation with the US over Cuba and badly needed Chinese support. Thus, the Chinese were able to neutralize one superpower quite effectively.

As for the other superpower, the Chinese were deeply worried about the attitude of the US. In late 1961, the KMT leader Chiang Kaishek stated that 1962 would be a decisive year and that 'we can no longer vacillate or hesitate to perform our duty.' The Chinese noticed that recruits for the Taiwanese Army were called up one year ahead of schedule along with delayed de-mobilization, and a special budget to fund war time mobilization was also enacted. Also, an 'invasion tax' had been levied on industries located in Taiwan.[90] The US had appointed as their Ambassador to Taiwan a retired Navy Admiral who had considerable experience in amphibious warfare. So disturbed were the Chinese that, on 29 May, 1962, FM Chen Yi publicly stated that they expected a US supported invasion from Taiwan. The PLA rushed 100,000 troops, including five first grade divisions to the coastal provinces of Fukien and Chekiang. A foreign Ambassador in Beijing privately described the Chinese leadership's state of mind as 'panicky' over the prospect of an attack from Taiwan.[91]

To ascertain what was in the American mind and to gauge their intentions, the Chinese Ambassador to Warsaw, Wang Bingnan was recalled from leave and hastily dispatched to Warsaw with the instructions to meet his US counterpart forthwith. On 23 June, 1962, Chinese Ambassador Wang Bingnan, at his initiative, met US Ambassador John Cabot at Warsaw. Ambassador Wang claimed that Beijing had noted preparations in Taiwan for a landing on the mainland. Ambassador Cabot, who was unaware of any such preparations based on his brief from the State Department, conveyed to his Chinese interlocutor that '*he had been authorized to state that the US Government had no intention of supporting any GRC [Taiwan] attack on the mainland under existing circumstances.*' Ambassador Wang could not believe his ears, and to make sure he heard it right, requested the US Ambassador to repeat this assurance once again. The US Ambassador duly obliged.[92] Earlier, just to make sure that the Chinese received the message, the US took the unprecedented step of requesting the British to convey a similar message to the Chinese through their Mission at Beijing.[93] The Chinese could not believe their good fortune. Wang later admitted that this assurance that he obtained from the US played a 'very big role' in China's decision making process when it took the decision to attack India.[94] The reason why the US took such a stand was that it felt that any move to encourage the Taiwanese to take military action would only result in the two Communist giants—the Soviet Union and China—coming together again. This was something that US policy makers wished to avoid desperately.

What Ambassador Cabot told Ambassador Wang was publicly confirmed by President Kennedy to newsmen on 27 June, 1962. The Chinese breathed a huge sigh of relief, for they had anticipated trouble on two fronts. Once their fears of trouble from the KMT subsided, they were then able to concentrate fully on the Indian frontier. As the situation in coastal China eased, the Chinese rapidly reinforced their troops in Tibet with battle hardened Korean War veterans. And they now began to plan for the assault on Indian positions with the full confidence that both super powers had been effectively neutralized. All that was needed now was a suitable time, taking into consideration existing international situation. The US clarification given to China on 23 June, 1962, appears to have been the tipping point.

The rules for engagement for the Chinese PLA were now changed. The Indian side noticed that Chinese troops were now violating the line that Zhou had indicated in his letter of 17 December, 1959, as constituting the boundary in the Western sector [The 1956 Line], and moving beyond it.[95] They now began to aggressively confront Indian troops. The result was that for the first time since the Kongka La incident in October 1959, Chinese troops, on 21 July, 1962, opened fire on an Indian army patrol in the Chip Chap valley that resulted in two casualties.[96] The warning that a change in Chinese attitude and policy had taken place had been delivered. In addition, the Chinese wished to demonstrate that they could 'neutralize' any Indian post at will. Both the intended warnings were misread by the Indian leadership.

It is, indeed, strange that the Indian leadership that prided itself on understanding the international situation was blissfully unaware of the momentous change that had taken place in the international situation. They continued to behave as if nothing was going to happen, firm in the belief that China would not attack India and, at the very worst, some local skirmishes might take place on the border. This belief was fairly widespread, both in political circles as well as within the military establishment. The Galwan valley stand-off, which took place earlier, confirmed this view. To be fair, the Indian leadership was not alone in this assessment. Even the US National Intelligence Estimate [31 May, 1962] also made the following assessment, which was in line with the Indian belief: It stated that:

> India's attempt to force Chinese withdrawal from forward positions...will probably result in border clashes, *though the odds are against any major military escalation* [emphasis added].

While posturing on the frontline continued, serious efforts were also made simultaneously to dampen the situation. At the urging of Krishna Menon, Nehru now considerably softened his stance. In June 1962, Indian CDA in Beijing was instructed to meet Zhou and inform him that India would be prepared to send a ministerial-level delegation to Peking to discuss, *without pre-conditions*, all bilateral problems and disputes [emphasis added]. As Zhou was unavailable, FM Chen Yi received the Indian CDA and poured cold water over Nehru's initiative by bluntly stating that '*it was not acceptable unless the Government of India unequivocally and publicly withdrew all fictitious and false claims on Chinese territory. The present proposal was...a trap and, therefore, not acceptable.*'[97] As news of Nehru's conciliatory gesture inevitably became public, he was roundly criticized in the Indian press for 'breaking faith' and for bringing 'dishonour.'[98]

Not to let matters rest, the Government of India, on 26 July, 1962, sent to Beijing a formal proposal that 'as soon as the current tensions eased and an appropriate climate is created, negotiations could begin on the basis of the Report of the Officials of 1960.'[99] Even a modest Chinese conciliatory response would have helped Nehru to resist internal pressures. However, the Chinese for reasons best known to them chose to go public, with FM Chen Yi, once again, in a broadcast over the Italian-Swiss Radio on 3 August, 1962, threatened that 'no force in the world could oblige us to do something of this kind.' What he meant was that even after negotiations began, the Chinese would never make one sided withdrawals from its own territory '*neither in the past nor in the future*' [emphasis added]. The Chinese followed it up with a formal note on 4 August, 1962, insisting that 'there need not and should not be any pre-condition for such discussions.'[100] Before sending the formal note, Zhou called the Indian CDA in Beijing and accused India of the following:

> India had not only inherited Britain's imperialistic legacy but had adopted similar imperialistic claims, tactics and attitudes. India had given shelter to that 'renegade' Dalai Lama and more than a hundred thousand anti-Chinese rebels in India and had given facilities to the Tibetan rebels and Kuomintang thugs and other foreign mercenaries to attack and destabilize Tibet and the lawful presence of the Chinese. China had evidence that American CIA was financing, arming and guiding these heinous anti-Chinese activities. Nehru was either not aware or pretended not to know about such activities against China. India had allowed the installation of modern devices to spy on China.[101]

When asked why he had not spoken or written to Nehru about such serious allegations when he had evidence in his possession, Zhou evaded the question and replied that 'Nehru had lost control over his Government and the people of India had lost faith in their Government.'[102] The Chinese had probably already made up their mind to use force and were only waiting for a suitable opportunity. Zhou's bluster to the Indian CDA would indicate that the situation in Tibet would remain a key factor for the Chinese.

On the other hand, still firmly of the belief that the Chinese would not take any serious military action, Nehru told US Ambassador Galbraith, as late as 6 August, 1962, that he expected talks to take place with the Chinese after the Commonwealth PM's Conference in September 1962. The Foreign Secretary, MJ Desai, was to lead the talks with the Chinese from the Indian side. There was no inkling of a massive Chinese thrust across the border. None of the Indian agencies had detected any massing of Chinese troops!

The Chinese cleverly masked their real intentions by maintaining a diplomatic facade of reasonableness. This line was evident in the formal reply sent by the Chinese Government on 4 August, 1962.[103] If there were to be no Chinese withdrawals even after negotiations, then the only surmise that the Indian leadership could make was that the Chinese were not serious about negotiations. The Indian side, therefore, had no options but to revert to its earlier position that there could be no negotiations 'unless the status quo of the boundary in this region that had been altered by force since 1957, be restored.'[104] Nevertheless, not to completely cut off any hopes for negotiations, the Indian side proposed on 22 August, 1962, that the Government of India would be glad to receive 'a representative' to discuss essential preliminary measures. By September 1962, the Chinese attitude had perceptibly hardened.

On 8 September, 1962, skirmishes broke out on the border in the Eastern sector and a serious clash occurred on 11 September, 1962, near Dhola post. For the first time since the Longju incident in 1959, Chinese troops crossed the McMahon Line. On 13 September, 1962, the Chinese sent a 3-point proposal. In it they proposed that armed forces of both countries withdraw 20 kilometres along the entire Sino-Indian border based on the line of actual control. Secondly, further discussions should be held 'quickly' on the basis of the 1960 Report of Officials 'without setting any pre-conditions.' Thirdly, the Chinese formally proposed that talks could begin first in Beijing on 15 October, 1962, and later, in New Delhi.[105]

The Indian response was very measured, too. On 19 September, 1962, India said that it was prepared to hold discussions provided the status quo was restored in the Western sector 'which had been altered by force in the last few years.' India was agreeable to begin talks in Beijing on 15 October, 1962, and then later, in New Delhi.[106]

On 3 October, 1962, China sent yet another proposal, after it had launched probing attack across the McMahon Line. This time, the Chinese wished to discuss the 'entire boundary' and begin discussions on 15 October in Beijing on the basis of the Report of the Officials of the two sides, and that neither side will 'refuse to discuss any question concerning the Sino-Indian boundary that may be raised.'[107] India responded on 6 October, 1962, that while it was prepared to begin discussions, it would do so 'as soon as the latest Chinese intrusions South of the McMahon Line have been terminated.'[108]

Krishna Menon left for New York on 17 September, 1962, to attend the UN General Assembly, and returned to India only on 30 September, 1962. Nehru left Delhi on 8 September, 1962, to attend the Commonwealth PM's Conference and after visiting Paris, Lagos and Accra, returned only on 2 October, 1962, but left again on 12 October, 1962, for Colombo and returned to Delhi only on 16 October, 1962. Two of the most important officials at the Army Headquarters, Lt. Gen Kaul, Chief of General Staff, was on holiday in Kashmir till 2 October, 1962, and the Director of Military Operations [DMO] was on a cruise on the aircraft carrier Vikrant! All were blissfully unaware that momentous decisions were being taken in Beijing to use force. Meanwhile, in the absence of both the PM and the Defence Minister, major decisions remained pending, whilst Chinese troops massed on the borders ready to strike.

The Chinese did not have to wait too long for good fortune to smile and for a suitable time to arrive. They had been preparing and waiting patiently for the right moment to arrive. It seems that a final decision to attack was taken at a meeting on 6 October, 1962, presided over by Mao and attended by members of the Central Military Commission.[109] The decision was to launch a co-ordinated attack on both the Western and Eastern sectors and to 'inflict a massive blow.'[110]

That the Chinese military action was only a 'self-defence' measure as claimed by the Chinese was a sham, a deception, a propaganda exercise and quite absurd. Four facts clearly bring this out. On 7 July, 1962, the Chinese Ambassador in

Moscow told his Pakistani counterpart that China was going to teach India 'a lesson,' which the Pakistani Ambassador duly relayed to the British Ambassador in Moscow.[111] It is not known if the British forewarned Nehru based on this intelligence. Similarly, Zhou told the Soviet Ambassador in Beijing, Chervonenko, on 7 October, 1962, that 'India was preparing to attack China' and that 'if they attack us, we will resolutely defend ourselves.'[112] Secondly, all communications to the Indian Mission at Lhasa were cut on 9 October, 1962. No one was allowed to enter the Mission. All local staff members were withdrawn. Later, the Chinese were to explain this by stating that the Lhasa Telegraph Office experienced 'circuit failure.'[113] Thirdly, Indian POWs reported on return to India that the Chinese PLA had stationed interpreters in Tibet who spoke *every* major Indian language! They also saw at first-hand how well stocked and prepared the Chinese were. They had even prepared POW camps well before hand. The Chinese now admit that they had well prepared POW camps at Qiongqiong and Longzi.[114] Fourthly, the Chinese attack began *simultaneously in all sectors of the border, both in the West and in the East, at the same time [5 a.m. IST on 20 October, 1962] and completely synchronized as per Beijing time* [emphasis added]! Incidentally, the Indian CD'A in Beijing was called by a Vice-Minister of Foreign Affairs on 21 October, 1962, and handed over a protest note that India had 'invaded' Tibet and launched large scale attacks at 4.30 am on 20 October, 1962! However, the BBC quoting Chinese officials, also broadcast the Chinese allegation. The question is how did the BBC and the Chinese Government *know at the same time* about India's alleged attack? There is no doubt that it was a pre-planned, premeditated and a well-organized assault. Even Maxwell admits that the Chinese ploy of calling this military action as 'self-defence' was a 'fabrication' and to say that the Indians launched an attack in the Western sector was 'grotesque.'[115] The contrast with the confusion on the Indian side could not have been starker.[116]

The Chinese timed the initiation of their massive offensive both in NEFA and Ladakh very carefully with the developments in the Soviet-US stand-off over Cuba. Later the US Secretary of State, Rusk, told Nehru that the Chinese may have timed their massive assault on India with the knowledge that a Russian build-up was occurring in Cuba. They may have considered whether the missile plot succeeded or failed, the US would most likely be fully focused on the Cuban crisis and thus would not be able to take any action in Himalayas. Rusk told Nehru that '*China had intelligence personnel in Cuba and doubtless knew what was up*' [emphasis added].[117]

If further proof is needed, look at the sequence of events. On 11 September, 1962, the US called up reservists. On the same day, the Chinese began encircling Indian forward positions on the Namka Chu. On 20 October, 1962, President Kennedy issued an order for the quarantine of Cuba and on 22 October, 1962, it came into effect. On 20 October, 1962, the Chinese launched their massive assault on Indian positions. On 24 October, Tawang fell to the Chinese and on the same day, Zhou issued his three point proposal.

Due to the events in Cuba and fearing the prospects of a clash with the US, Soviet Russia decided to side with China. At meetings on the 11 and 14 October, 1962, the Central Committee of the CPSU felt that 'India's demands...are insulting for the PRC...we are disappointed with Nehru.'[118] Thus, it was no surprise that on 25 October, *Pravda* urged India to accept Zhou's 'proposal' [of 24 October] terming it as 'constructive.' *Pravda* declared that the McMahon Line was 'notoriously the result of British imperialism and consequently illegal.' But what was most opportunistic and even galling were Soviet Russia's attempts to placate the Chinese by disclosing sensitive military intelligence on India. On 5 November and also on 11 November, 1962, the Soviet Ambassador to China, Chervonenko, met Zhao Yimin and handed over intelligence on India. Not only that, on 3 November, 1962, Chervonenko met Zhang Hanfu and handed over copies of exchange of letters between Nehru and Khrushchev as also contents of exchanges between Indian and Soviet officials. [119] A clear breach of diplomatic confidentiality and, in the circumstances, not a very friendly attitude towards India!

In addition, the entire Soviet Politburo turned out for the farewell banquet given by Khrushchev for departing Chinese Ambassador Liu Xiao and his wife. In his speech, Khrushchev proposed that both countries issue a declaration 'tomorrow' that the Soviet Union would stand-by China in the event of a China-India war. He also offered to suspend the sale of MiG-21 jet fighters to India 'till after border tension was eliminated.' Other Politburo members indicated to Ambassador Liu that Khrushchev's proposal reflected the approval of the Presidium of CPSU. Liu Xiao reported the proposal to the leadership in Beijing, but was told not to respond.[120]

However, on 25 October, 1962, the Soviets decided not to contest the quarantine of Cuba, shied away from a confrontation with the US and decided to enter into talks. On the next day [26 October, 1962], the US announced that it recognized the McMahon Line as the traditional and generally accepted international border between India and China,[121] which meant that by being *South* of the McMahon Line, the Chinese were actually in violation of an international border.

As tensions between the two super powers eased, the Chinese now had a serious problem on their hands. They were over extended and with winter fast approaching, something dramatic had to be done. By early November 1962, Soviet Russia realizing the folly of its earlier position, had also changed track.[122] In an apparent political U-turn, Khrushchev shortly thereafter, informed the Indian Ambassador in Moscow that while Russia would not supply arms to either side, yet it would honour all its existing commitments to supply arms to India, such as transport planes and including the MIG factory.[123] Earlier, the Soviets had decided to put on hold vital supplies for India in deference to Chinese sensitivities. 'Why has it changed?' asked the Chinese Vice-Foreign Minister Zhang Hanfu from the Soviet Ambassador; no doubt deeply perplexed. Zhang answered the question himself, 'it was because of the [changed] situation in Cuba.'[124]

On 19 November, 1962, after receiving desperate appeals from Nehru in the form of two letters, the US put four squadrons of USAF in the Philippines, 300 transport planes and 14,000 troops on a forty eight hour alert. A US Carrier Task Force with aircraft carrier 'Enterprise' in the lead was ordered into the Bay of Bengal. The sending of the naval force was a signal from the US that, apart from military aid, the US was 'prepared to intervene with air power to protect Indian cities if the Chinese continued their advance.' President Kennedy made the forceful assertion that 'we regard this as more than a border squabble,'[125] although the earlier assessment had been that because of the difficult terrain the fighting would be confined only to the border areas.

As the quarantine of Cuba ended on 20 November, 1962, the Chinese read the signals correctly. The international situation had now once again turned decisively in India's favour. They realized that they could not go any further and hastily declared a unilateral cease fire on the same day, and declared that their troops would *withdraw back North of the McMahon Line* [The last Chinese troops left by 2 March, 1963] [emphasis added]. With this, the Chinese had gained not an inch of territory in the Eastern sector. The Chinese decision came as a complete surprise to the Indian leadership, although the Pakistani biographer of Ayub, Altaf Gauhar, claims that Ayub knew of the impending cease-fire announcement by the Chinese at least 48 hours before it was made.[126] If true, this would show that high-level co-ordination between China and Pakistan already existed or alternatively, Pakistanis were simply boasting!

To the Chinese the chief purpose of the 1962 conflict was neither territorial nor related to the boundary question. It was, to put it in the words of the then Chinese President Liu Shaoqi 'to demolish India's arrogance and illusions of grandeur. China had *taught India a lesson* [emphasis added] and would do so again and again' [To Sri Lankan leader Felix Bandaranaike].[127] Liu repeated the same line to the Swedish Ambassador. Mao confirmed this line of thinking when he told a Nepalese delegation in 1964 that the 'major problem between India and China *was not the McMahon Line, but the Tibetan question. In the opinion of the Indian Government, Tibet is theirs*' [emphasis added].[128] Mao had clearly discounted the territorial aspect of the conflict when he volunteered to the then Soviet Chargé d'affairs, Sergei Antonov that '*never, under any circumstances, will move beyond the Himalayas. That is completely ruled out. This is an argument over inconsequential pieces of territory.*'[129] Recent Chinese commentaries quote Mao's belief that the 'real target' was not Nehru *but the US and the Soviets that had been plotting behind the scenes against China.*[130] And an official Chinese publication published recently further amplifies the same theme as:

> The declaration [of cease-fire] of the Chinese Government was a serious blow for anti-China plan of America and Soviet Union and their strategic

> design in Asia, it also the shattered American and Soviet Union's attempts to be benefitted from Sino-Indian border conflict. Just as soldiers of Chinese Frontier Forces said, 'this time when Jawaharlal Nehru is hit then his pain is seen on the faces of Kennedy and Khrushchev.'[131]

In addition, it was the Chinese belief that this knock-out punch would keep the Sino-Indian frontier quiet for a considerable length of time to their immense advantage, discourage any Indian 'meddling' in Tibet and 'to strike peace with its neighbour.'[132] It was hoped that Tibet would, thus, be pacified.

So if what Mao told Antonov and the Nepalese and what Liu Shaoqi told Bandaranaike is correct, then the whole issue was not about the boundary question or India's forward movement in the Western sector or the territorial aspect of the boundary dispute, but something quite else. Mao even blamed Nehru for the clashes and said that he [Nehru] was using them for the following reasons:

> First, he is trying to deliver a blow to the Communist Party of India; second, to ease for India the conditions for the receipt of economic aid from the Western powers, in particular from the USA; and third, to obstruct the spread of influence of the CPR and the socialist camp on the Indian people.[133]

Mao wanted to 'wake up' Nehru and to try to detach him 'from the influence of the super powers.'[134] Mao also showed his contempt for Indian soldiers by sarcastically referring to them as 'bean-curd' soldiers. Was it then a misperception that led to the initiation of armed action?

Nehru himself felt that the border clashes had more meaning than mere squabbles for territory. In this respect, both India and China seem to be on the same wave length for both discounted the territorial aspect of the conflict. 'Countries do not take such action involving dangerous consequences without a much deeper reason', wrote Nehru to the Chief Ministers.[135] The primary objective was the removal of India as a power as it had become an obstacle 'in the way of China becoming a great power' as also the elimination of India's non-aligned policy would force India to join 'the Western camp.' This would also prove that 'Soviet policy was wrong.'[136] Nevertheless, for Nehru, the Chinese attack was a shattering blow, particularly to his reputation as a leader who 'understood China.' It also brought to an end his dream 'of a resurgent Asia with friendship between India and China with their fourteen hundred million people at its core.'[137] Zhou maintained that 'in this struggle against Indian reactionaries, [the 1962 conflict] we still made the US the most conspicuous target.'[138] He changed his tune when relations with the US improved and confessed to Kissinger during a conversation on 23 February, 1972, during President Nixon's visit, that:

> He [Nehru] was so discourteous he wouldn't even do us the courtesy of replying, so we had no choice but to drive him out.

Hardly a reason for going to war! In their personal animosity towards Nehru, there is no doubt that the Chinese leaders were of one view [F Bandaranaike's report 12 January, 1963]. Significantly, neither to Kissinger nor to Nixon did Zhou ever mention that the core of the problem was a border dispute! It would thus seem that the Chinese were well aware that they had initiated the conflict for reasons other than solving a border dispute.

Militarily the 1962 conflict was an unqualified success for Chinese arms. It was for the first time that the Chinese had projected their power on the subcontinent and South of the Himalayan crest.[139] But the end result for China was not as gratifying as has been assessed. For one, the Chinese leadership, because of the international situation rapidly turning adverse for China, thought discretion to be the better part of valour and quickly decided to withdraw their troops *North* and behind the McMahon Line. The Soviet view was probably quite accurate when Khrushchev taunted the Chinese in a report to the Supreme Soviet on 21 December, 1962, in which he derisively pointed out that 'China had desisted from further hostilities apparently because India had started to receive support from the US and British imperialists who were supplying it [India] with arms.' And as Khrushchev taunted the Chinese once again:

> China is now withdrawing its troops essentially *to the same line at which the conflict broke out.* Would it not have been better not to have advanced from there? [emphasis added][140]

The Chinese realized that if the armed conflict continued, it might turn into a large scale war. Hence, the Chinese took the decision to withdraw unilaterally from territory *South* of the McMahon Line. An additional factor was that with winter setting in rapidly and with an extended and a tenuous supply line, it would have been extremely difficult to maintain troops far and across the McMahon Line. The Chinese were also unsure of the Tibetan reaction. Should trouble break-out in Tibet, a large number of troops would then be required for internal security. Additionally, at the extended points reached by Chinese troops on 20 November, 1962, it was easier for India to mobilize larger forces, including heavy artillery and tanks. Thus, with over extended supply lines, Chinese forces would have been, for the first time, in a precarious and disadvantaged position. While Indian troops might not have fought well on the high mountains, nevertheless, they would be more than a handful if fighting took place on the plains. The outcome may not have been as predictable as before.

The net gain in terms of territory for China was an insignificant 2,000 square kilometres of alpine desert in Ladakh within their first and second claim lines, with nothing to show for their exertions in the East. While the withdrawal may be clothed in whatever terms the Chinese may like, the hard fact remains that they could not even hold on to Tawang. Had the Chinese stopped after capturing Tawang, as they did, and not penetrated further into Indian Territory after 24 October, 1962; it would have been extremely difficult for India to dislodge them. For one, world public opinion would not have been so deeply aroused, the Western powers would not have taken the issue so seriously and the Chinese supply line would not have been over-extended. It would have been seen as just another border skirmish. Public opinion in the world would have easily accepted it. And the Chinese would have retained the immensely important and strategic area of Tawang. That would have been a real gain! It was a major Chinese tactical mistake. In any event, by first crossing the McMahon Line and then retreating *North* beyond the McMahon Line on the conclusion of hostilities, the Chinese only served to further reinforce the validity of the McMahon Line as the international frontier between India and China. It also indicated that the Chinese accepted the McMahon *alignment.*

In the early days, the US attitude and position on the border question was ambivalent and far short of Indian expectations. On 12 November, 1959, the acting US Secretary of State Herter, publicly proclaimed that the US had not taken 'any side on the border dispute' and *as far as the legalities of rival border claims were concerned the US had 'no views'* [emphasis added]. As a result of the conflict, the US recognized, on 26 October, 1962, the McMahon Line as the international boundary line. This was a huge political gain for India. In addition, the US was conscious that it had to bolster India's position, for it could not, for Western strategic interests, let democratic India 'collapse' in the face of Chinese aggression. This policy position was reiterated in a Memo from Robert Komer, National Security Staff, to President Kennedy, wherein he stressed that 'we must stiffen Indian determination.'[141]

The British PM, MacMillan in a letter to Nehru on 23 October, 1962, confirmed the validity of the McMahon Line,[142] and the British Government took a step further than even the US position when the then Foreign Secretary, Lord Home, told the Foreign Press Association that 'we have taken the view of the Government of India on the present frontiers and the disputed territories belong to India.'[143] This statement of support was later reiterated by Lord Home, the British Foreign Secretary, at the UN, prompting the Chinese FM, Chen Yi, to remark that Lord Home's attitude proves that 'Indian reactionaries and British imperialists are jackals of the same liar.' For the former imperial power on the sub-continent to give such unqualified support to the Indian case was indeed hugely important. It was a distinct political gain for India.

The Chinese were livid over these developments. FM Chen Yi felt the Western powers had not given due consideration to the sense of national pride and self-respect of the Chinese people in seeking to recognize the McMahon Line as the international border. When the Chinese Ambassador, Wang, remonstrated with his US interlocutor, Ambassador Cabot, at their meeting at Warsaw on 13 December, 1962, about the change in the position of the US on the McMahon Line, Cabot said that in the US view it was clear that China, by military action had taken territory that had long been in Indian hands. Cabot also conveyed that

Map 3: Line Reached at End of Conflict in Western Sector—1962

while the US had no particular view on the merits of the border dispute, yet its policy was that 'any settlement' must be one 'which India could accept with honour.'[144] The US felt that this Chinese 'blunder' had opened for them an unprecedented opportunity[145] to 'win' over India to its side. This also led to shoring up of Western, particularly US, support for India. It was obvious that Chinese aggressiveness on the border had paid no political dividends, but on the contrary only helped to bolster Western support for India and to confirm US suspicions about Chinese belligerence.

On the other hand, the US was also keen to fulfil its own agenda at the earliest. Firstly, the US was keen to see the political demise of Krishna Menon, and his departure was seen as a very welcome relief and a distinct political gain. As Galbraith noted in his communication of 13 November, 1962, to Kennedy:

> The departure of Menon is an enormous gain. I have little doubt that in recent years, he was an immediate and efficient channel of communications to the Soviets and possibly even to the Chinese... Many people here think that in recent years, whenever the Chinese penetrated a little further in Ladakh, Menon arranged some shooting on the East Pakistan border as a diversion. I have no doubt that the march on Goa last year was timed to take people's minds away from the anti-Chinese syndrome which was developing as the result of last summer's penetrations. It worked. Within a few days, last December, China disappeared from the headlines and the liberating forces of Menon became the center of attention.[146]

Secondly the State Department felt that 'India's new anti-China pro-West turn can give us a major breakthrough in Asia,' and as Komer of the National Security Staff wrote to President Kennedy, the 'sheer magnitude of the opportunity handed us by Peiping [Beijing]'[147] was too good to miss. This, in turn, opened another opportunity for the US to attain its long held objective to strive for an India-Pakistan rapprochement in the sub-continent. This would eventually lead to enormous pressure both, by the US and the British, on India to compromise on the Kashmir issue. At the same time, President Kennedy felt that linking US military aid to India with a settlement in Kashmir was pushing things too far, for it risked squandering considerable Indian goodwill that the US had accumulated, and if the US pressed too hard, there was also the additional risk that it might precipitate a Sino-Indian reconciliation.[148]

At the same time, the US was also not that keen that the friction and hostility in Sino-Indian relations, particularly over the boundary issue, should end soon. The more bitter the quarrel and so long as it remained within manageable bounds, the more it would be to the strategic advantage of the US. As Komer [NSC staff] wrote in a Memo to Kennedy:

> Thus, it is as much in our strategic interest to keep up a high degree of Sino-Indian friction as it is to prevent it from spilling over into large scale war.[149]

The Chinese attack managed to arouse unprecedented nationalistic fervour in India. No Government, even if it wanted to settle for terms that seemed reasonable, short of a complete Chinese withdrawal, would be in a position to do so. The stalemate on the border would, thus, continue indefinitely. The Indian Army was rapidly expanded and rebuilt. The defence budget was nearly doubled. Thus, when the next major clash took place on the Sikkim-Tibet border at Nathu La in 1967, not only did the Indian Army hold its own, but no ground was yielded and no position lost.[150] Six new mountain divisions were raised and a reinforced and a rearmed Indian Army, with modern equipment, now stood at the borders. This development caused the Chinese to once again remonstrate with the US. At Warsaw, Ambassador Wang protested again and accused the US of 'goading India into provocations' by equipping six mountain divisions for Himalayan fighting and 'considering equipping two more and indulging in joint manoeuvres.'[151] Clearly, the Chinese had not anticipated such a development.

While there was understandable awe at the ease with which the Chinese Army had sliced through Indian defences, very few countries supported the Chinese position on the boundary dispute. Even Maxwell admits that 'the border war was almost universally reported as an unprovoked Chinese invasion of India...and confirmed the general impression that Peking pursued a reckless, chauvinistic and belligerent foreign policy.'[152] China lost its 'under-dog' role as a victim of imperialist diplomacy and, by its action, only reinforced the image that successive US spokesmen had projected of an 'aggressive, ruthless China.'[153] Perhaps Pakistan was the only country that was overjoyed at the humbling of India, and this was to lead it into committing a serious miscalculation when it tried to grab Kashmir by force in 1965. Most South-East Asian countries moved closer to the United States in fear of China's military power. Except for Egypt and Yugoslavia, few other Non-Aligned countries supported India in its hour of crisis. Support for India came mainly from Western countries, but this as India soon discovered, also carried a price tag.

Soviet Russia's prestige in India also fell rapidly and they only recovered their position due to inept policies followed by Western countries. As for India-China relations, they went into deep freeze to the strategic disadvantage of both. China now had hostile borders not only in the South and South-West, but in addition to coping with US power on its Eastern sea board soon had another hostile border with the Soviet Union in the North and North-West. The Peking Review of 19 July, 1963, admitted that both the US and Soviet Russia were giving military and economic aid to bolster India and that the 'Nehru Government thought that it had isolated China.' Fierce rhetoric pouring out from Beijing could not obscure the fact that soon after the border conflict, China faced hostility from all three major powers on its periphery. Not a great gain either!

The conflict of 1962 solved nothing. China now had declared adversaries on all its major frontiers.[154] Despite demonstrating their military strength vis-à-vis the Indian Army, the Chinese still could not pacify Tibet. Rebellion continued to simmer. Tibet remained an occupied region and the Chinese could only maintain their rule based on their military domination. If the Chinese had hoped that the border conflict with India would help pacify the Tibetans, they were in for a rude shock. It remained as troublesome as before. Thus, for all the reasons that China started the border conflict, none seemed nearer a solution. Even Zhou admitted to Nehru in a letter on 3 March, 1963, that 'use of force can settle no question between us,' and that ultimately the boundary question 'will have to be settled peacefully in the end.' Zhou also conceded that between India and China instead of 'peaceful co-existence,' there now would be 'long armed co-existence.'[155] A freeze in the relationship set in that was to last for decades. As Nehru, with great prescience, told colleagues in early 1963 that it will take 'more than a quarter of a century to return to any substantive negotiations, provided the Chinese did not attack India again.'[156] In present day writings, with considerable hindsight, some Chinese analysts feel that the Sino-Indian border war was 'an unfortunate tragedy between two formerly colonized and oppressed states.'[157] Some even admit that 'China not only failed to get back its lost territory, but created a new rival. This was unexpected.'[158]

To the vast number of Indians, the Chinese became synonymous with perfidy, never to be trusted again. The Chinese had managed to turn a friendly Nehru and India into an implacable foe. They never realized the depth of revulsion that their military action had caused in India. Rather than fracturing Indian polity, they managed to unite almost all sections of Indians against themselves.

And the Chinese seemed to have validated, with their military action, the Duke of Wellington's observation that 'the outcome of a successful military expedition in Asia was often no less embarrassing than a defeat.'[159]

CHAPTER 6

The Last Years of Nehru and Boundary Negotiations [1962-64]

'Nothing in my long political career has hurt and grieved me more than the fact that the hopes and aspirations for peaceful and friendly neighbourly relations...which we worked so hard ever since the establishment of the PRC should have been shattered by the hostile and unfriendly twist given in India-China relations during the past few years'

—Nehru to Zhou Enlai, 27 October, 1962.

On 20 October, 1962, the Chinese launched their full scale attack across the McMahon Line in the Eastern sector and against Indian positions in the Western sector. Within a period of four days the Chinese had eliminated practically all Indian posts in the Chip Chap Valley and North of Pangong Lake in the Western sector. Daulat Beg Oldi was evacuated and not captured by the Chinese. Thus, all posts that were within the Chinese claim line of 1960 had been captured by Chinese troops.[1] In the Eastern sector, by 24 October, 1962, the Chinese reached the Northern banks of Tawang Chu and had captured Tawang. At this point, they were at least about 20 to 30 kilometres across and South of the McMahon Line. Thereafter, a lull followed, possibly because the Chinese needed to re-group. In such mountainous terrain, supplies had to be provided to the troops mostly by porters and the Chinese took the opportunity to quickly build a road from Bumla to Tawang to ease their supply line.

Utilizing the opportunity so offered as a result of a military necessity, Zhou on the 24 October, 1962, sent yet another proposal to Nehru.[2] Summoning the Indian CDA in Beijing, Zhou basically made three points. Firstly, both sides should affirm that the Sino-Indian border question should be settled 'peacefully through negotiations,' both sides should respect the 'Line of Actual Control along the entire Sino-Indian border,' and their armed forces respect and withdraw 20 kilometres from 'this line.' Secondly, Zhou stated that China was willing to withdraw its 'frontier guards' in the Eastern sector *North* of the 'Line of Actual

Control' and at the same time, both countries would agree to not cross the 'Line of Actual Control' in the Western and middle sectors. Thirdly, Zhou once again suggested talks at the PM's level. Zhou also made a 'personal' appeal to Nehru to respond in a 'positive and constructive' manner. Zhou also vehemently denied to the Indian CDA that he had ever told Nehru in 1960 that China would maintain the status quo in the Eastern sector.[3] Here, it seems that PM Zhou was being economical with the truth for had Mao not, in the presence of Zhou, assured Khrushchev in Beijing on 2 October, 1959, that 'the McMahon Line with India will be maintained?'[4] Had Zhou also not written to Nehru on 17 December, 1959, that 'the Government of the People's Republic of China will absolutely not allow its armed personnel to cross this line [McMahon] in waiting for a friendly settlement?'[5]

Nehru's reply was sent on the 27 October, 1962, and was rather mild in tone. Nehru insisted that the situation as it existed prior to 8 September, 1962, i.e., before the current hostilities commenced, be restored. On that condition being met, India was prepared to welcome a delegation or Zhou himself to facilitate a peaceful settlement of 'our differences.' India was not sure where the LAC now stood, for it was only much later on 4 November, 1962, that Zhou clarified that by the LAC they meant in *the East it coincides with the McMahon Line and in the West and in the middle sector, it coincides with the 'traditional' boundary as put forth by the Chinese*. Zhou further classified that the LAC they now proposed was basically the same from which he had proposed a mutual 20 kilometre withdrawal in all sectors in his letter of 7 November, 1959. This later became identified as the LAC that existed on 7 November, 1959. A firm feeling amongst policy planners in India was that the Chinese first 'grabbed' territory, then paused, re-grouped and thereafter proposed talks and insisted that the new 'Line of Actual Control' be maintained! It was nothing but an attempt to legitimize the seizure of additional territory.

Thus, if the Chinese could accept the McMahon Line as the LAC in the Eastern sector and presumably were prepared to go back *North* of the line, then why could they not go back to where they were on 8 September, 1962, the date on which the first skirmishes took place, both in the Eastern and Western sectors? In any case, in the Western sector there was no such LAC, that existed on 7 November, 1959. All that existed on 7 November, 1959 were a series of posts, and it was only by using 'imagination' that they were theoretically joined together by drawing an imaginary line to form the so-called LAC of 7 November, 1959! The significance of 7 November, 1959 being that it was on this date that PM Zhou addressed a letter to Nehru first proposing that both sides withdraw 20 kilometres from the McMahon Line in the East, and in the West from the line that each side exercised 'actual control.' And for propaganda purposes, 7 November, 1959 *gave the impression* [emphasis added] that the Chinese were willing to go back *even further* than they were on 8 September, 1962!

Zhou, further in his communication of 4 November, 1962, flatly refused to go back to positions held on 8 September, 1962, as demanded by Nehru in his letter of 27 October, 1959 by asserting that this would be 'unfair and pregnant with the danger of conflict.' Zhou alleged that to accept to go back to the positions held on 8 September, 1962, would mean that in the Eastern sector 'Indian troops would actually be North of the McMahon Line *as Kechilang River [Namka Chu River] was North of the McMahon Line as per the co-ordinates given in the McMahon map* [emphasis added]. As for Aksai Chin in the Western sector, Zhou blandly stated that 'it had always been under China's jurisdiction and accused India of setting up 40 military strong-points 'east' of the 7 November, 1959, line. Having rejected outright Nehru's proposal to go back to the line of 8 September, 1962, Zhou appealed to Nehru to accept his 3-point proposal of 24 October, 1962.

On 14 November, 1962, Nehru responded to Zhou's clarifications of the 7 November, 1959, LAC, made vide his communication of 4 November, 1962. Nehru felt that the assertion that the LAC of 7 November 1959, in the middle sector, coincides with the traditional customary boundary is 'absolutely without foundation.' *China had never been South of the main Himalayan crest* [emphasis added]. To accept that 'the armed forces of both sides withdraw 20 kilometres from the LAC of 7 November, 1959, all along the Sino-Indian border' as now defined by Zhou, would, Nehru stressed, leave the entire 'Indian frontier defenceless and at the mercy of any fresh invasion by an aggressive and arrogant neighbour.' For example, Nehru pointed out that even in the Western sector, this new proposal would mean accepting Chinese occupation of an additional '5,000-6,000 square miles.'

As far as the Eastern sector was concerned, Nehru emphasized that as on 8 September, 1962, no Chinese troops had crossed the India-China frontier, as defined by India, along the highest watershed in accordance with the 1914 Simla Convention. As such, the Thagla ridge was South of the McMahon Line. Nehru accused China of having taken a 'cold-blooded' decision in total disregard of all principles governing relations between sovereign Governments.

Nehru now made a concrete proposal. In the Eastern sector, Chinese troops should go back to positions held on 7 November, 1959, that is, on the other side of the boundary along the Himalayan watershed which they had crossed on 8 September, 1962. In the middle sector, the position would remain the same; that is Chinese troops to be North of the highest watershed. In the Western sector, Chinese troops were to go back to a line connecting Spanggur post to Khurnak Fort to Kongka La [pass], and then Northwards join the main Aksai Chin road. Indian troops would go back to where they were on 8 September, 1962.

Meanwhile, on the ground, while diplomatic notes were being exchanged, the Chinese continued their massive push further into Indian Territory. No further exchanges at the PM's level took place till the cease fire announcement. Indian policy makers felt that by making successive cease-fire proposals during the conflict the Chinese were using deceptive diplomatic language to secure physical control of areas that China had never been in possession of, and which she had now acquired through the use of force. The Chinese never had any serious intent at negotiations.

On 19 November, 1962, Zhou summoned the Indian CDA in Beijing again and in a 45-minute monologue, harangued him as follows:

> Zhou's relationship with Nehru, the glorious friendship with India, the fight against imperialism, the Bandung Conference, Asian-African solidarity, intrigues by imperialistic countries to separate India and China, Nehru being misled by wrong advice and allowing himself to be aligned with the US and receiving vast quantities of military aid and advice. That Nehru should realize all this when there was still time to stop the war and negotiate.[6]

Zhou requested that his message be conveyed to PM Nehru.

When the Indian CDA informed Zhou that the Indian Embassy's telegraphic facilities were cut as of 20 October, 1962, and therefore, how could he send messages to Delhi, Zhou feigned ignorance. Curiously, before the CDA returned to his office, the facilities were restored.

On 20 November, 1962, Zhou summoned the Indian CDA again. This time, FM, Chen Yi, was also present, as were camera men and Chinese journalists. Zhou read out the Chinese unilateral cease-fire proposals. These were [a] Beginning 00.00 hours on 22 November, 1962, a unilateral cease fire would come into effect. [b] Beginning 1 December, 1962, Chinese troops would withdraw to 20 kilometres behind the LAC of 7 November, 1959. In the Eastern sector, this would mean behind the McMahon Line. Zhou claimed that, thus, the Chinese forces would be 'far behind the positions prior to 8 September, 1962.' Then Zhou asked the CDA to convey to Nehru his earnest request to turn to 'a new page of peace, friendship and co-operation' between India and China. While Zhou was trying to convey his message of 'peace', unknown to the Indian CDA, the Chinese had already briefed foreign correspondents stationed in Beijing at least half an hour earlier on their cease-fire proposals!

Earlier, in his letter of 4 November, 1962, to Nehru, Zhou had sarcastically noted that 'I believe the Indian Government must be having in its possession the original map of the McMahon Line. According to the original map, the Western-end of the McMahon Line starts at latitude 27°44.6′N [The Indian position was that the McMahon Line began at latitude 27°48′N]. Therefore, Zhou noted that the Namka Chu valley, Dhola post, Khinzemane, Thagla ridge where hostilities commenced on 8 September, 1962, were all *North* of the McMahon line, as per the co-ordinates of the McMahon map. That being so, Zhou levelled the accusation that it was Indian troops that had first intruded into Chinese territory. As the McMahon Line was not demarcated on the ground, the location of any point could only be clarified or fixed by reading off the longitude and latitude from the original McMahon map. Therefore, China was within its rights to initiate a 'defensive counter attack' as Indian troops were *North* of the so-called McMahon Line as per the McMahon map co-ordinates. Zhou's letter was followed by a note from the Chinese Foreign Ministry on 26 November, 1962, stating that the Indian position that the McMahon Line should follow the '*highest ridge*' in the Thagla area was an 'entirely groundless assertion.'[7] [Note: The Chinese, to obfuscate the issue used the word 'highest ridge' and not 'watershed.']'[8]

What Zhou perhaps 'forgot' to mention was the fact that the original McMahon map also has two place names mentioned in this sector, namely, the Tibetan village of Le which is shown *North* of the McMahon Line and the Indian village of Pangchen which is shown *South* of the McMahon Line. Logically speaking, therefore, the McMahon Line should lie somewhere in between these two villages.

The Indian point of view was that Henry McMahon, as emphasized in the Simla Conference minutes, had intended *to follow the main watershed* that exists in this region. There are a series of ridges here that run roughly in the East to West direction. As the ridge at latitude 27°48′ North is higher than the ridge at latitude 27°45′ North, logically, therefore, the alignment of the McMahon Line should be *moved North* by 3 minutes. If so, this would then correspond to the Thagla ridge. In addition, during 1953, there is official correspondence available that shows an exchange between Chinese officials stationed at Tsona and the Assistant Political Officer stationed at Tawang that clearly indicates that the boundary stones put up by Pangchen villagers were acceptable to the Tibetans, who were willing to pay for utilizing pastures on the Indian side. Significance lies in the fact that the Chinese accepted that Pangchen was an Indian village.

In order to further clarify the situation in the official level talks held in 1960, the Indian side had, in a meeting on 27 June, 1960, urged the exchange of large scale maps by both sides so that full information about the McMahon Line alignment would be readily available. The Chinese side rejected this suggestion and only provided a map of 1″=8 miles, and on 27 June, 1960, noted that there was no further need for 'exchanges.' Clearly, the Chinese were not willing to undertake clarity on such a vital issue, for reasons that can only be suspect.

Some apologists for China, without going into detail, have nevertheless, bought the Chinese line without question.[9] According to them, the Chinese approach seems to be 'sound' both 'practically and legally.' Fair enough, but then why not extend the same logic of the Chinese approach to the entire length of the McMahon Line? If that were to be done, to go by the coordinates of the original McMahon map, then the Sino-Indian boundary line in the areas of both Migyitun and Tulung La would be *advanced even more further North*, thereby including both these areas in India. In the area East of Tsari Sarpa, the Sino-Indian boundary, going by the original McMahon map co-ordinates, would advance by at least 11 kilometres to the North, *which would mean the inclusion into India of a total of additional Tibetan territory of at least 112 square kilometres* [emphasis added]!

So when in response to Zhou's seemingly disarming assertion, Nehru, in his letter of 14 November, 1962, put this question to him that the Chinese cannot have it both ways—either accept the McMahon Line alignment on the basis of the principle of highest watershed or go by the strict co-ordinates of the original McMahon map to determine the LAC—the Chinese, realizing the folly committed by their Prime Minister, demurred. If they accepted the alignment of the McMahon Line based on the highest watershed principle, then clearly they had crossed the McMahon Line and attacked Indian posts [Dhola, Namka Chu etc] in September 1962, thus clearly being the aggressors and nullifying their entire propaganda effort. Alternatively, if they accepted the alignment of the McMahon Line based on the 'strict co-ordinates' principle, they would lose about 112 square kilometres of territory! Not surprisingly, therefore, Zhou never responded to Nehru on this point, perhaps deeply embarrassed, and preferred to down play the uncomfortable query by asking the Chinese Ministry of Foreign Affairs to reply [Memo dated 20 December, 1962]. To hide their embarrassment, the Chinese Foreign Ministry obfuscated and responded that as the Eastern sector of the Sino-Indian boundary had not yet been 'defined'; so the question of which 'principle' China accepts 'does not arise'![10] The question is: then why raise the issue and that, too, at PM's level? It was obviously done only to confuse the gullible and for scoring propaganda points.

Soon after the fighting stopped, a conference of six Afro-Asian Non-Aligned nations [Burma, Cambodia, Ceylon, Ghana, Indonesia, and UAR] took place in Colombo from 10-12 December, 1962, to try and resolve the Sino-Indian border imbroglio. The conference put forward the following proposals, which would henceforth be known as the Colombo Proposals. What were these Colombo proposals? The substance of the Colombo proposals were:

> In the Eastern sector, the Chinese were to withdraw North of the McMahon Line and Indian troops could move right up to the Line. In the Western sector [a] Chinese forces were to withdraw 20 kilometres from the line of actual control [LAC] as it existed on 7 November, 1959, and [b] pending a final solution of the border dispute, the area of Chinese withdrawal was to be a demilitarized zone, to be administered by civilian posts of both sides, without prejudice to claims.

Clarifications were made subsequently by the Ceylon [Now Sri Lanka] PM. The proposals that emerged were that in the Western sector, China would withdraw 20 kilometres as proposed by Zhou in his letters of 21 and 28 November, 1962, to Nehru. Indian forces were *not to move forward.* To administer the DMZ that thus emerged as a result of Chinese troop withdrawals, both sides were to have civilian posts only to be set up *after an agreement between the two sides.* In the Eastern sector, Indian forces could move right up to the LAC, i.e., the McMahon Line, except in two areas: the Thagla ridge and Longju. In the middle sector, the Colombo Powers proposed that the status quo be maintained.

While India accepted the Colombo proposals *in toto* after clarifications by the Colombo Powers, the Chinese, in their memorandum of 6 January, 1963, and letter dated 8 January, 1963, to the Ceylon PM, made essentially two reservations. These were [a] the stipulation that Indian troops should not move forward in the Western sector *should apply to the entire border and not to the Western sector only.* And [b] that China was prepared not to set up any posts in vacated areas under dispute, provided Indian troops or civilians did not enter these areas. It was also clarified that these proposals were to aid in the consolidation of the cease-fire and a means by which both India and China could negotiate the settlement of the border dispute, and were not border settlement proposals per se.

India insisted that before negotiations could begin, China would have to accept the Colombo proposals *without any reservations.* India knew full well that the Chinese would find it difficult to accept the Colombo proposals after the clarifications had been given to both the countries. China, on the other hand, felt that its reservations could be discussed when the negotiations began and that such negotiations need not be held up on this score. The Chinese view was that the Colombo proposals contained 'contradictions and fallacies in logic,' and that Nehru had used these 'ambiguities' to his advantage to say that they met the Indian demand for a restoration of the situation as it existed on 8 September, 1962. In such circumstances, it was 'impossible for China not to maintain its own interpretations or not to have reservations.'[11] To needle the Chinese further, Khrushchev wrote to the Colombo powers supporting their recommendations! Later, the Soviets were to use the fact of Chinese ambivalence towards the initiative of the Colombo powers to castigate China in their polemical battle. As the *Pravda* of 19 September, 1963, reported:

> The Colombo proposals represented the friendly desire of states that were sincerely trying to help find a mutually acceptable solution to the border dispute. Unfortunately, the voice of reason expressing the will of the people of Asia and Africa was not heard in Peking.... [China] is in fact ignoring their efforts and making no move to apply the proposals.

While discussions were still continuing on the Colombo proposals, Zhou took an unusual step in that he summoned the Indian CDA in Beijing on 7 January, 1963, and said that as the CDA was returning to New Delhi for 'consultations,' he would like to send a very private, verbal message that was only for Nehru's ears. The message was: [a] for the next three months both countries should desist making negative statements against each other. [b] Nehru and he [Zhou] should meet as soon as possible, away from the press and publicity, in an agreed place, in order to exchange ideas for an agreed and joint action to defuse the situation. When Nehru was informed personally by the Indian CDA of Zhou's offer, Nehru's comment, after much deliberation and thought, was that matters had 'gone too far' and that 'no one in India would stand any more of China's bluff.'

As neither side was prepared to budge from its position, a deadlock ensued. Thus, the efforts of the Colombo powers did not succeed in unravelling the border dispute. Having achieved its goals by force of arms, China was most reluctant to move forward in settling the dispute, unless it was on its own terms. This posture was confirmed when Zhou wrote to Nehru on 3 March, 1963, stating that 'China is willing to wait with patience.' China further confirmed this stance when on 20 April, 1963, it informed India that 'it is entirely meaningless for Indian notes to repeat over and over again the hackneyed phrases that were refuted long ago' and if India continued to send similar notes, the Chinese Government 'will reply no more.'[12] Further, on 9 October, 1963, in a note, the Chinese Government emphasized that China was no longer interested in talks.[13]

The Chinese position was that 'it can be foreseen that no result will be obtained *even though boundary negotiations are held'* [emphasis added]. In other words, if India did not settle on Chinese terms, the Chinese would not respond and India could keep on waiting ad infinitum! The Chinese assessment was that it was indeed very unlikely that India would accept such terms. If one of the objectives of China taking the path of conflict in September/October, 1962, was to coerce India to the negotiating table *on its own terms*, then that aim, too, remained unfulfilled. China's policy now was to freeze the newly arrived at 'line of actual control' [LAC] and wait for further events to unravel. In the meanwhile, the unsettled conditions could always be used to bring pressure on India.

On 10 December, 1962, Nehru speaking in the Lok Sabha and in his letter to Zhou dated 1 January, 1963, and in subsequent communications, offered to refer the whole dispute for a decision on the merits of the case to the International Court of Justice [ICJ] at the Hague, which is an 'impartial world tribunal.'[14] Perhaps Nehru was aware that earlier also, when the British Envoy to China, Sir John Jordan, had challenged the Chinese Vice-Minister, Chen Lu, in December 1919, to submit the 'whole Tibet question' to the League of Nations, Chen Lu had responded that 'China had no faith in the League of Nations; since *in this as in other matters, might was still right*' [emphasis added].[15]

Zhou, in his response of 20 April, 1963, flatly turned down Nehru's proposal on the grounds that 'complicated questions involving sovereignty, such as the Sino-Indian boundary question, can be settled only through direct negotiations between the two parties concerned and absolutely not through any form of arbitration.' But why is China so wary of referring the Sino-Indian boundary question to any form of arbitration or the International Court of Justice? Was Zhou already aware that a few months earlier, on 15 June, 1962, the ICJ had delivered a judgment in the Cambodia/Thailand case [The Preah Vihear case] that wholly negated the Chinese case on the Sino-Indian boundary issue?

On 26 October, 1946, the then Chinese Government informed the UN Secretary General that China *recognizes ipso facto the compulsory jurisdiction of the International Court of Justice* in conformity with Article 36, paragraph 2 and 3 of the statute of the ICJ [emphasis added]. As soon as the People's Republic took the Chinese seat in the UN, including the permanent seat in the Security Council, the Government of the People's Republic on, 5 December, 1972, completely repudiated the previous commitment of its predecessor Government. It informed the UN Secretary General that China '*does not recognize the statement made by the defunct Chinese Government on 26 October, 1946*' [emphasis added]. The reasons for the Chinese reneging on previous commitments are obvious.

Firstly, China is not confident that its claims on the boundary dispute with India can withstand international judicial scrutiny. Its legal case is far weaker than India's. China knows that in the ICJ, claims based on treaties are particularly persuasive and that this rule holds even when agreements are unclear or incomplete. The ICJ ruling in the boundary dispute in the case of Thailand/ Cambodia [The Preah Vihear case] is hugely relevant. In it the ICJ held that in the interests of 'certainty, stability and finality of frontiers,' a map, even *if it is an unsigned map* [emphasis added], is valid evidence. But the more important point accepted by the ICJ was that as Thailand had not expressed any dissent for a long period of time, this constituted tacit acceptance, acquiescence of the map. The ICJ held that even though the map had no 'binding character', nevertheless, since there was '*no reaction from the Siamese [Thai] authorities, they must be held to have acquiesced*' [emphasis added]. Further, the ICJ added that 'a party...which by its silence maintained an attitude manifestly contrary to the right it is claiming before an International Tribunal is precluded from claiming that right' [*Vinire contra factum proprium non valet*]. Thus, held Justices Alfaro and Fitzmaurice, 'silence is tacit recognition' [1962, ICJ].

The position of China with regard to the McMahon map and the McMahon Line is uncannily similar to that of Thailand. China never protested or raised the issue of the McMahon map or the McMahon Line from the time it was signed in 1914, till Zhou first raised it in a letter to Nehru on 23 January, 1959, and even here, he spoke of 'taking a realistic attitude towards the McMahon Line.' In addition, China had recongnized the Burmese section of the McMahon Line. For years, China's main concern had been not the McMahon Line but the boundary between Outer Tibet and Inner Tibet. Even after the People's Republic was established in 1949, the new Government of China never raised the issue till considerably much later. China was well aware of Nehru's statement made in the Indian Parliament that 'map or no map, McMahon Line was our boundary.' They were aware of the provisions of the Indian Constitution [6th Schedule] explicitly incorporating NEFA within India. When India expelled the Tibetans from Tawang, China said nothing and never protested. Thus, by its conduct and the silence that it maintained, China indicated acquiescence or estoppel.

Thus, if we are to go by the ruling of the ICJ in the Preah Vihear case and this is then taken as a precedent, China's case in the Eastern sector becomes completely untenable [McMahon map/McMahon Line]. There are other similar decisions that confirm the ICJ judgment [Alaska Boundary Dispute, 20 October, 1903, the Guatemala-Honduras Boundary Arbitration, the Anglo-Norwegian Fisheries Case 1951, the Case Concerning Sovereignty over Certain Frontier Land 1959]. It is for this reason that China denounced the principle of *estoppel* as 'absurd', but in the light of international case law the Chinese view appears rather odd.

Secondly, China is aware that some of the maps published in China, including official maps, have shown the Sino-Indian boundary alignment as largely conforming to the Indian version. The important maps so listed are: [1] A 6th century Chinese map showing the KuenLun mountains as the Southern limits of Sinkiang [2] Map from Nei fu yu tu, 1760 [3] Hsi yu tu chih, 1762 [4] Ta ching hui tien, 1818 [5] Hsinchiang chih lueh, 1821 [6] Hsi yu shui tao chi, 1824 [7] Hsinchiang Tu Chih, 1911 [8] Official Chinese map of Hung Chun of 1893, handed over to the British Government [9] The Peking University Atlas published in 1925 and [10] Postal Atlases of China of 1917, 1919 and 1933. During the 1960 Official-level talks with the Chinese, the Indian side produced 36 official Indian maps and 8 official Chinese maps to support its case. The Chinese could refer to only 13 official Indian maps and none official Chinese maps to support its case. Thus, international case law as it exists, is not favourable to China's position, particularly as it pertains to the McMahon Line. The reasons are obvious for China never invoked any sustained objections to the McMahon Line till 1959 in order to maintain its claims and even in specific situations, when it was required to do so, China faltered.[16]

Even after the establishment of the People's Republic in 1949, the Chinese position in the Western sector continued to be legally full of contradictions and confusion. Take the case of the Chang Chenmo valley between the Lanak La [Pass] and Kongka La [Pass]. In 1950, a map published in People's China showed the whole of the Chang Chenmo valley as within Indian Territory. In 1951, the 'New Map of China' showed an alignment cutting across the Shyok valley. Similar was the position in maps published in 1953 and 1956, which showed a part of the Chang Chenmo valley in India. And to add to the confusion, Zhou, in his letter of 17 December, 1959, to Nehru, confirmed that the alignment shown in a Chinese map published in 1956 was correct, whereas Chinese officials in 1960 produced yet another version! The Chinese tried to cover-up this obvious discrepancy by accusing India of 'trying to exaggerate the divergences of delineation of Chinese maps.' If there are no divergences, as claimed, then why did Chinese officials not say in the 1960 talks that the position as indicated by Zhou in his letter of 17 December, 1959, to Nehru stands, i.e. the 1956 line? Why did they have to produce yet another—a 1960 version? Some well-known fellow travellers bought [the Chinese] line too[17] that these 'divergencies' were non-existant! [See Map 4] The fact is that these 'divergences' amount to several hundred square miles![18] Further, the fact is that *it was only at the 6th Meeting of officials held on*

Map 4: Chinese Claim 'Lines' of 1956 and 1960 in the Western Sector

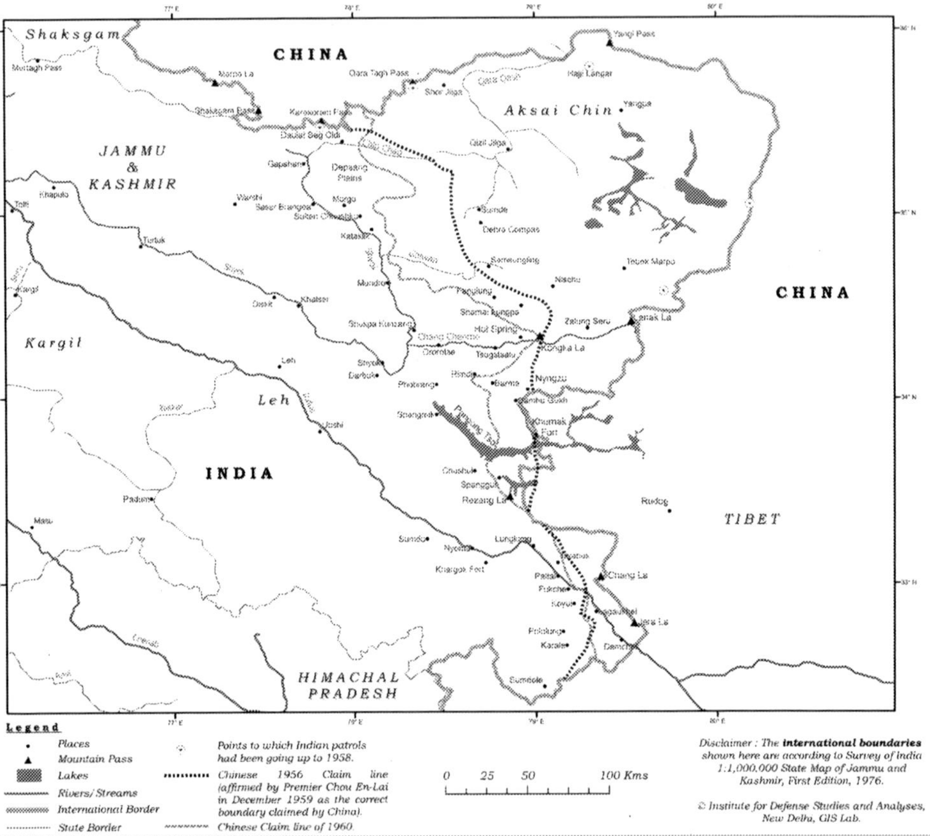

27 June, 1960, that for the first time the Chinese submitted an authorized map showing its version of the whole alignment of the Sino-Indian boundary [emphasis added]. Did the People's Republic of China not know where its boundaries were till then? The flexibility shown by China cartographers would indeed make a mockery of China's claims that its border alignment was 'rock-solid'? What would the ICJ have made of this?

Thirdly, it would open up the debate on whether Tibet has an international personality or not, and whether it was capable of entering into agreements on its own. Much of the Chinese case is actually Tibetan. If the ICJ were to rule, as had the International Commission of Jurists, that Tibet had been an independent personality and that, between 1911 and 1950, it was free from any vestige of Chinese control, it would seriously upset the Chinese position. [19] The so-called 'liberation' of Tibet in 1950 would then be automatically labelled as an 'invasion,' and Tibet an 'occupied country.' China can under no circumstances even remotely risk such an outcome.

Some foreign apologists of the Chinese contend that the Chinese turned down Nehru's offer due to the presence of a Taiwanese judge on the bench of the International Court.[20] This reasoning is rather odd, for the Taiwanese judge on the International Court of Justice was none other than the redoubtable Wellington Koo. It is well known that Wellington Koo had fought all his life for the territorial integrity of China. Koo was often lauded as one of the builders of modern China and, despite serving the Republic of China [Taiwan], was to receive a personal invitation from Mao to visit China in February 1972. It was also noticeable that when the US recognized the McMahon Line as the international border, the Taiwanese Embassy in Washington issued one of its very rare 'Protest Notes' to the United States Government. In fact, Li Zhongren, the former acting President of the Nationalist [KMT] Government on mainland China, wrote to the *New York Times* [NYT] in November 1962 that 'the Chinese, including those not on the mainland, feel that the border issue has transcended mere ideological differences: it has become something involving their territorial sovereignty as well as their national integrity and honour. No Chinese, regardless of political beliefs, will ever subscribe to the validity of the McMahon Line.' The undeniable fact is that even up to present times, the Taiwan Chinese remain even more forthright and adamant in pushing the Chinese case than their political opponents sitting in Beijing. It was apparent that not to go to the ICJ was just an excuse, for the Chinese knew of the weakness of their case. And it was convenient to utilize the myth of a Taiwanese Judge not to do so!

The Chinese were never enamoured of international law, for as the *People's Daily* [18 September, 1957] explained in an article entitled 'Refute the Absurd Theory Concerning International Law,' that:

> International law is one of the instruments of settling international problems. If this instrument is useful to our country, to socialist enterprise, or to the

> peace enterprise of the people of the world, we will use it. However, if this instrument is disadvantageous to our country, to socialist enterprises or to the peace enterprises of the people of the world, we will not use it and should create new enterprises to replace it [emphasis added].[21]

Thus, the reasons why the Chinese rejected Nehru's offer are fairly obvious. And what did the Chinese think about arbitration? The Chinese instead hurled abuse on the International Court of Justice [ICJ], with the *People's Daily* of 27 July, 1966, accusing the ICJ of being a 'shelter for gangsters.'

As anger mounted in India over the Chinese military action, India took another step that in the long run was perhaps not so fortuitous. On 3 December, 1962, the Indian Government informed the Chinese Government that effective from 15 December, 1962, India was withdrawing its Mission at Lhasa and Shanghai and asked the Chinese to withdraw their Missions from Calcutta and Bombay.[22] The withdrawal of the Mission from Lhasa meant that the last point of contact with the Tibetans was snapped. Although the Chinese had made it very difficult for the Mission to function effectively, nevertheless it was an important post, a potent symbol of India's links with Tibet, and it played a very useful role in that it monitored events taking place in Tibet. Similarly, the offices of the trade marts at Gartok, Gyantse and Yatung were also closed. With this, all official contacts between India and Tibet came to an end. Any residue influence that India retained in Tibet was thus eliminated. It was indeed an act of total misplaced patriotism.

Just a week before China launched its attack on India on 20 October, 1962, Sino-Pakistan talks opened in Beijing to settle the boundary between POK and China. Earlier, the Pakistanis had watched carefully the course of Sino-Indian negotiations on the Sino-Indian border, and were also perturbed as Chinese maps had shown large areas of Hunza as parts of China. Pakistan first made informal overtures to China to negotiate a boundary agreement towards the end of 1959,[23] but the Chinese were hesitant as they did not wish to jeopardize their relations with India. The first Pakistani formal note requesting for border talks was sent to China on 28 March, 1961.[24] China, ever watchful of events, did not formally reply till 27 February, 1962.

During Nehru's visit to Pakistan to sign the Indus Waters Treaty in September 1960, Nehru raised, in a meeting with Ayub at Murree on 22 September, 1959, the question of boundary with China. Ayub in response, then referred to the possibility of talks between Pakistan and China, and Nehru even requested a map showing the proposed alignment. Nehru told Ayub that India had in its possession old papers that indicated that the Mir of Hunza's claims had been turned down by the British.[25] In his meeting with Ayub, Nehru did not express any apprehension about the prospects of Pakistan-China border talks.

Later, Nehru clarified that he had spoken to Ayub 'because we thought that any action which they might take should be in line with the action we were taking in regard to this border and that there should be no conflict.' Publicly, however, Nehru took a stance that tried to show Pakistan in poor light. He told a press conference on 18 January, 1961, that 'Pakistan does not know very much about the border...their knowledge is extremely limited.' Recalling the Murree talks, Nehru told the Rajya Sabha on 3 May, 1962, that 'I found that they knew less than I did even on that side of the border.' And further to the Lok Sabha [7 May, 1962], Nehru added that 'the British Government, after due enquiry, had not accepted the Mir of Hunza's claim to that particular grazing area and, therefore, refused to intervene in the matter. This refers to a particular spot, a grazing area, and not to the whole frontier.' Nehru claimed that Ayub agreed with him and the latter had said that 'if the British Government had given it up, we cannot lay claim to it.'

The US was sufficiently perturbed at Sino-Pak developments for Ayub to take the initiative to explain to Harriman the reasons why Pakistan had decided to talk with the Chinese on the border question.[26] Ayub clarified in a meeting with Harriman on 22 March, 1961, that the decision to enter into talks with the Chinese was so as to 'avoid trouble' and not with any desire to embarrass the Indians. As Sino-Pak talks gathered momentum, it became obvious that the Chinese not only wished to settle their common 'border', but also endeavoured to drive a wedge between India and Pakistan. Timings of decisions were the decisive factors. The 3 May, 1962, announcement that negotiations were to start between Pakistan and China was timed to put pressure on India. To make doubly sure that the message was not lost, the Chinese, on 31 May, 1962, informed India in a formal note that it had never accepted that Kashmir was under 'Indian sovereignty.' Pakistani Ambassador to the US, Aziz Ahmed, admitted as such when he told Secretary Rusk that the timing of the move was 'entirely at the initiative of the Chinese and that he had no doubt that the Chinese had taken this step to put pressure on India.'[27] Later, the Pak Foreign Minister also admitted that 'an enemy's enemy is a friend!'

Thus, when the announcement of the Sino-Pak Agreement was made on 26 December, 1962, the timing of it was designed to annoy the Indians and to sabotage Indo-Pak talks that were on the anvil under the auspices of the Western powers. As could be expected, India angrily denounced the Agreement, stating that neither Pakistan nor China had any *locus standi* as Kashmir was legally and constitutionally a part of Indian Territory.[28] India recognized that the Chinese were out to destroy 'the accord and amity that had been developing between India and Pakistan.'[29] Between 1962 and 1965, India sent eight protest notes to the Chinese on this issue, but to no avail. The perception in India was that this Agreement represented a deliberate hostile act against India. The Chinese response was to deny the allegations and to state that the issue of 'ownership' of Kashmir had not been decided, for Article 6 of the Agreement recognized this problem and that this issue was to be settled between India and Pakistan.[30]

India maintained that earlier the Chinese position had been that negotiations with any authority in *de facto* control of territory without *de jure* control was 'not permissible.'[31] PM Zhou and the Polish PM had also, in a Joint Statement, issued on 11 April, 1957, stated that 'the Kashmir issue should not be allowed to be *made use of by external forces to create tension*' [emphasis added]. The Chinese had also informed India on 31 May, 1962, that the Chinese attitude was of 'never getting involved in the dispute over Kashmir.'[32] This position of ambivalence was partly due to Beijing's fear that third party meddling in Kashmir would set a bad precedent. Zhou clarified China's hesitancy due to its fear that a more forthnight stand on Kashmir might provoke India to make 'similar claims on Tibet.' Therefore, while expressing openly its support to national liberation movements across the globe, China was careful to limit its support to Pakistan's case on Kashmir to 'moral support.'

The Chinese position changed in 1964, by when the Chinese were confident that they had sufficiently brow-beaten India and could with impunity support the Pakistani line of 'self-determination of the Kashmiri people.' It was obvious that China was now seeking to play a major role in the affairs of Kashmir. The old princely state of Jammu and Kashmir had an area of 222,236 square kilometres of which 106,567 square kilometres was with India, 78,114 square kilometres with Pakistan [POK] and 38,000 square kilometres was under Chinese occupation. An additional 5,180 square kilometres was ceded by Pakistan to China. For all practical purposes, China now became a factor in the eventual settlement of the Kashmir dispute. [Map 5]

Ayub admitted to the British High Commissioner to Pakistan, Sir Morrice James, that 'the Chinese had deliberately tricked the Pakistanis by issuing the announcement when they did in the hope of creating bad blood between India and Pakistan.'[33] The Western powers accepted this farce. On the other hand, 'the timing of the announcement,' said Nehru, was designed to 'prejudice the outcome of the joint talks on Kashmir.'[34] That nothing came out of the Indo-Pak talks was in a sense a result of Chinese manoeuvrings on the border. At crucial moments of the talks, Chinese intervention ensured that little progress was made. The Chinese succeeded in their attempts in widening Indo-Pak differences and in keeping tension alive. Nehru's assessment was spot on.

It was obvious that neither third party intervention in the form of Colombo proposals nor the efforts of the Western powers to forge closer ties between India and Pakistan had got very far. Another effort was made by yet another interested third party. Lord Bertrand Russell of UK, the eminent philosopher, sent two emissaries—Schoenmen and Pottle—who arrived in China on 9 July, 1963, after they had met Nehru. They were personally received by Zhou on 12 July, 1963. According to the Chinese, Schoenmen told Zhou that Nehru had asked him to convey orally to the Chinese the following:

Map 5: Jammu& Kashmir [India]

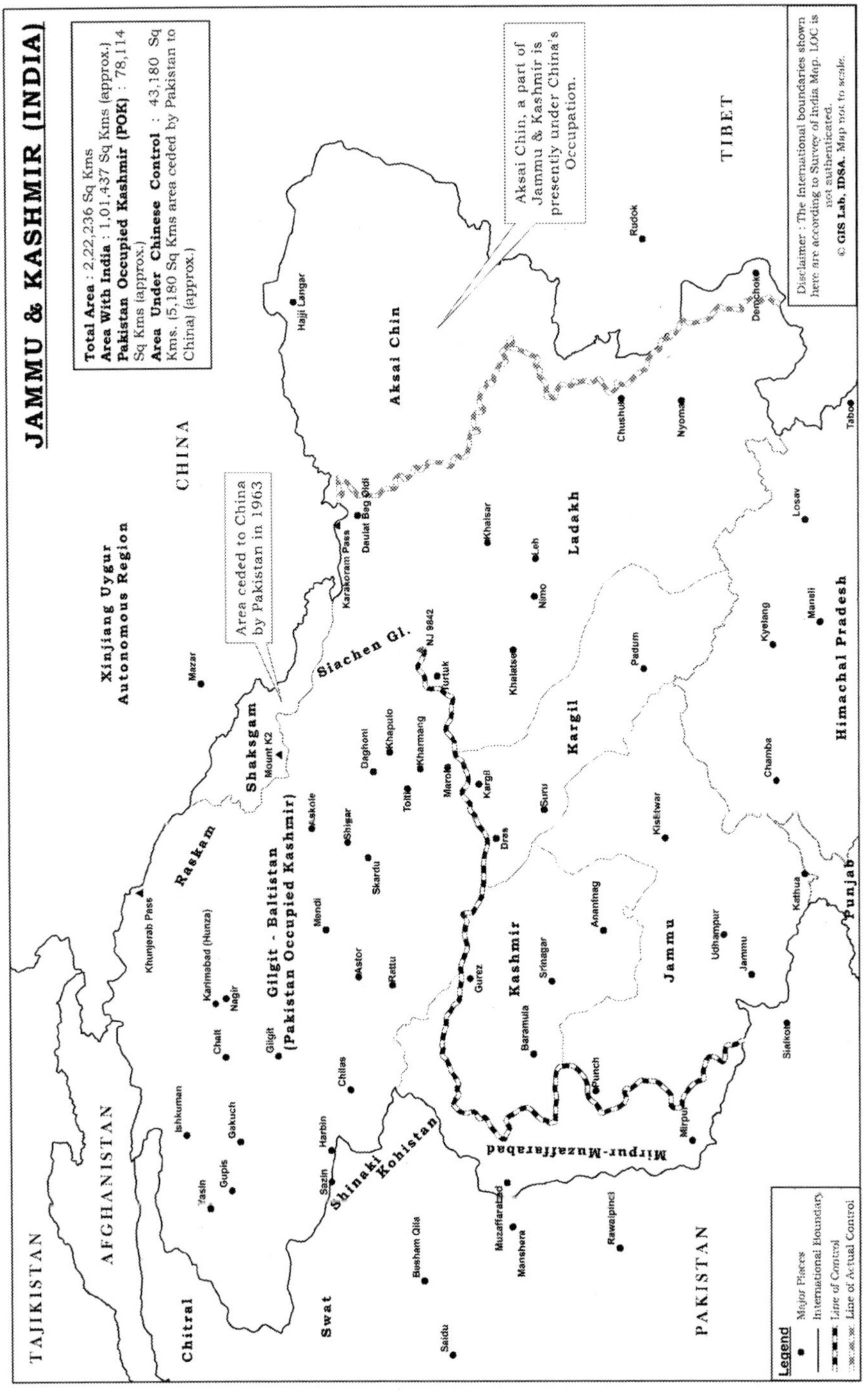

> If China would agree that the strip formed by China's 20 kilometre withdrawal in the Western sector of the Sino-Indian border becomes a no-man's land and be vacated of all civilian posts, he would not request any civilian posts be placed there and India would hold negotiations with China. PM Nehru further said, for his part, he did not want such talks to fail but wanted to discuss the whole question of the boundary and that in the talks, there would be give and take.

In a further meeting with Chinese officials on 13 July, 1963, Scheonmen apparently changed his stance. He now told the Chinese that it was not Nehru who conveyed the above but he himself who had suggested it. The Chinese grew suspicious of the motives of the two emissaries and told them that it was for India to 'advance such ideas *as its own proposals*' [emphasis added]. The Chinese also conveyed the above conversations to India in the form of a memorandum dated 21 July, 1963. India responded rather quickly to the Chinese and, on 30 July, 1963, informed them categorically that 'no such message of any kind was given by the Prime Minister of India to these two gentlemen', although it was not denied that they had met PM Nehru earlier. It was later learned that the two gentlemen had indeed met Nehru on the persuasion of Krishna Menon, but were not given any 'message' for the Chinese.

Nehru was by now convinced that the struggle with China was bound to be a long term one. Quite uncharacteristically, he wrote an article for *Foreign Affairs* magazine [April 1963] in which he called for the *strengthening* of the Indian Army and for *expanded production of arms and equipment* [emphasis added]. Nevertheless, in April 1964, just a month prior to his death, Nehru made one last effort. He suggested that India was prepared to surrender its claim to establish an equal number of posts in the 20 kilometre demilitarized zone in the Western sector, provided China removed its posts, too. In this way neither country would have any posts in the demilitarized zone. Nehru's feeling was that with this idea, the main Chinese reservation had been met and he hoped that China would make such a proposal.[35] As no such proposals were forthcoming from the Chinese, the position, therefore, remained stalemated as before with no forward movement. This was Nehru's last effort to find common ground with China on the boundary question.

After Nehru's death, the new PM Shastri made another effort at resolving the deadlock. On 25 September, 1964, Foreign Minister Swaran Singh told the Lok Sabha that 'we are willing to regard the vacation of the seven Chinese posts in this area, should the Chinese undertake it, to be substantial compliance with the conditions set forth in the Colombo proposals. If China agrees to this, we are willing to enter into negotiations.' He further added 'we accept the modification that instead of an equal number of posts in the DMZ, the Chinese should remove theirs.' He also indicated that India would be willing to enter into negotiations on the boundary issue 'in the manner envisaged in the Colombo proposals.'[36]

The Chinese rejection was swift. A Chinese Government statement of 9 October, 1964, stated categorically that 'India's demand for Chinese withdrawal of seven posts as a pre-condition for negotiations is utterly unreasonable...the land on which these civilian posts are situated has always been Chinese territory. What right has India to ask China to withdraw? As if to confirm the obvious, Zhou told the NPC on 21 December, 1964, that 'we will not withdraw a single one of these seven civilian posts.' Zhou deemed India's proposals as 'entirely unreasonable.' The Chinese were in no mood for a compromise to start the negotiations.

India's new PM, Shastri, explained the situation to the Lok Sabha on 24 December, 1964. He said that India was 'willing to agree to there being no posts of either side in the DMZ.' However, as China had not agreed to this formulation, the 'question of negotiations does not arise.'

A total impasse had, thus, been reached and negotiations for solving the border question were put in deep freeze. It was clear that with China having achieved its territorial and other objectives by a force of arms, it had very little incentive left to enter into negotiations. In any case, China was soon convulsed in the throes of an internal upheaval known as the Cultural Revolution, and had little time for anything else. There was to be no further movement on boundary negotiations for several years. The stalemate was thus complete.

CHAPTER 7

The Interregnum [1964–80]

From the end of hostilities in 1962 till 1980, there were no formal negotiations between India and China on the border question. The main sticking point continued to be India's insistence that China accept the Colombo proposals *in toto*, whereas China said that it had accepted them 'in principle', but continued to maintain two reservations. The crux of the matter was in the Western sector. In this sector, the Colombo proposals were that as a result of Chinese withdrawal, a DMZ to a depth of 20 kilometres would emerge and that in this DMZ, both sides could maintain civilian posts *to be decided jointly as to where they would be located* [emphasis added]. The Chinese, on the other hand, not only unilaterally decided the location of their posts, but categorically stated that the DMZ was Chinese territory. They refused to have any posts from India located in the DMZ. Even Nehru's compromise offer, just before his death, of having no posts by either country in the DMZ was peremptorily turned down. Thus, the impasse continued.

Meanwhile, there were numerous protest notes from either side alleging violations of the line of actual control [LAC]. As the LAC was never demarcated on the ground, each side had its own perceptions of where the line actually was. This was perhaps the main reason why there continued to be acrimonious exchanges on violations. Sometimes the intrusions were deliberate to test the response of the other side. Intrusions were alleged by both sides not only on the ground, but by aircraft as well. In acrimonious notes to each other, both would deny any such intrusions vociferously. Thus, tension between the two countries could be kept alive or dampened depending upon the frequency, depth and extent of the violations. More often than not, tension on the LAC was retched up or down to score political points or to persuade the other party to follow a particular policy. The Chinese began to use this lever ever so frequently. Time and again, tension on the border was totally unrelated to events on the border itself. The Chinese surmised that they had found a 'weapon' with which they could browbeat India whenever they wished to do so.

The opportunity for the Chinese to test the efficacy of this policy arrived sooner than they probably had expected. Ever since the debacle of Indian arms in 1962, the Pakistanis felt that their moment of opportunity had arrived to wrest Kashmir by force of arms from India. The Sino-Pak Border Agreement had cemented the relations between the two countries. Serious consultations took place on the next steps to be taken when Ayub visited China [2-9 March, 1965], and received an exceptionally full ceremonial treatment. The first indications of a security tie-up between Pakistan and China came in the summer of 1963, when Ayub made the statement on 8 July, 1963, that 'smaller nations of Asia would look to China for protection against India.' The CIA also sensed that Sino-Pak collusion was in the offing. Reports were being received by the CIA, since early 1964, of a possible 'secret Sino-Pakistan Mutual Defence Agreement of some kind.' It was felt whether this Agreement existed or not, 'some secret understanding did, indeed, exist.'[1] The plan to infiltrate mujahedeen into Kashmir was probably known to the Chinese, for during his visit to Pakistan in February 1964, Zhou talked of 'joint fighting tasks,'[2] and co-operation in the security field was almost certainly a topic for discussion. Two 'reliable and sensitive' reports received by the US indicated that both Bhutto and Foreign Secretary Aziz Ahmed knew of a 'secret memorandum' that Ayub had written on his talks with Zhou, and that an 'understanding' did indeed exist between China and Pakistan relating to actions that either side might take in case the other was involved in military conflict with India.[3] As the plan progressed, so did the belligerency in the tone of Chinese notes to India on the border.

Apart from numerous intrusions in the Western sector, one area of concern was the Sikkim-Tibet boundary. Fortunately for India, this was the only boundary fully recognized by the Chinese and demarcated on the ground. This area, which abutted on the 'chicken's neck,' was vital to India, for through this narrow piece of territory ran the only land-link between India and its North-Eastern territories. Any pressure at this point meant that India could not withdraw troops from this area in case trouble erupted in Kashmir. The Chinese knew this, too. Therefore, the Chinese decided to start to build their case by alleging that India was violating this boundary by building structures *beyond the line* [emphasis added]. With this verbal belligerence, the Chinese hoped to achieve three main objectives. Firstly, it would impress their Pakistani 'partners' that they were serious associates. Secondly, it would enhance China's prestige in Pakistan. Thirdly, it would keep India off balance and yet not commit them to any military action.

The pattern of Chinese accusations of alleged violations by Indian troops along the Sikkim-Tibet border took a dramatic upswing as fighting broke out in Kashmir in August 1965. Chinese notes now began to end with threats and warnings that 'if India does not stop acts of aggression and provocation it must bear full responsibility for the consequences that may arise.'[4] As the fighting on Western front entered a decisive stage, the Chinese issued another threat on 8 September, 1965, that if India did not dismantle 'all aggressive military structures' on the Sikkim-Tibet boundary and 'stop all its acts of aggression and provocation against China in the Western, middle and Eastern sectors' it would be responsible for 'the consequences.' China had now decided to expand the threats from the Sikkim-Tibet border to all along the Sino-Indian border[5] and in a Chinese Government statement on 7 September, 1965, made the astonishing claim that '*India's aggression against any one of its neighbours concerns all its neighbours*'! In other words, the Chinese was now asserting their rights to interfere in the affairs of the Indian sub-continent.

Whilst Chinese rhetoric against India went into full propaganda drive, they were extremely careful not to commit anything more than that to Pakistan. FM Chen YI was present in Karachi on 4 September, 1965, where Bhutto met him and briefed him extensively with maps on how the hostilities with India over Kashmir were proceeding. Chen Yi was full of bluster in urging the Pakistanis to attack Indian positions, but when Bhutto finally raised the question: Would the Chinese open a front on the Sino-Indian border? Chen Yi demurred. After dodging the question several times, he finally told Bhutto that he had no authorization to say anything but would submit the issue to PM Zhou![6]

To diffuse the situation on the Sikkim-Tibet border, India offered to the Chinese that an 'independent and neutral observer' could visit the border and see for himself the actual situation that prevailed. Not unnaturally, the Chinese were not interested, for their motives were entirely different. In a most curious interpretation of their claim of 'non-involvement' in Kashmir, as conveyed to India in their note of 31 May, 1962, the Chinese now re-interpreted the same note to suggest that by 'non-involvement' they meant that the Kashmir question should be settled on the basis of respect for 'the Kashmiri people's right of self-determination.'[7] Here was another example of Chinese 'double-talk.' The timing of this clarification is most important, for on this date [16 September], the Pakistanis were wavering whether to continue the conflict with India or to settle for a ceasefire [By this time all of Pakistan's hopes had been dashed]. In the same note, the Chinese also alleged that India had constructed 56 structures along the Sikkim-Tibet border and 'threatened and demanded that within *three days* they should be dismantled or face grave consequences.' The last threat was intended to egg on the Pakistanis to continue the fighting *by suggesting* that the Chinese were ready to intervene. There were credible reports that indicate that both Ayub and Bhutto flew secretly to Beijing on the night of 19/20 September, 1965, to elicit Chinese support by requesting them to open another front on the Sino-Indian border. It is unclear whether the Chinese refused to accede to Ayub's request or whether Ayub himself had second thoughts.[8] Ayub would also have been aware of Rusk's threat that if he created a situation which produced a China intervention then he would have 'alienated himself from the West.' Rusk insisted that this was 'a reality.'

Both Soviet Russia and the US were sufficiently alarmed at what they thought were Chinese pretexts of utilizing differences over the Sino-Indian boundary to meddle in the Indo-Pak conflict. On 13 September, 1965, Soviet Russia had already warned 'those whose inciting statements, whose policy help fan the conflict, must be warned by the entire world, by all states, that they thereby assume a heavy responsibility for such a policy, for such actions for trying to push India and Pakistan towards an aggravation of the conflict.' Beijing could not have missed the Soviet intent conveyed in the statement.

The US Government was even more forthright. The US issued two explicit warnings to the Chinese. On 15 September, 1965, Secretary of State Rusk made a public statement warning the Chinese to stay out of the conflict between India and Pakistan.[9] On the same day, the US Ambassador to Poland, John Cabot, was instructed to meet the Chinese Ambassador to Poland, Wang Guoquan, and warn him as follows:

> Regarding recent unfounded allegations conveyed to India with a threat of military action, the US Government deplored even the making of such threats which if pursued, could create a most dangerous situation which it would be difficult to confine to the areas or parties initially affected [10]

On 15 September, 1965, the Indian Ambassador to the US, BK Nehru, met US Secretary of State Dean Rusk and orally requested him that the US Government make a formal statement warning China that the US will intervene if China attacks India and that the US will come to the assistance of India. Rusk listened, but was non-committal, for the US was not keen to get into a fire fight with the Chinese over sub-continental issues, involved as it was with the Vietnam problem.

Nevertheless, the Chinese realized that they were now up against the two super powers that were both of the same opinion. As the Ta Kung Pao of Hong Kong (a pro-Chinese newspaper) noted 'what warrants attention is the fact that not only is US Imperialism supporting Indian aggression, *but also some people who call themselves Marxists-Leninists*' [emphasis added]. It was a bitter pill to swallow, and the Chinese now fell back on bluster and verbal threats. As the fortunes of the Pakistanis faded, so did the verbal belligerence of Chinese notes to India dramatically increase. In a note delivered at midnight of 16 September [trying to make it look dramatic] to the Indian CD'A at Beijing, the Chinese demanded that India immediately stop 'provocations' and dismantle 'military structures of aggression *built on Chinese side of the Sikkim border*' [emphasis added] or face 'grave consequences.' A time limit of three days was given [i.e., 19 September]. Faced with a determined India, now conscious of the support of the two super powers, both Pakistan and China caved in. For the Chinese, it was humiliating to first extend the ultimatum by another three days to 22 September and then finally to abandon it. With a fine sense of humour the Indian PM, Shastri, suggested that if the so-called structures were on the Chinese side as alleged by them, then they were welcome to demolish them by themselves! If they wanted India to do so then Indian troops would have to cross over into Tibet to carry out the task!

The Chinese ploy of using pressure on the boundary to fulfil larger political objectives had dismally failed. China's disappointment was reflected in Vice Premier Bo's address to a visiting Pakistani delegation when, on 29 September, 1965, he told them that the 'struggle is not yet over, but has entered a new phase.'[11] A perceptive US Consul-General in Dacca noted the following:

> Chinese prestige has collapsed in East Pakistan. Faced with the united military opposition of the US and USSR, China was afraid to move against India. Despite brave words... China merely blustered when the chips were down.[12]

The Sino-Pak understanding was shown for what it was worth—nothing but a self seeking agreement. Pakistan caved in when Rusk threatened that if Ayub created a situation that produces a 'Chinese intervention, then he will have alienated himself from the West' and that '*not one thin dime for a country* that suggests or encourages aggressive policies of Red China' would be available.[13] China, on the other hand, conscious of the fact that both the super powers were of one view, did not wish to risk an adventure whose outcome could have been extremely risky. Quietly, it first extended the ultimatum by three days and then unilaterally declared that its objectives in Sikkim had been met, swallowed a bitter pill and quietly ended its threats.

The events of 1965 showed that India was not as isolated as China had thought, and that Pakistan was not yet ready to sacrifice its relationship with the West for China's sake. When the Indo-Pak cease-fire was announced, the Chinese voice was checked and became muted. All that China could do was to make scornful comments about Indian border violations and about the 'cowardice' of Indian soldiers. It was obvious that China had gained nothing from inciting Pakistan, and few failed to discern that its policy of intimidating India on the border had failed. China's policy was further in tatters when Pakistan accepted arch rival Soviet Russia's proposal to meet India at Tashkent 'under Soviet auspices' to settle Indo-Pak disputes. China's propaganda machine became unusually muted and fell back to publishing vitriolic articles critical of India.

China was sufficiently perturbed at the turn of events for the Chinese FM, Chen Yi, to summon the Pakistan Ambassador to China and warn him that Tashkent was 'casting a shadow over Sino-Pak relations.'[14] And to make matters worse, a day before Zhou was to arrive in Pakistan in July 1966, Foreign Minister Bhutto, considered to be pro-Chinese in orientation, was sacked by Ayub. *Dawn* of Karachi remarked that this sacking [of Bhutto] 'signalled a change' of Pak policy. Despite its support to Pakistan during the 1965 war by verbal sabre-rattling along the Sino-Indian border, China now faced the prospect of Pakistan slipping out of its orbit. At the same time, China watched with consternation when PM Kosygin visited Pakistan in April 1968 and offered military aid to Pakistan in order to wean it away from the tight embrace of Beijing. The Chinese now resorted to bluster and instead accused India of forming 'an open military alliance with US Imperialism and Soviet Revisionism *directed against China and*

Map 6: India-China Border. Map of Nathu La, Jelep La

India's other neighbours' [emphasis added]. Far from cementing its relationship with Pakistan, China now was clearly worried at the prospect of joint US-Soviet action against it.

Having failed to achieve its objectives during the Indo-Pak conflict, the Chinese once again tried to keep tension alive with India, particularly along the Tibet-Sikkim border. It may be noted that the Sikkim-Tibet boundary is not only recognized by the present Government of the People's Republic of China, but this boundary is also demarcated on the ground. Therefore, there is no ambiguity on its alignment. That China chose this area to raise the temperature illustrates the point that even if the entire Sino-Indian boundary was fully negotiated and settled by both sides and demarcated on the ground, the Chinese would still have no hesitation in raising an issue, if they so wished, to attain their political objectives elsewhere.

On the Sikkim-Tibet border, the Chinese started feverish construction activity to build roads right up to the border-line. Soon, the Chinese opened a new phase of hostility towards India by installing loudspeakers at selected points on the border and started broadcasting virulent anti-Indian propaganda. Perhaps this had more to do with internal reasons, for the Cultural Revolution was at its height. Fortunately for India, most of the Chinese broadcasts were in such highly Sanskritised Hindi that very few Indian troops posted at the border actually understood what the Chinese were saying.[15] With the Cultural Revolution raging on mainland China, these antics of extremely doubtful value were designed more to impress the leadership back on the mainland of their 'revolutionary' spirit rather than to achieve anything substantial on the Sino-Indian border.

Nevertheless, the Chinese were also keen to test the state of readiness of the Indian Army. Accordingly on 11 September, 1967, the Chinese suddenly opened fire on an Indian patrol party near the Nathu La [Pass] [On Tibet-Sikkim border]. For several days the firing went on and, at one stage, it became very intense when heavy artillery opened up on both sides. Most of the Chinese bunkers on the North side and in depth were completely destroyed. Several curt diplomatic notes were exchanged between the two sides. Finally, when peace returned some days later, Indian troops had not yielded any ground and neither had the Chinese been able to capture any Indian position. Casualties were heavy on both sides, with India reporting a loss of 88 killed and 163 wounded. Chinese losses were estimated at 300 killed and about 450 wounded. Thereafter, an uneasy lull prevailed in the area. A situation of no peace—no war thus prevailed.

This was also the period when China was fully involved with the 'Cultural Revolution' and, due to extensive internal problems thus created, there was little time to consider serious foreign policy issues. The Chinese Foreign Ministry came under the control of fiery Red Guards for several days, with the Foreign Minister Chen Yi himself and other leading officials facing humiliation at their hands. Almost all Chinese Ambassadors abroad except one [Huang Hua in Cairo] were withdrawn. It was during this period that Chinese foreign policy suffered serious reverses in Africa, at Algiers and with the overthrow of President Sukarno in Indonesia, it lost a kindred soul. Subsequently, the Chinese were appalled when several hundreds of overseas Chinese were massacred in Indonesia and their Embassy at Jakarta was unceremoniously thrown out.

The intensification of the US-led war in Vietnam, coupled with deteriorating relations with Soviet Russia, forced the leadership in China to introduce the PLA into the governing system to restore order from the chaos of the Cultural Revolution. However, clashes took place with Soviet Russia along the disputed border in the North-East, the most serious of which was the Damansky/Chen Pao clash along the Ussuri River, where the Chinese suffered several hundred casualties. The Chinese were apprehensive of what the Soviets might do, particularly after the Soviet invasion of Czechoslovakia in 1968 and the initiation of the Brezhnev doctrine. Aware of threatening noises emanating from Moscow on the use of nuclear weapons, the Chinese were seriously alarmed. In a meeting with Kosygin at Beijing airport, Zhou accepted the proposal for both countries to restore Ambassadorial level relations and to open border negotiations. The Chinese realized that they could make little headway in normalizing relations with socialist countries till its estrangement with the Soviet Union continued. The only friends that China had were Albania and Pakistan.

Thus, as the decade of the sixties neared its end, China recognized its fragile position as its political adversaries continued to mount pressure. At loggerheads with the Soviets in the North, the situation in the South from the Chinese point of view was also rather precarious. With India, there appeared to be no movement at all. The US war effort in Vietnam had intensified. A US inspired coup was engineered in Cambodia, which led to the ouster of Sihanouk and his subsequent exile in Beijing. With a hostile nuclear armed Soviet Russia to the North and a hostile nuclear armed US Pacific Fleet deployed all along the Eastern Sea Coast, the Chinese recognized the seriousness of their position. At this point in time, the US viewed China as an implacable enemy.[16] China, aware of the evolving situation, signalled its precarious position when Zhou told Vietnamese PM Pham Van Dong on 29 April, 1968, that 'the US has been half encircling China and now the Soviet Union is also encircling China. The circle is getting complete.' The Chinese leadership and policies had, indeed, landed it in a very difficult situation.

Earlier, Zhou had met Ayub on 2 April, 1965 in Karachi and, conscious of China's deteriorating security environment, had requested that a message be conveyed to President Johnson. The message was:

> [a] China will never provoke a war with the US; [b] China means what it says; [c] China will honour whatever obligations it has undertaken; and [d] China is prepared for an escalation and if it comes to a conflict, there will be no limits.[17]

Unfortunately, Ayub's visit to the US was cancelled, but that did not deter the Chinese. They decided to use the British channel instead. Chen Yi summoned a startled British CDA, Donald Hopson, on 31 May, 1965, and much to the latter's surprise, requested that the above points be conveyed to the US. The British duly obliged and the Chinese message was conveyed to President Johnson.

While the Chinese were busy trying to convey messages of peace to the Americans, the Vietnamese were getting increasingly worried at the Chinese attitude. General Vo Nguyen Giap, the famous Vietnamese general and the victor against the French at Dien Bien Phu, recalled the following:

> that the Chinese Government told the US that if it did not threaten or touch China, then China would do nothing to prevent the attacks on Vietnam. It is like telling the US that it could bomb Vietnam at will as long as there was no threat at the Chinese border.[18]

This period was also quite barren in Sino-Indian relations. The worsening domestic situation in China, which was over shadowed by the rise and subsequent defection of Defence Minister Lin Biao, tense relations with the Soviet Union in the wake of the invasion of Czechoslovakia, and the war in Vietnam set different priorities for China. Nevertheless, the Chinese continued to mount vicious propaganda attacks against India. One particularly nasty piece in the People's Daily lampooned the Indian PM, Mrs. Gandhi. The Chinese characters used for Indira Gandhi, 'Ying di la Gandi' were changed to 'Mei di la Gandi' meaning 'pulled by the US'! Mahatma Gandhi's birth centenary, which fell in 1969, was totally ignored by the Chinese.

In order to break out of its perceived encirclement, the Chinese now sought an opening both with India and the US. In early 1970, a US table-tennis team was invited to visit China, signalling a thaw in the relationship. It was also at this time that China made an overture to India in the hope that at least this would keep its South-Western border with India quiet. The Chinese would no doubt have also noticed that, officially, India took no sides in the Sino-Soviet border dispute and that there was a certain amount of disenchantment creeping within the Indian establishment over Soviet Russia's decision to supply arms to Pakistan. When Mrs. Gandhi protested to Kosygin in a personal letter on 10 July, 1968, against Soviet arms supply to Pakistan, she received a reply in general terms that did not indicate any change in Soviet policy. Mrs. Gandhi also publicly aired the feeling that ever since the Tashkent Agreement, there had been a 'shift' in Soviet thinking. The disenchantment in India over the Soviet decision to supply arms to Pakistan escalated to a level that some members of the ruling Congress Party called for the 'restoration of India's manoeuvrability by mending fences with China.'[19] Perhaps aware of such differences developing, the Chinese at the more optimistic level hoped to dent the close relationship between India and Soviet Russia.

Mrs. Gandhi, too, was keen to normalize relations with China. She realized that India could not retain its freedom of manoeuver if it was hemmed in by poor relations with China. As a first step, India stopped publishing the 'White Papers' on the border dispute. These annual publications, presented to Parliament, only led to China 'baiting' and a worsening of relations. Secondly, Mrs. Gandhi realized that it would be an 'over simplification' to regard poor relations with China *as merely the result of a border dispute* [emphasis added]. Simultaneous or subsequent developments—such as China's systematic support of Pakistan against India, her provocative criticism of India for being 'subservient' to the US and Soviet Russia, indicated that the border dispute was the outcome of a more complex policy followed by China that required an equally more broad based approach. Mrs Gandhi also declared that 'we do not have hostile intentions towards China.'[20] Thirdly, Mrs. Gandhi took the decision to abandon the Colombo proposals '*in toto*' but moved only very incrementally. The first hint of this came at a press conference on 1 January, 1969. In response to a question, she made a statement, which amounted to saying that the Indian Government would be prepared to try ways of solving conflicts with China through talks *which were not based on any preconditions* [emphasis added]. Asked whether India would no longer insist on the '*in toto*' formula, she replied 'that is not what I meant. What I meant is that we are stuck in a particular position. That does not solve our problem with China. We should try to find a way of solving this problem.' When a persistent questioner demanded a 'straight answer', she replied, 'unfortunately straight answers are not possible.' FM Dinesh Singh expressed similar sentiments when he told Parliament on 8 April, 1969 that 'we have a long frontier with China. We would like to reduce tension along this frontier.' The Chinese, quick off the mark, too sensed an opening.

On 1 May, 1970, Mao met the Indian Charge d'Affairs at Beijing at the Tienanmen and told him the following:

> We cannot go on quarrelling like this. We must become friends again. We will become friends again. [Women puhui zhei yang chao xiaqu. Women yingai yao zuo pengyu. Women yiding zuo pengyu.]

India's response was hesitant, for unknown at that time except within a very small and a tight circle, India was quietly negotiating a treaty with the Soviets and did not wish to jeopardize its outcome. While China waited for a more positive response, events in Pakistan overtook Mao's gesture. With Pakistan's crackdown in East Pakistan [Now Bangladesh], war clouds appeared on the horizon. The signing of the Indo-Soviet Treaty on 9 August, 1971, completely changed the situation once again. While *Pravda* termed the Indo-Soviet Treaty as a 'deterrent against the hegemonic goals of China', China did not criticize the Indo-Soviet Treaty till as late as 7 December, 1971. In fact, when Bhutto led a high powered Pakistani delegation to China and pleaded that the Indian Army was in battle positions against *both* wings of Pakistan, all that the Chinese FM, Ji Pengfei, said was, 'that the Pakistani people should make *joint efforts to overcome difficulties and solve their own problems*' [emphasis added].[21] Qi Pengfei also told the Pakistanis that China would support Pakistan 'to defend state sovereignty and national independence.' The key phrase 'territorial integrity' was deliberately left out in the hope that the implications of this would be understood in New Delhi. Later, even Bhutto was to admit in an interview with C L Sulzberger that China had turned down Pakistan's request for a defence pact.[22] Nevertheless, once Indo-Pak hostilities commenced, China as before was firmly, but only verbally, supportive of Pakistan. But this time China had the additional support of the US. And once again, the key pressure point against India was the unsettled boundary between India and China.

In the Indo-Pak conflict over Bangladesh, the US, fearing the dismemberment of Pakistan and the collapse of the Pakistani Army, urged the Chinese to militarily intervene on Pakistan's behalf. On 10 December, 1971, Kissinger met Chinese Ambassador to the UN, Huang Hua, at a secret CIA 'safe house' in New York. To impress the Chinese, Kissinger handed over a 'Top Secret' dossier of US intelligence as well as photographs to show that the US was moving naval ships to the Bay of Bengal to intimidate India. Kissinger told the Chinese:

> If the People's Republic of China were to consider the situation on the Indian sub-continent a threat to its security and if it took measures to protect its security, the US would oppose efforts of others to interfere with the People's Republic.[23]

Kissinger later reported to Nixon that he had asked for this meeting with the Chinese to suggest 'Chinese military help to Pakistan.' Kissinger had clearly misjudged Chinese intentions, for the Chinese did not yet fully trust the US nor did they want to shut the door completely with India.

In tandem with what Kissinger told Huang Hua, the Pakistani Foreign Secretary summoned the Chinese Ambassador to Pakistan to meet him on 12 December, 1971. Sultan Khan reinforced what Yahya Khan had earlier requested the Chinese that 'nothing less than Chinese intervention against India would do.' Later, the Chinese Ambassador brought back the Chinese reply. The Ambassador said while China would continue to support Pakistan 'morally, economically and politically, *its capacity to intervene was limited*' [emphasis added]. For emphasis, the Chinese Ambassador stressed, 'please do not pin much hope on it.'[24] Later, on 16 December, 1971, *Xinhua* made it clear that there would be no Chinese military intervention.

China could not have acted otherwise. The Chinese were conscious of their long lines of communication under severe winter conditions in Tibet, the disarray in the PLA following the defection of Defence Minister Lin Biao and, sensing a possible clash with Soviet Russia, their best troops had to be deployed at the Sino-Soviet border. Therefore, the Chinese could only resort to bluster. Apart from making the usual hard line statements about the Sino-Indian boundary, specifically the Sikkim-Tibet border, the Chinese did nothing on the ground. In fact, the

Chinese had already hinted that they would do nothing militarily when a senior official of the Chinese Foreign Ministry told the Indian CDA at Beijing, 'Mr. CDA *need not worry* for China will act in accordance with international law' [emphasis added]. Much to Kissinger's chagrin, US intelligence discerned no unusual Chinese military activity along the Sino-Indian border.

It took some time for the bitterness over the Bangladesh events to die down. When the events in Sikkim led to the merger of that state with the Indian Union, China again bitterly attacked India. At first, the Chinese leadership was a bit perplexed at the turn of events. They suspected a Soviet 'hand' behind this move by India. Coming close on the heels of the events that led to the independence of Bangladesh, the Chinese suspected that this was yet another attempt by the *Soviets in collusion with India* to 'encircle' China [emphasis added]. The *People's Daily* reflected this view when it stated that 'facts have once again shown that Soviet revisionist, social imperialists and Indian expansionists constitute a serious threat to the independence and sovereignty of South Asian countries, and are the cause of the unstable situation in the South Asian subcontinent.'[25] Still not sure of the reasons, the Chinese leader Deng Xiaoping met Kissinger on 27 November, 1974, and queried him: 'Why did they have to annex it? Indian policy is *most peculiar* for they already had military control, and after annexation, their military position has in no way strengthened.' Nevertheless, Chinese kept up the anti-Indian verbal barrage. A statement of the Government of the People's Republic of China issued on 29 April, 1975, vowed that 'it absolutely does not recognize India's illegal annexation of Sikkim and firmly supports the people of Sikkim in their struggle for national independence and in defence of state sovereignty against Indian expansionism.' Although harsh language was used by China, it was all verbal bombast. China did not cause any problems on the border, even though Indian and Chinese soldiers were within a handshake distance of each other at several points.

Nevertheless, both sides appeared keen to normalize relations. Each had reasons of their own. China had recognized Bangladesh as an independent country. Soon, the idea was mooted that, as a first step, diplomatic representation in respective capitals should be upgraded to Ambassador-level. The last Indian Ambassador to China had completed his term and a new one was never appointed. A similar position prevailed as far as China was concerned. As such, technically, there had been no withdrawal of Ambassadors. The moot point was that if India took the initiative, would China respond in the same manner? It was suggested that since India had been the first not to appoint a new Ambassador, it was for India to take the initiative. Vice Foreign Minister Han Nienlong told the Indian CDA in Beijing on 26 January, 1976, that, should India decide to take the initiative, China would similarly respond. Eventually, India took the initiative and appointed an Ambassador in 1976 and, as informally agreed earlier, China reciprocated soon thereafter.

The defeat of Mrs. Gandhi in 1977 came as a welcome surprise for Chinese leaders. They never expected that she would lose the elections. The Chinese reading of the situation was that this electoral defeat of Indira Gandhi was a 'set-back for the Soviets.'[26] They detected in the newly installed Janata Party leaders' claim of initiating a policy of 'genuine nonalignment' a move away from a close relationship that India had with Soviet Russia. They tried to influence this trend by adopting a twin track policy. Firstly, to test India's reaction, Deng Xiaoping gave interviews to two prominent Indian journalists in which he made an offer to settle the boundary question on the basis of a 'package deal.' Essentially, what Deng was offering was that the existing 'line of actual control' be converted into the Sino-Indian boundary; although it must be emphasized that China never spelt out the details of the offer. Therefore, the assumption was that China would also keep the additional territory that they had captured in 1962 and settle along the LAC that came into existence at the end of the conflict in 1962. Secondly, to create a favourable public opinion in India, the Chinese leadership toned down its strident and vociferous backing of Pakistan on the Kashmir issue. This was only a tactical step, for in case it was so required, a hard line posture could easily be resumed. Incidentally, there were press reports that Deng had suggested that the Kashmir dispute be settled between Indian and Pakistan on the basis of the Line of Control [LC].[27] Thirdly, the Chinese allowed Indian ships to visit Chinese ports for the first time since the conflict of 1962.[28]

As a part of the new approach, a Chinese delegation led by Wang Bingnan, Head of the Chinese People's Association for Friendship with Foreign Countries, visited India and met both PM Desai and FM Vajpayee. Interestingly, Wang also called on former PM, Mrs. Gandhi. During his visit, Wang extended an invitation to Vajpayee to visit China on behalf of the Chinese Foreign Minister. A further initiative followed in September 1978, when Huang Hua and Vajpayee met in New York, the first such meeting of the two Foreign Ministers since 1962. Soviet Russia was not amused at China's efforts and dubbed them as an 'evil campaign to dupe New Delhi.'[29] It was an attempt to 'weaken Indo-Soviet friendship.'[30] Vajpayee was forced to reassure the Soviets that his forthcoming visit to China would in no way affect India's friendship with the Soviet Union, and that India had her own experience with China and would keep 'her eyes and ears wide open.'

Nevertheless, the Janata Party leadership remained keen to re-build the relationship with China. There were signals that China was also inclined to revise some of its earlier attitudes towards India. Vajpayee took the initiative to visit China—essentially a leap of faith and became the first Indian leader to do so since the conflict of 1962. Earlier, Vajpayee had hinted to the Chinese that India could normalize relations with China without a resolution of the boundary issue. [31] However, during formal discussions with Huang Hua, the boundary issue was discussed, but beyond re-stating positions taken during the 1960 official level talks, there was no progress. It was during Vajpayee's talks with Deng Xiaoping in February 1979 that the latter once more put forward the 'package proposal;' that is, to accept that the boundary dispute is a legacy of history and that it could be settled along the 'Line of Actual Control.' Deng's view was that India 'controlled' areas were rich in natural resources whereas the Chinese held areas were neither economically 'useful' nor were they habitable. Vajpayee had no specific brief on how to respond to this offer, but reacted by re-stating India's well known position. Deng then said that if it was not possible to accept his proposal on the boundary, then this issue should not 'prevent us from improving relations in other fields.' Vajpayee, perhaps not too sure of domestic support, only reiterated the centrality of settling the boundary issue first and at an early date.

For all its talk of 'genuine non-alignment', the Janata Government was soon to learn lessons the hard way. The Chinese, while Vajpayee was in China, made it a point to support the Pakistani position on Kashmir. 'We have done so in the past and will continue to do so in the future.' Although, even before Vajpayee's visit diplomatic efforts were made to commit the Chinese not to open hostilities against Vietnam while Vajpayee was in China, the Chinese remained non committal. Far from diluting friendship with Soviet Russia, an absolute necessity both strategically and militarily, the Janata Government found itself in a messy situation. While Vajpayee was still in China, the Chinese attacked Vietnam and termed its attack as 'teaching a lesson', to Vietnam. This was the same terminology that they had used against India in 1962! Whether this was a deliberate affront remains a moot point. Parliament in India was so incensed at Chinese temerity that the Rajya Sabha unanimously condemned China for 'continuing its policy of seeking to settle its disputes with neighbours through the use of force.'[32] Even the Soviet leader, Brezhnev, was annoyed and told Desai that 'your FM's visit to China was not well received by our public. I do not know how your people reacted to it, but our people took it ill.'[33] Thus, the Janata Government's efforts to promote a settlement of the border issue by trying to create a favourable climate came to nothing, and it fell from power soon afterwards.

The return of Mrs. Gandhi to power in 1980 saw a shift in the way she saw the security situation. She took a very clinical view. The trauma of the military defeat in 1962 at the hands of the Chinese had begun to fade. Indian policy planners now assessed that as far as the international situation was concerned, the two super powers, although still mutually antagonistic to each other, were developing relations with China on a differing path. Sino-US relations were blossoming and both were working in tandem, as witnessed in the Chinese decision to attack Vietnam. Sino-Soviet relations, though still tense and stalemated, were also showing the first signs of a thaw. The Soviet invasion of Afghanistan had clearly upset the delicate balance in South Asia. Mrs. Gandhi told Brezhnev that while India would not openly criticize Soviet intervention in Afghanistan, it would certainly have an 'adverse' effect on India's security. Mrs. Gandhi was clearly worried at the massive flow of lethal arms from the US and China to Pakistan and nuclear and missile proliferation from China to Pakistan. The US National Security Directive of 3 July, 1979, authorizing joint US-Pakistan operations in Afghanistan, upset the delicate balance in South Asia. This would be to the strategic disadvantage of India. Therefore, India could not support Soviet intervention, although this was never publicly stated.

In the meanwhile, the Soviets had been pressing India to support their proposal for 'collective security' for Asia. In a series of speeches [7 June, 1969; 20 March, 1972; 21 December, 1972], Brezhnev had outlined the Soviet proposals, but Mrs. Gandhi understood that this was anti-China in its intent. The Chinese took the 'collective security' proposal to mean a Soviet attempt to 'encircle' China. 'The collective security proposal,' thundered the *People's Daily*, was an 'anti Chinese military alliance which Brezhnev had picked from the garbage heap of the war-monger, Dulles.'[34]

Under the circumstances, Mrs. Gandhi began to look for new strategic openings to enhance India's options. Therefore, the opening to China became important as it gave India a chance to assess the new Chinese leadership under Deng Xiaoping, and to explore the prospects of a boundary settlement. The Indian leadership did not expect an immediate breakthrough nor did they feel that China would be any more accommodating than she was in the 1950s. It was clearly understood that a constraint that existed would be the Soviet attitude to Sino-Indian border talks, if and when they took place. India could not ruffle Soviet feathers un-necessarily, given the vital military supply relationship, the fact that the Soviet Union was India's largest trading partner and Soviet political support for India's position on Kashmir and other issues was vital.

Nevertheless, Mrs Gandhi was keen to underscore to other powers that India did, indeed, have other options and that the Sino-Indian window was not permanently closed. To test the waters, a senior official was sent by Mrs. Gandhi to China in early 1980 to explore the possibilities of moving forward. Taking advantage of an invitation to visit North Korea, the senior official stopped over in Beijing for talks with the Chinese. The talks covered essentially the same ground that was done during Vajpayee's visit in 1979, and the Chinese once again reiterated the 'package proposal.' The Chinese, too, wary of Soviet intentions, felt the need to broad base their options. As vital economic reforms initiated by Deng Xiaoping were underway, the Chinese, too, needed a peaceful border on its South-Western flank. FM Huang Hua, for the first time since 1962, attended the Indian Embassy Republic Day Reception at Beijing on 26 January, 1980. Beijing Review of 4 February, 1980, also hinted at an improvement of relations.

On 21 June, 1980, Deng Xiaoping met an Indian journalist, Krishna Kumar, Chief Editor of the Vikrant [Defence News Service], and conveyed the following for the settlement of the boundary issue:

in a packaged way... I mean according to the Line of Actual Control. If both of us stand to this point, then this question can be solved with one sentence.... I think you can pass this message to Mrs. Gandhi.

Deng further added that in the past, there were many points of difference but that 'they are narrowing.' In order to ensure that his message reached Mrs. Gandhi, Deng received in Beijing, G Parthasarthy, a former Indian Ambassador to Beijing and a known close advisor to Mrs. Gandhi, and conveyed that 'it [the boundary dispute] is not difficult to settle, so long as both sides take reasonable measures.' PM Zhao Ziyang told GK Reddy of The Hindu that there was a need to arrive at a 'fair, reasonable and comprehensive' settlement.

An opportunity for opening a dialogue soon arrived, when Mrs. Gandhi met Chinese leader, Hua Guofeng in Belgrade at Tito's funeral. At the meeting in Belgrade, both sides decided to exchange visits at Foreign Minister's level. It was during FM Huang Hua's visit to Delhi in June 1981, postponed from August 1980, that a decision was taken to resume border talks. It was the first time since 1962 that a Chinese Foreign Minister had visited India. Mrs. Gandhi highlighted the importance of the visit with the remark that 'the big thing is that after so many years, a Chinese leader has come to India.'[35] *The People's Daily* [6 July, 1981] remarked that as long as both sides were 'sincere,' the Sino-Indian border problem can be solved 'fairly and reasonably.' Thus, after a gap of nearly 20 years, both sides decided to resume discussions on the boundary issue at the Vice Minister/ Secretary level.

As anticipated by the Indian leadership, the Soviet Union was clearly unhappy at the turn of events. Mrs. Gandhi had on 8 May, 1980, taken the precaution of confirming to Brezhnev that '*India would not improve its relations with China at the cost of its friendship with the Soviet Union*' [emphasis added].[36] At the end of Huang Hua's visit to India, *Pravda* noted that Sino-Indian talks had yielded, 'no agreement or even a joint communiqué.... Beijing's emissary in the face of India's firm demand was forced to agree to official talks for the settlement of the border issue.' Nevertheless, despite Mrs. Gandhi's assurance, the Soviets 'warned' India during President Reddy's visit to Moscow that 'China's smile diplomacy was a ruse to make its territorial gains permanent through gradual normalization.' At the same time, the Soviets also used the carrot of generous economic and military assistance to try and dissuade Mrs. Gandhi from moving closer to China. Economically, the Soviets offered a loan of 7.8 billion roubles, increased oil supplies and agreed to boost trade to US $13.3 billion. Militarily, the Soviets offered licensed production of T-72 Tanks and MiG-27 fighters.[37]

But Mrs. Gandhi held fast to her opening to China despite apparent Soviet unhappiness and economic/military generosity.

CHAPTER 8

Negotiations are Resumed, the Wangdung Incident and PM Rajiv Gandhi's Visit to China [1980–1989]

After a gap of almost 20 years, both India and China agreed once again to sit across the table to hold 'purposeful discussions to arrive at a settlement' of the vexed boundary question. This was as per the understanding reached during the visit of Chinese FM, Huang Hua, to India. There were no pre-conditions or specific terms set by either side for the resumption of the talks. India had largely abandoned the position that China must accept the Colombo proposals *in toto* before talks could commence.

As India was now entering into boundary negotiations with China, it was evident that the trauma of the 1962 conflict had begun to fade. Indian policy planners undertook a series of assessments on the current international situation, the South Asian scene, particularly developments in the India-Pakistan context and what could be the future prospects of relations with China. The two super powers, though, still mutually antagonistic, had developed relations with China, but on differing trajectories. Whilst the Sino-US bilateral relationship continued to blossom, as witnessed in their joint efforts to support Pakistan during the 1971 crisis, the Sino-Soviet relationship, though, stalemated at the moment, saw the first beginnings of a thaw. PM Mrs Gandhi was very wary of the floodgates of lethal arms supplies that threatened to flow to Pakistan from both the US and China as a result of Soviet intervention in Afghanistan. Therefore, the opening to China became important for it gave India the opportunity to, firstly, assess the new leadership of Deng Xiaoping and, secondly, to explore the possibilities of a boundary settlement. The Indian leadership was sanguine enough not to expect an immediate breakthrough in the boundary talks and neither did it expect that the Chinese would be any more forthcoming than they were in the 1950s. Mrs Gandhi was conscious of the constraint that existed in the form of Soviet attitude to the opening with China, for the military supply relationship was vital for India. Nevertheless, the Indian leadership was keen to demonstrate that its China option was there and that the Sino-Indian window was not permanently closed. This was intended not only as a reminder to the two super powers, but also to South Asian countries as well, particularly Pakistan.

The first meeting of the renewed Sino-Indian border talks took place in Beijing from 10-14 December, 1981. In the first meeting, both sides propounded some general principles that should be kept in mind while searching for a boundary solution. None of these principles were such that went beyond expressing general concerns and attitudes. Nevertheless, the Chinese once again put forward the 'package proposal.' It was essentially the same proposal that Deng Xiaoping had publicly aired through the medium of two Indian journalists and had earlier also conveyed to former FM Vajpayee. When the Indian side requested for cartographic examination of the Chinese proposal, it was turned down by China. The Indian side suspected that the Chinese were non-serious about settling the boundary issue and were, thus, not really interested in pushing forward the 'package proposal.' They were probably only assessing what would be India's reaction. FM Narasimha Rao, accordingly, informed Parliament that 'the Government of India never accepted the premise on which it is based [the package proposal] namely, that the Chinese side is making a concession in the Eastern sector by the giving up of territory which they allege is illegally incorporated into India. Nevertheless, we welcome the prospect of the Eastern sector being settled without any particular difficulty.'

FM Rao's statement indicated acceptance of one half of Deng's offer, but that is not what the Chinese had in mind. As the Indian side appeared 'unenthusiastic' to the Chinese about its 'package proposal', the Chinese suggested that the boundary issue be set aside and relations developed in other areas so as to complete the normalization process. However, India held firm to the belief that a settlement of the boundary issue was central to any normalization, and suggested that the Colombo Proposals could form a convenient starting point. The Chinese rejected this idea, for according to them, the Colombo Proposals were by now 'outdated.' At the end of the first round of talks, the Indian view was that these talks were 'exploratory' and, therefore, no meaningful bargaining could be expected. FM Rao informed Parliament that 'it was not our anticipation that it would be possible to make substantive progress in the first round...we may, however, regard the fact of the meeting itself the first on this subject in twenty years as a positive step.' FM Rao indicated that India was keen to continue negotiations. The Chinese, on the other hand, sounded more positive and *Xinhua* quoted Chinese Foreign Minister, Huang Hua, to say that 'the talks that Chinese and Indian officials are now holding on the boundary and other bilateral matters will surely have a positive influence on furtherance of friendly and co-operative relations between the two countries.'

Meanwhile, the Chinese pressed for early resumption of the second round of talks, despite being told that the Indian leader [Secretary] was under orders of transfer and that a new Secretary had not yet arrived. To accommodate the Chinese request, the second round was held at New Delhi from 17-20 May, 1982. On the eve of the meetings, both sides informed the press what they had in mind. The Chinese Vice-Foreign Minister, Fu Hao, reaffirmed China's unwillingness to accept the McMahon Line and hinted that the border negotiations could well be a lengthy process. In the meanwhile, he pressed for expanding cultural, scientific and trade ties. India reiterated that a lack of progress on the boundary issue would inhibit expansion of links in 'other fields' and that the McMahon Line was the boundary in the Eastern sector and the incorporation of Sikkim into India was 'not open to debate.'

In the second round of formal talks, China once again pleaded for an overall settlement essentially along the 'line of actual control,' a position very similar to the one taken in the first round of talks. China also reaffirmed its position that if it was not possible to settle the boundary issue, then it should be put aside and progress made in other areas such as trade, cultural, etc. India rejected the Chinese approach and insisted the settlement of the boundary was the main issue and a first priority. The failure of the Chinese to push forward the 'package deal' probably convinced the Chinese leadership that they would not be able to budge the Indian side into accepting their proposition. The Chinese also realized that for Sino-Indian relations to normalize some progress was also necessary on Sino-Soviet relations so as to lessen Soviet hostility to a rapprochement between China and India. But at this point, Sino-Soviet relations still remained frozen. However, soon after the conclusion of the talks with India, the *People's Daily*, in a hardening of Chinese stance, claimed that the border issue is the result of 'imperialist aggression and expansion against China.' It further went on to say that 'China is the victim, for it has never occupied an inch of Indian Territory.' In other words, there would be no unilateral concessions. It would seem that from this point onwards, the Chinese, while remaining conscious of the need to keep the dialogue with India going, were not expecting any forward movement in the negotiations. Their strategy was to develop relations in other fields and push the boundary issue on to the back burner.

Just three months after the conclusion of the second round of border talks, both China and Pakistan signed a Protocol opening the Khunjerab Pass along the Karakoram highway to commercial traffic. India protested to both countries as this was an area under illegal occupation of Pakistan. The Chinese reterated their known stand. As if to underline a hardening of Chinese stance, the then PM, Zhao Ziyang, clarified in October 1982 that while working for a comprehensive settlement, China would 'not make any unilateral concessions nor would it compromise its sovereignty.' In the Asian Games held at New Delhi in 1982, China vehemently protested at the participation of tribal dancers from NEFA [Arunachal Pradesh] and said that this was a 'deliberate step to propagate India's sovereignty over the state and to legalize it...the territory has been illegally occupied by India.' India turned down the protest in equally strong language.

While both sides exchanged sharply worded protest notes, neither felt that the dialogue should be abandoned. The third round was slightly delayed to allow for frayed tempers to cool, but took place in Beijing in early 1983 [29 January to 3 February, 1983]. Both in the third round and in the fourth round [24-30 October, 1983], it looked as if some progress was discernible, although the two sides were nowhere near reaching an agreement on a common set of principles. Sensing that it might just be possible to reach agreement based on the 'swap' formula, the Chinese reluctance to conduct the boundary negotiations on a sector-by-sector basis, as proposed by India, seemed to lessen. The Chinese informally sounded the Indian side on possible countours of a settlement based on the 'swap' formula, but with additional Chinese concessions in the Western sector. The Chinese proposal was never formally discussed, nor was the Indian response conveyed. Nevertheless, on 17 November, 1983, FM Rao informed the Indian Parliament that China had agreed to the Indian proposal for a 'sector-by-sector' approach and that this would be 'married' to the Chinese proposal of a 'package deal.' The Chinese agreement for a 'sector-by-sector' consideration was on the understanding that any agreement reached on a particular sector would be valid only if an agreement was reached *on the whole boundary together.* In other words, there would be no piecemeal agreements. It was also agreed in this round that attempts at normalization in 'other' spheres could proceed further.

Just prior to the fifth round of talks [9-15 September, 1984], Chinese leaders told the visiting West Bengal Chief Minister, Jyoti Basu, that there was no immediate prospect of a settlement of the border dispute. The Chinese also published an *Encyclopaedia of Tibetan History* that showed large parts of India, Nepal and Bhutan as parts of Chinese territories. No doubt this was intended to cause offence to the Indian side. Nevertheless, at the fifth round, it was agreed that, irrespective of the failure to reach an agreement on a common set of principles that were to define boundary making, the two sides could proceed directly for substantive discussions on a 'sector-by-sector' basis. India continued to maintain its position that unless there was a 'just and satisfactory solution to this question, our efforts to achieve full normalization of relations will continue to be handicapped.'[1]

The sixth round of talks were held in New Delhi from 6-11 November, 1985. This was the crucial round, as it was expected that serious negotiations would now commence on a sector-by-sector basis. The Indian side proposed that negotiations begin with the Eastern sector and this was accepted by the Chinese. However, the Chinese made it clear that the Eastern sector did not include the Sikkim-Tibet border. The Indian side, on the other hand insisted that the Sikkim-Tibet border was part of the Eastern sector. The crucial point, however, was that there was no dispute on the Sikkim-Tibet border, as China had already recognized this alignment and the Chinese Government had formally conveyed this as well. The impasse was broken when the Chinese side continued to ignore that this was part of the Eastern sector and the Indian side continued to maintain that it, indeed, was a part of this sector. Each side listened in silence when the other referred to this issue. And each side ignored the others position.

The feeling on the Indian side was that this Eastern sector was not very complicated for although the Chinese had said they would not accept the McMahon Line, yet they had largely respected the McMahon *alignment and, even after violating it in the 1962 conflict, had retired North of the McMahon Line after the conflict ended* [*emphasis added*]. In any case, India was in possession of the entire territory. Confidence on the Indian side was high as the Soviet Union had, just prior to the sixth round, published a fresh set of maps *that showed for the first time ever that the McMahon Line was the international boundary between India and China.* Thus, for the first time ever, both the super powers—the US and Soviet Russia—accepted the McMahon Line as the international border between India and China in the Eastern sector. This was a huge political gain for India.

The Chinese were aware that *at the very minimum*, India would insist that in the Eastern sector, the McMahon Line be recognized as the international boundary and if that presented 'problems' for the Chinese, then the McMahon *alignment* could be accepted, perhaps under a different nomenclature. The Indian side was conscious that the Chinese were 'allergic' to the name McMahon, since it reminded them of colonial times but, on the other hand, the Chinese had—by and large—accepted the McMahon alignment as in the case of the China-Myanmar boundary agreement. The Chinese were also aware that if differences in the Eastern sector were mutually satisfactorily resolved, then India would at once begin to press hard that the 'gains' of the 1962 conflict in the Western sector be reversed. To forestall any such demand, the Chinese decided to radically change their previously held position on the Eastern sector and accordingly decided to modify their tactics.

Even before detailed discussions opened within the boundary sub-group, the Chinese showed their hand by taking a completely different attitude in the preliminary meeting at the Vice-Minister/Secretary level. The Chinese leader Vice Minister Liu Shuqing blandly stated that as the Eastern sector was the area of the *largest* dispute, India would have to give *concessions* in the Eastern sector and in return China would give *concessions* in the Western sector! [emphasis added] Liu emphasized that this was what the actual meaning of the Chinese phrase 'mutual understanding, mutual adjustment meant.' This new Chinese position was a complete reversal of the line taken by Zhou that the 'biggest' dispute was in the Western sector and not in the Eastern sector. When the Indian side enquired from Liu as to where in the Eastern sector the concessions being demanded were located and what extent/area did the Chinese have in mind, Liu blandly replied that first India would have to accept the principle, just expressed, and then only would China give the necessary clarifications. The Chinese would *not even clarify whether the concessions demanded in the East had to be equal in area to what they would grant in the West, or whether there was some fixed ratio involved* [emphasis added]. Chinese Vice-Minister Liu was emphatic that he would give no further clarifications. In direct contradiction of China's earlier stated position, publicly expressed at the level of PM Zhou, the Chinese Vice-Minister, Liu, now maintained that the Eastern sector was the 'most disputed' area.

This new Chinese position was in contradiction to all their previously stated positions, and came as a rude awakening for Indian negotiators. It would be recalled that on 23 January, 1959, Zhou, in his letter to Nehru, had categorically stated that the Chinese Government 'finds it necessary to take a more or less realistic attitude towards the McMahon Line.' Later, in April 1960, Zhou in his famous six points, had referred to the need to take into account the sentiments of each country towards the Himalayas and the Karokorams. In his interaction with the press in New Delhi on 25 April, 1960, Zhou had expressly stated that 'there exists a relatively *bigger* dispute in the Western sector.' [emphasis added] Thereafter, every time the 'package proposal' was made by successive Chinese leaders, they had always proposed a settlement along the 'Line of Actual Control' or in other words, the status quo. The assumption was that by making such an offer, the Chinese were conceding that the entire 'disputed' area in the Eastern sector would go to India. As the Chinese on several occasions confirmed that the 'Line of Actual Control' in the Eastern sector mainly coincided with the McMahon Line, *they had never before* demanded 'concessions' in the Eastern sector as a price for settling the boundary issue!

Therefore, what the Chinese Vice-Minister Liu Shuqi was now demanding was indeed something very new and very unique. The Chinese knew that no Indian Government could ever accept such a proposition and hope to survive. The Chinese had probably come with the intention of scuttling the boundary talks. *The Hindu* of 11 November, 1985, correctly assessed the situation when it published a report stating that the Chinese had hardened their stand by asking for territorial concessions in the East. It was on this point that the negotiations very nearly completely broke down.

The feelings on the Indian side ran high at this outrageous demand, and it took several private meetings with the Chinese in the Foreign Secretary's office to bring the talks back on the rails. Fortunately, as the talks were held in Delhi, it was possible to discuss this issue at the highest levels. The Chinese Vice-Minister was also anxious that the talks not break down completely. The talks on the boundary did resume at the sub-group level, but were pro-forma in nature, with both sides adopting rigid positions. Both reiterated the known hard line position of earlier years. Instead of progress, the talks had regressed with no solution in sight. It was obvious that a stalemate had occurred. By making such demands that no Government in India could reasonably accept, it was perhaps what the Chinese anticipated for with no forward movement possible, India would be forced to put the boundary issue aside. The Chinese were adopting a stance that ensured that the boundary issue was put on the back burner. However, the Chinese were quite willing to develop relations in other areas and stated so in the talks.

The negotiating stance on both sides, thereafter, began to harden. The Indian position was reiterated that unless the boundary issue was resolved there could be no progress, and Rajiv Gandhi confirmed this stance to the Rajya Sabha when he said that trade relations with China would depend on 'progress on the border issue.'[2] In mid-June 1986 the Chinese went officially public with what they had said at the sixth round of talks when Vice-Minister Liu Shuqing told the press that India would have to make 'concessions' in the East for China to make 'concessions' in the West.[3] It was probably the Chinese assessment that to make this stance public, opinion in India would solidify against any such deal and thereby negate any Indian pressure on them to settle the boundary issue. The influential Chinese journal *Guoji Wenti Yanjiu* also published an article stating that the Eastern sector was the 'most controversial of all the three sectors.' It was perhaps, also the assessment of the Chinese leadership that the new Government of Rajiv Gandhi would not be able to deliver a settlement based on the status quo, for they reasoned that if the redoubtable Mrs. Gandhi was unable to do so, how could Rajiv Gandhi do so?

It was clear from the position taken by the Chinese at the end of the sixth round of border talks that an impasse had been reached and that the time had come to take major decisions on how to proceed further. While border talks could continue for the sake of keeping lines of communication open and the public remain satisfied that talks were continuing, no further progress could be expected. Either the level at which the talks were held would have to be raised, which would entail involving either the Foreign Ministers or political level special representatives, or that the boundary issue would have to be set aside as the Chinese desired. In addition, it was felt that if the boundary negotiations could not go forward, then steps should be taken at the very least to demarcate the LAC, build on confidence building measures [CBMs] and try and ensure that peace and stability was maintained all along the LAC. Internally, therefore, this was a period when intense consultations became necessary so that major decisions could be taken.

The seventh round of talks were held in Beijing from 21-23 July, 1986, and were devoted entirely to the confrontation that had developed along the Sumdorong Chu in the Eastern sector. The Chinese continued to maintain that the area which they had occupied [Wangdung] was *North* of the McMahon Line even going by the co-ordinates of the McMahon map and, therefore, India's protests were meaningless. The Indian position remained the same—that the Chinese had violated the McMahon Line and that Chinese troops were *South* of the Line and, hence, they should withdraw North to their previously held positions. As neither side budged from its stated position, a stalemate ensued. The Chinese, on the other hand, tried to internationalize the boundary issue by circulating a Xinhua note with two background commentaries at the UN in New York. This was the first time that either side had tried to involve the UN in the boundary issue. India simply ignored the Chinese attempt and nothing tangible came out of the Chinese initiative.

At the eighth round held in Delhi from 11-15 November, 1987, there were very little discussions on the boundary question; although other issues of importance in the international sphere as well as trade and cultural issues were discussed. The leader of the Chinese delegation, Vice-Minister Liu Shuqing brought a formal letter of invitation from the Chinese PM, Li Peng, for PM, Rajiv Gandhi, to visit China. As it became increasingly certain that Rajiv Gandhi was inclined to accept the invitation and visit China, it was decided to await the outcome of the visit before any new initiative could be taken on the boundary issue. Meanwhile, preparations began in earnest for this path breaking visit.

Chinese policy during the eight rounds of border talks was based in the main on two aspects. The first was to get India to agree on a 'package deal' on the lines of that offered to Vajpayee by Deng Xiaoping in 1979, and later publicly articulated to an Indian journalist Krishan Kant, the Editor of Vikrant on 21 June, 1980. Secondly, if India was not in a position to accept the package offer, then Chinese policy was to quietly bury the border issue and nudge India towards the development of relations in all other sectors.[4] This is how matters stood just prior to Rajiv Gandhi's visit to China. Both sides awaited the outcome of Rajiv Gandhi's visit to China and for new directions on how to proceed further. Chinese tactics had effectively stalemated any prospects of a solution to the boundary issue.

The Wangdung Incident

Sometime in the early 1980s, a decision was taken by the Government of India that patrolling by Indian security forces should be undertaken right up to the international border in the Eastern sector, i.e., the McMahon Line. The practical effect of this decision was that Indian security agencies would be able to position their personnel right up to the McMahon Line and thereby make India's position more stable and secure. However, the problem was that the Chinese did not recognize the McMahon Line, although they had made it known that they would respect the McMahon alignment by not crossing it. For the Chinese, there existed a 'Line of Actual Control' which in the main coincided, as they themselves clarified on several occasions, with the McMahon alignment. Secondly, it was not clear on the ground where exactly this alignment lay, for while the McMahon Line had been delineated on a map, it had never been demarcated on the ground. Thirdly, the McMahon Line was drawn on the original map on a scale of 1″=8 miles and was about 1/4″ thick, which, when transposed on the ground could mean a difference of several kilometres either way. Therefore, the only sure method of referencing it to actual ground positions was to link it to distinct geographical features that determined the main watershed in the region on the basis of which Sir Henry McMahon had originally drawn the Line. This method, too, in turn, created difficulties, for there were many such 'grey' areas which could not be determined whether they actually lay to the North or to the South of the McMahon alignment.

In order to clarify the situation and actually determine the ground position, Indian officials, on 27 June, 1960, at the 1960 official level talks, had repeatedly urged the Chinese that maps *on a large scale* be exchanged so that precise and full information would be available that showed the exact alignment in this area. The Chinese rejected the suggestion and only agreed to supply maps on the diminutive scale of 1″=80 miles and had blandly stated that 'there was no need for such an exchange.' The only inference that could be drawn was that either they were satisfied with the Indian position, or else did not wish for clarity; for they harboured aggressive designs and wanted to keep the border situation in a perpetual state of tension.

In order, therefore, to eliminate any misunderstanding, the Government of India took the decision that Indian security personnel should patrol right up to India's perception of the McMahon Line. From about the summer of 1982, a small detachment began patrolling the Thandrong pastures on the banks of the Sumdorong Chu, where herdsmen from the Indian side would come every summer. The security personnel and a handful of herdsmen would visit the area in the summer months and withdraw to more congenial positions in the winter, which were considerably South of the Sumdorong Chu, several kilometres behind the McMahon Line in the region. There were no Chinese protests at this movement on the Sumdorong Chu by Indian personnel when it was made in 1983. A seasonal post was established on 28 July, 1984. This procedure had been followed in 1984 and 1985 without any Chinese protest.

However, on 23 June, 1986, when Indian security personnel, as usual, moved towards the Sumdorong pastures they found to their consternation that the area was already occupied by about forty Chinese personnel, some in military uniform. They were soon reinforced and the Chinese strength went up to 200 military personnel. The Chinese were busy building permanent structures and their intentions did not appear peaceful. It was also discovered, a little later, that the Chinese had built a helipad near Wangdung and could, thus, supply their troops by air. The construction of permanent structures indicated that the Chinese were here to stay and would not withdraw as winter approached.

On 26 June, 1986, India protested to the Chinese Government on the intrusion and stated that the area, the Sumdorong Chu valley, was about 1-2 kilometres '*South*' of the McMahon Line and, as such, within India. The Chinese were asked to remove the intruders. On 8 July, 1986, the Indian protest was peremptorily turned down by the Chinese on the grounds that the area where Chinese were now positioned, even going by the coordinates of the 'so-called' McMahon Line, were '*North*' of the McMahon alignment. However, the Chinese stated that as the next round of border talks were due to be held at Beijing from 21-23 July, 1986, this issue could be discussed and added for emphasis, 'we propose to do so.' Meanwhile, the Chinese kept up the propaganda barrage by publishing two lengthy articles in the *Xinhua* [New China News Agency] and another on 22 August, 1986, entitled, 'On the true situation in Sumdorong Chu valley area on the Eastern sector of the Sino-Indian boundary', which largely reflected their stand-point.

Indian apprehensions of China's new found aggressiveness and not so peaceful intensions grew even more rapidly as the events of this incident unfolded. These apprehensions had been aroused somewhat earlier as China had during the sixth round of border talks at New Delhi [6-11 November, 1985], completely altered their stance and negotiating position on the Eastern sector. The Chinese position up to that point in time and as clarified at the level of PM, Zhou, had been that although China did not recognize the McMahon Line, they would nevertheless 'respect' the McMahon alignment. In his letter to Nehru on 23 January, 1959, Zhou had even gone further than this position and stated that 'on the one hand the Chinese Government finds it necessary to take a more or less realistic attitude towards the McMahon Line...and needs time to deal with the occasion' [Note: The qualifier 'so-called' before McMahon Line was not used by Zhou]. Zhou had even clarified during his visit to Delhi for the border talks with Nehru in April 1960 that the main dispute was in the Western sector and that the dispute in the Eastern sector was relatively 'small.'

During sixth round of talks [November 1985], the Chinese had demanded that India would have to give 'concessions' in the Eastern sector. Asked what was the 'extent' of the concessions and at what locations in the Eastern sector did they need the 'concessions', the reply of the Chinese leader, Liu Shuqing, was ambiguous in that India would first have to agree to the 'principle of concessions' and then would only China clarify as to the 'extent' of the concessions demanded. This was the real meaning of the principle of 'mutual accommodation, mutual understanding' that China so disarmingly propounded, and urged India to accept. Unofficial Chinese publications, with official connivance, no doubt, hinted that China would not be satisfied with anything less than the whole of Tawang!

With this background in mind, the Government of India, alarmed at Chinese intrusions, decided to rapidly reinforce its troops guarding the approaches to Tawang. The Indian Army moved quickly and in strength. Between the 18 and 20 October, 1986, a full brigade occupied Hathungla ridge above Sumdorong Chu. Unlike the mistakes of 1962, Indian troops never tried to hold the river-line, but stood firm on the high ground. By the time the Chinese crossed the Sumdorong Chu and moved uphill towards Lungrola/Hathungla, they were confronted by well dug—in Indian troops on the ridge line that had beaten them to the high ground. The Indian Brigade now occupied three important forward tactical features. These were Khyapho Ridge, Pt 4376 [Jimmy Top] and Tagra Raho.

Map 7: Chinese Intrusions in Sumdorong Valley[June 1986]

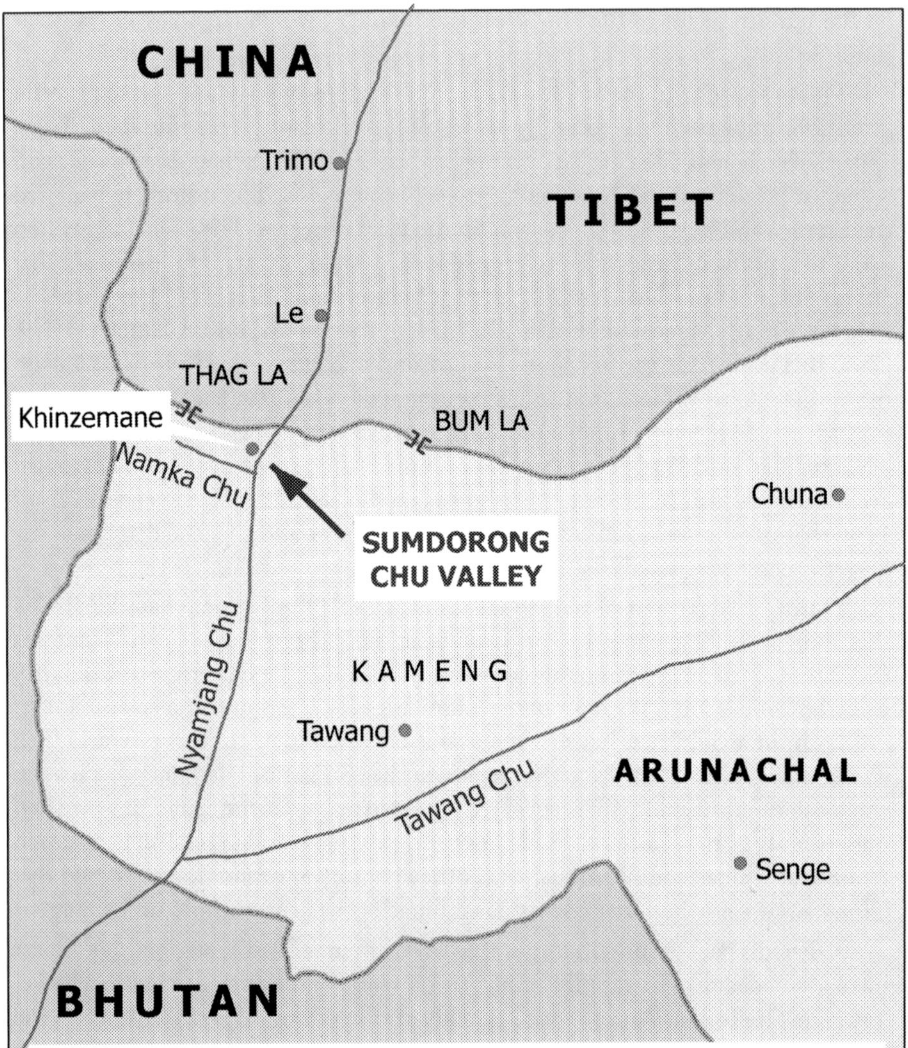

Sketch Map: Shows the Chinese Intrusion in Sumdorong Chu Valley (June 1986), which is part of the Tawang District of Arunachal Pradesh.

The Chinese were surprised and shocked at the speed and alacrity shown by the Indian Army. They had never anticipated such a movement. The Chinese could not go back and across the Sumdorong Chu as that would mean acknowledging a retreat, nor could they go forward as that would have meant certain defeat at the hands of superior Indian troops. The Chinese stood on the slopes, badly exposed, sulked and threw stones at Indian soldiers, but did not open fire or attempt a forward movement. They realized that they had been tactically out manoeuvred. For the first time in almost twenty four years to the day [20 October, 1962] when the 7 Brigade had been unceremoniously routed and evicted, Indian troops were in a position to evict forward Chinese posts. And for the first time ever in the Eastern sector, Indian troops had achieved local tactical superiority. The Chinese knew that they would have lost badly if fighting had erupted.

The Chinese leadership now attempted bluster in the hope that the new and untested Indian leadership under Rajiv Gandhi might falter. The Chinese leader, Deng Xiaoping, openly spoke of 'teaching India a lesson', trying to evoke memories of the 1962 conflict. There was speculation that messages were conveyed through the US 'warning' India, but in actual fact none were received in Delhi. When Rajiv Gandhi met President Reagan in 1987, the latter never mentioned a word about the incident or, for that matter about any such Chinese messages.

Nevertheless, India held firm and both sides reinforced troops on either side. The speed of the Indian deployment [Operation Falcon] made the Chinese realize that they could not deploy overwhelming numbers as that would take time and Indian troops, too, could be reinforced. The Indian Army utilized the opportunity to deploy tanks and armoured personnel carriers in both Ladakh [Western sector] and in Northern Sikkim. The Chinese never anticipated that this would happen. As the Indian Army had deployed in strength and with great speed, the Chinese realized that if any conflict ensued, the results would be quite different from those of 1962. And in any case, with winter approaching, there was little that could be done. The Chinese now proposed a flag meeting and it was held by local commanders on 15 November, 1986, where both sides agreed not to use force and that a political solution would be better.

Having successfully held the Chinese, India detected an opening and in December 1986, the Indian Parliament passed an Act transforming the North East Frontier Agency [NEFA] into the new state of Arunachal Pradesh, a constituent of the Indian Union. After all legal formalities had been completed, Arunachal Pradesh came into being in February 1987. Thus, no Government in India, even if it wished to, could hand over any territory in the Eastern sector without first moving a Constitutional amendment. A forceful message had been sent to the Chinese. Predictably, the Chinese erupted in rage, but as anticipated, reacted only verbally. The Chinese Ministry of Foreign Affairs issued a strong protest to India stating that, 'the establishment of an Indian State on Chinese territory illegally occupied constituted serious aggression against China's sovereignty and had deeply hurt the feelings of the Chinese people,' and that China would 'never recognize the so-called Arunachal Pradesh.' The high voltage Chinese reaction clearly indicated that their annoyance was at its peak at being clearly out-manoeuvred, both politically and militarily. The upshot was that reports were received that indicated that the Chinese Military Attaché in India, the Tibet District Military Commander and the Chengdu Regional Military Commander, were all transferred, perhaps for totally misreading the situation.

The Sino-Indian confrontation over the Sumdorong Chu was, as usual, not without international ramifications. Ever since the early eighties, one of the cardinal underpinnings of Sino-US relations, the anti-Soviet rationale, began to lose its sheen. The Chinese leaders had decided on a more accommodative policy towards Soviet Russia and publicly announced a policy of 'non-alignment' vis-a-vis the two superpowers. In time, high level overtures were made by both China and Soviet Russia. The Chinese indicated that they would not be averse to normalization of Sino-Soviet relations provided three conditions were met. These were [a] withdrawal of Soviet troops from Afghanistan. [b] Reduction of Soviet troops along the Sino-Soviet border and [c] an end to Vietnamese intervention in Cambodia. Later, the Chinese indicated that irrespective of the political conditions, they were prepared to revive economic, cultural and scientific relations. This enabled Vice Premier Arkhipov and Vice Premier Yao Yilin to exchange visits and trade substantially increased, did other contacts between the two countries.

By the time Soviet leader Gorbachov made his speech at Vladivostok on 28 July, 1986, Sino-Soviet relations had become demonstrably warmer. In his speech Gorbachov gave pride of place to China and called for better relations. He announced the acceptance of the Thalweg Principle [mid-channel] for the river boundary, withdrawal of six regiments from Afghanistan and commencement of thinning out of troops from Mongolia. At this point, the Chinese also softened their position. They hinted that only one condition really remained and that was the end of Vietnamese involvement in Cambodia, but significantly added that they would have no objection to the establishment of Soviet bases in Vietnam.

Nevertheless, the Chinese leaders were very keen to test Soviet sincerity. As usual, the Sino-Indian stand-off at Sumdorong Chu came in handy. For the Soviets, this presented the same dilemma that they had faced earlier in the early fifties—how to balance their time tested friendship with India with their very keen desire to normalize relations with China. Thus, when initial reports of the confrontation first came in, the initial reaction from Moscow was one of total silence. There were no statements either about the incident or of supporting India. During the 15th anniversary celebrations of the signing of the Indo-Soviet Treaty [9 August, 1986], the Soviet representative, SB Tatilaev, feigned ignorance of the incident under persistent questioning by Indian press representatives. The

Soviets, in a change of track, insisted that the Indo-Soviet Treaty was not specifically directed against 'any third country.'[5]

Soviet leader Gorbachov arrived in India in November 1986, ostensibly to reassure India. However, in his public statements, Gorbachov pleaded ignorance regarding the Sumdorong Chu incident. He insisted that better relations between the Soviet Union, China and India would be best so that 'no one will have to choose sides.'[6] In private conversation, Gorbachov however, assured the Indian leadership that the Soviet Union would not stand 'idly by' in case of threats to India's 'unity and integrity,' and that the Soviet Union would not take a 'single step that harmed India's real interests.' The Chinese understood Gorbachov's predicament and felt re-assured that he 'did not make public which side the Soviet Union would take *if India clashed with a third country*' [emphasis added].[7] Nevertheless, despite Gorbachov's private assurance to Rajiv Gandhi, the Soviets never clarified if clashes with China on the McMahon Line constituted a threat to India's 'unity and integrity.' The Soviets continued to maintain a policy of ambiguity.

Thus, Soviet Russian ambiguity over the events and the stand-off at the Sumdorong Chu left the Indian leadership dissatisfied. It did not go un-noticed that while the stand-off was nearing its peak, the Soviet Foreign Ministry announced in January 1987 the imminent withdrawal of a Soviet mechanized infantry division from Mongolia. This step was sufficient to allow the Chinese to redeploy their troops, possibly towards the Indian frontier. In February 1987, China and Soviet Russia held the first round of boundary talks for the first time in nine years. Clearly, the understanding between the Soviet Union and India was becoming brittle at the edges.

As for the other super-power, the US, it, too, did not wish to take sides. Therefore, if a military confrontation had ensued, both India and China would have been largely all on their own. Both India and China realized that there was little to gain in a military confrontation. Both would have suffered substantial setbacks. It was this realization that led to the momentous decision by Rajiv Gandhi to visit China.

Rajiv Gandhi's Visit to China

PM Rajiv Gandhi paid an official visit to China from 19 to 23 December, 1988. This was the first visit to China by an Indian PM in 34 years, and a major event in Sino-Indian relations. Nehru was the last Indian PM that had visited China in 1954. Meticulous advance preparations for PM Gandhi's visit were made, but reservations within sections of the ruling party persisted on both ideological considerations and the possible risks of an unpredictable outcome. Rajiv Gandhi had, however, firmly made up his mind that irrespective of the lack of a domestic consensus and differing risk perceptions, he would go ahead with his visit. His hands were considerably strengthened when the All India Congress Working

Committee on 5 November, 1988, urged the Government to 'seek a settlement based on mutual interest and acceptable to peoples of both countries through peaceful negotiations.' The significance of this resolution lies in the fact that it did not use the language of the 1962 Parliament resolution binding the Government to retrieve every inch of India's 'sacred soil.' Incidentally, in response to a message through a confidential private channel, the then President-elect of the United States of America—George HW Bush—conveyed his personal assessment to Rajiv Gandhi that the Chinese leadership would respond positively to his bold initiatives.[8]

During his visit, Rajiv Gandhi had extensive exchange of views on bilateral relations and international issues with Deng Xiaoping, Chairman of China's Central Military Commission, Chinese President Yang Shangkun and PM Li Peng. The discussions with Deng Xiaoping were the highlight of the visit. The extraordinarily long and warm handshake between Rajiv Gandhi and Deng Xiaoping manifested the truly historic nature of the visit and marked a turning point in the relationship. Deng told Rajiv Gandhi 'let both sides forget the unpleasant period in our past relations, and let us treat everything with an eye on the future.' Keeping the spirit of Deng's remarks in mind, the two sides agreed to restore, improve and develop good neighbourly relations between China and India on the basis of the 'Five Principles of Peaceful Coexistence,' and held in-depth talks on the Sino-Indian boundary issue. Li Peng stated China's position on the boundary issue and stressed that 'mutual understanding and mutual accommodation' was the only way to resolve this issue. The two sides agreed to settle the boundary issue through peaceful and friendly consultation. It was agreed that while seeking a solution to the boundary issue, the two countries would actively develop bilateral relations in other fields and create an atmosphere and conditions conducive to a 'fair and reasonable' settlement of the boundary issue. The two sides decided to take concrete steps towards this end and decided to set up [a] a joint working group on the boundary issue and [b] a joint group at the ministerial level on economic, trade and science and technology.

The decision to develop relations and seek normalization *without first settling the boundary issue was a major break from past policy* [emphasis added]. Up to this point, India had always insisted that before any normalization could take place, the boundary issue had to be first settled. This decision signified recognition that the settlement of the boundary issue was not imminent, would be of long term duration and in the circumstances of the international situation then prevailing, it would not be in India's interests to further delay normalization of relations with China. It also signified that the two sides had taken a basic decision to move away from hostility and confrontation to a policy of détente and dialogue. It was hoped that the development of India-China relations in various fields would eventually create a climate conducive to a settlement and that in the meanwhile, both sides would continue to work for maintaining peace and tranquillity all along the borders. The mandate of, and the concept of the 'joint' working group on the boundary was thus different from that of earlier boundary negotiations. This time, it was hoped that both sides would *work together* [emphasis added] to settle the boundary issue. Rajiv Gandhi's visit to China belied all apprehensions about the outcome and, in fact, exceeded expectations in terms of atmospherics. Rajiv Gandhi's visit symbolized a general movement away from hostility to one of dialogue and detente. Even the Soviet press, till this point hostile to any Sino-Indian rapprochement, lauded the visit, calling the event 'of exceptional importance' and that this would not only be beneficial for both India and China but 'would make a contribution to the cause of peace in all Asia.'[9] The decision, therefore, to normalize relations with China represented a correct reading of the evolving international situation. The collapse of the Soviet Union a few years down the road further underlined that the change of policy initiated by Rajiv Gandhi had been correct. The Indian leadership had read the evolving international situation well and had taken a basic decision that normalization of relations with China could not be delayed any further. It was also correctly surmised that a solution to the boundary issue would not be forthcoming easily or soon and, therefore, it was better to stabilize the situation to avoid any confrontation. That had been the lesson of the Sundorong Chu incident.

The Chinese thinking was that Rajiv Gandhi had decided to visit China because of the growing rapprochement between the Soviet Union and China. The Chinese also surmised that India would now move away from basing its case solely on historical documents/legal treaties/tradition to a position based more on 'political' parameters and present day security interests. In other words, India had moved closer to the Chinese position. In their assessment the Chinese were not too far away from predicting accurately the evolution in the Indian position.

CHAPTER 9

CBMs/Joint Working Groups/Special Representatives [1990 to Present]

Soon after the conclusion of Rajiv Gandhi's successful visit to China, the euphoria generated as a result dissipated rather quickly largely on account of internal developments within both India and China. Rajiv Gandhi and the Congress Party lost the 1989 general election and were replaced by an unsteady coalition. In China, internal dissent leading to large scale demonstrations culminated in the Tienanmen tragedy, where hundreds perished as a result of a vicious onslaught by the PLA on unarmed civilian demonstrators. This action completely paralyzed the decision making functions of the Chinese Government for a considerable length of time. In view of the brutal crackdown, China faced stiff opprobrium from the international community. But India did not issue any condemnatory statement on the Tienanmen incident. This was also the time when large scale disturbances erupted in the Kashmir valley. Both India and China exercised considerable restraint, a fact noted by decision makers in both countries. Thus, for about two years, there was little progress on the boundary issue as both sides had their hands full with domestic issues.

This was also the time when the Cold War ended and India had to rethink its security policies, particularly after the collapse of the Soviet Union. This rethink had already been initiated during Rajiv Gandhi's time, as it became apparent that a major realignment of forces was taking place in the international arena. The steady rapprochement of Sino-Soviet relations that became evident in the public domain, starting with Gorbachov's speech at Vladivostok on 28 July, 1986; it was a major strategic dynamic that India could no longer ignore. Shortly thereafter with the collapse of the Soviet Union, the Soviet factor that weighed heavily on Sino-Indian relations disappeared. The US emerged as the sole surviving super-power with its political, economic and military power at its zenith. This aspect could also no longer be ignored.

The US decision to resume arms supplies to Pakistan, its temporizing over the Kashmir issue and its decision to limit the transfer of high technology to

India raised serious questions in Indian perceptions on the efficacy of the US attitude towards India. India had to re-assess whether the US would continue to play its role as a friend. With the end of the Cold War, India had no other options but to alter its priorities and seek warmer relations with the US, considering the changed circumstances of the international situation. In addition, India faced growing international pressure in the areas of non-proliferation and alleged human rights violations in Kashmir. The indefinite extension of the Nuclear Non-Proliferation Treaty [NPT] in the mid-1990s, the opening of talks on the Comprehensive Nuclear Test Ban Treaty [CTBT] made it apparent that growing pressure from the international community would have to be met and that India would have to begin to look seriously at other options, as otherwise India risked marginalization.

Ever since the 1962 conflict, India had consistently maintained that a solution of the boundary question was a prior necessity for normalizing relations with China. India's insistence in this regard was one of the factors, although not the only one, that prevented the normalization of Sino-Indian relations. Although the two countries restored ambassadorial-level diplomatic relations in 1976, and in 1980, with the return to power of Mrs. Gandhi, agreed to begin talks on the border issue, India's principled stand point did not change. In his meeting with Vajpayee in 1979, the Chinese leader Deng Xiaoping had proposed a settlement of the Sino-Indian border dispute based on the concept of a 'package solution.' Alternatively, Deng had proposed that if it was not possible to resolve the border issue at an early date, then both countries should set it aside and consider cooperation in other areas. But it was not until Rajiv Gandhi's trip to China in 1988, *that India formally accepted the Chinese position* [emphasis added]. Thus, it was Rajiv Gandhi who initiated the process of normalization of bilateral relations, which successive Indian Governments later pursued and implemented after the Cold War ended *without insisting on a prior resolution of the border issue* [emphasis added].

Some elements in the Chinese leadership felt that India's pre-1988 insistence on not normalizing Sino-Indian relations until the border issue was settled was a tactical move, a 'bargaining chip' that India hoped to utilize to induce China to make concessions on the boundary issue. Thus, after Rajiv Gandhi's visit while negotiations on the boundary question continued apace, it became evident that the pace of normalization in other areas was proceeding much faster in that the two countries exchanged high-level visits, signed agreements in such areas as trade, technology, education and culture. It was notable that trade between the two countries grew exponentially over the next few years—from about US$ 200 million in 1988 to about US$ 670 million by 1993. This was also the period when India came under severe external foreign exchange pressure and needed time to settle its internal economic problems.

As India needed a peaceful, stable environment in which to concentrate on its economic recovery, ensuring peace and stability all along the Sino-Indian border became its primary goal in the early 1990s. The collapse of the Soviet Union had conclusively demonstrated that military might alone would not be able to ensure security and internal cohesion. On the other hand, India watched very carefully the peaceful rise of China, its high economic growth and smooth integration with the international economic system. With this, China was able to effectively neutralize any foreign threat to its stability and soon resumed normal relations with Western countries despite the terrible events that culminated in the Tienanmen massacres. All this did not go unnoticed amongst Indian policy makers. The key was the need for a peaceful environment in which economic development could take place unhindered.

China, too, was very keen to stabilize her South-Western border with India for it would help stabilize internal dissent in Tibet, contain Islamic extremism in Xinjiang [Sinkiang] as also free her to concentrate on what Deng Xiaoping asserted would be China's 'peaceful rise.' It was important in this context for China to give an impression to the international community that it *was not a belligerent power* [emphasis added]. In a sense between India and China, a certain parallelism in policy was evident, if not a convergence of interests. It was also quite evident that a solution to the boundary problem was not going to come any time soon. Therefore, short of a solution, the next best option would be to stabilize the border areas. It was towards this end that both countries now decided to concentrate their energies.

Nevertheless, their were some testy moments too. During President Venkataraman's visit to China [17-22 May, 1992] the Chinese, for reasons best known to them, conducted a nuclear test that put the President in an awkward position. On the other hand, when India apporached the Chinese in 1993 for supply of nuclear fuel for the Tarapur Atomic Power Station near Mumbai, the Chinese surprisingly agreed. With this, the Tarapur Plant continued to function, despite US unwillingness and French procrastination, although both countries had earlier agreed to supply the fuel.

Both India and China felt that the next important step, therefore, was to stabilize the Line of Actual Control (LAC) and eliminate as far as possible all disagreements over its alignment. Further, all attempts should be made to reach an agreement on preserving peace and tranquallity all along the LAC. And, finally, both sides should take measures to establish 'mutual trust' and 'confidence' along the LAC, preferably with an understanding between the two militaries. This tentative plan enabled both India and China to approach the issue with a common sense of purpose, whereby the two sides *worked together* to stabilize the Sino-Indian border areas and hopefully to create an atmosphere of reasonableness and peace that both sides could utilize later to build on—and to eventually find—an amicable solution to the boundary issue.

In the negotiations that followed in several meetings of the newly constituted Joint Working Group [JWG], the Chinese laid down three points. Firstly, they wanted that the 'forward' posts that India had established as a result of the Sumdorong confrontation [1986] be withdrawn. Secondly, they wished to make a separate reference to the Sikkim-Tibet boundary so that they could maintain their position on Sikkim. Thirdly, they held the view that maintenance of peace and tranquillity on the LAC should not automatically imply an agreement between India and China as to the *alignment* of the LAC.

The Indian response was that no withdrawal could be unilateral and that if any withdrawal took place, it would have to be mutual and specifics would have to be worked out on the basis of reciprocity. As for the Sikkim-Tibet boundary, India could not consider a separate reference—since Sikkim was a part of India. On the third point, India stated that what was required was an objective and precise demarcation of the LAC based on ground realities and not on territorial claims. The agreement on the LAC would not be considered as a substitute for a boundary settlement, since it would not touch on the claims of either side.

After several rounds of discussions, it was agreed that withdrawal of forward posts would be reciprocal and details would be worked out by experts. This was subsequently agreed in the JWG meeting in April 1995, when the two sides agreed to simultaneously disengage from four border posts. These new posts were now to be re-located at least one kilometre apart. As for reference to the Sikkim-Tibet boundary, it was subsumed in the general reference to 'all' sectors of the Sino-Indian boundary. As for the third point, it was agreed that this agreement was 'without prejudice' to the stand of either side on the Sino-Indian boundary question. However, the guiding principle was clear. The primary aim was to *defuse tension along the LAC, to reduce possibilities of a military confrontation and to create an atmosphere conducive to help settle the boundary question* [emphasis added].

The signing of the 'Agreement on Maintenance of Peace and Tranquillity along the Line of Actual Control in the Sino-Indian Border Areas' (7 September, 1993) and the 'Agreement on Confidence-Building Measures in the Military Field Along the Line of Actual Control in the India-China Border Areas' (December 1996) between the two Governments should be seen in this context. [See Annexures II and III] India saw these two agreements as, on one hand, ensuring that the two sides could work together to resolve the boundary issue peacefully without resorting to violence, and on the other, that the non-settlement of the Sino-Indian boundary dispute would not inhibit the development of bilateral relations between the two countries. The important point was that this was a move to stabilize and remove points of contention all along the Sino-Indian border areas.

Therefore, what was essentially worked out after a series of discussions reflected in a general sense the attitude of the two countries towards 'confidence building', 'military transparency' and 'verification.' The main points can generally be listed as follows:

[a] Neither side shall use or threaten to use force against the other and strictly observe and respect the LAC.

[b] Both sides shall keep their military forces in the border areas along the LAC to a minimum level.

[c] Establish communications between military commanders, including periodic meetings at designated points to resolve any local issue. In addition, an 'experts group' to meet to discuss implementation measures as also LAC delimitation.

[d] Limiting size of military forces within agreed zones along the LAC, including the number of main battle tanks, infantry combat vehicles, missiles, etc. In addition, to avoid large division-size exercises, prior notification of exercises involving more than a division and prohibiting combat aircraft within a 10 kilometre radius of the LAC became necessary.

The advent of the Vajpayee-led NDA Government in early 1998 brought some changes in policy towards China. Keen to refurbish its 'nationalist' credentials and based on a foreign policy outlook of a more assertive India, the Vajpayee Government decided that India should openly become a nuclear weapons power. With India having successfully conducted the Pokharan tests on 11 and 13 May, 1998, India emerged as a nuclear weapons power that had wide ramifications, particularly on its relations with China.

After the first nuclear test on 11 May, 1998, there was no reaction from the Chinese, ostensibly because they had been caught unawares. To explain the rational behind the nuclear test and to seek US 'understanding', Vajpayee wrote a letter on 11 May, 1998, to President Clinton in which, although not naming China directly, he sought to explain the test by stating that it was necessary to carry it out as India had an '*overt nuclear state on its borders that had committed armed aggression against India in 1962*' [emphasis added] and that although relations had somewhat improved yet '*an atmosphere of distrust persists mainly due to the unresolved border problem* [emphasis added].' The arrow clearly pointed towards the Chinese. The White House, for reasons best known to it, promptly leaked the letter which was published in the *New York Times* on 13 May, 1998. On its publication, the Chinese went ballistic and their reaction was furious.

After the second nuclear test on 13 May, 1998, the Chinese, by now fully prepared, issued a statement that was vitriolic. The Chinese Government 'is deeply shocked,' said the statement, and 'expresses its strong condemnation...the Indian Government, which itself has undermined the international effort in banning nuclear tests so as *to obtain the hegemony in South Asia in defiance of world opinion, has even maliciously accused China of posing a nuclear threat to India.* This is utterly groundless....this gratuitous accusation by India against China is solely for the purpose of finding excuses for the development of its nuclear weapons' [emphasis added].

The reasons for this harsh reaction are not far to seek. The Chinese were apprehensive and suspected that India was utilizing the nuclear tests to move politically and militarily closer to the US, and particularly to those elements within the US establishment that harboured 'anti-China' feelings. With the souring of US-China relations in the 1990s, China felt that the dissemination of information about the various 'threats' that China posed was nothing but an attempt by interested parties to rouse public opinion in a new effort at China's 'containment.' At another level, the Chinese also apprehended that this was an attempt by the Vajpayee Government to cement an Indo-US 'understanding' based on the so-called Chinese 'threat.'

The Chinese now reverted to following a twin track policy with India. Firstly, the Chinese decided to mobilize, in conjunction with other like-minded states, international public opinion against India's nuclear tests and to initiate action through the medium of the United Nations. Secondly, it decided that if relations with India were to move forward then India would have to 'untie the knot.' As President Jiang Zemin told AFP on 3 June, 1998, 'it was India that originated the tense situation in the region.'[1] In other words, India having tied the knot would have to publicly state that it did not apprehend any 'threat' from China. In the meanwhile, the Chinese decided to freeze all steps towards resolving the boundary issue and suspended the working of the Joint Working Group [JWG]. In line with its new stance, the Chinese refused to give dates for the 11th round of the JWG. As before, the Chinese once again decided to use as leverage the boundary issue.

Meanwhile, the Chinese, working jointly with the US, actively initiated steps to convene a meeting of P-5 Foreign Ministers. China along with the US sponsored UN Security Council Resolution 1172, *condemning* both the Indian and Pakistani nuclear tests. UNSC Resolution 1172 'demanded' that both India and Pakistan refrain from further tests, to immediately stop nuclear development programmes and to refrain from weaponization. When on 9 July, 1998, India proposed to China the conclusion of an agreement for the 'no-first use of nuclear weapons', it was met with a brusque rejection. The Chinese demanded that India first sign the NPT and the CBTD. Sino-US co-operation on South Asia reached its apogee when, on the conclusion of President Clinton's visit to China, the two countries issued on 27 June, 1998, the Sino-US Presidential Joint Statement on South Asia. In it both countries indicated 'shared interests' in a 'peaceful and stable South Asia' and in a 'strong non-proliferation regime' that had been put at risk by 'these tests,' and agreed to work 'closely together.' The common goal, as it was understood, was to force India to sign the NPT. Thus, through co-operation and co-ordination of policies with the US, China hoped to play an even bigger role in South Asian affairs and attempted to confine India's role to South Asia alone by bracketing it with Pakistan. It seemed as if the US was pushing for an active Chinese role to 'co-determine' the affairs of South Asia and wished to establish a 'condominium' with China. Incidentally, when Chinese President, Jiang Zemin, tried to obtain a similar joint statement with the Russians during his visit to Moscow in November 1998, the Russians turned him down for they did not wish to antagonize India.[2]

Meanwhile, India pushed hard for an understanding with the US of its nuclear policy. Eventually, Strobe Talbot and Jaswant Singh were named as the two interlocutors. Strobe Talbot and Jaswant Singh met fourteen times in ten locations in seven countries on three continents to conduct 'the most intense and prolonged set of exchanges ever between American and Indian officials in an attempt to pull back US policy from its pro-China orientation, to re-adjust its attitude towards India and to inject a sense of realism.' These talks were crucial and signalled the beginnings of a new understanding between the US and India. These important changes in US policy can be pinpointed to the effectiveness of these discussions. Despite Beijing's concerns to the contrary, the US began to show a degree of understanding of India's position and backed away from insisting on the full implementation of UNSC Resolution 1172. The US policy towards India also began to undergo a subtle change. The US began to lay emphasis on Indo-US bilateral co-operation. And an important aspect of the change was its concern at the un-relenting rise of China that increasingly outweighed its nuclear proliferation agenda. To induce such a dramatic shift in the outlook of US foreign policy towards India, South Asia and China was, indeed, a singular foreign policy success of the Vajpayee/Jaswant Singh team. It eliminated any hopes that China had of playing a 'co-partnership' role with the US in the affairs of South Asia.

The Indian leadership also moved deftly to allay Chinese anger, when PM Vajpayee's office in late October 1998 publicly stated that India did not see China as an 'enemy' and nor did it wish to enter into an arms race with China. When President Narayanan spoke to the Chinese Ambassador to India on the same lines, Beijing appeared to be mollified and allowed a pre-meeting of the JWG on the boundary issue to take place. A few days later, the Chinese FM, Tang Jiaxuan, announced that the JWG would resume work and the first meeting since the nuclear tests was held from 15-17th April, 1999. The Chinese had sensed that *with the US no longer interested in pushing India into a corner* [emphasis added], it was in their interests to resume a working relationship with India, particularly since India had made the necessary amends by publicly stating that it did not consider China as an 'enemy.'

The results of the India-US 'understanding' became apparent to the Chinese when the US adopted the Indian version that it was Pakistani 'adventurism' that had caused the Kargil conflict. China was wary of the 'understanding' developing between India and the US, particularly if India-Pakistan relations worsened to a point where China might be the only power that might have to physically intervene to rescue Pakistan. China did not wish to get involved in yet another India-Pakistan military conflict, for neither of the options that were available to her seemed palatable. If China was seen as not supportive enough of Pakistan, then its position in Pakistan would be seriously jeopardized. On the other hand, China did not wish to see any further consolidation of the emerging US-India understanding. China, therefore, decided that it would be best to localize the conflict, urge the restoration of a Indo-Pak dialogue and at the same time try and improve relations with India. Chinese FM Tang called for 'negotiations and consultations to seek an effective way to resolve the Kashmir issue *politically*' [emphasis added]. Implicit in this statement was the gesture to India in that there was no mention of 'UN Resolutions' and there was no element of support to Pakistan in its latest adventure. It was clear that China did not wish to take sides with Pakistan, although some Chinese publications, particularly those belonging to the PLA, continued to be hawkish and were decidedly pro-Pakistan. Perhaps for the first time since the 1962 conflict, China did not indulge in sabre-rattling on the border in support of Pakistan in the latter's latest confrontation with India.

The further normalization of relations between India and China was evident in that the Chinese agreed to receive the Indian FM, Jaswant Singh, who visited China from 15 to 17 June, 1999, even while the Kargil stand-off was still in progress. The Chinese FM acknowledged that Sino-Indian relations had entered a period of 'improvement' and that Jaswant Singh's visit was an important 'step in this process', but insisted that the prerequisite was that both countries do not consider each other 'a threat.' Jaswant Singh duly obliged and confirmed that the Indian Government 'does not think that China is a threat.' Having ensured that its 'minimum' condition was accepted, the Chinese agreed to a series of measures designed to improve relations. The foremost amongst these measures was the Chinese decision to give a clarification, in the JWG, of the precise alignment of the LAC along the Sino-Indian boundary. The Chinese also agreed to commence a strategic security dialogue with India, although the announcement was kept at a very low key so as not to arouse Pakistani suspicions.

Having committed to Jaswant Singh that they would initiate a process for the clarification and determination of the LAC in all sectors of the boundary, a meeting took place in March 2000, where maps of the middle sector were exchanged. On 17 June, 2002, both sides met again and maps of the Western sector were seen by both sides for about 20 minutes. Soon enough, the maps were hastily returned by both sides since these maps represented the maximalist positions which were clearly unpalatable. The major differences in determining the alignment of the LAC in the Western sector are in twelve areas. These are: Samar Lungpa, Trig Heights, Depsang, Kongka La [pass], Pangong Tso, Spanggur Gap, Mount Sajun, Dumchele, Demchok and Chumar.[3] Since neither side was in a position to reconcile the very wide and differing versions of the LAC in the Western sector, the process of exchange of maps on the LAC simply petered out and by 2005, it came to a complete halt. The maps of the Eastern sector were never exchanged or even glanced at. Thus, India would never know the extent of the 'concessions' that the Chinese had demanded as way back as 1985.

The next major development in the quest for a boundary solution took place during Vajpayee's visit to China in June 2003. The two sides signed the 'Declaration on Principles for Relations and Comprehensive Cooperation between China and India.' In the declaration, both sides reaffirmed that they would promote a long-term, constructive and cooperative partnership and emphasized that '*their common interests outweigh their differences*' [emphasis added]. On the security issue, both sides committed that they were 'not a threat to each other' and that neither side would 'use or threaten to use force against the other.' The latter, in fact, was a reiteration of the 1996 Agreement.

On an issue of considerable sensitivity for China, India conceded [recognized] that the *Tibet Autonomous Region* [*TAR*] *was a part of the territory of the People's Republic of China* [emphasis added] and that India would not allow Tibetans in India to engage in anti-China political activities. There was substantial criticism in India on the use of such terminology to describe the relationship between India and Tibet/China. The earlier formulation used by India had been that India considered Tibet to be '*an autonomous region of China.*' By stating that India now considered Tibet Autonomous Region [TAR] to be a part of the People's Republic of China [PRC] had certain distinct political connotations. [See Annexure IV] Firstly, it was now understood to mean that there was no 'invasion' of Tibet by China in 1950, since Tibet was considered to be a part of the PRC that had already been established in 1949. Secondly, China had lopped off considerable parts of erstwhile Tibetan territory and incorporated these into other provinces. Thus, by recognizing TAR, as opposed to Tibet earlier, India also recognized its new territorial limits and the incorporation of parts of Tibetan territory into other Chinese provinces, contrary to the position of the Dalai Lama. Thirdly, Chinese maps of TAR show Arunachal Pradesh, which by now the Chinese had started to refer as 'Southern Tibet', to be a part of TAR. Therefore, did Vajpayee inadvertently concede China's claims over Arunachal Pradesh?

On the other hand, China was keen to introduce two additional words into the text—'inalienable' and 'acknowledge.' The proposed Chinese sentence would have read thus: 'India *acknowledges* [instead of recognizes] TAR to be an *inalienable* [new word] part of the territory of the PRC.' India refused to accept this formulation. In international legal terminology, the word 'recognition' is a much milder form than the word 'acknowledge', although the Chinese word for both is the same [Chengren]. By insisting on the formulation as it stands, the Chinese may have possibly tied themselves up into legal knots. What if tomorrow the PRC collapses? And by refusing to add the word 'inalienable', India has limited its recognition of Tibet as a part of China *to the life of the PRC* [emphasis added]! A far better course for the Chinese would have been to insist that India *acknowledge that* Tibet had *always* been apart of China *as an autonomous province* rather than of the PRC, the latter being a term that, after all, refers only to a Government or a political system, but certainly not to a State.

There was considerable criticism in India that by agreeing to this formulation, Vajpayee had forgone India's position on the McMahon Line and thus eroded its claims to Arunachal Pradesh. This criticism was based on the assumption that the McMahon Line was a product of the Simla Convention, where Tibet had participated as an entity independent of China, on equal terms and in its own right. What should be noted is the fact that TAR was recognized as a part of People's Republic of China, *which only came into existence in 1949*—and thus Tibet's legal position as it obtained in 1914—when the Simla Convention was signed—*remained unaltered* [emphasis added]. This new Indian formulation on the status of Tibet was reiterated by India in the 11 April, 2005, Joint Statement, as also in the 21 November, 2006, Joint Declaration. Thereafter, there was no mention of the status of Tibet in the 15 January, 2008 'Shared Vision of the 21st Century' Statement, or in the 16 December, 2010, Joint Communiqué.

It was anticipated that as a quid pro quo, the Chinese would give recognition to Sikkim as a part of India. Hitherto, the Chinese position had been that India had 'forcibly' occupied Sikkim and they continued to treat Sikkim as an independent entity. During Vajpayee's visit, all that the Chinese were prepared to concede was to sign a memorandum on 23 June, 2003, between India and China on expanding border trade in which under Article 1, it was stated that, '*the Indian side designates Changgu of Sikkim state and the Chinese side Renqinggang of TAR as venues for border trade market.*' This formulation came under heavy criticism in India and PM Vajpayee was forced to issue a statement underlining the fact that the 'process' of Sikkim *not* being an issue in Sino-Indian relations had begun. The Chinese Foreign Office spokesman, on the other hand, denied that there had been any change in the Chinese position, asserting that it was an issue 'left over by history.' Privately, Vajpayee was told that China would need 'some more time' before it changed its position on Sikkim.

On the border question, PM Vajpayee and PM Wen reiterated their determination to seek 'a fair, reasonable, and mutually acceptable' solution through consultations *on an equal footing* [a phrase supplied by the Chinese PM]. They agreed that, pending an ultimate solution, they should work together to maintain peace and tranquillity in the border areas, continue implementation of the agreements signed for this purpose, including the agreement to seek a clarification of the alignment of Line of Actual Control [LAC]. The two Governments agreed that special representatives would be appointed in an effort to seek an early settlement of the boundary issue and that they would explore '*from the political perspective' of the overall relationship, the framework of a boundary settlement.* [emphasis added]

This was a very important and a new formulation. In other words, the earlier Indian position that the Sino-Indian boundary was established by treaty, custom and usage was set aside and the brief for Indian negotiators now moved closer to the Chinese position that the Sino-Indian boundary be negotiated *afresh based on political parameters* [emphasis added]. This is what the Chinese had always wanted. Sensing that there may be an opening, the Chinese now began to court India with frequent high level visits, dialogues, offers of a strategic partnership and modest concessions on outstanding issues.[4] All these were gestures only, as no concrete proposals on solving the boundary issue were forthcoming.

The fall of the Vajpayee Government and the installation of the new Congress-led Government did not bring any substantial change in the negotiating posture adopted by India. As the boundary negotiations were now to be conducted as per 'political parameters', it became important, therefore, to settle and define what these parameters were and to come to a mutual agreement on them. PM Wen Jiabao's visit to India in April 2005 served as a catalyst for a distinct forward movement in border negotiations and this forward movement soon became visible.

The first step was for China to formally recognize that Sikkim was a part of India, as had been promised to Vajpayee during his visit in 2003. This step was now taken by China and, in a Joint Statement issued on 11 April, 2005, Article 13 of the Joint Statement reads as follows:

> Both sides reviewed with satisfaction the implementation of the memorandum on the border trade through the Nathula Pass between the Tibet Autonomous Region of the People's Republic of China and the Sikkim State of the Republic of India.

Thus, for the first time ever, the Chinese conceded that Sikkim was a part of India.

On 12 April, 2005, PM Wen handed over to PM Manmohan Singh a revised official map showing Sikkim as a part of India in full confirmation of the above statement. The Chinese Ambassador to India, Sun Yuxi told a press conference at the time of Wen's visit that the question of sovereignty over Sikkim had been 'completely settled.'[5] With this, the curtain finally came down with the official Chinese recognition of Sikkim as a part of India. The ambiguity that existed during Vajpayee's visit was removed and the verbal promise made by the Chinese leadership to Vajpayee was, thus, finally fulfilled.

However, the more important document that was signed on 11 April, 2005, was the agreement setting out the 'Political Parameters and Guiding Principles' for the settlement of the boundary question [Annexure V]. The significance of this Agreement lies in the fact that India finally abandoned Nehru's concept of the boundary that it was based on 'tradition, delimited by treaty, custom and usage and that it was a settled fact that required only minor rectifications.' By accepting that the boundary now be settled in 'a package way' was just what the Chinese had always wanted ever since Zhou's first assertions and later during his abortive negotiations with Nehru in April 1960. To the credit of the Chinese,

Map 8: Position of Tawang

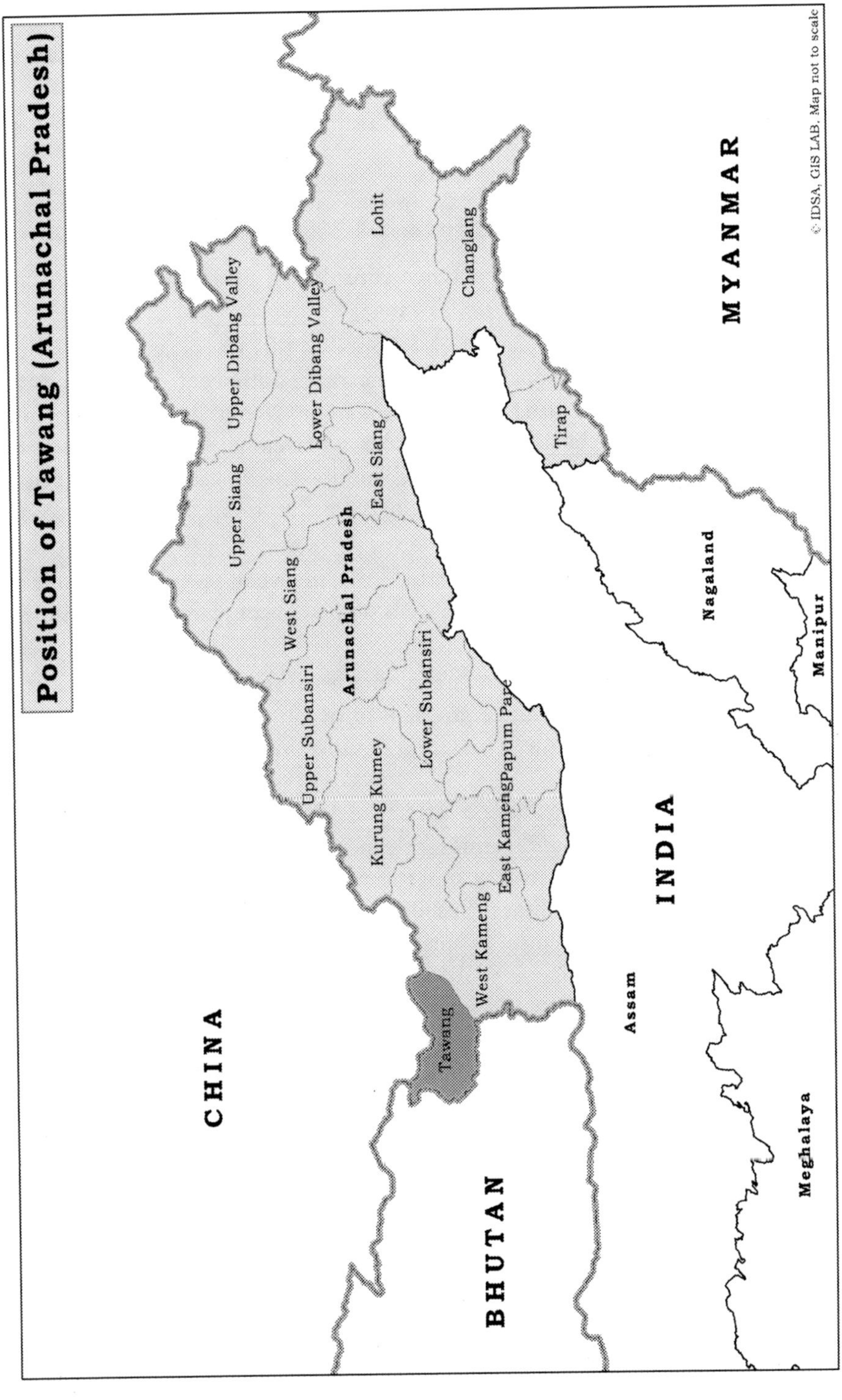

they had always maintained a consistent position throughout. It was India that changed its position. Nevertheless, it was a clear signal by India that it was now ready for a 'package deal.'

However, the most important article, from India's point of view, was Article VII, which stated as follows:

> In reaching a border settlement the two sides shall safeguard due interests of their settled populations in border areas.

Thus, Article VII assumes importance considering persistent Chinese claims, particularly those that centred on Tawang.

It was surmised by Indian interlocutors that this was a significant Chinese concession in that they had abandoned their earlier position of seeking 'concessions' in the Eastern sector in return for 'concessions' in the Western sector, as propounded first by the Chinese in the sixth round of talks in November 1985. The assumption, again, was that the Chinese had also abandoned their claims on Tawang and would, thus, settle for the status quo in the Eastern sector i.e. along the McMahon alignment.

Despite what was agreed as per Article VII, in several press articles emanating from China, the authors [no doubt with official encouragement] continued to make claims that:

[a] India controls 90,000 square kilometres of the 'richest part' of Tibet and the Himalayan region; equivalent to two and a half times Taiwan or the province of Jiangsu. The Chinese Government cannot easily 'give-up' this territory.

[b] China showed 'greatness' after the 1962 conflict by giving up land controlled by it and cannot be expected to show 'magnanimity' again. India lost an opportunity 'to settle' when Mao, Zhou or Deng were alive. Hu Jintao [then Chinese President and party leader] is not Mao or Deng.

[c] This issue is linked to sovereignty and territorial integrity of China and indicates the relative position of China in the global hierarchy and, therefore, China should not adopt any hasty step or make compromises on principles.

[d] A 'fair and reasonable' settlement implies that India will have to 'give up something to get something.' Ideally, China should get the entire area. It could, however, be split 50:50 like Heixiazi Island [Bolshoy Ussuriysky] was split between China and Russia.

[e] As a last resort, Beijing should at least recover Tawang, the Walong area along the Lohit Valley and Takpa Siri.

But why is Tawang so important for the Chinese and why is there continued insistence on its recovery?

Tawang is home to an important monastery. Inspired by the 5th Dalai Lama, Merag Lama Lodre Gyatson founded the monastery in 1681 and maintained ecclesiastical links with the great Drepung monastery at Lhasa till the Chinese take-over of Tibet. Presently, it is the only important Tibetan Monastery outside the control of Lhasa [and, therefore, China]. The 6th Dalai Lama [Tsangyang Gyatso] was born here and his foot-print is still displayed to the faithful.[6] The Chinese fear that in the future it could again play an important role in Tibetan religious affairs, particularly when the time comes to choose the next Dalai Lama. The Chinese fear is that when the time comes to choose the next Dalai Lama on the demise of the present one, could the Tawang Monastery not play a similar role?

Tawang is also very strategically located. As early as 1910, Sir Charles Bell had written about the importance of Tawang. He warned that:

> if the Chinese regain control over Tibet, later on they will pay special attention to the development and consolidation of the at—present thinly populated but warm and fertile districts in the South-West of Tibet, which are not far from Assam and from which districts, when developed, a considerable army could be fed.'[7]

Bell further elaborated and his prescience was most commendable that,

> the resulting growth of Chinese power in Tibet... China had very little power and there were no signs of her being aggressive on the Indian frontier...the position in now completely changed. China is becoming every year more formidable as a military power. She has seized power in Tibet and is increasing her military strength there more and more. Only a narrow stretch of territory intervenes between her conquests and the plains of India. And these conditions apply to 1,100 miles of frontier, i.e. from the North West corner of Nepal to the North-East corner of Assam. It is of vital importance to keep China and all foreign powers out of this narrow stretch of territory.[8]

What Charles Bell wrote then, remains equally valid even today, if not with greater relevance!

As early as 1910-12, the British General Staff, too, foresaw the importance of Tawang for the defence of India when they opined in a memorandum on 1 June, 1912, that:

> The direction of the frontier line about Tawang requires careful consideration. The present boundary is South of Tawang, running Westwards along the foothills from near Udalgiri to the Southern Bhutan border and thus a dangerous wedge of territory is thrust between the Miri country and Bhutan. A comparatively easy and much used trade route traverses this wedge from North to South by which the Chinese would be able to exert influence or pressure on Bhutan, while we have no approach to this salient from a flank, as we have in the case of the Chumbi salient. A rectification of the boundary here is, therefore, imperative[9] [i.e. Tawang should be with India].

Sir Henry McMahon, too, recognized the importance of Tawang. Writing to the British Government in London on 8 July, 1914, he explained his decision to include Tawang inside Indian Territory as follows:

> This seems to us a natural watershed frontier, access to the shortest trade route into Tibet, and control of the monastery of Tawang which has blocked the trade by this route in the past by undue exaction and oppression. [Map 8]

Chinese claims to Tawang are in fact based on Tibetan claims and the Tibetans never seriously challenged the Indo-Tibetan boundary as agreed upon by them in 1914. In the past, it is true that the Tawang Monastery collected dues from the inhabitants, but these were religious dues and this fact did not confer any territorial sovereignty on the Tibetan Government. The Chinese delegate to the Simla Convention, Ivan Chen, supported this view.[10] And so did the then Chinese Foreign Minister, Sun Paochi who on 13 June, 1914, told the British Minister in Peking that 'the Tibetans affected to think that they had rights over all the places inhabited by Lamaists, but this was not so. The Lamas might have ecclesiastical authority but this did not necessarily mean that these places belonged to Tibet.'[11] At best, it can be said that Tawang was within Tibet's ecclesiastical orbit and nothing more.

The position remains the same today. The strategic nature and the importance of Tawang remains undiminished and that is why the Chinese are adamant that Tawang should be returned to Tibet. They have clearly understood and recognized its religious importance and its strategic and military significance. If they were to succeed in beguiling India to vacate Tawang by dangling the carrot of a border settlement, the military position of India in the North-East would clearly become quite untenable.*

Another important agreement signed during Wen's visit was the Protocol on the 'Implementation of Confidence Building Measures in the Military field along the Line of Actual Control [LAC] in the Sino-Indian Border Areas.' This Protocol lays down modalities for the implementation of several measures contained in the Agreement of 1996 on Military CBMs along the LAC in the India-China Border Areas. The salient features of the Protocol include:

- Details on avoiding the holding of large-scale military exercises in close proximity of the LAC as per the 1996 Agreement and in case an exercise is being conducted, to provide relevant information to the other side;
- Dealing with air intrusions as per the provisions of 1996 Agreement;
- Procedure to be followed by both sides in the eventuality of their border personnel coming in face-to-face contact as a result of differences in the alignment of LAC or any other reason;
- Holding of additional meetings at the existing three border personnel meeting points, namely, Spanggur, Nathu La and Bumla to celebrate

*The issue of Tawang is referred to in chapter 3 also.

National Day or Army Day of each side;

- Extension of the mechanism of border meeting points to Kibithu-Damai in the Eastern Sector and the Lipulekh Pass in the Middle Sector;
- Exchanges between the relevant Military Regions of China and Army Commands of India;
- Exchanges between institutions of training, sports and culture of the two armed forces.

It was hoped that with this additional protocol in place, the chance of hostilities breaking out would be considered remote and that the border areas would remain sufficiently safe and secure. Thus, at the end of Wen's visit, what was put in place was a three-tier structure. At the apex were the negotiations taking place at the 'special representatives' level based on 'agreed parameters and guiding principles.' At the second level were the detailed and comprehensive negotiations taking place within the Joint Working Group comprising of officials, experts and technical personnel. At the third level were the periodic contacts between the two armed forces and particularly across the LAC, where any local issue was resolved by the local commanders at the local level.

In a bid to further consolidate the arrangements along the LAC, both sides felt that encouragement should be given for greater contacts between the armed forces of the two countries. These were given concrete shape during the visit of the then Defence Minister, Mukerjee, to China, when the first ever MOU on Defence was signed on 29 May, 2006. This MOU explicitly mentions 'frequent exchanges' by instituting an annual defence dialogue, joint military exercises and cooperation in 'search and rescue', counter-terrorism and anti-piracy operations. Such exchanges were first proposed by Li Peng during his visit in 2001. It was hoped that such exchanges in the military field would further help in stabilizing the border areas. For the Chinese, a commentator in the *PLA Daily* felt that through such exchanges 'we can learn from foreign armies *and get acquainted with their advanced military theories and equipments and try and find out our own weaknesses and deficiencies*' [emphasis added].[12] Specifically from India, the Chinese PLA were anxious to learn Indian Army tactics in counter-insurgency operations in Kashmir and to assess its combat readiness.

However, soon after the departure of Chinese PM Wen from India, Manmohan Singh arrived in Washington in July 2005 for what was to be a landmark visit. In the Joint Statement issued on 18 July, 2005, it was stated that:

> President Bush conveyed his appreciation to the Prime Minister over India's strong commitment to preventing WMD proliferation and stated that as a responsible state with advanced nuclear technology, India should acquire the same benefits and advantages as other such states. The President told the Prime Minister that he will work to achieve full civil nuclear energy cooperation with India as it realizes its goals of promoting nuclear power and achieving energy security. The President would also seek agreement from

> Congress to adjust US laws and policies, and the United States will work with friends and allies to adjust international regimes to enable full civil nuclear energy cooperation and trade with India [emphasis added].

Separately, it was conveyed by the US State Department that the US will help India become a major 'world power' in the 21st century.

This landmark strategic agreement was a defining moment in Indo-US relations that would have having far reaching strategic consequences. There were two important facets of this agreement. Firstly, a belated acceptance of India as a 'responsible state with advanced nuclear technology' amounting to a tacit US recognition of India's status as a de facto nuclear weapons power outside the NPT and secondly, an undertaking by the US that it would work with its friends and allies to 'adjust international' regimes, thereby eliminating discrimination faced by India in the conduct of its nuclear policy. With this significant help from the US, India had taken a giant step out of nuclear apartheid that it had been pushed into. This agreement was not only based on common values, but on common interests and these included a practical programme for joint action. The two countries also agreed to upgrade their 'strategic partnership' into a '*comprehensive strategic partnership*' [emphasis added].

Following this major initiative, President Bush, on a visit to India, signed the 'Civil Nuclear Energy Co-operation Agreement' between the two countries with PM Manmohan Singh on 2 March, 2006. In December 2006, the US Congress passed the 'Indo-US Peaceful Atomic Co-operation Act,' which allowed civilian nuclear commerce for the first time in thirty years. In April 2007, the US, Indian and Japanese Navies carried out their first ever trilateral joint naval exercises. With Japan also, India entered into a '*comprehensive strategic partnership*' and it was envisaged that meetings, every alternate year, would be held at PM's level. An annual strategic dialogue was also initiated with Japan in 2007 at the Deputy Minister/Secretary level.

All these major strategic developments did not escape the notice of Chinese policy planners in Beijing. They had noticed that in May 2002, a contingent of US Special Forces had landed in Agra and had taken part with Indian troops in exercises for two weeks, for the first time in 39 years and that India was one of the first countries to welcome the US Missile Defence Plan. This indicated that military cooperation between the two countries had already reached a high level. *The People's Daily* mocked at these trilateral exercises between India, the US and Japan by asking the question, '*A goodwill* joint naval drill'?[13] Military co-operation also grew steadily and China noticed that the *quality* of US arms sales to India showed a marked improvement. According to Chinese analysts, the US was trying to consolidate the US-India relationship by focusing on three key areas. These were defence, energy and economic relations. In line with this thinking, the US wished to form a strong politico-strategic partnership with India by emphasizing shared democratic values, common interests in combating global terrorism, achieving energy security, expanding bilateral trade and maintaining regional stability. The two countries already had extensive interdependence in software development, service out sourcing and infrastructure and manufacturing investments.[14]

But perhaps the most significant aspect of this growing cooperation, apart from the nuclear deal, was enhanced defence and space cooperation, and the emerging US-India military ties that spanned from arms sales to joint military exercises. In this context, Chinese sources pointedly referred to a October 2002 Pentagon report on Indo-US military relations that indicated a major shift of US policy towards India, defining and recognizing it as a major rising power, and helping India to achieve that status. During Defence Minister Mukherjee's June 2005 visit to the United States, the two countries signed a 10-year Defence Cooperation Agreement under which the US would provide a broad range of defense technology and military assistance, including fighter aircraft.[15] Chinese analysts suggested that the reason for the US policy change from 'restriction and control' to one of 'relaxation and even preferential treatment' for India was largely driven by a desire to balance China's growing power. At the same time, India's growing defense budget and arms acquisitions made it an attractive customer for US arms exports.[16]

Few strategic analysts in Beijing were ready to believe that the upgrading of US-Indian strategic ties would not impact adversely on China and that this would not produce consequences that were inimical to China. The fact that the US would help India to become a major world power in the 21st century and should this become a reality, the Chinese concluded, could only be at their expense. There was visible uneasiness in China at the prospect that India could 'band-wagon' with the US to 'encircle' China. The Chinese were concerned with any US initiative, particularly in the Asia-Pacific region, that included India but left out China.

The first indication that China was seriously concerned at developments between the US and India came in May 2007. The Chinese Foreign Minister, Yang Jiechi, told then Indian FM Mukherjee at their meeting in Hamburg that 'the mere presence of populated areas [in Arunachal Pradesh] would not affect Chinese claims on the boundary.'[17] When Manmohan Singh met the Chinese President, Hu Jintao, at Hamburg during the G-8 Summit in June 2007, the former tried to assert that a consensus had already been reached on Article VII of the 'Guiding Principles' and that this consensus could not be changed. In reply, Hu merely contended himself by invoking the spirit of peace, friendship, equality, mutual benefit and mutual understanding and did not revoke the line taken by his Foreign Minister.[18]

Thus, it seemed that, once again as it had done so many times before, the Chinese had decided to utilize the unsettled border as a part of coercive diplomacy to put 'pressure' on India. They had decided to disabuse Indian interlocutors of any notion that the Chinese demand for 'concessions' in the Eastern sector was a thing of the past when they agreed to Article VII of the 'guiding principles' that emphasized that 'settled populations' would not be disturbed. The Chinese now began to lay stress on Article V of the 'guiding principles' that referred to 'national sentiments' and stressed that they could not give up their position in the Eastern sector in line with these sentiments. Just as Zhou had written to Nehru in 1959 that 'China could not disgrace itself by selling out its territory of 90,000 kilometres, the size of the Chinese province of Chekiang',[19] how could the present Chinese interlocutors hurt 'national sentiments' by ostensibly 'gifting away' such large chunks of territory in the Eastern sector?

Thus, the whole premise on which Article VII of the 'guiding principles' stood in the minds of the Indian interlocutors was nullified [emphasis added]. China, it seemed, had decided that the best way to dissuade or coerce India from entering into strategic co-operation with the US, to China's detriment, was to signal conclusively that there would be 'consequences' and that India should be made aware of them. And, as usual, the Chinese thought that the best way to do this was to remind India of its vulnerabilities in the Sino-Indian border areas. The Chinese had, therefore, once again adopted a hard-line posture on the boundary question in order to 'coerce' India to follow a particular foreign policy line.

It came as no surprise, therefore, that in May 2007, a visa was denied to an IAS officer of Arunachal Pradesh to visit China on the plea that 'he did not need a visa to visit his own country'! It was designed to irritate India. China, however, was prepared to issue 'stapled' visas to other visitors from Arunachal Pradesh. A similar issue was raked up by the Chinese for India citizens from Jammu & Kashmir. China, also in violation of the spirit of the 1994 Agreement, began aggressive patrolling along the LAC, leading to several violations. If any reminder was necessary, the Chinese Ambassador to India, Sun Yuxi, just prior to Chinese Communist Party [CCP] leader and President, Hu Jintao's visit to India in November 2006, publicly laid claim to Arunachal Pradesh in what was termed as a diplomatic gaffe, but in reality was deliberate, intentional and a well-considered move designed to cause maximum irritation to India. According to Ambassador Sun, 'it is our position that the whole of the state of Arunachal Pradesh is Chinese Territory and Tawang is only one of the places in it. We are claiming all of that.' Ambassador Sun's remarks were never repudiated by the Chinese Foreign Ministry, but on the other hand, were extensively quoted by Chinese bloggers. At the same time, the Chinese stepped up their already close military links with Pakistan with expanded nuclear trade. China agreed to supply two new nuclear reactors. These were ostensibly for power generation purposes, but clearly outside the Nuclear Suppliers Group [NSG] system. The supply of nuclear and missile technology by China to Pakistan is to strike at the heart of the security system of India. As for Pakistan's complicity in the Mumbai terror attacks [26/11/2008], China maintained a deafening silence.

While closely analysing and criticizing the evolving Indo-US relationship, the Chinese also took care not to destabilize her own vast linkages with the US. The Indian assessment was that the US engagement with China was, indeed, very broad-based and that it would be extremely difficult for either the US or China to seriously jeopardize this relationship. Apart from a high level 'strategic and economic' dialogue, there is also a Joint Commission on Commerce and Trade, where meetings take place on an annual basis. Institutionally, there are 93 such bilateral mechanisms where consultations are held on an annual basis by Cabinet level officials, including a bilateral US-China dialogue on South Asia. It is one of China's major diplomatic goals to persuade the US to revert to a system whereby both countries can 'jointly' exercise influence over events in South Asia. And China will continue to create 'uncertainties' in the Sino-Indian border areas, just to 'remind' India that it could face 'a problem' should it align itself too closely with US strategic policies.

At present, even after fifteen rounds of talks at the 'special representatives' level, there is only but glacial movement forward towards a settlement of the boundary issue. It is but to be expected, given the nature and complexities of the international situation. The fact that there is little progress is also underlined in that the very concept of having 'special representatives' for discussing the boundary issue has been considerably diluted. This has been done by introducing discussions on 'strategic matters' in their deliberations. This would indicate that perhaps very little time is devoted for discussing the boundary issue for there is hardly any discernible forward movement. Presently, it is reported that the Chinese have used the mechanism of 'political' parameters to put forward their plea for the incorporation of nearly 60,000 kilometres of the Eastern sector, including Tawang, with Tibet,[20] on the plea that its incorporation is needed for 'political' purposes, since the 6th Dalai Lama was born there and that Tawang hosts one of the more important Tibetan monasteries. Not surprisingly, while the very institution of the Dalai Lama is abused almost daily by the Chinese, yet in the name of this very institution, Tawang is demanded from India! The Chinese have cleverly utilized Article III of the 'guiding principles,' which states that both sides will 'make meaningful and mutually acceptable adjustments to their respective positions on the boundary so as to arrive at a package settlement to the boundary question' to coax India into giving further concessions and, at the very least, to concede the Tawang tract.

As the Chinese attitude stiffened and became more obdurate by reverting to old hard line positions, the realization grew in India that there was no easy solution available and that this question is not likely to be decided any time soon. Therefore, India decided not to take any chances and it became imperative to strengthen its defences, particularly in the Eastern sector. It is proposed that two new additional army divisions be raised for Arunachal Pradesh. Advanced Sukhoi fighter jets are now stationed at Tezpur. It is proposed to construct 26 new strategic border roads. In Ladakh, old and presently disused airfields have also been activated. Both the PM and the External Affairs Minister have insisted on visiting Arunachal Pradesh, despite severe criticism by the Chinese media. The Dalai Lama visited Tawang and, much to the discomfort of the Chinese, declared that it belonged to India!

Thus, the present picture is much the same as it has been earlier. The two countries are no nearer to a solution to the boundary solution, despite 15 rounds of talks at the special representatives level. Nevertheless, the talks will continue as it politically suits both countries to do so and it constitutes an important channel of communication.

As far back as 1959, Nehru had recognized that 'the Sino-Indian border, even at the best of circumstances, will remain a frontier of dangerous potentialities.'[21] Nehru also correctly surmised that the border dispute was 'relatively easy to solve', but felt that the Chinese had kept this dispute alive and that the attack on India [1962] was part of a larger plan to humiliate India.[22] Therefore, Nehru's assessment was that this conflict with China was a 'long term affair' and that 'we must be prepared for it and shoulder the burdens that it necessarily brings to us.'[23] Perhaps even Nehru never really anticipated that after nearly six decades, several rounds of negotiations at various levels, the two countries are no nearer a solution than they were earlier. He probably also never anticipated how right he would be.

As for the Chinese, they, too, were candid when the former PM Wen Jiabao admitted towards the end of 2011, 'it may not be possible *to ever* [emphasis added] fully solve the boundary question.' That possibly is a fair assessment and perhaps the most accurate statement issued so far. It is also a very conclusive statement.

CHAPTER 10

Why is There No Settlement So Far?

Whenever a situation arises where fundamental policy decisions have to be taken, strategic analysts and policy makers, well versed in matters of state, invariably take a fairly hard and dispassionate look, particularly at the internal and external ground realities, before recommending a change in policy to their respective political leaderships. Of particular interest is whether such a change in policy, subtle or otherwise, would lead to greater advantage or whether a change would end in a distinct disadvantage. Timing is also very important. No policy decisions are taken in isolation for there are invariably wide repercussions; nor are they taken in a vacuum. This applies equally to the Sino-Indian border question and, hence, it has been quite evident over the years that a solution is not a mere technical matter, but rather a political and a strategic issue whose ramifications go well beyond the bilateral field. If the Sino-Indian boundary question was merely a technical matter, it would have been resolved a long time ago.

It goes without saying that there are political factors present, both in India and China, that do favour a solution, but perhaps only under certain circumstances. What would be those circumstances and do they exist at present? In other words, a solution must be assessed as a distinct overall gain. It goes without saying that this gain *must be mutual,* for otherwise the aggrieved party would have little interest in taking the settlement process forward. In the Sino-Indian context, it appears that policy makers, more so on the Chinese side, *may have taken the decision that the present status quo is perhaps preferable than opting for a solution* [emphasis added]. A settlement may be politically or strategically unwise or the price to pay maybe far too high. Therefore, it is important to assess what does a settlement entail and whether it is in the national interests of the two countries to do so. Or alternatively, does the present stalemate remain an acceptable outcome and the preferred option. What, then, are the reasons for opting for the present status quo?

A question that is often asked is if bilateral negotiations are not making the desired progress, should the two countries not opt for the involvement of third parties? Perhaps a third party could coax the two countries to reach a settlement. In the international community [including the UN Charter] and in authoritative textbooks on international law, five distinct methods are recognized for the peaceful settlement of international disputes. These are: bilateral talks, good offices, mediation, arbitration and a judicial settlement under ICJ jurisdiction. The first mode of bilateral talks is the preferred method adopted by both India and China currently.

The second mode is to utilize the 'good offices' of another power to resolve the dispute. In this case, the power offering 'good offices' acts essentially as a go—between without offering a solution. For this mode to be successful the state offering 'good offices'—*must have a substantial stake in the settlement of the dispute* [emphasis added]. In its own assessment its involvement should result in a significant enhancement of prestige, additional accretion of power or perhaps even economic/commercial advantage. It is highly unlikely that any state would undertake such a task if there was no substantial gain for itself. Additionally, it would most certainly need to be trusted by both parties as well.

The third mode is mediation. Mediation differs from 'good offices' in that a mediator offers a solution during the course of negotiations, but without any commitment by the disputants to accept the mediator's proposals. Mediation also occurs as a result of a request by both the disputants to assist them to find a solution to the dispute. There is also no advance commitment by the parties to the dispute of any kind.

The fourth mode is arbitration. This involves a submission by both parties to an impartial arbitrator or a body of arbitrators. Sometimes, both parties select one arbitrator each and a third is a joint selection or has the approval of both. The outcome of the dispute is settled *as per the provisions of international law* [emphasis added]. This mode differs from a judicial settlement in that each of the disputants has to some extent a say in the selection of arbitrators.

The fifth mode is for the disputants to go for an outright judicial settlement by submitting their respective case before the International Court of Justice [ICJ], where the dispute will be settled by a judicial verdict based on the principles of international law. The ICJ decision need not be unanimous and most cases are decided on a majority basis. Several states have opted for this mode of settlement, but both China and India have expressed reservations. China has not as yet accepted the Optimal System under Article 36(2) of the ICJ Statute. India has accepted, but with the reservation that disputes concerning the status of its territories and delimitation of its boundaries would be outside the purview of the ICJ. Nevertheless, nothing prevents both India and China from following ICJ case law to settle their dispute,[1] or from taking the initiative to jointly or singly approach the ICJ. Nehru had offered to Zhou to go to the ICJ in 1963, but his offer was hastily turned down.[2]

It must be emphasized that each dispute is rather unique. No one particular mode can be prescribed for all. In this sense, the Sino-Indian border question, too, is unique and a solution would, therefore, have to be found within the ambit of the evolving relationship between the two countries. *So far, neither India nor China have opted for any other method except the bilateral mode for the settlement of the dispute*, deeming the issue to be far too important to involve third parties [emphasis added]. No other state has been officially involved in helping to reach a settlement. Thus, a settlement, if and when it is arrived at, would necessarily be as a result of bilateral negotiations.

Present day Chinese strategists while referring to the boundary dispute also make it a point to emphasize that China-Pakistan relations, Tibet and the Dalai Lama and India's propensity to seek enhanced strategic and security links with countries of East Asia under the aegis of US 're-balancing' towards Asia, are important factors that China takes into account while determining policy. What worries them is that India may abandon its strategic autonomy and ally with the US to 'contain' China. They discern that a growing number of Indian strategists, as well as large sections of influential Indian media, are promoting the case for alignment with the US.[3] In the Chinese mind, the link between a boundary settlement and these strategic factors is, therefore, well established. On each of these issues, China first seeks satisfaction.

There is no other state in the world that has longer contiguous land frontiers than China: a total of about 22,000 kilometers, of which about nearly 19,000 kilometers traverse China's minority areas.[4] When the People's Republic was founded in 1949, China's borders were delimited by three types of lines and land boundary disputes existed with almost every neighbour. These were boundary lines under old treaties ratified by previous Chinese Governments, traditional borders and lines of actual control. At present, China has a land border with 14 states, although India considers the China-POK border to be illegal—since the whole of Jammu and Kashmir is a part of India and, therefore, Pakistan has no common border with China. According to India, China's land borders should, therefore, be with only 13 states. The People's Republic of China ratified its first land boundary agreement on 4 January, 1961, with Burma [Now Myanmar]. Thereafter, China has settled its land boundaries with Nepal [1961], Mongolia [1962], North Korea [1962], Pakistan [1963] and Afghanistan [1969]. With these settlements, nearly one-half of China's total boundary line was covered. After a lull of some two decades, China further signed land boundary agreements with Laos [1991], Russia [1991, 1994 and 2004], Kazakhstan [1994], Kyrgyzstan [1996], Vietnam [1999] and Tajikistan [1999]. Thus, of the 14 states that have land borders with China, 12 have finally and conclusively settled their border disputes with the People's Republic, [5] although there continues to be a doubt whether the land border with North Korea has been finally settled, with both sides claiming sovereignty over the Baitoushan/Paektu-san [White Head

Mountain] area. While the settlement of China's land borders has shown progress, China's maritime boundaries continue to remain in dispute mainly in the East and South China Sea areas.

In recent times, China has fought border skirmishes with the then Soviet Union, Vietnam and India. With the settlement of boundary disputes with the states comprising the former Soviet Union and Vietnam, *India and Bhutan remain the only states that have continuing land border disputes with China* [emphasis added]. As regards Bhutan, China alleges that it is still under 'India's firm control' and that India will not allow it to 'freely engage in diplomatic relations with China and solve the border issue.'[6] At dispute is the Chinese demand for an additional 269 square kilometers in North-Western Bhutan, adjoining the strategic Chumbi valley, in exchange for 495 square kilometers in the remote and wild Northern areas near Northern Bhutan that China is willing to concede. Thus, the Sino-Indian boundary question is perhaps the most important and only dispute that remains to be settled despite decades—long period of negotiations that have taken place between the two countries. [Map 9]

It is, indeed, an anomaly as to why there is no settlement with India when all other similar boundary disputes with other states have been settled. It is not as if there are no solutions possible, but there has to be a will, a reason and an inclination to settle. And it is not technical reasons that are holding up a settlement. While assessing the prevailing reality along the Sino-Indian border, three factors need to be kept in mind. Firstly, in the Western sector, the Chinese are in possession of territory up to their stated claim line. Secondly, India is in no position to evict them physically by using military force. Thirdly, although India is in possession of territory in the middle and Eastern sectors, the Chinese would like to take possession of even larger chunks of Indian controlled territory, particularly in the Eastern sector. Maybe these are negotiating tactics, but it cannot be discounted that these continue to be strategic Chinese aims, for the Chinese have *not* surrendered their claims to the whole of Arunachal Pradesh in the Eastern sector or, for that matter, to the smaller pockets in the middle sector. The Chinese know that short of use of force, with all its concomitant consequences, India will not give up its position in the middle and Eastern sectors.

The Chinese even decline to demarcate a mutually determined 'Line of Actual Control' all along the Sino-Indian border so that untoward incidents, including military clashes, can be avoided. In the Chinese mind, therefore, the settlement of the border issue with India cannot be divorced from regional, political and larger strategic issues confronting it. In fact, if the regional, political and strategic issues with India were amicably resolved, a boundary settlement would inevitably follow. Ever since the boundary issue came to the fore and even at present, *this dispute is utilized by China for trying to coerce foreign policy changes by India that often have nothing to do with the dispute itself* [emphasis added]. China has used the threat of intrusions across the LAC—as part of coercive diplomacy—in order

Map 9: Disputed Areas Between Bhutan and China

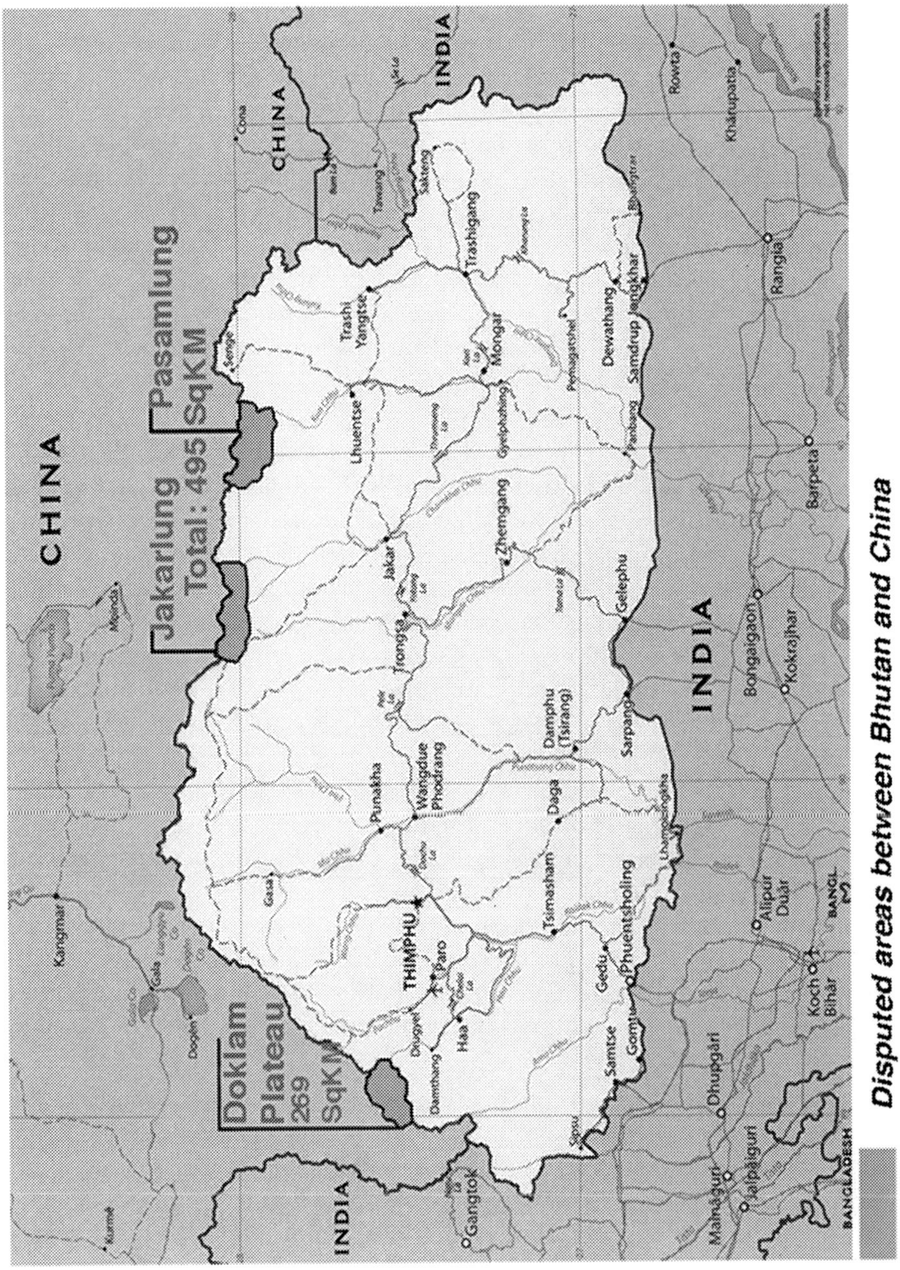

to influence decisions in a way most desirable for it. And that is also the principal reason why China does not desire an early conclusion, except perhaps completely on its own terms. It is too valuable a coercive diplomatic asset to give up. As an article in the Hong Kong based newspaper *Wen Wei Po* put it, 'while New Delhi was quick to express hope to see both sides try harder to resolve their border dispute....China has implemented a policy of good neighbourliness and incessantly extended its hand of friendship to India...India has adopted a policy, a mega-strategy of restraining China with the United States on the one hand and imposing economic and trade restrictions on the other. In this situation, *China does not need to rush for a quick solution to its boundary dispute with India*' [emphasis added]. In other words, a boundary settlement is only possible if India were to remain within the 'red-lines' drawn by China.

From the Chinese point of view, the most significant factor in Sino-Indian relations that still remains unresolved is the issue of Tibet. Although over the years India has officially accepted that Tibet is an autonomous region of China and has repeatedly stated so, yet doubts about India's intentions continue to linger in the Chinese mind. Even the Chinese military action in 1962 was attributed not to the legality—or otherwise—of the McMahon Line, but as Mao Zedung told a Nepalese delegation in 1964, to the fact that 'in the opinion of the Indian Government, Tibet is theirs.' Further, China justified military action in 1962 by observing that 'the Indian ruling circle had taken the mantle of the British imperialists' and had begun to '*regard China's Tibet as an Indian sphere of influence*' [emphasis added].[7] This Chinese paranoia about India's intentions towards Tibet continues still, for whenever a Sino-Indian joint statement is envisaged, the Chinese insist that a sentence be incorporated stating that 'Tibet is a part of China.' In the past, Chinese rhetoric always attributed continuing discontent in Tibet to Indian 'machinations' rather than to their own repressive policies. Presently, they also blame the Dalai Lama. The decision by the Indian Army to raise a new strike corps for operations in the North would have done nothing to lessen Chinese apprehension about the intentions of India. Further, the Chinese see India's move to bolster its military strength as 'sourced in a larger plan by the West to contain China.'

Despite enormous efforts put in over the years, China has still not been able to pacify Tibetan aspirations for complete autonomy or even independence. China has tried everything from brutal crackdowns to economic sops and, yet, the Tibetan yearning for independence has just not died down, to its utter exasperation. China faces a crisis of credibility in Tibet even after a half century of so-called 'democratic reforms.'[8] Sometimes, even Chinese officials, in candid moments, admit that although their economic strategies have been a success, yet their political strategy for ensuring stability has been a dismal failure.[9] The Chinese received a rude awakening just prior to the Beijing Olympic Games in 2008, when extensive disturbances erupted in Tibet. The Tibetan protests in 2008 were the largest and most widespread since the exile of the Dalai Lama in 1959. Since 2009 nearly 126 Tibetans have self-immolated in protest against Chinese rule. Those that have left a record of their intentions call for the return of the Dalai Lama to Tibet, of the independence of Tibet and of their frustrations as an occupied people.[10] The Chinese, in their paranoia, suspect an Indian 'hand.' And the recent unrest amongst the Uighur population in Xinjiang [Sinkiang]—where riots broke out protesting Chinese rule—has done nothing to lessen Chinese obsession with so called 'out-side interference.' Nearly 200 people died in the riots of July 2009.[11] Sometimes Tibetan protests are subtle, such as displaying pictures of the Dalai Lama in prayer rooms, writing protests in poetry and music[12] or turning towards the South [Dharamsala where the Dalai Lama resides] in the presence of Chinese officials, and bowing their heads in silent prayer. Nothing irritates Chinese officials more!

China realizes that the Sino-Indian boundary is in actual fact largely the Tibet-India boundary, except for a short length that abuts Xinjiang. There are no old Tibetan maps that show the Southern boundary of Tibet with India! However, much China may obfuscate, the issue today, but for the period 1911 to 1951, China was totally absent from the scene and Tibet was independent all but in name. There was not a single Chinese soldier or administrator present in Tibet and there was no effective Chinese control anywhere near the Tibet-India boundary. China is aware that the majority of Tibetans still yearn for such a period to return. Even Mao Zedung admitted in the 6 April, 1952, CCP directive that, 'while several hundred thousand Han people live in Sinkiang, there are hardly any in Tibet, where our army finds itself in a totally difficult minority area' and that there was 'no social basis or popular support for the Communist liberation of Tibet.'

History shows that Inner Asia—with Tibet located at its strategic epicenter—has suffered from periodical political upheavals. In the past, Tibetan cultural and religious influence in Central Asia was significant. That is the reason why China was in such haste to conclude boundary agreements with the successor states of the Soviet Union in Central Asia. In China's Xinjiang province, communities overlap with those in the states of Central Asia and their cultural, religious and ethnic affinities with their kin across borders are strong. The commitment of these communities to the Chinese Central Government is rather weak. Therefore, administrative and political control in Xinjiang becomes problematical and cannot be divorced totally from the events in the Central Asian Republics. It is for this reason that the Chinese realize that a strong Chinese military presence is necessary both in the Western and South-Western areas of China. So long as strong Chinese military garrisons dot the Tibetan landscape and are present in strength along the Indo-Tibet border, India will always remain concerned and wary. Similarly, strong Indian Army units stationed along the contentious border will always remain a cause for worry for the Chinese, lest India be tempted to interfere in the internal affairs of Tibet and beyond. The Chinese are aware of the specially trained Indian Army units, manned mainly by Tibetans, which are located close on the Indian side of the border.

The Dalai Lama lives in exile in Dharamsala [India] along with thousands of his followers. He is the center of the Tibetan community, the person to whom the Tibetans look for guidance in all things. They give to him a faith and a belief and a trust unparalleled in other relationships.[13] China watches the Dalai Lama's every move with anxiety. The Dalai Lama can still initiate sufficient turmoil in Tibet to cause the Chinese anxious moments. The Chinese are aware that with the increasing high profile the Dalai Lama has attained internationally, the cause of the Tibetans will not die down completely. The Dalai Lama's prestige—both in the Buddhist world and elsewhere—is very high and polemical attacks by the Chinese on his persona are seen by the Tibetans as contempt for their way of life and their dignity. The Chinese are aware of the moderation exercised by the present Dalai Lama, although they will never admit it, but are acutely embarrassed by the rise of the militant Tibetan Youth Congress [TYC], whom they equate with al-Qaeda.[14] What irked the Chinese was that elections were held for the Tibetan 'Government-in exile' in India in 2011, after the Dalai Lama announced that he had given up his political role and that India did nothing to stop the holding of such elections. In contrast, no such elections are ever held in the Chinese controlled Tibetan Autonomous Region [TAR].

The Internet and Communication Technology [ICT] revolution and instant information thus generated through the internet and social media carry the Dalai Lama's messages, even to those inside Tibet, and have added to Chinese ire. The Tibetan cause has received widespread coverage through this new medium and the Chinese are wary of its potential to influence politicians, civil society and other influential entities, particularly in Western countries. The issue of Human Rights is increasingly becoming an important foreign policy tool. The Chinese are conscious of the fact that with an aging Dalai Lama, the question of his succession also has the potential of generating sufficient unrest within Tibet to cause them immense worry. If the new Dalai Lama is 'discovered' in India and continues to reside in India, he may turn out to be even more intransigent and intractable than the present Dalai Lama. Therefore, as in the past, China would need the co-operation of India. What better way than to remind India not to play the 'Tibetan card' than to continue to keep the boundary question unsettled and underscore the Chinese potential for damaging Indian security in the Northern areas, just in case it becomes necessary to coerce the 'co-operation' of India?

The Chinese have always had a fine tradition of strategic thought and perhaps one of the subtlest. In the 5th century, Wang Jingze, a Chinese strategist, reportedly compiled a list of 36 stratagems and one of the listed stratagems [No. 3] is 'to kill with a borrowed knife.' As it has always been one of China's important strategic objectives to keep Indian influence confined to the South Asian region, what better way than to utilize the services of a willing accomplice such as Pakistan? It is, therefore, not without reason that China has assiduously forged an 'all weather' relationship with Pakistan, much to the detriment of Indian interests. There is no other state in South Asia that has been lavished more attention by China than Pakistan. China probably expects that Pakistan would follow 'its line' in its confrontation with India. There are two important aspects of this relationship that worry India. These are the nuclear issue and the massive arms supply from China to Pakistan. It is these that encourage Pakistan to adopt an intransigent and a hostile attitude towards India and thus keep India 'occupied' with developments within South Asia, much to the strategic advantage of China.

China played a central role in helping Pakistan to become a nuclear weapons state. In keeping with this role, China is helping Pakistan to increase its nuclear energy output from 770 megawatts to 8,000 megawatts by 2030. China is helping Pakistan to develope the fastest growing nuclear arsenal in the world.[15] Failing to achieve what was done for India by the US, Pakistan has looked to China to fill the void and China, in turn, has given ample indication that it was ready to do so. The Chinese do not buy the thesis that nuclear co-operation cannot be extended to Pakistan on the same basis as India because India and Pakistan are 'different states with different histories and, therefore, different needs.' China stands for equivalence between India and Pakistan and has criticized the 'discriminatory' nature of the NSG waiver given to India and demanded that the same be given to Pakistan. Having 'fathered' Pakistan's nuclear weapons program, China now intends to 'grand-father' Pakistan's civilian nuclear program in an attempt to beat the NSG guidelines, and has reportedly agreed to supply six new nuclear reactors. The Chinese are well aware that Pakistan's nuclear weapons systems are India-centric and, despite that, have supplied Pakistan's main delivery systems, including 34 short range M-11 ballistic missiles, in 1992.[16] There is no doubt that China will continue to be the final arbiter of the pace of Pakistan's nuclear weapons development.

China is also the main military weapons supplier to the Pakistan Army. According to SIPRI, nearly 55 per cent of China's arms exports go to Pakistan. China's arms exports world-wide rose by an unprecedented 162 per cent for the period 2008-2012 and China has replaced the UK as the fifth largest arms exporter in the world.[17] The Chinese supply everything from fighter aircraft to missiles to naval vessels to Pakistan. The aim is to ensure that India always has to face a two front threat. Thus, China does not wish that the threat to India should dissipate either from the Pakistan front or from the Sino-Indian border. As Pakistan is the only South Asian state that can offer military resistance to India and China does not wish to give up its strategically pivotal position in Pakistan, it cannot therefore, come to terms on a unilateral basis with India by resolving the Sino-Indian boundary question, for the position of Pakistan would in that case become untenable, as it would face increased military pressure from India. Under present circumstances, Pakistan is too valuable an ally and China does not wish to alienate its friendship with Pakistan built with such diligent effort. On the other hand, a recent trend that is quite discernible is the strengthening of the links between China and Pakistan, particularly in the crucial Northern areas of Pakistan where there are reports of the presence of PLA units. The strategic interests of both China and Pakistan coincide in South Asia. As the former Chinese PM, Wen Jiabao, told the then Pakistani PM, Gilani, that China is willing to work with Pakistan—*to safeguard our common interests as all-weather strategic partners.*[18] Clearly, the reference to 'common interests' can only mean 'containing' India jointly! China is not, at present, willing to concede to India any strategic space nor does it wish for India to become the pre-eminent and unchallenged military power in South Asia, for that would mean the elimination of Chinese influence in South Asia. China would have no strategic space left in South Asia.

Any strategic analyst sitting in Beijing would realize that in any Sino-Indian stand-off, the role of the US would be crucial. The US is still the only super power that is capable of doing a power projection in any part of the world and has enormous economic and military leverage. Both India and China consider their respective bilateral ties with the US to be by far the most important of any relationships. China has watched with some anxiety the US urge India to play a greater role in the Indo-Pacific region. As US Deputy Secretary of State William Burns put it, 'India's strong presence in the Indian and Pacific Oceans is a source of comfort and affirms its potential as a net security provider in the maritime domain.'[19] Therefore, the way Indo-US relations develop in the future is of great strategic significance for China. Chinese analysts pinpoint three areas in which the US was trying to consolidate its relationship with India. These are defence, energy and economic relations. They realize that if both the US and India work in tandem, they have the capability of upsetting the Chinese power calculus, particularly in the larger Indo-Pacific region. In the future, the Asian strategic landscape is likely to dominated by three powers; the US, China and India. It is obvious that a combination of any two can easily overwhelm the third. China is aware that in Asia, India is the only major continental rival left that is capable of 'balancing' China.

Of major concern to China is the burgeoning Indo-US military co-operation. Since 2002, the US and India have conducted over 50 military exercises, including joint naval exercises, high altitude operations, air combat and warfare and exercises in covert warfare demonstrating how far the relationship had developed in such a relatively short period of time.[20] Co-operation in missile defence was discussed and agreed in the Policy Defence Group, and in 2008, India announced that plans for integrated missile defence system to be constructed with US assistance that would become operational by 2011.

In October 2002, a Pentagon report indicated a major shift in US policy attitudes towards India by defining and recognizing India as a major rising power and *helping India to achieve that status.* The 10-year Defence Framework Co-operation Agreement, signed in 2005, calls for expanded joint military exercises, increased defence related trade and provision by the US to India a broad range of defence technology and military assistance, including space and other hi-tech areas. Recently, after a meeting of the two National Security Advisors in Washington, it was decided that both India and the US had decided to move from a buyer-seller situation to actually developing, co-producing various defence acquisitions involving technology transfer *at much higher levels than before* [emphasis added].[21]

Chinese analysts suggest that the year 2005, when negotiations for Indo-US Civil Nuclear Agreement began, was the tipping point. US policy changes from one of 'restriction and control' to one of 'relaxation' and even 'preferential treatment' for India was, thus, the logical conclusion and was largely driven by the US desire to balance China's growing power and to 'contain' it and make India a strategic counter-weight to China.[22] The Chinese felt that India's move to bolster its military strength was 'sourced in a larger plan by the West to contain China.' As the *People's Daily* put it:

> Although both sides say the agreement has nothing to do with China...the China factor is only too obvious. Both [the US and India] felt keenly uneasy about China's development, though neither of them mentioned it. US neo-cons have long been insisting that long term threat is from China, while India apparently senses that China is a neighbor stronger than itself in both economic and military strength.

Few Chinese strategic analysts are ready to believe that this up-gradation of Indo-US ties would not impact adversely on China's interests and produce results that were inimical to it. The Chinese calculation is that the US decision to help India become a major Indo-Pacific power can only be at their expense. There is visible uneasiness and discomfort in China at such a prospect. Some even see the development of Indo-US military ties as a part of the larger US policy to re-pivot to Asia and an attempt to 'band wagon' or 'coerce' Asian countries into joining in the 'containment' of China. As the *People's Liberation Army Daily* put it, 'the US is laying out forces across the Asia-Pacific region in advance to contain the rise of China.'[23] Not all the blame is put at the door of the US, for India, too, is seen as a willing accomplice. It is felt that India 'needs to show its value' to the US plans to counter and contain China, so that it could garner US military support and [thus] help raise its international status. Indian troop escalation on the border between India and China is aimed at 'meeting the requirements of the US and then getting support from the US.'[24]

Therefore, there are two main policy options before China. The first is to continue to use coercive diplomacy to 'threaten' India with incursions across the LAC in the India-China border areas to 'remind' India that if it aligns itself too closely with US interests, it would be very vulnerable in the face a belligerent China. As an article in the *People's Daily* in 2005 put it:

> China has to make it clear to India the price to be paid for taking what America offers.

And that:

> New Delhi had to be taught the 'costs' associated with trampling on China's vital security interests.

In such a scenario, China cannot afford to settle the border question, for how else would it be able to mount incursions across the LAC to coerce India to be more accommodating? The greater the ambiguity about the alignment of the LAC, the greater the opportunity this presents for China to utilize this issue to browbeat India.

The second view is that India is too large a country and too proud of its independence and strategic autonomy for it to become a camp follower of the West. Therefore, it is the assessment of this point of view that India would not become a 'client' state of the West and turn against China. However, this appears to be a minority view and expressed more in hope for it is often qualified by reiterating that this does not mean that India has a policy that is 'friendly and constructive towards China,' and that India has 'good reason to adopt the policy of containing China.' Why India should adopt this policy of containment is answered by the Chinese commentators themselves. They aver that as there are 'considerable disputes' between India and China—including territorial disputes, the issue of Tibet, Pakistan and the Indian Ocean[25]—India would be tempted to join in the containment policy followed by the Western powers, particularly the US. The reference to the Indian Ocean is indeed of significance for this alludes to China's discomfiture over Indo-US Naval co-operation and China's Malacca dilemma.

The last Quadrennial Defence Review [QDR] released by the Pentagon in 2010 contains the assessment that as India's military capabilities grow, it would '*contribute to Asia as a net provider of security in the Indian Ocean and beyond*' [emphasis added].[26] President Obama further emphasized the same theme in January 2012 in a document entitled 'Sustaining US Global Leadership: Priority for 21st Century Defense,' in which he stressed that the United States was investing in a long-term strategic partnership with India to 'support its ability to serve as a regional economic anchor *and security provider in the broader Indian Ocean Region*' [emphasis added]. India appeared to accept this role when Manmohan Singh alluded to the fact that India was situated at the cross-roads of Asia and astride one of the busiest sea-lanes of the world. Manmohan Singh said 'we have to assume our responsibility in the Indian Ocean region and *are well positioned to become a net provider of security in our immediate region and beyond*' [emphasis added].[27] It is this common strategic thinking of both the US and India that worries the Chinese, for this can easily be converted, in the future, into something much more robust and potent, particularly in the Indian Ocean area.

The Indian Ocean covers about 20 per cent of the world's surface. It is the third largest of the world's five oceans. The Indian Ocean Rim countries have a population of approximately 2.6 billion, or 39 per cent of the world's people. The Indian Ocean accounts for 50 per cent of the world's container traffic and Indian Ocean ports handle about 30 per cent of global trade. Around 66 per cent of the world's seaborne trade in oil transits the Indian Ocean. Roughly 55 per cent of known oil reserves, and around 40 per cent of gas reserves are in the Indian Ocean region.[28] The US believes that India, as the largest democracy in the world, with suitable maritime capabilities could play an important role in the protection of these arteries of the global economic engine. For both the US and India, the stability and viability of Sea Lines of Communications [SLOC] in the Indian Ocean area is also an important strategic objective.

It was the then Chinese leader, Hu Jintao, who first referred to China's 'Malacca dilemma' [马六甲困境] [Ma liu jia Kunjing] in November 2003 in a speech to high level cadres attending a meeting on economic issues. Hu maintained that 80 per cent of China's trade, including oil imports, passes through the Malacca Straits and that 'certain powers have all along encroached on and tried to control navigation through the Strait.'[29] At the heart of the matter is China's Malacca dilemma.

The Malacca Straits are a shallow and narrow waterway linking the Indian Ocean with the South China Sea. At some points it is only 23 metres deep. At its narrowest point, the navigable channel is about 1.5 to 2 kilometres wide and yet it is one of the busiest waterways in the world.[30] Nearly 60,000 ships, including huge oil-tankers carrying oil from West Asia to major oil consuming nations of China, Japan and South Korea, navigate through the Straits on an annual basis. At current trends, nearly 80% of China's oil imports are expected to pass through this route. China relies heavily on imported oil, gas and other natural resource commodities to feed its growing economy and these are mainly transported by sea. It is expected that China's imports of crude oil may exceed 300m tons by 2013 and by 2030, nearly 75% of its oil consumption would be based on imported oil. Today, China is the world's second largest importer of oil after the US and it has even overtaken Japan. Nearly 10% of China's total energy consumption is based on imported oil. As the global GDP doubles over the next 17 years, China will come to own a quarter of the world's merchant fleet.[31]

A Chinese newspaper in 2004 stated that 'it is no exaggeration to say that whosoever controls the Straits of Malacca will have a stranglehold on the energy route to China.' Chinese think tanks, in their discussions, use the term 'control' by India over the Indian Ocean and view Indian deterrence from different angles, including Indian maritime capabilities singly or jointly with the US Navy. As a Chinese commentator put it:

> According to US geo-strategic desires, in order to push India to integrate into its system to contain China, the US encourages India not only to move East, but also brings up the concept of an Indo-Pacific region to justify India's intervention in Asian-Pacific affairs.[32]

In case the Straits of Malacca were ever to be blockaded, it would mean a detour of at least three to four days extra steaming by ships and that also not through very safe waters. Whatever both the US and India may say, the Chinese are sceptical of their attitude for the two countries have sufficient naval fire power to cause acute embarrassment to China bound shipping in case it ever became necessary. It is for this reason that China watches each joint exercise between the US and Indian Navies with such trepidation and if the Japanese or the Vietnamese Navies were to join in, Chinese paranoia would become even that much more acute. This was recently demonstrated when a Chinese naval ship buzzed an Indian naval ship INS AIRAVAT on a goodwill visit to a Vietnamese port.

Deeply aware of their vulnerability, the Chinese have already started to take effective counter-measures to obviate such a necessity. Firstly, the Chinese have already enhanced the capacity of their strategic oil reserves, with the location and exact quantities stored in the strategic reserves considered to be a state secret. But most important of all, China is building new oil and gas pipelines right across the central Euro-Asian heartland as well as from Myanmar to Southern China. The importance of these oil and gas pipelines across the Euro-Asian heartland and Myanmar lies in the fact that most, if not all, would be immune from hostile military action.

Realising the importance of obtaining access to Central Asian oil and gas resources, the Chinese moved quickly, as a first step, to conclude boundary disputes lingering from the Soviet era with the former Soviet Republics of Kyrgyzstan, Tajikistan and Kazakhstan. Having settled the debilitating and vexed boundary disputes, China began negotiations for crude oil and gas supply arrangements with the countries of Central Asia. Negotiations began first with Kazakhstan and by 2004, construction of a 900 kilometre long oil pipe line costing about US $700 m commenced, which would join Atyrau in Kazakhstan with Alashankou in Xinjiang [Sinkiang]. Construction was completed by December 2005. This pipeline can carry 240,000 bbl/d of crude oil and it is expected that its capacity would be further enhanced to nearly double its present capacity by 2014. China began importing Turkmen gas at the end of 2009 and expects to increase supplies as the pipeline capacity and production levels increase. In July 2007, China signed a 30-year gas purchase agreement with Turkmenistan to take 1,100 Bcf/y. China and Turkmenistan signed another agreement in late 2011 that could add another 1,200 Bcf/y, bringing the total potential volume of gas exports to China to nearly 2,300 Bcf/y.[33] From here it would link up with the existing Chinese pipeline system. Thus, both crude and gas from Central Asia would soon be fuelling the engines of the Chinese economy and its growth centres situated along its Pacific coastline.

But by far the most important development has been the construction of the Russian Eastern Siberian-Pacific [ESPO] pipeline which commenced on 27 April, 2009. This became possible as a result of an agreement between Russia and China, under which China would offer Russian firms long term credit amounting to US$ 25 billion in return for which Russia would supply 300 mt of oil through this pipeline for the period 2011 to 2030. Russia is building the Eastern Siberia-Pacific Ocean pipeline in two stages, with the first phase [2757 kilometres, 600,000 bbl/d] completed in September, 2010. Once completed, this pipeline will deliver crude oil from Eastern Siberia to Russia's Pacific Coast, giving Russia's crude oil easier access to Asia-Pacific markets. It is expected to be completed in 2018 and it will transport 1.6 million bbl/d of crude oil. The Russians have built a new oil terminal port at Kozmino Bay on the Pacific coastline.[34] At a point near Skovorodino inside the Russian Far East, this pipeline is barely 40 kilometres away from the Chinese border and a branch is being built to supply crude oil to China directly and latest indications are that this section of the pipeline is ready for commissioning. Thus, Russia can supply Siberian crude independently to China as well as to Japan and South Korea without any political implications. In addition, Russia and China are presently negotiating for the construction of two gas pipelines that would carry, when completed, 69 b/cm of gas from Russia to China. These developments are symptomatic of the growing political, military and economic synergy between Russia and China. China today is one of the most significant and largest purchasers of Russian military hardware and these purchases include state of the art military systems.

With Myanmar, too, the Chinese have been quick off their feet. The South-East Asia Pipeline Co., an affiliate of the China National Petroleum Co. [CNPC], signed a deal with the Myanmar National Oil and Gas Co. to build two pipelines [Oil and Gas] from the Myanmarese port of Kyaukpyu situated on the West coast of Myanmar to Ruili in Yunan Province of China. From there the pipelines can be extended to feed, besides Yunan, other Southern Chinese provinces of Guangdung, Guangxi and Hunan. The two pipelines are 2,520 kilometres in length and are expected to carry 200,000 bbl/d of crude oil and 420 bcf/y of gas on an annual basis and have recently been completed.[35] Along with the oil and gas pipelines, China has also undertaken to build a rail link from the West coast of Myanmar to the Yunan province of China. It is said that the alignment of this railway line will be the same as of the oil pipeline. With such measures China hopes to minimize the economic impact of disruptions that can occur to its sea-borne energy flows.

Apart from taking measures to free themselves to some extent from the vulnerabilities that face them at present times, the Chinese have also undertaken a programme to strengthen their naval capabilities. The Chinese Navy is fast developing a blue water capability so as to be able to do a power projection in the South China Sea, as also at the Eastern mouth of the Malacca Straits. With the acquisition of an aircraft carrier [Soviet origin Varyag], the Chinese Navy is no longer merely a coastal force capable of defending the Chinese coastline only. China's naval modernization effort encompasses a broad array of weapon acquisitions, including anti-ship ballistic missiles (ASBMs), anti-ship cruise missiles (ASCMs), land-attack cruise missiles (LACMs), surface-to-air missiles, aircraft, submarines, destroyers and frigates, patrol craft, and amphibious ships. In addition, observers believe that China may soon begin (or already has begun) construction of indigenous aircraft carriers. China's naval modernization effort also includes reforms and improvements in maintenance and logistics.

Reports indicate that the PLA Navy possesses some 75 principal surface combat vessels, more than 60 submarines, 55 medium and large amphibious ships, and roughly 85 missile-equipped small vessels. The Navy has now completed construction of a major naval base at Yulin, on the Southern tip of Hainan Island. The base is large enough to accommodate a mix of attack and ballistic missile submarines. China continues to produce a new class of nuclear-powered ballistic missile submarine (SSBN), JIN-class (Type 094) SSBNs will eventually carry the JL-2 submarine-launched ballistic missile with an estimated range of some 7,400 km. The JIN and the JL-2 will give the PLA Navy its first credible sea-based nuclear capability.[36]

A recent study concluded that a 25 percent contraction in oil supplies would mean that China would suffer an annual reduction of 1.2 percent to 1.4 percent of its economic growth rate. Thus, the energy contraction would be a most severe economic setback for China and likely to cause maximum damage.[37]

Another factor that has dampened enthusiasm for a boundary settlement with India has been the rise of nationalism in China. China has utilized and promoted the concept of nationalism in an effort to dampen any attempt at internal dissension or a challenge to the rule of the CCP. This spirit of nationalism has been deliberately fostered and has its origins in modern times in the 4 May, 1919, movement. The link between Chinese nationalism and the question of a boundary settlement with India was raised as early as in 1959 when Zhou alluded to it in his letter to Nehru on 8 September, 1959. Zhou referred to this aspect when he stated that territory South of the McMahon Line that China claimed was a 'piece of territory...as big as 90,000 square kilometers. Mr. Prime Minister *how could China agree to accept under coercion such an illegal line which would have it relinquish its rights and disgrace itself by selling out its territory—and such a large piece of territory as that?'* [Emphasis added][38] The Mao-Zhou leadership was strong and charismatic enough to keep nationalism in China on a tight leash, to use it when required, but also retained sufficient authority to affect a compromise wherever required.

When Deng Xiaoping first started his reform movement in 1978, there was stiff opposition from old CCP hardliners and skepticism within the general Chinese public about the efficacy of these reforms. The Chinese people wondered whether yet another calamity like the 'Cultural Revolution' was about to be inflicted on them. It was Deng who devised the strategy of targeting Japanese 'atrocities' during the Second World War as a means to divert public attention from the economic reforms that he was about to launch. In 1989, a conscious decision was taken by the leadership that pragmatic nationalism would supplement Communist ideology to help keep the people with the CCP and the Chinese state.[39] The identification of the CCP with nationalism would thus make any criticism of the CCP seem 'unpatriotic', particularly after the horrific Tienanmen massacres in 1989. The Chinese leaders deliberately promoted the line that China will never again be subjected to 'humiliation and insult' as it was in the past. In other words, China would not accept 'unequal treaties' imposed by imperial powers in the past. Therefore, how can China sign away any territory, such as 'Southern Tibet'/ Arunachal Pradesh that it so vociferously proclaims as belonging to China? Having hardened its own position by referring to Arunachal Pradesh as 'Southern Tibet', how can the present leadership now agree to part with a slice of Tibet, which would effectively suggest a partition of Tibet between China and India? Having natured the force of nationalism for their internal political purposes, how can the present Chinese leadership, who by no means possess the charisma of a Mao Zedung, barter away Chinese territory? They can do so only at the cost of their own political prestige and at their own peril. The Chinese leadership is aware of the developing fragile nature of the internal situation, made even more acute by the need for economic reforms to sustain growth. Therefore, it is obvious that extreme reluctance exists for them to take any step that their political opponents might accuse them of 'selling out' Chinese territory.

In the early 1980s, when the Chinese leader Deng Xiaoping offered to settle the boundary issue by way of a 'package deal' and when the Chinese interlocutors pressed for a 'package solution' during the first two rounds of the boundary negotiations [1980-81], it was just possible that a boundary settlement might have been negotiated. To be fair, however, the *Chinese never officially put in concrete terms as to what they meant by a 'package deal' and what would be the territorial contours of such a deal* [emphasis added]. It would certainly have meant that India would have to surrender all claims to the Aksai Chin area and it might also have involved some concessions along the McMahon Line, but there was never any clarity offered by the Chinese. But considering the constraints, both internal and external, the Indian leadership was not ready to give-up its position in the Western sector, nor grant any concessions in the Eastern sector. This was made clear by the then Indian Foreign Minister, Narasimha Rao, in Parliament. The reasons why this is so are rather profound and have deep strategic implications for India.

As for Indian apprehensions, at the heart of the matter is *India is not at all sure that a boundary settlement with China will bring it peace and stability all along the border areas and that China will not violate it as and when it finds it necessary to do so* [emphasis added]. Even with a boundary settlement, China will still not lose the option of pushing non-state actors across the new boundary line to aid insurgency in the North East areas of India. Nor will China be inhibited from supplying arms to insurgents across the new line or through Myanmar into Indian Territory. These fears are real and not without foundation, for India has seen China's 'all weather friend' Pakistan do exactly the same across the well-defined, mutually agreed and demarcated on the ground LOC in Jammu and Kashmir. There are sustained reports that Chinese intelligence agencies continue to have regular interaction with insurgent leaders from India's North East and that supply of lethal weapons to insurgent outfits such as ULFA, NSCN, UNFL and PLA of Manipur continues unabated. The supply of arms was confirmed by the Minister of State, Ramachandran, in a written reply to Parliament [Lok Sabha][40] Earlier, this issue of arms supply to insurgents had been brought to the attention of the Chinese during talks at the 'special representatives' meeting on 16-17 January, 2012. To illustrate the point with concrete evidence, the Indian side handed over copies of ULFA Chief, Paresh Barua's air-line travel tickets, period of stay etc. in Yunnan.[41]

India is also aware of the Chinese propensity of taking military action and designating it as 'teaching a lesson.' The Chinese are the originators of this new military thesis and have practiced it, as they themselves claim, against India in 1962 and against Vietnam in 1979. Even if total credence is given to the Chinese claim that its military action in 1962 against India was across undetermined borders, what is to be made of Chinese military action across the Sino-Vietnam border? The 1,272 kilometer long Sino-Vietnam border was basically determined by the 1887 Sino-French Agreement and demarcated on the ground in 1895. The differences that remain are only minor, relating to confusion in the understanding of the language of the Agreement itself and in no case extend beyond 60 square kilometers and about 30 meters near the Friendship Pass. In any case, China has not claimed that it has 'lost' any territory to Vietnam.[42] Thus, if China mounted a military operation across internationally recognized borders in the case of Vietnam, what would prevent it from undertaking similar action against India, even if Sino-Indian borders were to be settled and internationally recognized? India cannot afford to let its guard down and would, therefore, have to continue to maintain sufficient troops all along the boundary and maintain their combat readiness. The question that then arises with Indian policy planners is: after having agreed to a compromise solution, what then is the 'peace dividend'? Does a settled boundary bring any additional or enhanced security that India seeks over the present status quo? If the answer is problematical or cannot be answered in unequivocal terms, then it may be better to maintain the present position.

Any settlement of the Sino-Indian boundary presents two major legal problems to India. The first relates to the issue of Jammu and Kashmir. India claims sovereignty over the whole of Jammu and Kashmir and, therefore, cannot agree to let the boundary along the Pak-occupied Kashmir [POK]-China be set aside. The Chinese refuse to discuss any territorial settlement West of the Karakoram Pass with India [POK-China]. In present times to needle India, the Chinese sometimes also say that the Sino-Indian boundary does not include the portion that falls in Jammu and Kashmir, since the legal status of Kashmir is in 'dispute.'

Secondly, even considering that this legal tangle can be suitably resolved by the use of ambiguous language, the Supreme Court of India has held in the Berubari case that not an inch of Indian Territory can be ceded from the Union without a Constitutional amendment. Considering that any settlement would have to involve a compromise and considering the fractured nature of Indian politics, can any Government, no matter of whatever hue, be confident that it can obtain the necessary votes for a Constitutional amendment?

As Indian policy planners look at the internal situation in China, they are not yet totally convinced that the situation is stable enough for the CCP and its leadership to undertake a major initiative to settle the boundary issue with India at this juncture. Internally, China is still in a combustible state; some scholars even refer to it as 'fragile.'[43] In April 2013, the CCP Central Committee General Office issued '*Document No.9*' to party high level cadres in which it enumerated 'the perils' facing the party and the Government.[44] These 'perils' itemized the dangers and were entirely related to the internal political and economic situation prevailing in China. The most important related to the slowing down of economic growth, corruption, inequality, human rights and the desire for Western style democracy. The fear expressed in *Document No.9* was that the Chinese people might start agitating for a liberal democratic state rather than a Communist state.

China's recent meteoric rise as an economic power-house was largely based on the same model that Japan had followed earlier. Although the time lines are different, China's spectacular growth was export-driven utilizing low-cost labor to drive manufacturing. China opted for under-valuation of its currency to provide Chinese exporters with a distinct competitive advantage. Exports were promoted at the expense of household income and consumption. China encouraged a high domestic savings rate and used these savings to finance investment. China has consistently generated large trade surpluses which are invested overseas, primarily in US Government securities, to avoid upward pressure on its currency. In order to remain competitive, China relies on low cost labor to assemble or manufacture products for export using imported materials. China's attempts at innovation and hi-tech manufacture are still nascent. The problem now is that with the economy of the US growing ever so slowly and those of the EU and Japan largely stagnant, China's main export markets are dwindling with concomitant results for its economy. With a slowdown in the demand for China's exports, it is estimated that this would result in the Chinese economy growing at an annualized rate of only 5 per cent in the second half of this year.[45] China has tried to minimize the effects on its economy by following a credit driven investment strategy, but authorities also admit that this has increased domestic imbalances and resulted in unproductive investments and loan losses of state-owned banks. The reality is that a significant part of China's growth since 2007-08 may just be an illusion. Its headline growth of 8-10 per cent since then has been driven by new lending averaging 30-40 per cent of GDP. Up to 20-25 per cent of these loans may prove to be non-performing, amounting to losses of 6-10 per cent of GDP. If these losses are deducted, Chinese growth is appreciably lower.[46] The rich Chinese seem to be voting with their feet by emigrating out of China. An estimated 14 per cent whose net worth is more than US $ 10 million have already left. Despite restrictions imposed by the Bank of China on capital currency movement, an estimated US$ 3.77 trillion has moved out of China in the last decade.[47]

With economic growth slowing down, the foremost problem that China faces today is internal security. There are thousands of riots every year primarily in the rural areas prompted by land seizures by corrupt officials. There are about 200 million internal migrant workers that are treated as second class citizens as they are denied health care facilities, on par with local residents, and their children often end up in sub-standard schools. This dichotomy of approach has led to glaring 'inequality.' The Gini Co-Efficient for China, the internationally accepted measure of inequality within a country, was between 0.46 and 0.49 in 2007, the highest for any Asian country[48] and could be approaching 0.61.[49] According to the UN, if the Gini Co-Efficient touches 0.44, danger signals on internal stability should start flashing. This inequality is further highlighted by the fact that the richest 10 percent in China own 45 percent of the country's wealth, whereas the poorest 10 percent own only 1.4 percent![50] At the same time, large income disparities exist between urban and rural residents, between regions and in minority areas. This income disparity is a source of widespread discontent and social protest.[51] Therefore, it comes as no surprise that China's budget for internal security [US$ 124 billion] is more than its defence budget [US$ 119 billion].[52] There is no doubt that public cynicism, which is on the increase, erodes popular support for the Chinese Communist Party [CCP].

Another factor that threatens internal stability is the existence of widespread corruption in China. According to Transparency International Index [TNI], of the most corrupt countries in the world, China stands at the 80th position out of 176 countries. It is still slightly better than India which stands at the 94th position.[53] That China has managed to maintain high growth rates despite widespread corruption does not mean that in the future such corruption would not cause considerable economic damage. Although the present leadership has made it a point to fight corruption, there are still many within its fold who feel that stringent action might harm the CCP's prestige. Party officials are loathe to give up power and the resulting discretion that has allowed them to build huge personal properties and massive economic gains for spouses and children.[54]

China's population dividend is also fast disappearing, although presently people aged 60 and above constitute only 15.5 per cent of the total population, yet by 2050, the elderly will be nearly 40 per cent of the total population.[55] Thus, it is becoming an aging society. While its overall population might remain roughly constant due to its one child policy, its working population is expected to drop by 1.5 per cent annually; thus, by 2025, China's working population will only be 56-58 per cent of its overall population, making it one of the oldest populations in the world.[56] That this will have a negative impact on its economic growth is almost inevitable, apart from the difficulty of finding fresh recruits for the PLA. Even if China changes its population policy it will be decades before the effect is felt.

The unprecedented rise of China as an economic power also has had its adverse side-effects. China faces monumental environmental degradation. Today, China is home to 16 of the world's most polluted cities and only 1 per cent of China's estimated 560 million urban dwellers breathe air as per international standards. Nearly 2/3rds of China's cities fail to meet air quality standards set by the Chinese Government themselves, resulting in a plethora of diseases for its citizens. Nearly 70 per cent of China's two major rivers—the Yangtze and the Huang He—are polluted as a result of illegal waste disposable practices.[57] In 2007, China surpassed the US as the largest emitter of green-house gases and also has the dubious distinction of being the world's largest emitter of carbon dioxide. It is estimated that about 25 per cent of China's land area is now a desert.[58]

Much as Chinese policy planners recognize that the only outside power that is able to decisively influence the course of events in the Sino-Indian context is the United States, so do Indian policy planners. While China remains wary of the attitude of the US, the Indian leadership is also not sanguine whether the US will come to its help in the event of a Sino-Indian confrontation. One close look at various facets of the dynamics of the Sino-US relationship would make this dilemma clear. As far as the Sino-Indian border is concerned, the US recognizes the McMahon Line as the international boundary in the Eastern sector, but has no position as far as the Western sector is concerned.

The Sino-US relationship is, indeed, vast and varied. Apart from a high level 'strategic and economic' dialogue at Cabinet level that is held annually, there are 91 other bilateral institutional arrangements where exchanges take place between the two countries. There is a bilateral dialogue on South Asia where all subjects including military and strategic are discussed. No two other countries have any such similar arrangements. The two way trade with the US has risen from US$ 375 billion in 2009 to US$ 600 billion in 2012. Chinese investment has doubled in the US in the last two years. There are at present about 194,000 Chinese students studying in the US, up from 67,000 students in 2008. Conversely, there are over 20,000 US students studying in China. Chinese business and tourist arrivals have risen from 400,000 in 2008 to over 1.5 million at present. It is estimated that by 2017, this figure is likely to reach 4 million or about 10,000 arrivals every day![59] The Chinese President and CCP leader Xi Jinping has been advocating a 'new' relationship with the US by underlining three basic principles. These are [a] No conflict and no confrontation, [b] Mutual respect, and [c] Win-win co-operation which means that each side abandon a zero sum mentality and *accommodate each-others interests as also deepen shared interests* [emphasis added].[60] In other words, what China would dearly wish for is a 'co-equal' partnership with the US. There is no such desire for a similar relationship with any other country in Asia, including India.

What Indian planners discern is that both China and the US are in a tight embrace from which to disentangle would be critically injurious to both. Therefore, will the US come to the aid of India in a confrontation with China is a moot point. In that case, can any serious planning be made on the basis of this premise?

Thus, the Sino-Indian relationship is a very complex issue. There are areas of contention as well as areas of co-operation. The boundary problem is not the only issue; it is not a stand-alone issue, nor a mere technical problem. In finding a solution, both India and China may first have to define the very nature of their world view, particularly as it pertains to Asia and whether there is any meeting point. On many occasions, the Indian PM, Manmohan Singh, has reiterated that there is sufficient space for both to grow, but is China ready to accept a 'co-equal partnership' with India in Asia? Reading from what the Chinese State Councilor, Yang Jiechi, wrote in his thesis entitled, '*Innovations in China's Diplomatic Theory and Practice under New Conditions,*' the Chinese leadership considers itself *on par with the US* and *its policy is to seek an accommodation with the US on that basis.* India is not even mentioned in this article. Therefore, the only conclusion that can be inferred is that *China is not yet ready to accept that India has a co-equal role to play in the affairs of Asia* [emphasis added].

The fact remains that there is continued strategic mistrust between the two countries, with no sign of any approaching convergence. Therefore, China will continue its policy of keeping India strategically confined to South Asia with the active assistance of Pakistan, and strategically imbalanced by continuing incursions across the LAC on the border. In such an event, there is little chance that there will be any meaningful forward movement in the settlement of the boundary dispute between India and China. It is not that 'fair and reasonable' solutions are not available, but for China it is too valuable an instrument of coercive diplomacy to give up. Despite India agreeing to settle the boundary issue in 'a package way,' there are few signs that China is willing to settle the boundary issue unless India completely subscribes to China's world view and agrees to remain within the 'red lines' that China set for it. As that is unlikely to happen, the stalemate, therefore, is likely to continue.

NOTES

Chapter 1

1. Oppenheim, *A Treatise on International Law* (London: Longmans, Green & Co., 1905), pp. 451-52.
2. Sir Thomas Holdich, "Political Boundaries," *Scottish Geographical Magazine*, vol. 32, issue 11 (1916), p. 501.
3. Owen Lattimore, *Inner Asian Frontiers of China* (2nd edn., New York: American Geographical Society, 1951)
4. Lord Curzon, *Frontiers*. "Romanes Lecture" (Oxford: Clarendon Press, 1907). See Also. Alastair Lamb, *Asian Frontiers: Studies in a Continuing Problem* (London: Pall Mall, 1968).
5. Sir Henry McMahon, *Journal of the Royal Society of Arts*, vol. 84 (1935), p. 2.
6. Sir Olaf Caroe, "Geography and Ethics of India's Northern Frontiers," *The Geographical Journal*, vol. 126, No. 3 (September 1960), pp. 298-306.
7. Morris Rossabi, *China and Inner Asia* (London: Thames & Hudson, 1976), p. 20.
8. Carol McGranahan, *Empire and the Status of Tibet: British, Chinese and Tibetan Negotiations 1913-14*, in Alex McKay, ed. The History of Tibet, vol. 3: The Modern Period 1895-1959 (London: Routledge Curzon, 2003), p. 268.
9. Sir Alfred Lyall, *The Rise of British Dominions in India* (London: John Murray, 1893), Chapter 18, p.340.
10. British and Foreign State Papers, 1894-95, pp. 292, 379.
11. Sir Francis Younghusband, *The Heart of the Continent* (London: John Murray, 1896) Reprinted by Scriber, New York.
12. Sir Charles Bell, "North-East Frontier of India," *Journal of the Royal Central Asian Society*, vol.17, Issue 2 (1930), pp. 221-225.
13. The Lytton Papers, No. LyP/518/4, p. 1013.

Chapter 2

1. Jawaharlal Nehru, *The Selected Works of Jawaharlal Nehru* [SWJN], (New Delhi: JLN Memorial Fund], vol. 25, p. 429.
2. British Foreign Office Tel No. 371-84457, quoting Nehru speaking to Indian Army Officers in Srinagar.
3. Sir Charles Bell, *Tibet, Past and Present* (London: Clarendon Press, 1927), p. 111.
4. Letters to Chief Ministers, 1947-64, vol. V (1958-64), pp. 228-29.
5. FRUS 1943 (China), p. 626. British Embassy, Washington Aide Memoire No. 893.24/1594 dated 19 April 1943 to the US Department of State.
6. C. Brandt, B. Schwartz, J.K. Fairbank, *A Documentary History of Chinese Communism* (Cambridge, Massachusetts: Harvard University Press, 1952), p. 64.
7. Edgar Snow, *Red Star over China* (New York: Random House, 1938), p. 444.
8. M Taylor Fravel, *Strong Borders Secure Nation: Co-operation and Conflict in China's Historical*

Disputes (Princeton: Princeton University Press, 2008), p.72. See also Ni Fuhan, Huang Ke. *The Peaceful Liberation of Tibet/Heping Jiefang Xizang (Lasa: Xizang renmin chubanshe, 1995)*, p.47.

9. Note Verbal from the Foreign Ministry of the People's Republic of China to the Government of India, dated 10 November 1950.
10. P. Mehra, *Tibet* (Delhi: Oxford University Press, 2011), p. 244.
11. Younghusband Collection, MSS EUR/F-197/105,44. [Statement of Tashi Lama to Bogle].
12. Melvyn Goldstein, *History of Modern Tibet 1913-1951: The Demise of the Lamaist State* (University of California Press, 1989), p.2.
13. Van Walt van Praag, *The Status of Tibet* (Boulder Colorado: Westview, 1987), p. 107.
14. FRUS 1949, vol. IX, p. 1065. US Department of State. (Bureau of Far Eastern Affairs, Memo No. 693.0031 Tibet/1-849 dated 12 April 1949 from Ms. Ruth Bacon to Chief of Division, Chinese Affairs).
15. Satow to Lansdowne Memo No. FO 535/5, Enclosure 4, No. 95, dated 17 November 1904 [Conversation between Sir Ernest Satow and Prince C'hing].
16. India Office Records [IOR]: L/P&S/10/265, 1912.
17. Sir Charles Bell, *Tibet, Past and Present* (London: Clarendon Press, 1927), p.247.
18. Premen Addy, *Tibet on the Imperial Chessboard: The Making of British Policy towards Lhasa 1899-1925* (New Delhi: Academic Publishers, 1984), p. 91. [L/PS/7/151 No.182. Curzon to Hamilton].
19. Ibid., p. 130.
20. Secretary of State for India, Brodrick letter dated 5 August 1904 to Lord Ampthill, Acting Viceroy.
21. Hardinge Papers, *Memo by Lord Hardinge, Viceroy of India*, dated 1 February 1911.
22. Van Walt Van Praag, *The Status of Tibet* (Boulder, Colorado: Westview Press, 1987), p. 64.
23. Sir Olaf Caroe, Deputy Secretary, Foreign Department, government of India Memo No. Pz 2785/36 dated 9 April 1936 to Walton, India Office, London.
24. HMG, Memo No. F493-X dated 17 August 1937.
25. Public Record Office (London: India Office to Foreign Office, FO 371/20964 dated 21 June 1937)
26. FRUS 1943 (China), p. 626. British Embassy, Washington Aide Memoire to US Department of State No. 803.24/1594 dated 19 April 1943.
27. Van Walt van Praag, op. cit., p. 79.
28. Public Record Office [PRO], *Jordan Papers* (Jordan to Langley, 13 November 1913).
29. Proceedings House of Lords 1840, appendix 1.
30. Michael Greensburg, British Trade and the Opening of China (Cambridge University, 1951)
31. Gregory Blue, "Opium for China," in Timothy Brook, Bob Tadashi Wakabayashi (ed.) *The Opium Regimes: China, Britain and Japan 1839-1952* (Berkeley: University of California Press, 2000), p. 31
32. British Foreign Office [FCO]. FO 371/35 755 dated 7 May 1943.
33. FRUS 1949, vol. IX, p. 1065. US Embassy, London Tel. No. 1841 dated 26 August 1947 to US Department of State, Washington.
34. Tsering Sakya, *The Dragon in the Land of Snows* (London: Pimlico, 1999), p.55.
35. Statement of Foreign Secretary David Miliband, 25 October 2008.
36. Cold War International History Project [CWIHP] 1995-96. On Mao's visit to Soviet Union, 1949-50.
37. Ibid.
38. FRUS 1951 [China & Korea, part-II], p.1683. Secretary of State to US Ambassador, Delhi Top Secret Tel. of 2 June 1951.

39. Alexandre I Andreyev, *Soviet Russia and Tibet* (Brill's Tibetan Studies Library, vol. IV, 2003), p. 390.
40. FRUS 1901, Affairs in China (1901), p.12. US Secretary of State Hay letter to European Powers dated 3 July 1900.
41. Public Record Office [PRO] File No. FO 535, vol. XII, Letter from US Commissioner to China, Rockhill to President Roosevelt dated 8November 1908. See also Jonathan Mirsky, 'Tibet: The CIA's Cancelled War' (China File/Asia Society, 9 April 2013).
42. FRUS China (1943), p. 630. Department of State Memo No. 893.24/1594 dated 15 May 1943 to British Embassy, Washington.
43. FRUS 1942 (China), p. 625.
44. FRUS 1943 (China), p. 629. Memo from Assistant Secretary of State, Berle to the Director of the Office of Strategic Services [Donovan].
45. FRUS 1943 (China), p.630.
46. US Department of State File No. 793.94/570.
47. FRUS 1945, vol. VII, p.770. Memo from President Truman to Gen. Marshall.
48. CWIHP/Diary of NV Roschin, Top Secret, Copy No. 4, 1 December 1949/Conversation with Zhou Enlai]
49. FRUS 1950, vol. 1, p. 388. National Security Policy; Foreign Economic Policy (Top Secret Report of the National Security Council, dated 25 August 1950).
50. FRUS 1949, vol. IX, p. 1065. Memo by Ms. Ruth Bacon of the Office of Far Eastern Affairs to the Chief of the Division of Chinese Affairs (Sprouse) dated 12 April 1949.
51. FRUS 1949, vol. IX, p.1071. US Ambassador to India, Henderson to Department of State, Washington Tel. No. 302 dated 12 April 1949.
52. John Knaus, *Orphans of the Cold War: America and the Tibetan Struggle for Survival* (New York: Public Affairs, 1999)
53. FRUS 1951, vol. VII, p. 1696. US Ambassador, Delhi to Secretary of State, Washington.
54. FRUS 1951, vol. VII, p. 1748. US Secretary of State to US Ambassador, Delhi Tel. No. 107 dated 12 July 1951 [US Archives:793B.00/7-1251]
55. FRUS 1958 60 [China], vol. XIX, p. 790. Secretary of State Herter to US Ambassador to India.
56. Department of State, Central Files: 793B.00/2-2060. Text of letter printed in Department of State Bulletin 21 March 1960, pp. 443-444.
57. Department of State to US Ambassador, Delhi Tel. No. 54905 dated 14 April 1970.
58. Nehru in *Foreign Affairs Record*, August 1958, p.145.

Chapter 3

1. Goldstein, *A History of Modern Tibet: The Demise of the Lamaist State 1913-51* (Berkeley: University of California Press), p. 31. See also Ji Youquan, *Bai Xue: jiefang Xizang jishi/ White Snow: A Factual Record of the Liberation of Tibet* (Beijing: Zhongguo wuzi, 1993), p.31.
2. Tsering Sakya, *Dragon in the Land of Snows: A History of Modern Tibet since 1947* (New York: Columbia University Press, 1999), p. 45. See also Zhang Guohua's account in Survey of China Mainland Press [SCMP] No. 2854 of 6 November 1962, p. 6.
3. National Archives [UK] British Foreign Office File No. 371-76314, Code 94, No. 1016. See also Tsering Shakya. op. cit., p.25.
4. FRUS 1950, vol. VI, p. 365. US Ambassador to London, Douglas to Secretary of State Tel. No. 3480 dated 20 June 1950.
5. FRUS (1950), Vol. 6, p. 613.
6. Panikkar, *In Two Chinas: Memoires of a Diplomat* (London: Allen & Unwin 1956), p102.

7. John Lall, Aksai Chin and the Sino-Indian Conflict (Delhi: Allied Publishers Pvt. Ltd., 1989), p.233.
8. Soviet newspaper *The New Times* No.47 [1950], p. 21
9. Memo No. F-2-1022 dated 15 December 1950. Sir E Dening to Sir W Strang.
10. FRUS 1950, vol. VI [East Asia and the Pacific], p. 185. Memo of Conversation between Sir E Dening and US Ambassador to Thailand, Stanton.
11. Selected Works of Jawaharlal Nehru [SWJN]—Series II, vol. 15(2), p. 444. Nehru to Panikkar Tel. of 25 October 1950.
12. Amiya and BG Rao, *Six Thousand Days: Nehru, Prime Minister* (Delhi: Sterling Publishers 1974), pp. 98-99.
13. *Pioneer*, 31 October 1950.
14. Jiang Siye, Li Hui, *A History of the Counter Attack War in Self-Defence along the Sino-Indian Border* [*HCAWSDSIB*] (Beijing: Military Science Publication), Chapter 2, Section1. [Original in Chinese].
15. Goldstein, op. cit., p. 708. FCO File No. FO 371/84454.
16. FRUS 1950, vol. VI [China], p.578. US Ambassador Henderson to Secretary of State [20 November 1950].
17. Goldstein, op. cit., p. 729. Instructions were read out by Bajpai, MEA Secretary General to British High Commissioner who then conveyed them to London. FCO No. 371-84455 refers. See also Tsering Sakya. op. cit., p.59; as also SWJN—Second Series, vol. 15(2).
18. FRUS 1951, vol. VII, p. 1528. US Embassy, London to Secretary of State, Washington Tel. No. 3803 dated 9 January 1951.
19. Goldstein, op. cit., p. 718. Tel. dated 14 November 1950 from Sir Gladwyn Jebb to Foreign Office, London inFCO File No. 371-84454.
20. FCO to UK High Commissioner, Delhi Tel. No.2538 dated 10 November 1950 in FCO File No. 371/84454.
21. Goldstein, op. cit., p. 734. Minute by RH Scott, FCO No. 371-84455 dated 28 November 1950.
22. Goldstein, op. cit., p. 718.
23. FRUS 1950, vol. VI, p. 603. US Ambassador, Delhi to Secretary of State, Washington. Letter No. 793B.00/12-1850 dated 18 December 1950.
24. FRUS 1951, vol. VII, p. 1529.
25. Sardar Patel Correspondence 1945-50. Edited by Durga Das (Ahmedabad: Navjivan Publishing House, 1974), vol. X, p.335. Nehru's reply of 18 November 1950 at p. 341.
26. Transfer of Power 1942-47: The Mountbatten Viceroyalty, India Office Records, p. 156. Top Secret Letter No. F.7-NEF/46 dated 8 April 1947 [Fry to Hopkinson].
27. CS Jha, *From Bandung to Tashkent: Glimpses of India's Foreign Policy* (Delhi: Sangam Books, 1983), p. 44.
28. SWJN-Second Series. vol.15 [2]. Note dated 18 November 1950, pp.342-47.
29. Michael Brecher, *Nehru: A Political Biography* (Boston: Beacon Press, 1962), p.590.
30. Speech by Nehru in Parliament on 17 March 1950.
31. Nehru's Letter to B Shive Rao MP dated 23 June 1953.
32. Judith Brown, *Nehru: A Political Life* (Delhi: Oxford University Press, 2003), p. 317.
33. Nehru, *A Bunch of Old Letters* (Bombay: Asia Publishing House, 1958), pp. 385-86. Mao's letter to Nehru dated 24 May 1939.
34. Joan Robinson, "The Chinese Point of View," *Journal of International Affairs* [40] April, pp. 232-244.
35. McGhee, *On the Frontline in the Cold War* (Westport, Connecticut: Praeger Publishers, 1997), p. 52.
36. FRUS 1949, vol. VI, pp. 1750-52. Memo of Conversation between Nehru and Truman.

37. Richardson, *Tibet and its History* (London: Oxford University Press, 1962), p. 173.
38. British CDA Beijing to FO, London letter No. FT 1068/3 dated 23 March 1950.
39. FRUS 1950 (East Asia and the Pacific), vol. VI, p.613 Henderson to Eliot Weil, Tel. No. 795.00/12-3050 dated 30 December 1950.
40. The Truman Library/George M Elsey papers.
41. FRUS 1949 (China-Part-II), vol. IX, p. 1097. Henderson to Secretary of State Tel No. 893.00/12-3049 dated 30 December 1949.
42. Edwin Martin, *Divided Counsel: Anglo-American Response to the Victory of the Communists in China* (University Press of Kentucky, 1986), pp.119. See also The Truman Library: The George Elsey Papers.
43. BN Mallik, *My Years with Nehru: The Chinese Betrayal* (Delhi: Allied Publishers Pvt. Ltd., 1971), p. 80.
44. Roby Barret, *The Greater Middle-East and the Cold War: US Policy under Eisenhower and Kennedy* (IB Taurus &Co. Ltd., 2007), p.279.
45. FRUS 1949, vol. IX, p. 1086. US Ambassador to India, Henderson to Secretary of State Tel. No. 893.00/12-149 Tibet dated 1 December 1949.
46. FRUS 1950, vol. V, p.1445.
47. FRUS 1949, vol. IX, p. 1091. US Embassy, London to Department of State Tel. No. 4903 dated 12 December 1949.
48. Goldstein, op. cit., p.136. Memo from RM Belcher to DD Kennedy No. 793B.00/6-255 dated 18 June 1951.
49. Foreign Office, London. Internal Memo to Sir E. Dening dated 2 August 1950.
50. John Knaus, *Orphans of the Cold War: America and the Tibetan Struggle for Survival* (New York: Public Affairs, 1999), p.53.
51. British Foreign Office Internal Memo, dated 23 October 1950. R Scott to Sir Sterndale-Bennet.
52. Goldstein, op. cit., p. 620. National Archives, Kew, File No. 371-84465, Code FT File 1192.
53. Goldstein, op. cit., p. 756. FCO File No. 371/93002 contains note sent by British Official on meeting with US Embassy Official.
54. Nehru to MEA Secretary-General. Note dated 9 July 1949.
55. British High Commissioner, Delhi to Secretary of State for Commonwealth Relations, Philip Noel-Baker letter No. F943/1015/10 dated 15 January 1949.
56. Escott Reid, *Envoy to Nehru* (Delhi &Toronto: Oxford University Press, 1981), p.55.
57. Apa Pant, *Mandala: An Awakening* (Delhi & Calcutta: Orient Longmans, 1978).
58. McGhee Papers, The Truman Library. Memo of Conversation between Nehru and McGhee on 14 March 1951.
59. Panikkar's Tel. to Nehru dated 6 January 1950 and to Foreign Secretary Menon dated 20 February 1950.
60. Tsering Sakya, op. cit., p 90.
61. Richardson, op. cit., p 189.
62. British Foreign Office. Internal Memo by P. Scott No. FT/10310/29 dated 31 May 1951.
63. Letter to Chief Ministers dated 25 March 1959 (vol. 5, 1958-1964), p228.
64. FRUS 1951, vol. VII, p. 1529. US Ambassador Henderson to Secretary of State Tel. of 25 January 1951.
65. FRUS 1950, vol. VI, p. 603. US Ambassador Henderson to Secretary of State Tel. of 18 December 1950.
66. Apa Pant, op. cit., p 116.
67. NR Pillai, "Middle Ground Between America and Russia: An Indian View," *Foreign Affairs*, January 1954.

68. SWJN-SS, vol. 15 (pt-2), p 348.
69. White Paper III, p.93.
70. BN Mallik, op. cit., pp. 179-80.
71. Lorne J. Kavic, *India's Quest for Security* (Berkeley: University of California Press, 1967), p. 95.
72. SS Khera, *India's Defence Problems* (Bombay: Orient Longmans, 1968).
73. Yang Yizhang, Dangdai Zhongguo (Beijing: Congshu Bianji Bu, 1991), pp. 202-209.
74. SWJN-SS, vol. 18, p.471.
75. John Lall, op. cit., p.236.
76. Note by S Dutt to Nehru. The S Dutt Papers, Jawaharlal Nehru Memorial Library [JNML].
77. Panikkar, op. cit., p. 175.
78. S Dutt, op. cit., p. 87.
79. Richardson, op. cit., p. 196
80. SWJN-SS, vol. 18, Tel. No. 212 dated 17 June 1952.
81. SWJN-SS, vol. 18, Tel. of 18 June 1952. Nehru to Panikkar.
82. SWJN-SS, vol. 16(2), p. 643. Tel. No. 327 of 28 September 1951. Panikkar to Nehru.
83. Escott Reid. op. cit., p. 34.
84. Ibid., p 95.
85. Panikkar, "The Defence of India and Indo-British Obligations," *International Affairs*, vol. 2 (January 1946), pp 85-96.
86. FRUS 1951, vol. VI (pt-2), p. 2188. US Ambassador, Chester Bowles reporting to State Department on conversations with Nehru.
87. S Gopal, *Nehru* (Harvard University Press, 1984), p.278.
88. BK Nehru, *Nice Guys Finish Second* (India: Viking, 1997), p. 381.
89. BM Kaul, *The Untold Story* (Delhi: Allied Publishers Pvt. Ltd., 1967), p. 209.
90. Nehru's note to CD Deshmukh dated 26 January 1952.
91. Crocker, *Nehru: A Contemporary's Estimate* (New York: Random House, 1966), p156.
92. Sir Paul Gore-Booth, *With Great Truth and Respect* (London: Constable, 1974), p.295.
93. McGarr, *The Cold War in South Asia; Britain, the US and the Indian Sub-Continent 1945-65* (Cambridge: Cambridge University Press, 2013), p. 162. Sir Paul Gore-Booth to Saville Garner on 15 December 1962., DO196/209.
94. FRUS 1961-62. Vol XIX, Document No. 164. US Ambassador Galbraith to Kennedy dated 6 August 1962.
95. Dwight D Eisenhower, *The Eisenhower Diaries* (New York: WW Norton & Co. 1981), p.300.
96. Zins, Boquerat, *India in the Mirror of Foreign Diplomatic Archives* (Delhi: Manohar, 2004), p. 108. British High Commissioner, Delhi to CRO London, No. FY 1192/102 of December 1953.
97. Ibid., p. 108. No. F16460/6/65 dated 13 November 1948.
98. BM Kaul, op. cit. p209.
99. FRUS 1952-54. vol. IX (Pt-2), Africa and South Asia, p 1720.
100. FRUS 1952-54, vol. XI, p. 1701. US Ambassador Allen to Secretary of State Tel. No. 493.919/7-2853.
101. FRUS 1952-54. vol. IX, pp. 119-21. Africa and South Asia
102. Dennis Kux, *India and the United States: Estranged Democracies 1941-91* (Washington: National Defense University Press, 1992), p. 107.
103. Galbraith, *A Life of our Times* (New York: Random House, 1982), p.403.
104. Dennis Kux, op. cit., p 106
105. Cold War History, Vol. 11, Issue 2/2011, Cold War Cooperation: Chinese Foreign Ministry Files. FMPRC File No. 204-00007-15(1). Memcon: Mao-Nehru Second Talk, 23 October 1954.

106. FRUS 1952-54. vol. IX (Pt-I), pp. 131-34. Memo Dulles-Ayub talks.
107. Richard Aldrich, Michael Coleman, *Britain and the Strategic Air Offensive against the Soviet Union: The Question of Air Bases in South Asia 1945-49* (History No.242, vol. 74, 1989), pp. 400-26.
108. *New York Times* [NYT], 5 November 1953.
109. Sir Anthony Eden, *The Full Circle* (London: Houghton Mifflin, 1960), p.9.
110. W. Barnds, India, Pakistan and the Great Powers (New York: Praeger,1972), pp. 100-102.
111. Nehru speaking in the Lok Sabha, 22 February 1954.
112. Robert McMahon, *The Cold War in the Periphery* (New York: Columbia University Press, 1994), p 339.
113. Chinese Foreign Ministry File No. 204-00007-15(1). Memcon: Zhou-Nehru Second Talk, October 1954.
114. Robert McMahon, op. cit., p.190.
115. Dana Schmidt, "Pakistan to get Arms," *New York Times*, 14 February 1954.
116. Robert McMahon, op. cit.
117. Ibid, p. 207.
118. Stephen Cohen, *India: Emerging Power* (Washington: Brookings Institute, 2001), pp. 39-40.
119. Chinese Foreign Ministry File no 204-00007-15(1). Memcon: Zhou-Nehru Second Talk October 1954.
120. FRUS 1951 vol. VI, p. 217. CIA Memo 1951.
121. Sardar Patel Correspondence, vol. X, p. 334. (Navjivan Publishing House, 1974).
122. FMPRC File no.204-00007-15(1). Memcon Zhou-Nehru Second Talk October 1954.
123. Liu Xuecheng, *Sino-Indian Border dispute and Sino-Indian Relations* (Lanham, Maryland: University Press of America, 1994).
124. British High Commissioner, Delhi to CRO London. Top Secret Letter of 12 May 1951.
125. *Selected Works of Mao Zedung* [SWMZ]: *On Diplomacy*, p. 134.
126. Ibid., pp. 126-135.
127. S Dutt, op. cit., p. 83.
128. Liu Xuecheng, op. cit.
129. SWJN-SS, vol. 25, p. 467.
130. Richardson, op. cit., p. 197.
131. HCAWSDSIB, Chapter2,Section 1.
132. Tsering Sakya, op. cit., p.118.
133. TN Kaul, *A Diplomat's Diary* (Delhi: MacMillan, 2000), p.197.
134. Goldstein, op. cit., p.471.
135. Breacher, *India and World Politics* (Westport, Connecticut: Praeger,1968), p.140.
136. Nehru speaking in the Lok Sabha on 10 May 1954.
137. Richardson, op. cit., p.174.
138. S Dutt, op. cit., pp. 87-90.
139. Srinath Raghavan, *War and Peace in Modern India* (Ranikhet: Permanent Black, 2010), p. 241. File No. 371-110647.
140. SWJN, vol. 25, p. 420.
141. Letters to Chief Ministers dated 1 July 1954.
142. Foreign Affairs Reports, October 1954, p. 126.
143. TN Kaul, op. cit., p. 64.
144. Cold War History, op. cit., 20 October 1954.
145. White Paper VI.
146. White Paper VI, p. 96.
147. Ibid., p.99.

148. PM Zhou Enlai at a Press Conference at Calcutta on 9 December 1956.
149. Department of State, Intelligence Report dated 25 February 1957.
150. Crocker, op. cit., p. 99.

Chapter 4

1. SWJN-SS, vol. 26, p. 477.
2. Liu Peihua, *A Short History of Modern China* (Beijing: 1954).
3. S S Khera, op. cit., p. 157.
4. Goldstein, op. cit., p.74.
5. SWJN-SS, vol. 26, pp. 481-84.
6. R. Guha, *J Nehru and China: A Study in Failure?* Harvard-Yenching Institute Working Paper Series.
7. Ya Nanze, "Gandi furen zishu," [My Truth] (Beijing: Contemporary Publishers,1985), p. 72, quoted in Tan Chung, Across the Himalayan Gap: An Indian Quest for Understanding China (Delhi: Indira Gandhi National Centre for Arts), p. 409.
8. Writings of Mao Zedung 1949-76. Mao's Tel. to CPI leader Ranadive on 19 November 1949 quoted by People's Daily of 20 November 1949.
9. Brecher, op. cit., p.141.
10. Letters to Chief Ministers 1947-64, vol. IV, p.82.
11. *Cold War History*, vol. 11, issue 2/2011. Cold War Co-operation. New Chinese Evidence on Nehru's 1954 visit to Beijing. Memcon Zhou-Nehru Second talk, 11-15/FMPRC 204-00007-05, 20 October 1954.
12. Appadorai, *India in World Affairs* (Delhi: Sterling Publishers, 1975), p. 230.
13. Proceedings of Lok Sabha, 2 March 1955/Part 1, vol.1, No. 7, Col 381.
14. CS Jha, op. cit., p. 83.
15. Breacher, op. cit., p. 141.
16. Escott Reid, op. cit., p. 60.
17. MEA File No. E12 (109), NGO 56 and E12 1132/NGO/59.
18. S Gopal, *Nehru: A Biography* [vol.3] op. cit., p. 35.
19. J Lall, op. cit., p. 244.
20. S Gopal, op. cit. , p. 35.
21. Apa Pant, op. cit. , p. 71.
22. Dawa Norbu, *China's Tibet Policy* (Richmond: Curzon, 2001), p. 230
23. White Paper I, p.1.
24. WP I, p.3
25. WP I, p. 6
26. Lt-Gen Baljit Singh, "Face to Face with the PLA," *India Defence Review*, 22 September 2012.
27. S Dutt, op. cit. , p.115.
28. *Times of India*, Kalimpong, 9 April 1953.
29. S Dutt papers, JNML [Dalai Lama to Foreign Secretary].
30. Li Peisheng, Li Guozhen. *Pingxi Xizang Panluan* [*Suppressing the Tibetan Revolt*] (Lasa: Xizang renmin chuban she, internal circulation, 1995), p17. See also M Taylor Fravel. *Strong Borders, Secure Nation: Co-operation and Conflict in China's Territorial Disputes*(New Jersey: Princeton University Press, 2008), p. 75.
31. Report of the International Commission of Jurists, 8 August 1960.
32. Record of Talks between Nehru and Zhou at Sutlej Sadan, Nangal and on train from Nangal to Delhi on 31 December 1956 and 1 January 1957. MEA file No. E12(109)NGO 56 and E121132 NGO 1959 at SWJN-SS, vol. 36.

33. Richardson, op. cit., p. 203.
34. Apa Pant letter to MEA dated 31 December 1956.
35. HCAWSDSIB, op. cit., Chapter 2, Section1(F).
36. Wilson, *Zhou—A Biography* (Viking,1984), p.210.
37. Nehru Notes, Charitang, 28 September 1958. [JNML]
38. The Johnson Library, National Security File pertaining to the 303 Committee.
39. Dawa Norbu, China's Tibet Policy (Richmind Survey: Curzon Press, 2001), p. 268]
40. Crocker, op. cit., p. 107.
41. Jagat Mehta, *Negotiating for India: 1958-78* (Delhi: Manohar, 2006), pp. 59-60.
42. Escott Reid, op. cit., p. 60.
43. S Gopal, op. cit., p. 33
44. Foreign Secretary to Nehru, note dated 13 November 1959.
45. Nehru Speeches, 1957-63, p. 206.
46. FRUS 1961-63, vol. XXII, pp. 365-367. Problems and Prospects of Communist China. US National Intelligence Estimate No. NIE 13-63 dated 1 May 1963.
47. Galbraith, op. cit., p. 412.
48. Mao to Kissinger, Beijing 27 November 1973.
49. MacFarquar, *Origins of the Cultural Revolution* (Oxford University Press, 1997), vol.1.
50. Dr Li Zhisui, *The Private Life of Chairman Mao* (New York: Random House, 2011), p. 306.
51. Yao Shujie, "A Note on China's Famine in 1959-61," *Journal of Political Economy.*
52. Frank Dikotter, *Mao's Great Famine: The Final Tally* (London: Bloomburg,2010)
53. CIA/ Special National Intelligence Estimate No. 13-61 dated 4 April 1961 on Economic Situation in China.
54. Marshall Green, Report of the US Consulate-General, Hong Kong.
55. World Bank, World Development Indicators.
56. Embassy of India, Beijing DO Letter No. 1-CS(2)/57 dated 21 May 1959. [Available at JNML]
57. MacFarquar, op. cit., p 297.
58. British Foreign Office [Northern Department] Note No. NS 1033345/105 dated 6 October 1959.
59. Lorenz Luthi. *The Sino-Soviet Split: Cold War in the Communist World* (Princeton University Press, 2008)
60. The Cambridge History of China.
61. Pravda, 20 July 1958.
62. Foreign Exchange Reserves had gone down to Rs. 544 crores. After allowing a minimum of reserves at Rs 400 crores and Rs 40 crores as minimum working balance, the Reserve Bank was left with Rs 100 crores only. Of these there was a commitment to pay Rs 91 crores for Rourkela plant. Thus only Rs 10 crores was left. [Letters to Chief Ministers: 1947-57, vol. IV, p. 469.]
63. Letters to Chief Ministers: 1954-57, vol. IV, p. 468.
64. FRUS 1955-57 [South Asia], vol. VIII, Document 5. National Security Document No. 5701 of 10 January, 1957.
65. Dennis Kux, *Estranged Democracies 1941-91* (Diane Publishing, 1992), p.150.
66. Frankel, *India's Political Economy 1947-77: The Gradual Revolution* (Delhi: Oxford University Press, 1978)
67. Kennedy, The Strategy for Peace (Popular Library, 1961), p. 143.
68. Nehru Tel. to Krishna Menon dated 18 September 1957.
69. Wilson, op. cit., p.224
70. Zagoria, *Sino-Soviet Conflict: 1956-61* (Oxford, 1962), p. 280.

71. Allen Dulles [CIA Director]. 418th Meeting of the National Security Council on 10 September 1959. Eisenhower Library/Whitman File.
72. Khrushchev *Remembers—The Last Testament* (Boston: Little, Brown 1974), p 311.
73. Wilson, op. cit., p.210.
74. Richardson, op. cit., p. 206.
75. Foreign Secretary to Consul-General, Lhasa Tel. of 19 March 1959.
76. S Dutt. op. cit., p.150.
77. John Garver, *Sino -American Alliance: Nationalist China and American Cold War Strategy*(East Gate Book, 1999), p.175.
78. Crocker, op. cit., p.106.
79. Xizang Xingshi Wenwu Jiaoyu di Jiben Jiaocai (Lasa: 1960). Political Department of the Tibetan Military District, 1960. Quoted in "The Tibetan Distance Movement and the Role of the CIA" by J Narbu (Ed.) Robert Burnet, p. 186.
80. Xiaoyuan Liu, *Recast all Under Heaven: Revolution, War, Diplomacy and Frontier China in 20th Century* (New York: The Continuum International Publishing Group, 2010), p. 220. See also *Pingxi Xizang Panluan,* p. 99
81. SWJN-SS, vol. 47, p. 479. Rajendra Prasad to Nehru, 29 March and 1 April 1959 and Nehru's replies 30 March and 2 April 1959.
82. Government of Pakistan Handout No. E 2741 dated 27 May 1960.
83. GAOR, Session 14, Plenary Meeting 832, 20 October 1959, p. 483.
84. Survey of China Mainland Press [SCMP] No. 2005, dated 4 May 1959, p. 34.
85. *Peking Review* [28 July 1959], vol. 2, pp. 22-23.
86. AS Bhasin, *India-Pak Relations* (Delhi: Geetika Publications, 2013), vol. II, p. 743.
87. *Peking Review,* op. cit., pp. 18-19.
88. Ibid., p.10.
89. SWJN-SS, vol. 49, p. 545.
90. B N Mullik, op. cit., p. 621.
91. S Dutt, op. cit., p. 94.
92. L Rushbrook Williams, The State of Pakistan (London: Faber & Faber,1955/1962),
93. FMPRC, op. cit. Memcon Zhou-Nehru Second Talk.
94. F Grare. *Pakistan in the Face of in the Afghan Conflict: 1979-85* (India Research Press, 2003), p. 32.
95. FRUS, 1958-59. vol. XIX, p. 588.
96. Zhao Weiwen, *Yin-Zhong guanxi fenglun yu, 1949-99/Record of the Vicissitudes of India-China Relations, 1949-99* (Beijing: Shi shichubanshe, 2000), pp.124-129. See also Yang Gongsu. *Xin Zhongguo Duiwai Zhangce/New China Foreign Policies(unpublished manuscript)*, pp.68-69.
97. 403rd Meeting of the National Security Council on 23 April 1959.
98. Liu Wusheng, Du Hongqi, eds, *Zhou Enlai Junshi Huodong Jishi, 1918-75/Chronicle of Zhu Enlai's Military Activities* (Beijing: Zhongyang Wenxian Chubanshe, 2000), vol. 2, p. 497.
99. Zhou Enlai, *Wenjiao wenxian/Zhou Enlai's Diplomatic Papers* (Beijing: Zhongyang wenxian,1990), p.282.
100. S Gopal. op. cit., vol. III, p.362. Tel from Ambassador Parthasarthy to Foreign Secretary dated 21 March 1959.
101. Wu Lengxi, *Yi Mao Zhuxi/Remembering Chairman Mao* (Beijing: Xinhua,1995), p.282.
102. Jagat Mehta, op. cit., p.65
103. White Paper I, p.76.
104. Cold War History, op. cit., Mao-Nehru talks, 23 October 1954.
105. SWJN-SS, vol. 49, p. 323. Nehru to Apa Pant Letter of 23 May 1959.
106. White Paper [WP]1, p. 77.

107. HCAWSDSIB, Chapter 2, Section(1)G.
108. Natwar Singh, *My China Diary* (Delhi: Rupa, 2009), p.102.
109. Zhou Enlai, op. cit., pp. 268-76. See also Garver. *Protracted Contest: Sino-Indian Rivalry in the 20th Century* (Seattle: University of Washington), pp. 61-62.
110. HCAWSDSIB, Chapter 2,Section 1.
111. WP 2, p. 53.
112. Report of the Officials of the government of India and the People's Republic of China on the Boundary Question [New Delhi: Government of India, Ministry of External Affairs, 1961], p. 273.
113. FRUS 1958-60. vol. XIX. 418 Meeting of the National Security Council.
114. Wu Lengxi, *Shinian Lunzhan: Zhong-Su guanxi huiyilu, 1956-66* (Beijing: Zhongyang Wenxian 1999), p. 212.
115. Watson, *Frontiers of China* (New York: Praeger, 1966), p. 119.
116. Alexis Brezhnev, *Kitai* [*China*] (Moscova: Mezhdunarodyne Otnosheniye, 1998), p.70.
117. Vladislav Zubok, *Khrushchev-Mao Conversations* (CWIHP: Issue No. 12/13 Fall/Winter, 2001), pp. 262-270.
118. Borisov, Koloskov, Roberts, *Soviet Union in World Politics* (CWIHP), p. 95. See also Wu Lengxi. op. cit. ,pp 208-217.
119. "Sugong lingdao tong women fenqi de youlai yu fazhan"/The Origins and Development of Differences between the Soviet leadership and us (Beijing: RenminChubanshe, 1965), p. 71.
120. Whiting, *The Chinese Calculus of Deterrence* (University of Michigan Press, 1975), p. 73.
121. Liu Xiao, *Chu Shi Sulian Ba Nian/Eight Years as Ambassador to Soviet Union* (Beijing: Zhonggong dangshi ziliao chubanshe, 1986).
122. CWIHP, Conversation of Khrushchev with Mao Zedung on 2 October 1959 at Beijing. Document No 3, Archive of the President of the Russian Federation, f.52, op.1, d.499, II. 1-33. Copy in Volkogonov Collection, Manuscript Division, Library of Congress, Washington. Translated by VladislavZubok.
123. HCAWSDSIB, Chapter 2, Section 1.
124. WP III, p.5.
125. S Dutt, op. cit., p. 137.
126. HCAWSDSIB, Chapter 3, Section 1.
127. Lt-Gen SPP Thorat, From Reveille to Retreat (Delhi: Allied Publishers Pvt. Ltd., 1986)
128. Zins, Boquerat, op. cit., p.111. British High Commissioner, Delhi to Foreign Office, London Letter No. FC 1091/45 dated 13 July 1960.
129. Ibid., p. 111. British High Commissioner, Delhi to Foreign Office, London Letter No. FC 1091/53 dated 21 October 1959.
130. FRUS 1958-60, vol. XIX, p.780.
131. Crocker, op. cit., p 100.
132. Wu Lengxi, op. cit., p. 210.
133. Letters to Chief Ministers, dated 1 October 1959, vol. 5, p.285.
134. CS Jha, op. cit.
135. Dawa Norbu, *Strategic Analysis* (Delhi: July 1988), p. 393.

Chapter 5

1. Lok Sabha Debates, Second Series, Vol. XIX, pp. 4629-32.
2. Indian figures are based on Ministry of External Affairs usage. Chinese figures based on 'History of Counter Attack War in Self Defence along Sino-Indian Border [HCAWSDSIB] Chapter II, Section I, Para 96 [Beijing: Military Science Publication, 1994]
3. White Paper III, p. 79. Note by Ministry of Foreign Affairs, China to Embassy of India, Beijing on 26 December 1959.

4. WP I, p.26
5. WP I, p. 29.
6. WP I, p.48.
7. WP I, p.52.
8. A brief Note, undated, NML, S Dutt papers, Subject File # 40, pp. 39-41.
9. FRUS 1958-60, vol. XV, p. 166. Editorial Note (68). Memo of 404 Meeting of National Security Council, 30 April 1959.
10. British High Commissioner, Delhi MacDonald to Commonwealth Relations Office [CRO] London letter No. PREM 11/2728 PRO dated 21 October 1959.
11. FRUS 1958-60. vol. XV,p.472.
12. SWJN-SS, vol. 47, SS, p. 450 (para 4).
13. WP I, p.55.
14. P Mehra, *The North-East Frontier: 1906-1914*(Delhi: Oxford University Press, 1980), p.105.
15. WP I., p.55.
16. Cunningham, *Ladak: Physical, Statistical and Historical* (London: WH Allen & Co., 1854)
17. WP II, p. 29.
18. P Mehra, op. cit., p.134.
19. Woodman, *Himalayan Frontiers* (London: Crescent Press,1969), p.181.
20. FRUS 1958-60. vol.XV, p.513.
21. WP II, p. 28
22. *Peking Review*, 13 September 1959
23. Cunningham. *Ladak 1854* (Reprint, Delhi: Sagar Publications, 1977), p. 261.
24. Lamb, *Britain and Chinese Central Asia* (London: Routledge and Paul, 1960), p.79.
25. British Foreign Office Note F. Pros/160-9 dated 30 December 1892.
26. Fisher, Rose and Huttenback, Himalayan Battleground (London: Pall Mall,1963), p. 62.
27. L/P&S/10/344. [File No.P.464/1913, Pt. 5] Proceedings of the 7th Meeting/Annexure 3. Chen to McMahon, 26 April 1914.
28. L/P&S/10/718. [File No. P.3260/1917 Pt.6] John Jordan to British Foreign Office No. 250 dated 30 June 1914 contains memo from WaiChiaoPu [Chinese Foreign Office] dated 29 June 1914 containing paragraph cited.
29. Aitcheson Treaties, vol. XIV, 1929 edition, pp.37-38.
30. Report of the Officials of the government of the PRC and the government of India (Peking; 1961/Chinese Report), p.30.
31. Sir Charles Bell, *Tibet, Past and Present* (Oxford: Clarendon Press,1924), p. 155.
32. Oppenheim. *International Law: A Treatise* (London: Longman, Green &Co 1955), pp. 874-5.
33. ICJ Reports 2002, pp. 685-6, para. 149.
34. Wu Lengxi, *Shinian Luzhan 1956-66/A Decade of Polemics*, vol.1, pp. 210-212.
35. Fravel, op. cit., pp. 84-85.
36. Nehru's letter to Chief Ministers, 1 October 1959, Vol. V, p. 285.
37. S Dutt, Record of Discussions between President Eisenhower and Nehru on 10 December 1959. (S Dutt Papers, JNML). See also FRUS 1958-60. vol. XV, p.523.
38. HCAWSDSIB, Chapter 3, Section 1, para 285.
39. WP III, p. 55.
40. WP III, p.53.
41. Hoffman, *India and the China Crisis* (Berkeley: University of California Press, 1990), pp. 82-85.
42. PN Kaul, *Record of Talk between the PM of USSR and the PM of India at the latter's residence* [*12 February 1960*] Subject File No.24 1960, S Dutt Papers, JNML.
43. Asian Recorder 1960, p.3177.

44. *People's Daily*, 17 Feb 1960.
45. Zhou Enlai Zhuan/Zhou Enlai's biography [Beijing: Peoples' Publishing House and Cultural Archive Publishing, 1989], Vol. 3, pp. 1517-23.
46. Zhou Enlai Nianpu/Chronical of Zhou Enlai Life [Beijing: Zhongyang Wanxian, 1997], Vol. 2, p. 312.
47. S Gopal, Op cit., p136.
48. Jagat Mehta, op. cit., p. 80.
49. British High Commissioner to CRO letter No. 1091/29 dated 27 April 1960.
50. British High Commissioner to CRO letter No. 1091/26 dated 2 April 1960. See also DO 35/8822 dated 12 April 1960.
51. BN Mullik, op. cit., p 273.
52. NML, PN Haksai papers, I & II unstatements, Subject Files, File No. 25, pp. 39-41. Tel No. 24452, Circular: HOMs from Foreign Secretary, dated 27 April 1960.
53. S Dutt, op. cit., p. 132.
54. British High Commissioner to CRO. FO/CRO No. 371/150440. TNA.
55. Lok Sabha Debates, Second Series, vol. 43, p.13, 791-804.
56. FRUS 1958-60, Vol. XV, p. 562.
57. Woodman, op. cit., p.272.
58. CIA Document E0129583.4 (b)(1). [Three part CIA Series on Sino-Indian Border Dispute]
59. CWIHP, Memo of Conversation between Soviet Ambassador and CCP General Secretary, Deng Xiaoping. AVRP(Foreign Policy Archives of the Russian Federation) f.0100op.53,p.8,d.454,II 165-9. Translated by Ben Aldrich-Moodie.
60. Fravel, op. cit., p 177.
61. MacMillan, *At the End of the Day 1961-63* (London: Macmillan, 1973), p.224.
62. Palit, *War in the High Himalayas: The Indian Army in Crisis 1962* (London: Hurst & Co Publishers, 1991), pp. 97-98.
63. Brecher, op. cit., p. 151.
64. Krishna Menon, *India and the Chinese Invasion* (Delhi: Contemporary Publications, 1963), p. 15.
65. Maxwell, *India's China War* (London: Jonathan Cape, 1970), p.221.
66. Whiting, op. cit., p. 11.
67. Government of India, 1963.
68. Durga Das, *India from Curzon to Nehru and After* (Delhi: Harper Collins, 2000), p. 361. Nayyar, *India the Critical Years* (Delhi: Vikas Publications, 1971), p. 160. T N Kaul. *Diplomacy in War and Peace* (Delhi: Vikas Publications, 1979), p. 13. Chester Bowles, *America and Russia in India* (Foreign Affairs, July 1971), p. 649.
69. Y D Gundevia, *Outside the Archives* (Delhi: Sangam Books, 1987), p. 211
70. Brecher, op. cit., p. 324.
71. Nayyar, op. cit., p. 133.
72. David Floyd, *Mao against Khrushchev: A Short History of the Sino-Soviet Conflict* (New York: Praeger, 1964), pp. 366-67.
73. Nayyar, op. cit., p. 133.
74. HCAWSDSIB, Chapter 3, Section 1, para 292.
75. CWIHP, Summary of Conversation between Chairman Mao and Soviet CDA Sergey Antonov on 14 October 1959. Top Secret, Copy 3. Journal of Antonov SF.
76. White Paper III, p. 55
77. FRUS 1961-63, South Asia. vol. XIX, Document 12, pp.30-31
78. Xu Zehao, Ed., Wang Jiaxiang Nianpu/Chronicle of Wang Jiaxiang's Life (Beijing: Zhongyang Wenxian Chubanshe, 2001), pp.486-89. See also Fravel. op. cit., p.100.
79. Robert Ross, Jiang Chengbin (Ed.), Re-examining the Cold War: US-China Diplomacy

1954-73 (Cambridge, Mass. University of Harvard Press, 2001), p. 304.
80. WP VI, p. 96.
81. WP VI, p. 99.
82. FRUS 1961-63. vol.XIX, South Asia, Document 145, p. 291.
83. McGarr, *The Cold War in South Asia: Britain, the US and the Indian Sub-Continent 1945-65* (Cambridge: Cambridge University Press, 2013), p. 154.
84. HCAWSDSIB, Chapter 3, Section 3(a), para 369.
85. Whiting, op. cit., p.74.
86. HCAWSDSIB, Chapter4, Section2, para 476.
87. Liu Xiao, *Chu Shi Sulian Banian/Eight years as Ambassador to Soviet Union* (Beijing: Dangshi Ziliao Chubanshi, 1986), p. 121.
88. S Gopal. op. cit., p.222.
89. Galbraith, *Ambassador's Journal* (Boston: Houghton Hifflin, 1969), p.431.
90. *New York Times*, 30 March 1962.
91. Whiting, op. cit., p. 67.
92. FRUS 1961-63. North-East Asia, vol. XXII, Document 131. Tel. No. 2136 from US Embassy, Warsaw to Department of State dated 23 June 1962.
93. FRUS 1961-63. North-East Asia, vol. XXII, Document 128. Tel from Department of State to US Embassy, London dated 22 June 1962.
94. Wang Bingnan, Zhong-Mei Huitan Jiunian Huigu/Recollections of Nine Years of Sino-US Talks (Beijing: Shijie Zhishi Chubanshe, 1985), pp. 85-90.
95. WP VI, p. 71.
96. WP VI, p. 92. See also S Gopal. op. cit., p.213.
97. PK Bannerji, My Peking Memoires (New York: Clarion Books,1990), pp. 51-52.
98. *Hindustan Times*, 10 August 1962.
99. WP III, p.4.
100. WP III, p.18.
101. PK Bannerji, op. cit., p.54.
102. Ibid.
103. WP VII, p. 17
104. WP VII, p. 37.
105. WP VII, p.73.
106. Ibid., p. 78.
107. Ibid., p. 98.
108. Ibid., p. 102.
109. Kissinger, *On China* (US: Penguin Group, 2012), p. 192.
110. MacFarquar, *The Origins of the Cultural Revolution* [3] (New York: Columbia University Press, 1974), p. 307.
111. British Ambassador, Moscow to Foreign Office, London letter No. FC 1061/46 dated 11 July 1962. See also. Max-Jean Zins, Gilles Boquerat. Ed. *"India in the Mirror of Foreign Diplomatic Archives."*(Foundation Books).
112. Zhou Enlai Nianpu/Chronical of Zhou Enlai Life, op. cit., p. 502.
113. WP VIII, MEA Memo to Embassy of China, 4 November 1962 and MFA, Beijing reply of 17 November 1962.
114. HCAWSDSIB, op. cit., *"Memorabilia of Sino-Indian Border conflict 1949-1963, year 1962,"* p. 446.
115. Maxwell, op. cit., p 372.
116. Dalvi, *Himalayan Blunder* (Delhi: Thacker, 1969), p.152.
117. FRUS 1961-63. vol. XIX, South Asia, Document 289, p. 573.
118. S. Radchenko, *Two Suns in the Heavens: The Sino-Soviet Struggle for Supremacy 1962-67*

(Stanford CA: Stanford University Press, 2009), p. 29 quoting Fursenko ed., *Presidium* TsK KPSS, 1954-64. 596,616.

119. CWIHP, Prozumenshikov, *New Evidence from Russian Archives* (Bulletin 8-9, Winter 1996-97), p. 253. S Radchenko, op. cit., p.30. [Based on Foreign Policy Archives of the Russian Federation. (a) AVP RF, Fond 0100, opis 55, Papka 480, Delo7, List 113 and (b) AVP RF, Fond 0100, Opis 55, Papka 480, Delo7, List 119].
120. Liu Xiao, op. cit.
121. FRUS 1961-63, vol. XIX, South Asia, Document 181. Department of State vide Tel No. 1663 dated 26 October 1962 to US Embassy, Delhi authorized recognition of McMahon Line as the international border between India and China.
122. See Pravda Article, 5 November 1962.
123. S. Gopal, op. cit., p. 226 quoting Tel from Indian Ambassador to Soviet Union TN Kaul to PM Nehru dated 9 November 1962.
124. Wang Dong, *The Quarreling Brothers: New China Archives and re-appraisal of the Sino-Soviet Split* (CWIHP: Paper No. 49, 7 July 2011).
125. FRUS 1961-62, vol.XIX , South Asia, Document 211.
126. Altaf Gauhar, *Ayub* (Oxford University Press,1996), p. 210.
127. Mastny, "The Soviet Union's Partnership with India," *Journal of Cold War Studies*, vol.12, No. 3 (Summer 2010), quoting tel. dated 11 January 1963 from PRC Foreign Ministry to all Chinese Embassies abroad.
128. Mao Zedung Sixiang [1949-68], Joint Research Service No. 61269 dated 20 February 1974.
129. Cold War International History Projects [CWIHP], Wilson Center, Journal of SF Antonov, Top Secret, Copy No. 3/Conversations with Mao/14 October 1959.
130. Hong Yuan, *The Global Times*, 28 June 2012.
131. HCAWSDSIB, Chapter 6, Section 1(b), para 1081.
132. Hong Yuan, op. cit., 28 June 2002.
133. CWIHP, Wilson Centre, Journal of SF Antonov, Top Secret, Copy No. 3/Conversation with Mao.
134. Ibid.
135. Jawaharlal Nehru, *Letters to Chief Ministers* dated 22 December 1962, vol. V, p. 540.
136. Ibid., p. 552.
137. CS Jha, op. cit.
138. Xiaoyuan Liu, op. cit. p.222.
139. Hilsman, *To Move a Nation: The Politics of Foreign Policy of the Administration of John Kennedy* (New York: Delta, 1967), p. 338.
140. Report to the Supreme Soviet, 12 December 1962.
141. FRUS 1961-63, vol. XIX, South Asia, Document 226.
142. McGarr, op. cit., p. 154. See also DO 196/165. The National Archives [TNA].
143. *Survey of International Affairs*, 1962, p.418.
144. FRUS 1961-63. vol. XXII, North-East Asia, Document 158.
145. FRUS 1961-63. vol. XIX, South Asia, Document 226.
146. FRUS 1961-63. vol. XIX, South Asia, Document 196.
147. FRUS 1961-63. vol. XIX, South Asia, Document 226.
148. McGarr, *The Cold War in South Asia: Britain, the US and the Indian Sub-Continent 1945-65* (Cambridge: Cambridge University Press, 2013), p. 182.
149. FRUS 1961-63. vol. XIX, South Asia, Document 226.
150. Bajpai, *China's Shadow over Sikkim* (Delhi: Lancer, 1999), p. 193.
151. FRUS 1961-63 vol. XXII, North-East Asia. Document 194.
152. Maxwell, op. cit., p. 423.
153. Whiting, op. cit., p. 161.

154. Kissinger, op. cit., p. 192.
155. Xiaoyuan Liu. op. cit., p 222.
156. PK Bannerji, op. cit., p. 101.
157. Hong Yuan, *The Global Times*, 28 June 2012.
158. Liu Zhongyi, *The Global Times*, 13 December 2012.
159. Lamb, op. cit., p.171.

Chapter 6

1. Woodman, op. cit., p. 285.
2. White Paper VIII, p. 1.
3. PK Bannerji, op. cit., p. 65.
4. See Chapter 4 (Notes at 122)
5. WP III, p. 55.
6. PK Bannerji, op. cit., p. 72.
7. WP VIII, p.23.
8. China has accepted the 'watershed principle' in the following cases. [a] Treaty of Nerchinsk, 27 April 1689 [b] Convention of Great Britain and China 1890: Article I [c] Convention between France and China, 20 June 1895 [d] Convention between Great Britain and China of 1894 and 1897: Article III, Para 3 [e] Boundary Agreement between Burma and China, ratified on 4 January 1961: confirming the McMahon Line section in Burma and [f] China-Nepal Boundary Agreement ratified in 1961.
9. Maxwell, op. cit., pp. 298-99.
10. WP VIII, p.42
11. FM Chen Yi, Interview to Swedish Broadcasting Service, *Survey of China Mainland Press* [SCMP], No. 2941, March 1963, p. 24.
12. WP IX, p. 2.
13. WP IX, p. 10.
14. WP VIII, p. 51.
15. British Foreign Office File No. FO 371-3689 F/4004/177338/10.
16. SP Sharma, "The India-China Border Dispute" *American Journal of International Law (AJIL) 1965*, vol. 59, p. 41.
17. Maxwell, op. cit., p. 209.
18. Fisher, Rose, Huttenback. op. cit., p 101.
19. CH Alexandrowicz, "The Legal Position of Tibet," *American Journal of International Law*, April 1954, vol. 2, pp. 265-274.
20. Maxwell, op. cit., p. 432.
21. Chen T'i-chiang, "*Refute the Absurd Theory Regarding International Law*," (Head of the Division of International Law, Chinese Academy of Sciences)
22. WP VIII, p. 122
23. Ayub, *Friends not Masters* (London: Oxford University Press, 1967), p. 162
24. *Dawn*, 3 March 1962.
25. Nehru Speaking in the Lok Sabha, 7 May 1962.
26. FRUS 1961-63, South Asia, vol. XIX, Document 11.
27. FRUS 1961-63, South Asia, vol. XIX, Document 126, p. 257.
28. WP IX, p. 2.
29. Ibid., p. 3.
30. Ibid., p. 1.
31. Ibid., p. 24.
32. WP VI, p. 100

33. Sir Morrice James. *Pakistan Chronicle* (Karachi: Oxford University Press, 1993), p. 90.
34. Nehru Speaking in the Lok Sabha, 3 March 1963.
35. Lok Sabha Debates, 1964, vol. 34.
36. Ibid.

Chapter 7

1. FRUS 1964-68, vol. XXV, South Asia, Document 186, p. 359. CIA Memo (OCI) No. 2316 dated 6 September 1965. See also Burce Reidel Avoiding Armageddon (Delhi: Harper Collins, 2013), p. 67.
2. *Dawn*, 25 February 1964.
3. US National Archives, CIA Research Tool (CREST). Memo dated 21 July 1965 from Thomas Hughes, Director of International & Research, Department of State to WF Raborn, Director of Central Intelligence.
4. WP XII, Chinese Note of 27 August 1965.
5. Ibid. Chinese Note of 8 September 1965.
6. I. Akhund, *Memoirs of a Bystander: A Life in Diplomacy* (Karachi ;Oxford: Oxford University Press, 1997), p.94.
7. WP XII, Chinese Note of 16 September 1965.
8. Altaf Gauhar, *Ayub Khan: Pakistan's First Military Ruler* (Karachi: Oxford University Press, 1996), pp. 252-53. See also Praveen Swami, *India, Pakistan and the Secret Jihad: The Covert War in Kashmir 1947-2004* (Delhi: Taylor & Francis, 2007), p. 63.
9. *The Washington Post*, 16 September 1965.
10. FRUS 1964-68. vol. XXX, China, Document 101
11. Sheldon Simon, "The Kashmir Dispute in Sino-Soviet Perspective," *Asian Survey*, March 1967, pp. 176-87.
12. US Consul-General, Dacca to Department of State, Airgram A-78 dated 23 September 1965. See also Crawford, *Pivotal Deterrance*, p. 157.
13. FRUS 1964-68. vol. XXV, South Asia, Document 214, p. 411.
14. SM Khan, *Memoirs and Reflections of a Pakistani Diplomat* (London: Centre for Pakistani Studies, 1997), p.161.
15. Statement of External Affairs Minister, Rajya Sabha 29 November 1966.
16. Kissinger. op. cit., p. 201.
17. CWIHP. Conversations between Chinese and Foreign leaders on the War in Indo-China 1964-77. Meeting between Zhou Enlai and President Ayub Khan at Karachi 2 April 1965. Working Paper No. 122, Conversation No. 6, p. 76.
18. Douglas Pike, *Vietnam, the Soviet Union: Anatomy of an Alliance* (Westview Press, 1987), p. 87.
19. *AICC Economic Review*, 1 August 1968, pp. 3-4.
20. *Indira Gandhi, Peoples and Problems* (London: Hodder& Stoughton, 1982), p. 75.
21. *Xinhua*, 5 November 1971.
22. *NYT*, 13 February 1972.
23. FRUS 1969-71, vol. XI, South Asia Crisis 1971, Document 274.
24. SM Khan, op. cit., p. 379.
25. *Peking Review*, No. 37, 13 September 1974, p. 12.
26 *Peking Review*, No. 14, 8 April 1977, pp. 23-24.
27. *Far Eastern Review*, vol. 108, pp. 26-27. "*A Thaw in the Himalayas*"
28. NYT, 24 June 1977, p. A-6.
29. *Izvestia*, 21 March 1978.
30. *Izvestia*, 29 September 1979.

31. Jagat Mehta. *Rescuing the Future* (Delhi: Manohar, 2008), p.323.
32. *The Statesman*, 23 February 1979.
33. The Morarji Papers (Humanities Press), p. 29.
34. *Peking Review*, No. 27, 4 July 1979, pp. 22-23.
35. *Times of India*, 28 June 1981.
36. Bhabani Sen-Gupta, *The Afghan Syndrome*, vol.2 (Delhi: Vikas Publishers, 1982), p. 133.
37. Robinson, "Soviet Union and Asia," *Asian Survey*, vol. 21, No. 1 and vol. 22, No.1, p. 26.

Chapter 8

1. Minister of State, Khurshid Alam Khan, *The Telegraph*, 2 April 1985.
2. *The Indian Express*, November 1985.
3. *The Times of India*, 11 June 1986.
4. Liu Xuecheng, *Looking Beyond the Sino-Indian Border Dispute* (Beijing: Chinese Institute for International Studies, 11 August 2011)
5. *Soviet Review*, vol. III, No. 35 (3 September 1986), pp. 20-21.
6. Foreign Broadcast Information Service (FBIS), 2 December 1986, pp. D2-D29.
7. Ibid, 19 December 1986. See also Liaowang 15 December 1986.
8. Ronen Sen, *The Telegraph*, 31 January 2012.
9. FBIS, 23 December 1988.

Chapter 9

1. FBIS—China, No. 98-154.
2. Susan Shirk, "One Sided Rivalry: China's Perceptions and Policies towards India" in Frankel and Harding (ed.) p. 93.
3. Sisir Gupta, *The Hindustan Times*, 14 June 2013.
4. Garver, Wang Feiling, *China's Anti-Encirclement Strategy* (Asian Security on-line Publications), 29 September 2011.
5. *News India Times*, 8 April 2005, p. 15.
6. Lamb, *The McMahon Line*, vol. 2 (London: Routledge and Kegan Paul, 1966), p. 294.
7. Woodman, *Himalayan Frontiers* (London: The Crest Press, 1969), p. 123. [Bell Papers, I.O.L. Eur. MSS. F.80.]
8. Ibid. [Bell to Foreign Department, government of India, dated 6 August 1910.
9. Lamb, *The McMahon Line*, vol. 2 (London: Rouledge & Kegan Paul, 1966), p. 305. Text of Note by Chief of General Staff is at Appendix 9, Woodman. op. cit., p. 370.
10. WP III, p. 93.
11. WP III, p. 93.
12. Sun Haiyang, *PLA Daily*, 2 July 2007.
13. *The People's Daily*, 21 April 2007.
14. Ibid., 6 March 2006.
15. Xinhua on Line. [Xinhua Wang].
16. Hou Hongyu, *An Analysis of Changes in US Arms Export Policy Towards India* (Beijing: Xiandai Guoji Guanxi/Contemporary International Relations).
17. Brahma Challeney, "China's Unprincipled Principles," *Asian Age*, 16 June 2007.
18. *Xinhua*, 7 June 2007
19. White Paper II, p. 30.
20. *Indian Express*, 2 December 2012.
21. Nehru, Letters to Chief Ministers dated 15 December 1959, vol. V, p. 337.
22. Nehru, Letters to Chief Ministers dated 22 December 1962, vol. V, p. 553.
23. Nehru, Letters to Chief Ministers dated 21 May 1963, vol. V, p. 594.

Chapter 10

1. Junwu Pan, *Towards a New Framework for Peaceful Settlement of China's Territorial and Boundary Disputes* (The Netherlands: Martinus Nijhoff Publishers, 2009), Chapter 7, p. 214.
2. White Paper VIII, p. 51
3. Liu Zhongyi, Visiting Fellow at the Centre for Strategic and International Studies (CIIS). "Sino-Indian Border Dispute and their Competitive Symbiotic Relationship," *Future Directions International,* 28 May 2013.
4. Judge Xue Hanqin [International Court of Justice]. "China and International Law: 60 Years in Review," *Chatham House,* 8 March 2013.
5. Ibid.
6. Liu Zhongyi, *The Global Times,* 4 August 2013.
7. "More on Nehru's Philosophy in the Light of the Sino-Indian Border Question," *People's Daily,* 27 October 1962.
8. Dr. Dibyesh Anand, Interview to Zee Television (Delhi: Zee.com), 19 November 2011.
9. Andrew M. Fischer, "The Geopolitics of Politico-Religious Protest in Eastern Tibet," Field-Spots, Cultural Anthropology-on-Line, 8 April 2012.
10. Carole McGranahan, "Opinion," *The Outlook (Delhi),* 22 October 2012.
11. *Hindustan Times,* 15 September 2013, p. 19.
12. Carole McGranahan, op. cit.
13. Ibid.
14. *Beijing Review,* 3 May 2008.
15. Bruce Riedel. "JFK Overshadowed," National Interest.org. See also Bruce Riedel. "Divided They Stand," *Indian Express,* 28 October 2013, p. 10.
16. Ahmed Faruqui, *The Complex Dynamics of Pakistan's Relationship with China* (Islamabad: Political Research Institute, Summer 2001), 27 October 2008.
17. SIPRI estimates quoted in the *Hindustan Times,* 19 March 2013.
18. *Xinhua,* 18 May 2011.
19. William Burns, US Deputy Secretary of State address to students of Pune University on 19 December 2011. (Rediff.com)
20. Lisa Curtis, *US-India Relations: The China Factor* (The Heritage Foundation), www.heritage.org/research/reports/2008.
21. *Business Standard,* 21 August 2013, quoting National Security Advisor, S Menon.
22. Mao Siwei, *The Global Times,* 25 February 2013.
23. Maj-Gen Luo Yuan, *People's Liberation Army Daily,* 11 January 2011. Quoted by Reuters/ Chris Buckley.
24. *China Youth Daily,* 16 November 2011. "*India Trying to Contain China by Ignoring Itself.*"
25. *People's Daily* on line, 22 January 2013. "*Will India Join in Strategic Containment of China?*"
26. Robert Gates. Quadrennial Defence Review. Press Trust of India quoted in Times of India 2 February 2010.
27. PM Manmohan Singh quoted in *The Hindu,* 23 May 2013.
28. Salman Khurshid, Julie Bishop, "Putting out to Sea a New Vision," *The Hindu,* 2 November 2013.
29. Marc Lanteigne. "China's Maritime Security and the Malacca Dilemma," *Asian Security,* vol. IV, No. II, pp. 143-161.
30. *International Herald Tribune,* 28 December 2000.
31. Brahma Chellaney. "Global Marine Trends 2030 Report," *The Hindu,* 5 November 2013.
32. Fu Xiaoqiang. "US-India Alliance Evidence of Wishful Thinking due to Different Calculations," *Global Times,* 12 August 2013.
33. US Energy Information Administration [Country Report: Turkmenistan, 2013]

34. US Energy Information Administration [Country Report: Russia, 2013]
35. *China Daily*, 20 October 2013.
36. US Department of Defence Report, 2011, "*Military and Security Development of PRC.*"
37. Rand Study (Santa Monica, 2003), pp.105-116, "*Lines Fault in China's Economic Terrain.*"
38. White Paper II, p.30
39. Zhao Suisheng. "Chinese Nationalism and its Bitter Orientations," *Political Science Quarterly*, vol. 115, No.1 (Spring 2000), pp. 1-33.
40. *Times of India*, 13 March 2013.
41. Sanjib Baruah, *Hindustan Times*, 13 February 2012.
42. Steven Hood, *Dragons Entangled: Indo-China and the China-Vietnam War* (New York: East Gate), p. 116.
43. Susan Shirk, *China: The Fragile Super-Power* (US: Oxford University Press, 2007).
44. Chris Buckeley. *New York Times*, 19 August 2013.
45. Hilda Wang, Lombard Street Research, *New York Times*, 11 September 2013.
46. Satyajit Das, *The Independent*, 11 June 2013.
47. Yanzhong Huang, "China: The Dark Side of Growth," *Yale Global*, 6 June 2013.
48. Asian Development Bank Report, 2007.
49. *The Economist*, 15 December 2012.
50. *The China Daily*, 19 June 2005.
51. John Knight, *World Bank Policy Research Working Paper* No. WPS 6482 of 13 June 2013.
52. *Reuters*, 5 May 2013.
53. Caroline Binham, *The Financial Times*, 5 December 2012.
54. Andrew Wedman, "Growth and Corruption in China," *China Research Centre*, vol. 11, no.2. (30 December 2012)
55. Robyn Mak, *Reuters*, 11 August 2013.
56. Michael Pettis, *Carnegie Europe*, 5 July 2013.
57. KS Kim, Renping Hao, Andrew Champeau, paper entitled 'Growth, Environment and Politics: The Case of China', presented at International Conference 'China and World Economy' at University of Washington, Seattle, 16-18 March 2012.
58. Alasdair MacBean, *China's Environment: Problems and Policies* (Oxford University Press), p.298.
59. Edward Gresser, "Lop sided Chinese-US Relations," *Yale Global* 9 May 2013.
60. Yang Jiechi [Former Foreign Minister of China and presently State Councilor] "Innovations in China's Diplomatic Theory and Practice under New Conditions". Signed article in CCP Magazine Qiushir [Seeking the Truth], published on 16 August 2013.

ANNEXURES

ANNEXURE I

Text of Letter published in the Correspondence of G.E. Morrison 1912-1920 by Hui Minlo/Google Books

663. From Chen i-fan Simla 10 November 1913.

Dear Dr. Morrison,

I should have written to you long time ago, had I not been pressed by the work of the Conference. I am here doing all the work myself and do not receive any outside assistance. On the point of my leaving Peking the present Foreign Minister recommended Mr. B.D. Bruce to me for service in Simla, but on arrival here some small difficulties were raised against his inclusion in my staff, and he was soon afterwards ordered to return to Darjeeling by the direct order of the I.G.

The first meeting of the Conference was opened on the 13th, and the Tibetan claims were then handed in. They consisted of five items as follows:

1. The independence of Tibet.
2. Extension of Tibetan territory including Kokonor and Batang and Lithang.
3. The revision of the Trade Regulations of 1893 and 1908 with England without China.
4. No Amban in Lhasa.
5. Freedom of intercourse between Lamas in China with Tibet.
6. Compensation to Tibet for what damages done there by the Chinese soldiers.

To these I presented my counter-proposals on the 30th ultimo after consultations with my Government and consisted of 7 items:

1. Chinese undertake not to convert Tibet in a province.
2. Chinese must have an Amban with an escort of 2600 soldiers.
3. China shall be the only intermediary for any negotiations between Tibet and any foreign power.
4. Amnesty granted to all those who have been imprisoned on account of well known sympathy. [This claim looks insignificant, but if carried through means a great deal to China for there are still many sympathisers of China in Tibet.
5. Clause 5 in the Tibetan claims can be discussed. [I want to use this as a lever for what I want in other respects.]

6. The Revisions of the Trade Regulations must be made with China on the basis of Article IV of the Adhesion Convention of April 27 of 1903.
7. A rough frontier delimitation includes Giamdu and Narguchuka

As you will see there must be a great deal of bluff on both sides, we have to claim Giamdu, though I have not the little of reason to think that such a demand can be entertained for a moment. *The reason that I did not put any claim for sovereignty over Tibet was simply because instead of gaining anything by that it would be supposed by the Indian Government that I had no intention of having the problem solved.* I hope you can see your way of approving the course of action I have taken in the matter. I am alone here, but I am fighting several opponents whom I will not particularize until I am face to face with you.

All the papers here approve the strong action taken by our President in regard to the Opposition Party of the well- known Kuomintang.

Believe me.

Yours Sincerely,
Ivan Chen

If you want to see the Tibetan claims and our counter proposal, you can [ask the] Wai Chiao Pu for them.
I.C.

ANNEXURE-II

Agreement on the Maintenance of Peace and Tranquility along the Line of Actual Control in the India-China Border Areas

September 7, 1993

The Government of the Republic of India and the Government of the People's Republic of China (hereinafter referred to as the two sides), have entered into the present Agreement in accordance with the Five Principles of mutual respect for sovereignty and territorial integrity, mutual non-aggression, non-interference in each other's internal affairs, equality and mutual benefit and peaceful coexistence and with a view to maintaining peace and tranquility in areas along the Line of Actual Control in the India-China border areas.

1 The two sides are of the view that the India-China boundary question shall be resolved through peaceful and friendly consultations. Neither side shall use or threaten to use force against the other by any means. Pending an ultimate solution to the boundary question between the two countries, the two sides shall strictly respect and observe the Line of Actual Control between the two sides. No activities of either side shall overstep the Line of Actual Control. In case personnel of one side cross the line of actual control, upon being cautioned by the other side, they shall immediately pull back to their own side of the Line of Actual Control. When necessary, the two sides shall jointly check and determine the segments of the Line of Actual Control where they have different views as to its alignment.

2 Each side will keep its military forces in the areas along the Line of Actual Control to a minimum level compatible with the friendly and good neighbourly relations between the two countries. The two sides agree to reduce their military forces along the Line of Actual Control in conformity with the requirements of the principle of mutual and equal security to ceilings to be mutually agreed. The extent, depth, timing, and nature of reduction of military forces along the Line of Actual Control shall be determined through mutual consultations between the two countries. The reduction of military forces shall be carried out by stages in mutually agreed geographical locations sector-wise within the areas along the Line of Actual Control.

3 Both sides shall work out through consultations effective confidence building measures in the areas along the Line of Actual Control. Neither side will undertake specified levels of military exercises in mutually identified zones. Each side shall give the other prior notification of military exercises of specified levels near the Line of Actual Control permitted under this Agreement.

4 In case of contingencies or other problems arising in the areas along the Line of Actual Control, the two sides shall deal with them through meetings and friendly consultations between border personnel of the two countries. The form of such meetings and channels of communications between the border personnel shall be mutually agreed upon by the two sides.

5 The two sides agree to take adequate measures to ensure that air intrusions across the Line of Actual Control do not take place and shall undertake mutual consultations should intrusions occur. Both sides shall also consult on possible restrictions on air exercises in areas to be mutually agreed near the Line of Actual Control.

6 The two sides agree that references to the Line of Actual Control in this Agreement do not prejudice their respective positions on the boundary question.

7 The two sides shall agree through consultations on the form, method, scale and content of effective verification measures and supervision required for the reduction of military forces and the maintenance of peace and tranquility in the areas along the Line of Actual Control under this Agreement.

8 Each side of the India-China Joint Working Group on the boundary question shall appoint diplomatic and military experts to formulate, through mutual consultations, implementation measures for the present Agreement. The experts shall advise the Joint Working Group on the resolution of differences between the two sides on the alignment of the Line of Actual Control and address issues relating to redeployment with a view to reduction of military forces in the areas along the Line of Actual Control. The experts shall also assist the Joint Working Group in supervision of the implementation of the Agreement, and settlement of differences that may arise in that process, based on the principle of good faith and mutual confidence.

9 The present Agreement shall come into effect as of the date of signature and is subject to amendment and addition by agreement of the two sides.

Signed in duplicate at Beijing on the Seventh day of September 1993 in the Hindi, Chinese and English languages, all three texts having equal validity.

[Signed:]

ANNEXURE-III

Agreement Between the Government of the Republic of India and the Government of the People's Republic of China on Confidence-Building Measures in the Military Field Along the Line of Actual Control in the India-China Border Areas

November 29, 1996

The Government of the Republic of India and the Government of the People's Republic of China (hereinafter referred to as the two sides), Believing that it serves the fundamental interests of the peoples of India and China to foster a long-term good-neighbourly relationship in accordance with the 'five principles of mutual respect for sovereignty and territorial integrity, mutual non-aggression, non-interference in each other's internal affairs, equality and mutual benefit and peaceful co-existence, Convinced that the maintenance of peace and tranquility along the Line of Actual Control in the India-China border areas accords with the fundamental interests of the two peoples and will also contribute to the ultimate resolution of the boundary question, Reaffirming that neither side shall use or threaten to use force against the other by any means or seek unilateral military superiority, Pursuant to the Agreement between the Government of the Republic of India and the Government of the People's Republic of China on the Maintenance of Peace and Tranquility along the Line of Actual Control in the India-China Border Areas, signed on 7 September, 1993, Recognizing the need for effective confidence building measures in the military field along the Line of Actual Control in the border areas between the two sides, Noting the utility of confidence building measures already in place along the Line of Actual Control in the India-China border areas, Committed to enhancing mutual confidence and transparency in the military field, Have agreed as follows:

Article I

Neither side shall use its military capability against the other side. No armed forces deployed by either side in the border areas along the Line of Actual Control as part of their respective military strength shall be used to attack the other side, or engage in military activities that threaten the other side or undermine peace, tranquility and stability in the India-China border areas.

Article II

The two sides reiterate their determination to seek a fair, reasonable and mutually acceptable settlement of the boundary question. Pending an ultimate solution to the boundary question, the two sides reaffirm their commitment to strictly respect and observe the Line of Actual Control in the India-China border areas. No activities of either side shall overstep the Line of Actual Control.

Article III

The two sides agree to take the following measures to reduce or limit their respective military forces within mutually agreed geographical zones along the Line of Actual Control in the India-China border areas:

(1) The two sides reaffirm that they shall reduce or limit their respective military forces within mutually agreed geographical zones along the Line of Actual Control in the India-China border areas to minimum levels compatible with the friendly and good neighborly relations between the two countries and consistent with the principle of mutual and equal security.

(2) The two sides shall reduce or limit the number of field army, border defence forces, paramilitary forces and any other mutually agreed category of armed force deployed in mutually agreed geographical zones along the Line of Actual Control to ceilings to be mutually agreed upon. The major categories of armaments to be reduced or limited are as follows: combat tanks, infantry combat vehicles, guns (including howitzers) with 75 mm or bigger calibre, mortars with 120 mm or bigger calibre, surface-to-surface missiles, surface-to-air missiles and any other weapon system mutually agreed upon.

(3) The two sides shall exchange data on the military forces and armaments to be reduced or limited and decide on ceilings on military forces and armaments to be kept by each side within mutually agreed geographical zones along the Line of Actual Control in the India-China border areas. The ceilings shall be determined inconformity with the requirement of the principle of mutual and equal security, with due consideration being given to parameters such as the nature of terrain, road communication and other infrastructure and time taken to induct/de-induct troops and armaments.

Article IV

In order to maintain peace and tranquility along the Line of Actual Control in the India-China border areas and to prevent any tension in the border areas due to misreading by either side of the other side's intentions:

(1) Both sides shall avoid holding large scale military exercises involving more than one Division (approximately 15,000 troops) inclose proximity

of the Line of Actual Control in the India-China border areas. However, if such exercises are to be conducted, the strategic direction of the main force involved shall not be towards the other side.

(2) If either side conducts a major military exercise involving more than one Brigade Group (approximately 5,000 troops) in close proximity of the Line of Actual Control in the India-China border areas, it shall give the other side prior notification with regard to type, level, planned duration and area of exercise as well as the number and type of units or formations participating in the exercise.

(3) The date of completion of the exercise and de-induction of troops from the area of exercise shall be intimated to the other side within five days of completion or de-induction.

(4) Each side shall be entitled to obtain timely clarification from the side undertaking the exercise in respect of data specified in Paragraph 2 of the present Article.

Article V

With a view to preventing air intrusions across the Line of Actual Control in the India-China border areas and facilitating overflights and landings by military aircraft:

(1) Both sides shall take adequate measures to ensure that air intrusions across the Line of Actual Control do not take place. However, if an intrusion does take place, it should cease as soon as detected and the incident shall be promptly investigated by the side operating the aircraft. The results of the investigation shall be immediately communicated, through diplomatic channels or at border personnel meetings, to the other side.

(2) Subject to Paragraphs 3 and 5 of this Article, combat aircraft (to include fighter, bomber, reconnaissance, military trainer, armed helicopter and other armed aircraft) shall not fly within ten kilometers of the line of actual control.

(3) If either side is required to undertake flights of combat aircraft within ten kilometers from the Line of Actual Control, it shall give the following information in advance to the other side, through diplomatic channels:

   a) Type and number of combat aircraft;
   b) Height of the proposed flight (in meters);
   c) Proposed duration of flights (normally not to exceed ten days);
   d) Proposed timing of flights; and
   e) Area of operations, defined in latitude and longitude.

(4) Unarmed transport aircraft, survey aircraft and helicopters shall be permitted to fly up to the Line of Actual Control.

(5) No military aircraft of either side shall fly across the Line of Actual Control,

except by prior permission. Military aircraft of either side may fly across the Line of Actual Control or overfly the other side's airspace or land on the other side only after obtaining the latter's prior permission after providing the latter with detailed information on the flight in accordance with the international practice in this regard. Notwithstanding the above stipulation, each side has the sovereign right to specify additional conditions, including at short notice, for flights or landings of military aircraft of the other side on its side of the Line of Actual Control or through its airspace.

(6) In order to ensure flight safety in emergency situations, the authorities designated by the two sides may contact each other by the quickest means of communications available.

Article VI

With a view to preventing dangerous military activities along the Line of Actual Control in the India-China border areas, the two sides agree as follows:

(1) Neither side shall open fire, cause bio-degradation, use hazardous chemicals, conduct blast operations or hunt with guns or explosives within two kilometers from the Line of Actual Control. This prohibition shall not apply to routine firing activities in small arms firing ranges.

(2) If there is a need to conduct blast operations within two kilometers of the Line of Actual Control as part of developmental activities, the other side shall be informed through diplomatic channels or by convening a border personnel meeting, preferably five days in advance.

(3) While conducting exercises with live ammunition in areas close to the line of actual control, precaution shall be taken to ensure that a bullet or a missile does not accidentally fall on the other side across the line of actual control and causes harm to the personnel or property of the other side.

(4) If the border personnel of the two sides come in a face-to-face situation due to differences on the alignment of the Line of Actual Control of any other reason, they shall exercise self- restraint and take all necessary steps to avoid an escalation of the situation. Both sides shall also enter into immediate consultations through diplomatic and/or other available channels to review the situation and prevent any escalation of tension.

Article VII

In order to strengthen exchanges and cooperation between the military personnel and establishments in the border areas along the Line of Actual Control, the two sides agree:

(1) To maintain and expand the regime of scheduled and flag meetings between their border representatives at designated places along the Line of Actual Control;

(2) To maintain and expand telecommunication links between the border meeting points at designated places along the Line of Actual Control;
(3) To establish step-by-step medium and high-level contacts between the border authorities of the two sides.

Article VIII

(1) Should the personnel of one side cross the Line of Actual Control and enter the other side because of unavoidable circumstances like natural disasters, the other side shall extend all possible assistance to them and inform their side, as soon as possible regarding the forced or inadvertent entry across the Line of Actual Control. The modalities of return of the concerned personnel to their own side shall be settled through mutual consultations.

(2) The two sides shall provide each other, at the earliest possible, with information pertaining to natural disasters and epidemic diseases in contiguous border areas which might affect the other side. The exchange of information shall take place either through diplomatic channels or at border personnel meetings.

Article IX

In case a doubtful situation develops in the border region, or in case one of the sides has some questions or doubts regarding the manner in which the other side is observing this Agreement, either side has the right to seek a clarification from the other side. The clarifications sought and replies to them shall be conveyed through diplomatic channels.

Article X

(1) Recognizing that the full implementation of some of the provisions of the present Agreement will depend on the two sides arriving at a common understanding of the alignment of the Line of Actual Control in the India-China border areas, the two sides agree to speed up the process clarification and confirmation of the Line of Actual Control. As an initial step in this process, they are clarifying the alignment of the Line of Actual Control in those segments where they have different perceptions. They also agree to exchange maps indicating their respective perceptions of the entire alignment of the Line of Actual Control as soon as possible.

(2) Pending the completion of the process of clarification and confirmation of the Line of Actual Control, the two sides shall workout modalities for implementing confidence building measures envisaged under this Agreement on an interim basis, without prejudice to their respective positions on the alignment of the Line of Actual Control as well as on the boundary question.

Article XI

Detailed implementation measures required under Article I to Article X of this Agreement shall be decided through mutual consultations in the India-China

Joint Working Group on the Boundary Question. The India-China Diplomatic and Military Expert Group shall assist the India-China Joint Working Group.

Article XII

This Agreement is subject to ratification and shall enter into force on the date of exchange of instruments of ratification. It shall remain in effect until either side decides to terminate it after giving six months' notice in writing. It shall become invalid six months after the notification.

This Agreement is subject to amendment and addition by mutual agreement in writing between the two sides.

Signed in duplicate in New Delhi on 29 November 1996 in the Hindi, Chinese and English languages. All three texts being equally authentic. In case of divergence, the English text shall prevail.

ANNEXURE-IV

Formulations/Statements on Status of Tibet by India

29 April 1954	Agreement Between India and China on Trade and Intercourse Between Tibet Region of China and India. *'Desirous of Promoting Trade and Cultural Intercourse Between the Tibet Region of China and India.....'*
23 December 1988	India-China Joint Press Communique *'The Indian Side Reiterates the Long Standing and Consistent Policy of the Government of India That Tibet is an Autonomous Region of China...'*
16 December 1991	India-China Joint Communique *[Same Formulation as Above]*
23 June 2003	Declaration on Principles for Relations and Comprehensive Co-operation Between India and China *'The Indian Side Recognizes that the Tibet Autonomous Region is a Part of the Territory of the People's Republic of China..'*
11 April 2005	India-China Joint Statement *[Same Formulation as Above]*
21 November 2006	India-China Joint Declaration *[Same Formulation as Above]*
15 January 2008	A Shared Vision for the 21st Century—India and China *No Mention of Tibet*
16 December 2010	India-China Joint Communique *No Mention of Tibet*

ANNEXURE-V

Agreement between the Government of the Republic of India and the Government of the People's Republic of China on the Political Parameters and Guiding Principles for the Settlement of the India-China Boundary Question

April 11, 2005

The Government of the Republic of India and the Government of the People's Republic of China (hereinafter referred to as the two sides), Believing that it serves the fundamental interests of the peoples of India and China to foster a long-term constructive and cooperative partnership on the basis of the Five Principles of Peaceful Co-existence, mutual respect and sensitivity for each other's concerns and aspirations, and equality, Desirous of qualitatively upgrading the bilateral relationship at all levels and in all areas while addressing differences through peaceful means in a fair, reasonable and mutually acceptable manner, Reiterating their commitment to abide by and implement the Agreement on the Maintenance of Peace and Tranquility along the Line of Actual Control in the India-China Border Areas, signed on 7 September 1993, and the Agreement on Confidence Building Measures in the Military Field along the Line of Actual Control in the India-China Border Areas, signed on 29 November 1996, Reaffirming the Declaration on Principles for Relations and Comprehensive Cooperation between India and China, signed on 23 June 2003, Recalling that the two sides have appointed Special Representatives to explore the framework of settlement of the India-China boundary question and the two Special Representatives have been engaged in consultations in a friendly, cooperative and constructive atmosphere, Noting that the two sides are seeking a political settlement of the boundary question in the context of their overall and long-term interests, Convinced that an early settlement of the boundary question will advance the basic interests of the two countries and should therefore be pursued as a strategic objective, Have agreed on the following political parameters and guiding principles fora boundary settlement:

Article I

The differences on the boundary question should not be allowed to affect the overall development of bilateral relations. The two sides will resolve the boundary question through peaceful and friendly consultations. Neither side shall use or threaten to use force against the other by any means. The final solution of the boundary question will significantly promote good neighbourly and friendly relations between India and China.

Article II

The two sides should, in accordance with the Five Principles of Peaceful Coexistence, seek a fair, reasonable and mutually acceptable solution to the boundary question through consultations on an equal footing, proceeding from the political perspective of overall bilateral relations.

Article III

Both sides should, in the spirit of mutual respect and mutual understanding, make meaningful and mutually acceptable adjustments to their respective positions on the boundary question, so as to arrive at a package settlement to the boundary question. The boundary settlement must be final, covering all sectors of the India-China boundary.

Article IV

The two sides will give due consideration to each other's strategic and reasonable interests, and the principle of mutual and equal security.

Article V

The two sides will take into account, inter alia, historical evidence, national sentiments, practical difficulties and reasonable concerns and sensitivities of both sides, and the actual state of border areas.

Article VI

The boundary should be along well-defined and easily identifiable natural geographical features to be mutually agreed upon between the two sides.

Article VII

In reaching a boundary settlement, the two sides shall safeguard due interests of their settled populations in the border areas.

Article VIII

Within the agreed framework of the final boundary settlement, the delineation of the boundary will be carried out utilizing means such as modern cartographic and surveying practices and joint surveys.

Article IX

Pending an ultimate settlement of the boundary question, the two sides should strictly respect and observe the Line of Actual Control and work together to maintain peace and tranquility in the border areas. The India-China Joint Working Group and the India-China Diplomatic and Military Expert Group shall continue their work under the Agreements of 7 September 1993 and 29 November 1996, including the clarification of the Line of Actual Control and the implementation of confidence building measures.

Article X

The Special Representatives on the boundary question shall continue their consultations in an earnest manner with the objective of arriving at an agreed framework for a boundary settlement, which will provide the basis for the delineation and demarcation of the India-China boundary to be subsequently undertaken by civil and military officials and surveyors of the two sides.

Article XI

This Agreement shall come into force as of the date of signature and is subject to amendment and addition by mutual agreement in writing between the two sides.

Signed in duplicate in New Delhi on 11 April, 2005, in the Hindi, Chinese and English languages, all three texts being equally authentic.

In case of divergence, the English text shall prevail.

For the Government of the Republic of India

For the Government of the People's Republic of China

New Delhi, April 11, 2005

Bibliography

A Tom Grunfeld. *The Making of Modern Tibet* (New York: East Gate/ME Sharpe Inc., 1996).

Alastair Lamb. *Britain and Central Asia: The Road to Lhasa 1767-1905* (London: Routledge & Kegan Paul, 1960).

____, *The McMahon Line: A Study in the Relations between India, China and Tibet, 1904-1914, Vol. I & II* (London: Routledge & Kegan Paul, 1966).

Alex MacKay. *Tibet and the British Raj: The Frontier Cadre 1904-47*(London: Curzon Press, 1997).

Amiya Rao, BG Rao. *Jawaharlal Nehru PM* (New Delhi: Sterling Publishers, 1974).

AO Cukwarah. *The Settlement of Boundary Disputes in International Affairs* (London: Manchester University Press, 1967).

Ayub Khan. *Friends not Masters: A Political Biography* (Karachi: Oxford University Press, 1967).

C von Furer- Haimendorf. *Himalayan Boundary* (London: Murray, 1955).

Chakravarthi. *The Evolution of India's Northern Borders* (Delhi: Asia Publishing House, 1971).

Chanakya Sen. *Tibet Disappears* (Bombay: Asia Publishing House, 1960).

Charles Heimseth, Surjit Mansingh. *A Diplomatic History of Modern India* (Bombay: Allied Publishers Pvt. Ltd., 1971).

Chester Bowles.*Promises to Keep: My Years in Public Life 1941-1969* (Delhi: BI Publications, 1972).

CIA Documents [Freedom of Information Act-Electronic Reading-Historical Collections].

Claude Arpi. *The Fate of Tibet: When Big Insects Eat Small Insects* (Delhi: Har-Anand Publications Pvt. Ltd., 1999).

Clive Christie. *Great Britain, China and the Status of Tibet 1914-21* (Modern Asian Studies, Vol. X, Issue IV, October 1976).

CP Fitzgerald. *The Southern Expansion of the Chinese People* (Canberra: Australian University Press, 1972).

Cunningham. *Ladak : Physical, Statistical and Historical* (London: W.H. Allen, 1854).

Curzon. *Frontiers* (Oxford: Oxford University Press, 1908).

Dalai Lama. *Freedom in Exile: The Autobiography of the Dalai Lama* (New York: Harper Collins, 1990).

——, My Land and My People (London: Weidenfeld& Nicholson, 1962).

David Sambaugh. *China Goes Global* (Oxford, 2013).

Dawa Norbu. *China's Tibet Policy* (Richmond, Surrey: Curzon Press, 2001).

Dennis Kux. *Estranged Democracies: India and the US 1941-1991* (Delhi: Sage Publications, 1993).

Donald Zagoria. *The Sino-Soviet Conflict 1956-61* (Princeton: Princeton University Press, 1961).

Dorothy Woodman. *Himalayan Frontiers: A Political Review of British, Chinese, Indian and Russian Rivalries* (London: The Crescent Press, 1969).

Edgar Snow. *Red Star over China* (London: Victor Gollancz Ltd., 1968).

——, *The Other Side of the River* (London: Random House, 1961).

Foreign Relations of the United States [FRUS].

Francis Watson. *The Frontiers of China* (London: Chatto&Windus, 1966).

Frank Dikotter. *Mao's Great Famine: The History of China's Most Devastating Catastrophe 1958-62* (New York: Bloomsbury Publishing, 2010).

——, *The Tragedy of Liberation: A History of the Chinese Revolution 1945-1957.*

Frederick Drew. *The Jummoo and Kashmir Territories* (London: Edward Stanford, 1875).

FS Aijazuddin. *The White House and Pakistan: Secret Declassified Documents 1969-74* (London: OUP, 2002).

G Narayan Rao. *The India-China Border: A Reappraisal* (Delhi: Asia Publishing House, 1967).

George Patterson. *Tibet in Revolt* (London: Faber & Faber, 1961).

Girilal Jain. *Panchsheel and After* (Delhi: Asia Publishing House, 1959).

GJ Alder. *British India's Northern Frontier* (London: Longman, Green &Co. Ltd., 1963).

GS Bajpai. *China's Shadow over Sikkim: The Politics of Intimidation* (Delhi: Lancer Publishers, 1999).

Heman Ray. *Sino-Soviet Conflict over India.*

Ji Youquan. *BaixueJiefang Xizang Jishi/White Snow: A Factual Record of the Liberation of Tibet* (Beijing: Zhongguo Wuzi, 1993).

JK Galbraith. *Ambassodor's Journal: A Personal Account of the Kennedy Years* (London: Hamish Hamilton, 1969).

John Dalvi. *Himalayan Blunder* (Bombay: Thacker & Co. Ltd., 1969).

John Garver. *Protracted Contest: Sino-Indian Rivalry in the 20th Century* (Seattle: University of Washington Press, 2001).

John Gittings. *Survey of the Sino-Soviet Dispute 1963-67* (London: Oxford University Press, 1968).

Judith Brown. *Nehru: A Political Life* (Delhi: Oxford University Press, 2003).

Kenneth Lieberthal. *Governing China* (Norton, 1995).

Khrushchev Remembers. *The Last Testament* (Boston: Little, Brown, 1974).

KM Panikkar. *In Two Chinas: Memoirs of a Diplomat* (London: Allen & Unwin, 1955).

KPS Menon. *Memories and Musings* (Delhi: Allied Publishers Pvt. Ltd., 1979).

Lorenz M Luthi. *The Sino-Soviet Split: The Cold War in the Communist World* (Princeton: Princeton University Press, 2008).

Lorne Kavics. *India's Quest for Security: Defence Policies 1957-65* (Berkeley: University of California Press, 1967).

Lt-Gen SPP Thorat. *From Reveille to Retreat* (Delhi: Allied Publishers Pvt. Ltd., 1986).

Margaret Fisher, Leo Rose and Robert Huttenback. *Himalayan Battleground: Sino-Indian Rivalry in Ladakh* (London: Pall Mall Press, 1963).

Melvyn Goldstein. *A History of Modern Tibet 1913-51* (Berkeley: University of California Press, 1989).

Michael Brecher. *Nehru: A Political Biography* (London: Oxford University Press, 1959).

____, *India and World Politics: Krishna Menon's View of the World* (London: Oxford University Press, 1968).

Michael C. van Walt van Praag. *The Status of Tibet* (Boulder, Colorado: Westview Press, 1987).

MJ Akbar.*Nehru: The Making of India* (London: Viking, 1988).

Morris Rossabi. *China and Inner Asia: From 1368 to the Present Day* (London: Thames and Hudson, 1975).

Nathan & Scobell. *China's Search for Security* (Columbia, 2012).

National Security Archives, The George Washington University.

Neville Maxwell. *India's China War* (London: Jonathan Cape, 1970).

Office of the Historian; United States Department of State.[Presidents Kennedy, Johnson and Nixon].

Orville Schell & John Delury. *Wealth and Power: China's Long March to the 21st Century* (Little Brown, 2013).

Owen Lattimore. *Inner Asian Frontiers of China* (Boston: Beacon Press, 1951).

Paul McGarr. *The Cold War in South Asia: Britain, the US and the Indian Sub-Continent 1945-65* (Cambridge: Cambridge University Press, 2013).

Premen Addy. *Tibet on the Imperial Chessboard: The Making of British Policy towards Lhasa* 1899-1925 (Delhi: Academic Publishers, 1984).

Rajeshwar Dayal. *A Life of our Times* (Delhi: Orient Longmans, 1998).

Report of the Officials of the governments of India and the People's Republic of China on the Boundary Question (Ministry of External Affairs, government of India, February 1961).

Richardson. *Tibet and its History* (London: Oxford University Press, 1962).

Robert McMahon. *The Cold War on the Periphery: the US, India and Pakistan* (New York: Columbia University Press, 1994).

Robert Sutter. *Chinese Foreign Relations: Power and Policy Since the Cold War* (Rowman & Littlefield, 2008).

Roedad Khan. *The British Papers: Secret and Confidential, India-Pakistan and Bangladesh 1958-69* (London: OUP, 2002).

Sir Basil Gould. *The Jewel in the Lotus* (London: Chatto & Windus, 1957).

Sir Charles Bell. *Tibet: Past and Present* (Oxford: Clarendon Press, 1924).

____, The People of Tibet (Oxford: Clarendon Press, 1968).

____, Portrait of the Dalai Lama (London: Collins, 1942).

SM Burke. *Pakistan's Foreign Policy: An Historical Analysis* (London: Oxford University Press, 1973).

SS Khera. *India's Defence Problems* (Bombay: Orient Longmans, 1968).

Stephen Cohen. *India: Emerging Power* (Washington: Brookings Institution Press, 2001).

Steven Hoffman. *India and the China Crisis* (Berkeley: University of California Press, 1990).

Sudhir Ghosh. *Gandhi's Emissary* (Calcutta: Rupa & Co., 1967).

Susan Shirk. *China: The Fragile Superpower* (Oxford, 2007)

____, Changing Media, Changing China (Oxford, 2011).

Suzanne Odgen. *China's Unresolved Issues* (Prentice Hall, 1995).

Thant Myint U. *Where China Meets India: Burma and the New Crossroads of Asia.*

Thomas Robinson and David Shambaugh. Ed. *Chinese Foreign Policy: Theory and Practice* (Oxford: Clarendon Press, 1994).

TN Kaul. *A Diplomat's Diary: 1947-1999* (Delhi: MacMillan India Ltd., 2000).

____, *Diplomacy in Peace and War* (Delhi: Vikas Publishers, 1979).

____, *India, China and Indo-China* (Delhi: Allied Publishers Pvt. Ltd., 1980).

____, *My Years through Raj to Swaraj* (Delhi: Vikas Publishers, 1993).

Tom Grunfeld. *The Making of Modern Tibet* (Delhi: Oxford University Press, 1987).

Tsepon WD Shakabpa. *Tibet: A Political History* (New Haven/London: Yale University Press, 1967).

Tsering Shakya. *The Dragon in the Land of Snows: A History of Modern Tibet since 1947* (London: Pimlico, 1999).

Tyabji. *Memoirs of an Egoist* (Delhi: Roli Books, 1988).

Walter Crocker. *Nehru: A Contemporary's Estimate* (London: Allen & Unwin, 1966).

Warren Smith. *Tibetan Nation: A History of Tibetan Nationalism and Sino-Tibetan Relations* (Colorado: Westview Press, 1996).

WF van Eekelen. *Indian Foreign Policy and the Border Dispute with China* (The Hague: MartinusNijhoff, 1964).

White Papers I-XIV (Ministry of External Affairs, government of India, New Delhi).

Xiaoyuan Liu. *Recast all Under Heaven: Revolution, War, Diplomacy and Frontier China in the 20th Century* (New York: The Continuum Publishing Group, 2011).

Xu Zehao. *Wang Jiaxiang Nianpu 1906-74/Chronology of the Life of Wang Jiaxiang 1906-74* (Beijing: Zhongyang Wenxian Chubanshe, 2001).

YD Gundevia. *Outside the Archives* (Hyderabad: Sangam Books India Pvt. Ltd., 1984).

Zheng Wang. *Never Forget National Humiliation –Understanding Chinese Nationalism.*

Index